Risk Financing

Risk Financing

Richard G. Berthelsen, JD, CPCU, ARM
Director of Curriculum
The Institutes

Michael W. Elliott, MBA, CPCU, AIAF
Director of Examination Development
The Institutes

Connor M. Harrison, CPCU, AU, ARe
Assistant Vice President
The Institutes

4th Edition • 8th Printing

The Institutes
720 Providence Road, Suite 100
Malvern, Pennsylvania 19355-3433

4th Edition • 8th Printing • February 2011

Library of Congress Control Number: 2006929350

ISBN 978-0-89463-297-6

Foreword

The Institutes are the trusted leader in delivering proven knowledge solutions that drive powerful business results for the risk management and property-casualty insurance industry. For more than 100 years, The Institutes have been meeting the industry's changing professional development needs with customer-driven products and services.

In conjunction with industry experts and members of the academic community, our Knowledge Resources Department develops our course and program content, including Institutes study materials. Practical and technical knowledge gained from Institutes courses enhances qualifications, improves performance, and contributes to professional growth—all of which drive results.

The Institutes' proven knowledge helps individuals and organizations achieve powerful results with a variety of flexible, customer-focused options:

Recognized Credentials—The Institutes offer an unmatched range of widely recognized and industry-respected specialty credentials. The Institutes' Chartered Property Casualty Underwriter (CPCU) professional designation is designed to provide a broad understanding of the property-casualty insurance industry. Depending on professional needs, CPCU students may select either a commercial insurance focus or a personal risk management and insurance focus and may choose from a variety of electives.

In addition, The Institutes offer certificate or designation programs in a variety of disciplines, including these:

- Claims
- Commercial underwriting
- Fidelity and surety bonding
- General insurance
- Insurance accounting and finance
- Insurance information technology
- Insurance production and agency management
- Insurance regulation and compliance
- Management
- Marine insurance
- Personal insurance
- Premium auditing
- Quality insurance services
- Reinsurance
- Risk management
- Surplus lines

Flexible Online Learning—The Institutes have an unmatched variety of technical insurance content covering topics from accounting to underwriting, which we now deliver through hundreds of online courses. These cost-effective self-study courses are a convenient way to fill gaps in technical knowledge in a matter of hours without ever leaving the office.

Continuing Education—A majority of The Institutes' courses are filed for CE credit in most states. We also deliver quality, affordable, online CE courses quickly and conveniently through our newest business unit, CEU.com. Visit www.CEU.com to learn more.

College Credits—Most Institutes courses carry college credit recommendations from the American Council on Education. A variety of courses also qualify for credits toward certain associate, bachelor's, and master's degrees at several prestigious colleges and universities. More information is available in the Student Services section of our Web site, www.TheInstitutes.org.

Custom Applications—The Institutes collaborate with corporate customers to utilize our trusted course content and flexible delivery options in developing customized solutions that help them achieve their unique organizational goals.

Insightful Analysis—Our Insurance Research Council (IRC) division conducts public policy research on important contemporary issues in property-casualty insurance and risk management. Visit www.ircweb.org to learn more or purchase its most recent studies.

The Institutes look forward to serving the risk management and property-casualty insurance industry for another 100 years. We welcome comments from our students and course leaders; your feedback helps us continue to improve the quality of our study materials.

Peter L. Miller, CPCU
President and CEO
The Institutes

Preface

Risk Financing is the text for ARM 56, one of the courses required for earning the Associate in Risk Management (ARM) designation. This text provides the reader with a comprehensive overview of techniques risk management professionals use to finance and manage risk. These techniques are often characterized as either retention or transfer, but actually incorporate elements of both.

The contents of *Risk Financing* can be summarized as follows:

- Chapter 1 provides an overview of risk financing, as well as a brief overview of the risk financing techniques described throughout the text. Additionally, the chapter describes how risk financing can be incorporated into the holistic approach to risk management—enterprise risk management.

- Chapters 2 and 3 describe insurance's usefulness as a risk financing technique. Risk financing techniques are often benchmarked against insurance.

- Chapter 4 presents loss forecasting in the context of an extensive case study. Organizations with firm expectations of their future losses are more capable of using risk financing alternatives to insurance.

- Chapter 5 describes self-insurance plans that enable an organization to pay for its own losses through a formal system. Self-insurance plans generally include a significant retention component.

- Chapter 6 describes retrospective rating plans. These are insurance plans in which the organization can pay a significant share of its own losses.

- Chapter 7 explains the operation of reinsurance and how it can be used to manage risk. Reinsurance enables insurers and captive insurers to operate within the limits of their financial resources.

- Chapter 8 describes captive insurance plans. Organizations that are willing to retain a significant share of their own losses in exchange for greater flexibility often form their own captive insurer to address their risk financing needs.

- Chapter 9 explains the operation and characteristics of finite and integrated risk financing plans. Often used by sophisticated, enterprise-focused risk management programs, these plans can include financial or market risks.

- Chapter 10 examines the product innovations that enable organizations to access the capital markets to finance risks that are traditionally covered by insurance (or reinsurance).

- Chapter 11 describes the uses of noninsurance contractual transfers of risk. These contractual agreements are normally incidental to another, larger transaction and can transfer either the loss exposure itself or the cost of recovering from a loss.

- Chapter 12 examines the six steps involved in purchasing insurance and other risk financing services. This chapter is most useful to risk management professionals who have already assessed their organization's loss exposures, evaluated risk financing alternatives, and determined that purchasing insurance is the most appropriate risk financing plan.

- Chapter 13 describes the process of allocating risk management costs, including the purpose of the process, which costs to allocate, and how the costs should be allocated.

For more information about The Institutes' programs, please call our Customer Service Department at (800) 644-2101, e-mail us at customerservice@TheInstitutes.org, or visit our Web site at www.TheInstitutes.org.

Richard G. Berthelsen, JD, CPCU, ARM

Michael W. Elliot, MBA, CPCU, AIAF

Connor M. Harrison, CPCU, AU, ARe

Contributing Authors

The Institutes and the authors acknowledge with deep appreciation the work of the following contributing authors:

Arthur L. Flitner, CPCU, ARM, AIC
Vice President
The Institutes

Melissa O. Leuck, ARM
Director
Weather & Commodity Risk Solutions
Gallagher Financial Products

Contents

Chapter 1

Direct Your Learning

Understanding Risk Financing

After learning the content of this chapter and completing the corresponding course guide assignment, you should be able to:

- Describe risk financing and its importance to organizations.

- Describe the following risk financing goals:

  - Paying for losses

  - Maintaining an appropriate level of liquidity

  - Managing uncertainty of loss outcomes

  - Managing the cost of risk

  - Complying with legal requirements

- Explain how loss characteristics affect risk financing technique selection.

- Explain how enterprise risk management provides a holistic approach to risk financing.

- Define or describe each of the Key Words and Phrases for this chapter.

Develop Your Perspective

What are the main topics covered in the chapter?

Loss assessment identifies loss exposures that should be treated with risk control and risk financing. Risk financing is usually applied to loss exposures that cannot be effectively treated through risk control.

Identify the risk financing techniques used by your organization as either transfer or retention.

- Which loss exposures make the most sense to transfer?
- Which loss exposures make the most sense to retain?

Why is it important to learn about these topics?

Few loss exposures can be effectively treated with risk control alone. Consequently, risk financing techniques must be selected and implemented in situations where they are most appropriate.

Consider the goals of risk financing.

- How effective is retention in maintaining an appropriate level of liquidity?
- How effective is insurance in managing uncertainty?

How can you use what you will learn?

Evaluate your organization's use of transfer and retention in financing risk.

- Why are most applications of risk financing measures a combination of retention and transfer?
- Would your organization benefit from adopting a holistic approach to risk management and, consequently, to its risk financing needs?

Chapter 1
Understanding Risk Financing

Risk management helps people and organizations realize the opportunities and avert the threats associated with risk. Risk assessment enables a risk management professional (any person who has responsibility under an organization's risk management program) to identify and analyze loss exposures for subsequent treatment. Loss exposures are conditions that could result in financial loss to an organization from property, personnel, liability, or net income losses.

The first two steps in the following six-step risk management process are key to a successful risk assessment:

1. Identifying loss exposures
2. Analyzing loss exposures
3. Examining the feasibility of risk management techniques
4. Selecting the appropriate risk management techniques
5. Implementing the selected risk management techniques
6. Monitoring results and revising the risk management program

Risk assessment leads to risk treatment, which is addressed in the remaining steps of the risk management process. Risks are usually treated with a combination of risk control and risk financing techniques. Risk control is a conscious act or decision not to act that reduces the frequency and severity of losses or makes losses more predictable. Although an organization can control most risk to some degree, it must finance its residual risk to mitigate its effect. This text describes the risk financing techniques that are available to most organizations.

This chapter defines risk financing and explains its importance to risk management. Risk financing goals must support both the organization's risk management goals and the organization's financial goals. Determining how to achieve these goals leads to the selection of appropriate risk financing techniques. This selection involves matching loss characteristics with the most appropriate risk financing technique. The chapter concludes with a discussion of enterprise risk management and its holistic approach to risk financing.

RISK FINANCING AND ITS IMPORTANCE

Risk financing
A conscious act or decision not to act that generates the funds to pay for losses or offset the variability in cash flows that may occur.

When examining the feasibility of risk management alternatives, a risk management professional should consider risk financing as well as risk control. **Risk financing** is a conscious act or decision not to act that generates the funds to pay for losses or offset the variability in cash flows that may occur. Risk financing techniques can be categorized into the following two groups:

1. Transfer, which includes insurance and noninsurance techniques that shift the financial consequences of loss to another party
2. Retention, which involves absorbing the loss by generating funds within the organization to pay for the loss

Many risk financing techniques involve elements of both retention and transfer. For example, insurance with a deductible entails retention of the deductible amount and transfer of losses above the deductible. Exhibit 1-1 shows the risk management techniques available for treating accidental loss exposures.

EXHIBIT 1-1

Risk Management Techniques

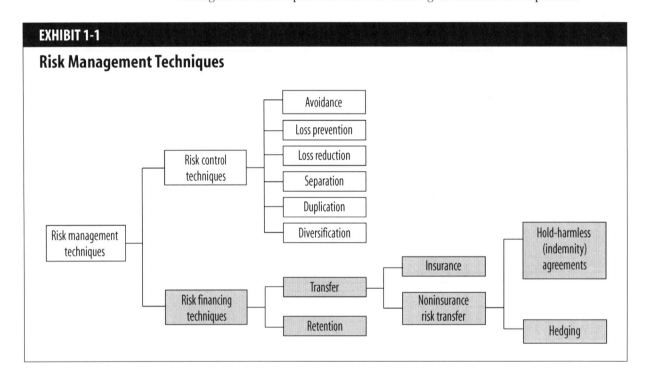

Transfer

Insurance
A risk financing technique that transfers the potential financial consequences of certain specified loss exposures from the insured to the insurer.

Transfer involves the transfer of risk through insurance and noninsurance techniques to shift the financial consequences of loss to another party. **Insurance** is a risk financing technique that transfers the potential financial consequences of certain specified loss exposures from the insured to the insurer. The insurance buyer substitutes a small certain financial cost, the insurance premium, for the possibility of a large uncertain financial loss, paid by the insurer. Although insurance is only one approach to risk financing, it is a vital component of a risk management program.

Insurance is essentially a funded risk transfer. By accepting a premium, the insurer agrees to pay for all of the organization's losses that are covered by the insurance contract. The insurer also agrees to provide services, such as claim handling and defense of liability claims.

Noninsurance risk transfer is a risk financing technique that transfers all or part of the financial consequences of loss to another party, other than an insurer. Contracts that are not insurance contracts but that transfer loss exposures are therefore considered noninsurance risk transfers. Some contracts deal solely with assigning responsibility for losses arising out of a particular relationship or activity. Under these contracts, which are known as **hold-harmless agreements** (also called indemnity agreements), one party (the indemnitor) agrees to assume the liability of a second party (the indemnitee). Exhibit 1-2 shows a hold-harmless agreement that might be included in a lease.

Noninsurance risk transfer
A risk financing technique that transfers all or part of the financial consequences of loss to another party, other than an insurer.

Hold-harmless agreement
A contract under which one party (the indemnitor) agrees to assume the liability of a second party (the indemnitee).

EXHIBIT 1-2

Hold-Harmless Agreement for Use in a Lease

To the fullest extent permitted by law, the lessee shall indemnify, defend and hold harmless the lessor, agents and employees of the lessor, from and against all claims arising out of or resulting from the leased premises.

Hedging is also considered a noninsurance risk transfer technique. **Hedging** is a financial transaction in which one asset is held to offset the risk associated with another asset.

Hedging
A financial transaction in which one asset is held to offset the risk associated with another asset.

Hedging is practical when it is used to offset loss exposures to which one is naturally, voluntarily, or inevitably exposed. For example, a newspaper publisher faces the loss exposure of newsprint price variability. To offset this loss exposure, the publisher might enter into a futures contract with its newsprint supplier to purchase a fixed quantity of newsprint over the coming year at a pre-agreed price. A **futures contract** is an agreement to buy or sell a commodity or security at a future date at a price that is fixed at the time of the agreement. If the market price of newsprint increases over the next year, the newspaper publisher has saved money by buying newsprint below the prevailing price. If the market price drops, the newspaper publisher's loss exposure is still reduced because it has eliminated the variability in the newsprint's cost. The same can be said for the newsprint supplier. Whether the newsprint supplier would have made more money or less money depends on the ultimate prevailing market price of newsprint, but, in either case, the futures contract reduces the cost's variability.

Futures contract
An agreement to buy or sell a commodity or security at a future date at a price that is fixed at the time of the agreement.

Retention

Retention is a risk financing technique by which losses are retained by generating funds within the organization to pay for the losses. Because retention can be the most economic risk financing technique available, it is sometimes preferred even when insurance or noninsurance transfer is available. Retention can also

Retention
A risk financing technique by which losses are retained by generating funds within the organization to pay for the losses.

be the risk financing technique of last resort; the financial burden of any losses that cannot be insured or otherwise transferred *must* be retained.

Retention can be planned or unplanned. These terms are defined as follows:

- Planned retention is a deliberate assumption of a loss exposure (and any consequential losses) that has been identified and analyzed. Planned retention may be chosen because it is cost-effective, convenient, or the only option.

- Unplanned retention is the inadvertent assumption of a loss exposure (and any consequential losses) because the loss exposure has not been identified or accurately analyzed. For example, many people inadvertently retain flood losses because they do not anticipate that the flooding caused by rain associated with the remnants of hurricanes will endanger their property.

Retention can also be complete or partial, defined as follows:

- Complete retention is the assumption of the full cost of any loss that is retained by the organization.

- Partial retention is the assumption of a portion of the cost of a loss by the organization and the transfer of the remaining portion.

Funding for retention differs as follows:

- Funded retention is the pre-loss arrangement to ensure that funding is available after a loss to pay for losses that occur.

- Unfunded retention is the lack of advance funding for losses that occur.

Pre-loss funding
A funded retention arrangement under which money to fund losses is set aside in advance.

Current-loss funding
A funded retention arrangement under which money to fund retained losses is provided at the time of the loss or immediately after it.

Post-loss funding
A funded retention arrangement under which the organization pays for its retained losses sometime after losses occur, using borrowing (or some other method of raising additional capital) in the meantime.

Three general methods can be used to pay for (fund) retained losses: pre-loss funding, current-loss funding, and post-loss funding.

1. **Pre-loss funding** is a funded retention arrangement under which the money to fund retained losses is set aside in advance. The principal advantage of pre-loss funding is that the money needed to fund losses can be saved over several budget periods. The principal disadvantage is that it ties up money that could otherwise be used by the organization and, consequentially, involves an opportunity cost for the organization. This reduction of available financial resources keeps pre-loss funding from being widely used.

2. **Current-loss funding** is a funded retention arrangement under which money to fund retained losses is provided at the time of the loss or immediately after it. Current-loss funding is the most commonly used and often the least expensive form of funding. Its main advantage is that it does not tie up funds before they are needed. Its principal disadvantage is that there may not be enough money in the current budget to cover the given loss and satisfy other cash flow needs.

3. **Post-loss funding** is a funded retention arrangement under which the organization pays for its retained losses sometime after losses occur, using borrowing (or some other method of raising additional capital) in the

meantime. For example, a building owner may have to take out a mortgage to fund the reconstruction of a damaged uninsured building. In such a case, the mortgage would be the post-loss funding instrument.

Advantages to using post-loss funding include the opportunity to pay the cost of retained losses over several years instead of all at once, and the need to use only the amount required to pay for retained losses. However, post-loss funding has several disadvantages. The organization using post-loss funding must pay interest on the borrowed funds. In addition, the loss event that produces the need to borrow may also reduce the organization's credit-worthiness, which increases the loan's cost. Although this disadvantage can be overcome by making pre-loss arrangements for a credit guarantee, such guarantees entail fees of their own. Also, guaranteeing post-loss credit may reduce the organization's capacity to borrow pre-loss funds for business operations.

Determining which risk financing techniques are appropriate requires the risk management professional to understand the organization's risk management program goals, which often may be broad and may be dependent on the successful implementation of both risk control and risk financing techniques. Additionally, risk management professionals must finance risk within the overall context of the organization's financial goals.

RISK FINANCING GOALS

The main financial goal of most publicly traded organizations is to maximize their market value by maximizing the present value of expected future cash flow. Future cash flow is a projection of the amount of cash that will flow into an organization in a given period less the amount of cash that will flow out of the organization during that same period. The present value of the future cash flow is derived by a calculation (called discounting) that accounts for the time value of money. In theory, investors value a publicly traded organization by projecting the size of its future cash flow. They then use a discount rate to adjust the expected cash flow to the present in order to estimate the organization's current market value.

The higher the risk associated with future cash flow, the greater the discount rate. The greater the discount rate, the lower the present value of an organization's cash flow and the lower the current market value that investors assign the organization. Therefore, increased variability in an organization's cash flow reduces the organization's market value.

To help increase its market value, a publicly traded organization should therefore carefully manage its cost of risk. (Although their overall goals may differ, privately held and not-for-profit organizations should also do so.) Managing the cost of risk involves minimizing the cost per unit of risk transferred and retaining risk when a sufficient return would result. The return from retaining risk can be measured in terms of the savings in risk transfer costs (assuming the organization has the option to transfer its risk).

To manage its cost of risk and maintain a tolerable level of uncertainty for retained losses, an organization should pursue risk financing goals. Common risk financing goals include the following:

- Paying for losses
- Maintaining an appropriate level of liquidity
- Managing uncertainty of loss outcomes
- Managing the cost of risk
- Complying with legal requirements

Paying for Losses

The availability of funds to pay for losses is particularly important in situations in which operations have been disrupted, such as when damaged property must be replaced. However, paying for losses is also important from other perspectives, such as public relations. For example, an organization does not want to tarnish its reputation by not paying liability losses that result from legitimate third-party claims.

Maintaining an Appropriate Level of Liquidity

Liquid assets are essential to paying for losses. A liquid asset is one that can easily be converted into cash. For example, marketable securities are liquid because they can readily be sold in the stock or bond markets. Some assets, such as machinery and equipment, are not liquid because they would be difficult to sell quickly.

When an organization retains its losses, it must determine the amount of cash it needs to pay for them and the timing of those cash payments. In deciding how to make its financial resources available to pay for its retained losses, an organization must consider its various sources of liquidity: the liquidity of its assets, the strength of its cash flows, its borrowing capacity, and (for a publicly traded organization) its ability to issue stock.

The higher an organization's retention, the greater the need for liquidity. Likewise, organizations that retain losses and have extensive loss variability and, consequently, greater uncertainty also need substantial liquidity.

Managing Uncertainty Resulting From Loss Outcomes

The relationship between uncertainty and the need for liquidity underscores the importance of managing that uncertainty. Managers of publicly traded organizations usually want to reduce the risks their organizations face. They believe that by being able to report steadily growing earnings to their stockholders, they maximize their organizations' market value. However, an organization often has difficulty determining the maximum level of uncertainty it can tolerate. Its maximum uncertainty level depends on a number of factors, such as its size, its financial strength, and its level of risk tolerance—for example, whether management prefers to accept risk in order to gain a possible benefit or whether management prefers to avoid risk despite the possibility of gain. An organization's maximum uncertainty level also depends on the degree to which its stakeholders are willing to accept risk.

Managing the Cost of Risk

Cost of risk is a concept that has historically been applied to hazard risk—that is, the possibility of accidental loss arising from property, liability, personnel, and net income loss exposures. Hazard risk contrasts with business risk (also called speculative risk), which presents not only the possibility of loss but also the possibility of gain. An organization usually seeks to minimize its cost of risk because any reduction in hazard risk expenses increases its net income. The following expenses form part of the cost of risk, regardless of whether losses are retained or transferred:

- Administrative expenses
- Risk control expenses
- Retained losses
- Transfer costs

Administrative Expenses

Administrative expenses include an organization's cost of internal administration and its cost of purchased services, such as claim administration and risk management consulting. Administrative expenses also include any insurance premium taxes paid. An organization should incur administrative expenses to the extent necessary to properly manage its risk financing program. Often, an organization can save administrative expenses by modifying procedures or eliminating unnecessary tasks. For example, some firms with a loss retention program save expenses by outsourcing the claim administration function.

Risk Control Expenses

Risk control expenses are incurred to prevent losses or reduce the severity of losses that do occur. An organization can best analyze its risk control expenditures by conducting a cost-benefit analysis. Resources should be allotted to a risk control measure as long as its marginal benefit exceeds its marginal cost. However, moral and ethical issues also influence the choice of risk control measures. For example, a risk control measure that cannot be justified by a cost-benefit analysis may be justifiable for humanitarian reasons, such as equipping corporate vehicles with anti-lock brakes and side-curtain air bags.

Retained Losses

Retained losses are a major component of an organization's cost of risk. When deciding whether to retain a loss, an organization can compare the projected cost of retaining the loss with the cost of transferring it.

Retaining some types of losses that have significant delays in claim reporting and settlement offers an additional benefit. Such losses, which include, for example, workers' compensation claims, are known as long-tail losses. Long-tail losses are not paid to claimants immediately, but instead are paid over time. Therefore, an organization can invest those amounts until losses are paid.

An organization should measure the value of such deferred loss payments when analyzing the cost of its loss retention program. Deferring loss payments lowers the organization's cost of risk. When deciding whether to retain or transfer its losses, an organization should also take into account the value of the cash flow benefit from retaining losses. A premium paid to an insurer to transfer losses is usually due at the beginning of the policy period, whereas retained losses are paid at later dates, generating a cash flow benefit to the organization and, therefore, lowering its present value costs.

Transfer Costs

Transfer costs are the amounts an organization pays to outside organizations to transfer its risk of loss. In the context of hazard risk, transfer costs are insurance premiums. In return for the premium, the insurer accepts the uncertainty of the cost of the insured's covered losses and agrees to reimburse the insured for covered losses or to pay covered losses on the insured's behalf.

By minimizing its transfer costs, an organization can maximize the net present value of its cash flow. It can minimize its transfer costs by employing an effective insurance broker or negotiating directly with insurers and other organizations that accept its risk of loss.

Although managing cost of risk is only one of several risk financing goals, it is the primary measure used by many organizations to gauge the effectiveness of the risk management program. Likewise, cost of risk serves, at least in part, as a personal performance measure for many risk management professionals.

Complying With Legal Requirements

Often, organizations are legally required to purchase insurance. For example, an organization that raises funds by issuing bonds may be subject to a covenant imposed by the bond purchasers that requires it to insure its property for a specific amount. The insurance laws of most states require organizations to purchase liability insurance for their vehicles or, alternatively, to qualify as self-insurers. Similarly, state workers' compensation statutes require most employers to purchase workers' compensation insurance or to qualify as self-insurers. Therefore, compliance with legal requirements is often a necessary risk financing goal.

Risk management professionals use risk financing goals to guide them in selecting appropriate risk financing techniques. However, the characteristics of losses associated with a particular loss exposure often direct the risk management professional to a particular risk financing technique.

RISK FINANCING TECHNIQUE SELECTION

Risk management professionals must consider the characteristics of the losses being managed when selecting appropriate risk financing techniques. These characteristics include loss frequency and loss severity.

Loss frequency is the number of losses that occur within a specified period. Loss severity is the amount of a loss, typically measured in dollars, for a loss that has occurred. Severity can be used to describe the size of an individual loss or a group of losses.

Most large organizations experience numerous relatively small losses. For example, large manufacturers may annually experience many minor injuries to their employees. Conversely, an organization may suffer a catastrophic loss, such as a large fire or a plant explosion, on an infrequent basis. Between these two loss extremes are medium-sized losses that may or may not occur regularly.

Exhibit 1-3 shows the general relationships among losses with different frequency-severity characteristics. The width of the triangle illustrates the relative frequency of losses at different severity levels. Usually, the more severe a loss is, the lower its frequency. The opposite is also true.

EXHIBIT 1-3

Frequency and Severity Characteristics of Losses

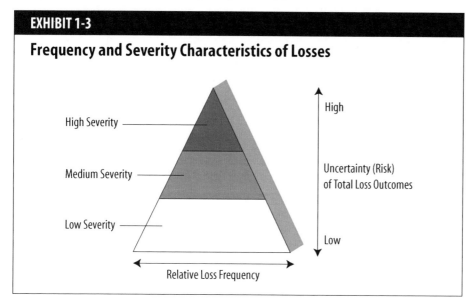

High-severity losses are relatively less frequent than low-severity losses.

Some categories of loss are not represented by the triangle. For example, organizations often experience losses that are characterized by both low severity and low frequency. Those losses are usually of little financial consequence. Organizations also could experience losses characterized by both high severity and high frequency. These losses are likely to be difficult to transfer and may bankrupt an organization.

The top segment of the triangle in Exhibit 1-3 represents catastrophic losses that are characterized by both high severity and low frequency. The cost of these losses is unpredictable, regardless of whether they are considered individually or as a group. Therefore, they present a high risk to organizations. Most organizations arrange to transfer these types of losses before they occur.

The bottom segment of the triangle in Exhibit 1-3 represents losses that are characterized by both low severity and high frequency. Organizations with a high frequency of losses find that low-severity losses, taken as a whole, are predictable. Therefore, organizations usually retain them. It follows that organizations with a low frequency of low-severity losses retain them as well.

The middle segment of the triangle in Exhibit 1-3 represents losses that are characterized by medium severity and medium frequency. Organizations may choose to either retain or transfer these losses, depending on their tolerance for risk and the cost of risk transfer.

"High," "medium," and "low" are relative terms that vary by organization. For example, "low" loss severity would probably be much smaller for a medium-sized organization than for a Fortune 500 organization. "Medium" loss severity for an organization that is financially secure with a high risk tolerance would probably be much larger than for an organization that is financially weak with a low risk tolerance. Therefore, the placement of the horizontal lines in the triangle varies by organization.

Exhibit 1-4 shows the relationships between risk financing plans and the frequency-severity characteristics of losses. In general, retention plans are used for low-severity losses, while transfer plans are used for high-severity losses. Because they combine retention and transfer, hybrid plans can apply to all losses, regardless of their severity. Hybrid plans combine the elements of both loss retention and loss transfer. For example, a large deductible insurance plan can be designed to cover all losses that fall within the triangle shown in the exhibit. Exhibit 1-5 categorizes the risk financing plans that are discussed in greater detail in subsequent chapters.

Loss characteristics correlate with the risk financing plans that are best suited to address them.

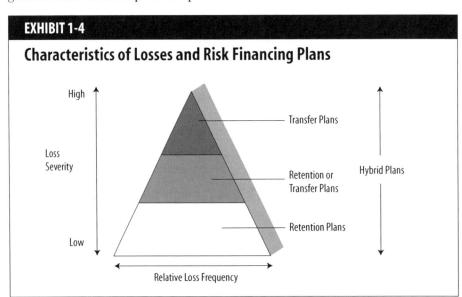

EXHIBIT 1-4

Characteristics of Losses and Risk Financing Plans

EXHIBIT 1-5

Categories of Risk Financing Plans

Retention Plans	Transfer Plans	Hybrid Plans
• Informal retention • Self-insurance	• Guaranteed-cost insurance • Insurance derivatives and insurance securitizations	• Large deductible insurance • Retrospective rating • Captive insurance • Pooling • Finite risk insurance

Hybrid plans include elements of risk transfer and risk retention.

The risk financing plans discussed in this text are described within the context of traditional risk management. However, many of these techniques can be used in the context of the broader view of risk management: enterprise risk management.

ENTERPRISE RISK MANAGEMENT: A HOLISTIC APPROACH TO RISK FINANCING

Many organizations now use a holistic approach to risk management called enterprise risk management (ERM). **Enterprise risk management (ERM)** is an approach to managing all of an organization's key business risks and opportunities with the intent of maximizing shareholder value. To realize this goal, ERM classifies risk into the following categories:

Enterprise risk management (ERM)
An approach to managing all of an organization's key business risks and opportunities with the intent of maximizing shareholder value.

- Strategic risks, which are those uncertainties associated with the organization's overall long-term goals and management

- Operational risks, which are those uncertainties associated with the organization's operations

- Financial risks, which are those uncertainties associated with the organization's financial activities

- Hazard risks, which are those uncertainties associated with the organization's reduction in value resulting from the effects of accidental losses

Strategic, operational, and financial risks are often called business risk because they arise from business activities. **Business risk** refers to risk inherent in the operation of a particular organization, including the possibility of loss, no loss, or gain. Risk management professionals often refer to business risk as speculative risk. For example, a hardware store owner would be engaging in business or speculative (strategic) risk when he purchases a large inventory of snow blowers in anticipation of a snowy winter season. Likewise, an organization that transfers funds between countries and consequently can incur a gain or loss from the transaction because of exchange rate differences is undertaking a business or speculative (financial) risk.

Business risk
Risk that is inherent in the operation of a particular organization, including the possibility of loss, no loss, or gain.

Enterprise risk management differs from traditional risk management in the following ways:

- Enterprise risk management encompasses both hazard risk and business risk; traditional risk management focuses on hazard risk.

- Enterprise risk management seeks to enable an organization to fulfill its greatest productive potential; traditional risk management seeks to restore an organization to its former pre-loss condition.

- Enterprise risk management focuses on the value of the organization; traditional risk management focuses on the value of the accidental loss.

- Enterprise risk management focuses on the organization as a whole; therefore traditional risk management is both its own discipline and part of the broader enterprise risk management discipline.

Pursuing ERM is a logical step for large organizations that can absorb substantial loss retentions, because different types of losses tend not to occur at the same time, so that gains in one area can offset losses in another. For example, property losses arising from hurricanes do not necessarily occur at the same time as losses due to increases in market interest rates. Therefore, an organization can reduce its costs by analyzing and managing its risks as a whole rather than by managing each source of risk separately.

Exhibit 1-6 illustrates the benefit of this holistic approach to risk financing. It shows possible outcomes for two sources of risk: hazard risk and interest rate risk. Hazard risk is a pure risk, so the possible outcomes are no loss, which is "good," or loss, which is "bad." Interest rate risk (a financial/market risk) is a speculative risk, so the possible outcomes are gain, which is "good," or loss, which is "bad."

EXHIBIT 1-6

Possible Outcomes From Two Sources of Risk[1]

		Hazard Risk (Pure Risk)	
		No Loss (good)	Loss (bad)
Interest Rate Risk (Speculative Risk)	Gain (good)	1 good-good	2 good-bad
	Loss (bad)	3 bad-good	4 bad-bad

An organization can reduce its costs by analyzing and managing its risks as a whole, rather than managing each source of risk separately.

An organization that analyzes each of its risks separately might transfer its losses that appear in quadrants two, three, and four, because a "bad" outcome is possible for each. However, an organization that adopts a holistic approach to risk financing might transfer only its losses in quadrant four, which includes a hazard risk loss and an interest rate risk loss in the same period. In quadrants two and three, "good" loss outcomes help offset "bad" loss outcomes, reducing the need to transfer the resulting risk.

When analyzing risk financing across their enterprise-wide risks, many organizations find inconsistencies in their approach to loss retention. For example, an organization that retains millions of dollars of risk on a daily basis in the foreign exchange market may find that it retains only $100,000 per loss under its property insurance policy. Taking a holistic approach to risk financing allows an organization to coordinate and possibly raise its combined overall risk retention level and therefore save money in the long run.

SUMMARY

Risk financing is a conscious act or decision not to act that generates funds to pay for losses or offset variability in cash flows that may occur. Risk financing complements risk control. Both risk control and risk financing are used by risk management professionals to treat loss exposures that have been identified as a financial threat to the organization. Risk financing techniques can be categorized into the following groups:

- Transfer, which includes insurance and noninsurance techniques to shift the financial consequences of loss to another party
- Retention, which involves absorbing the loss by generating funds within the organization to pay for the loss

Many risk financing techniques involve both of these elements. Insurance is a vital risk financing technique that transfers the potential financial consequences of certain specified loss exposures from the insured to the insurer. Noninsurance risk transfer is a risk financing technique that transfers all or part of the financial consequences of loss to another party, other than an insurer. Hold-harmless agreements and hedging are types of noninsurance risk transfer.

In cases in which no other alternative exists, retention can be the risk financing technique of last resort. Retention can be planned or unplanned; complete or partial; or funded or unfunded. Three general methods can be used to fund retained losses: pre-loss funding, current-loss funding, and post-loss funding. Pre-loss funding is a funded retention arrangement under which money to fund losses is set aside in advance. Current-loss funding is a funded retention arrangement under which money to fund retained losses is provided at the time of the loss or immediately after it. Post-loss funding is a funded retention arrangement under which the organization pays for its retained losses sometime after losses occur, using borrowing (or some other method of raising additional capital) in the meantime.

Risk financing goals should support the organization's risk management and financial goals. Common risk financing goals include paying for losses, maintaining an appropriate level of liquidity, managing uncertainty resulting from loss outcomes, managing the cost of risk, and complying with legal requirements. Risk management professionals use these risk financing goals to guide them in selecting appropriate risk financing techniques.

Loss exposures exhibit loss characteristics in terms of frequency and severity. Often, these characteristics direct the risk management professional to use a particular risk financing technique to treat them. Low-frequency/high-severity losses are most appropriately treated through transfer. High-frequency/low-severity losses are most appropriately treated through retention. High-frequency/high-severity losses are best avoided, whereas low-frequency/low-severity losses are usually of little consequence and are retained.

Many organizations use enterprise risk management (ERM) to treat their risk as a whole. Enterprise risk management is an approach to managing all of an organization's key business risks and opportunities with the intent of maximizing shareholder value. ERM differs from traditional risk management in scope. Traditional risk management, which deals only with hazard risk, is one component of ERM. Organizations that use ERM manage their risks as a whole, rather than separately.

Risk financing is an essential element of an organization's treatment of its loss exposures. Insurance, discussed next, is the most prevalent risk financing technique.

CHAPTER NOTES

1. Adapted from a lecture given on April 28, 1999, by Neil A. Doherty, professor of insurance and risk management, The Wharton School of the University of Pennsylvania.

Chapter 2

Direct Your Learning

Insurance as a Risk Financing Technique

After learning the content of this chapter and completing the corresponding course guide assignment, you should be able to:

- Describe the purpose and operation of insurance, including:
  - Risk reduction through pooling
  - Services provided by insurers
- Describe the characteristics of an ideally insurable loss exposure.
- Describe the types of insurance that address specific loss exposures.
- Describe the advantages and disadvantages of insurance.
- Define or describe each of the Key Words and Phrases for this chapter.

Develop Your Perspective

What are the main topics covered in the chapter?

This chapter examines insurance as a risk financing technique. Insurance can be used as a stand-alone risk financing technique to transfer risk, or as the risk transfer component of a hybrid risk financing plan.

Identify the distinction between pooling and insurance.

- How does pooling reduce risk?

- How does insurance differ from pooling?

Why is it important to learn about these topics?

Insurance is the principal means used by organizations to transfer risk. Risk management professionals must evaluate alternative risk financing techniques relative to insurance when choosing a risk financing technique.

Consider the advantages and disadvantages of insurance.

- How does purchasing insurance affect an organization's cash flow?

- How effective is insurance in lowering uncertainty to a tolerable level?

How can you use what you will learn?

Examine the loss exposures that your organization treats with insurance.

- Are there situations in which the insurance purchased does not provide complete risk transfer?

- Are there situations in which your organization is retaining a loss exposure for which insurance is available?

Chapter 2

Insurance as a Risk Financing Technique

Insurance is a component of most risk financing plans. Organizations that want the security and certainty of insurance can purchase an insurance policy that transfers hazard risk to an insurer.

Because its meaning depends on context, however, the term "insurance" can be confusing when used in relation to risk financing. Often, "insurance" is used to describe a risk financing plan in which the premium is a fixed amount; that is, the premium is not adjusted based on actual losses that occur during the policy period. In this context, an insurance plan transfers to the insurer the risk that an insured organization's losses will exceed the premium, which is based on average expected losses. These types of insurance plans are often referred to as guaranteed-cost insurance plans, because they guarantee, or fix, the amount of premium the insured organization will pay for the policy, regardless of the value of the actual losses the policy covers. Guaranteed-cost can be a misnomer, however, because various insurance pricing plans contain a loss-sensitive element that adjusts the price of insurance based on the amount of actual losses.

Insurance also is commonly used in connection with hybrid risk financing plans, such as large deductible plans and retrospective rating plans. These plans transfer to the insurer only part of the risk of loss, with the balance retained by the insured organization. Self-insurance plans for liability insurance, meanwhile, usually rely on excess liability insurance to provide the organization with risk transfer. Additionally, captive insurance plans often rely on a licensed insurer to serve as a fronting company for the captive insurer's activities. These plans usually involve the purchase of reinsurance, which can be characterized as "insurance for insurers." Reinsurance, as with excess liability insurance, provides the captive insurer with risk transfer. Because of such varied uses of insurance in risk financing plans, risk management professionals must understand how insurance works.

This chapter defines insurance and describes its purpose and operation. The concept of pooling underlies the operation of insurance and is essential to the evaluation of alternative risk financing plans that involve pooling, but not insurance. The characteristics of an ideally insurable loss exposure are also fundamental to understanding insurance and why some insurable loss exposures may be less desirable to an insurer. The chapter concludes by contrasting the advantages and disadvantages of insurance from the perspective of the organization and its risk management professional and summarizes the insurance coverages provided by the principal types of insurance.

PURPOSE AND OPERATION OF INSURANCE

Insurance is an important component of most risk financing programs. The purpose of insurance is to facilitate the spread of hazard risk among those that have similar loss exposures. Not only do insurers accept an organization's risk of loss, but they also provide services in areas such as risk control, claim processing, and legal advice. To some organizations, these specialized services may be as important as the risk transfer aspect of insurance.

Risk management professionals must understand why insurance works in order to adequately evaluate its effectiveness relative to other risk financing techniques that rely on risk pooling. Pooling is a fundamental risk management concept that is essential to the operation of insurance. Consequently, pooling should be understood on its own and in context with insurance.

Pooling[1]

Pool
An association of persons or organizations that combine their resources to economically finance recovery from accidental losses.

Unlike insurance, pooling reduces risk without transferring it. Generally, a **pool** is an association of persons or organizations that combine their resources to economically finance recovery from accidental losses. Pools reduce risk when the pooled losses are independent (or uncorrelated). Losses are independent when each loss occurs independently and they are not subject to a common cause of loss. For example, windstorm-related losses sustained by a building in California and by a building in Minnesota are uncorrelated because each building was damaged by a different windstorm. However, the windstorm exposures of two adjacent buildings are positively correlated, because both could be damaged by the same windstorm. The following examples demonstrate how pooling serves to reduce risk without actually transferring it.

How Pooling Reduces Risk

Suppose that two organizations—Galston and Atwell—are each exposed to the possibility of an accident in the coming year. Assume that each has a 20 percent chance of an accident that will cause a $2,500 loss and that each has an 80 percent chance of not experiencing an accident. Also assume that Galston's and Atwell's accidental losses are uncorrelated. Finally, assume that neither organization will have more than one accident during the year. Exhibit 2-1 shows the resulting probability distribution for each organization's accidental losses without pooling. (A probability distribution is a presentation of probability estimates of a particular set of circumstances and the probability of each outcome.)

EXHIBIT 2-1

Probability Distribution of Accidental Losses for Each Organization (Galston and Atwell) Without Pooling

Outcomes	Probability
$ 0	.80
$2,500	.20

Probability distributions can be used to calculate expected cost. Each organization has an 80 percent chance of no loss and a 20 percent chance of a $2,500 loss.

Because Galston and Atwell each face a 20 percent chance of having an accident that causes $2,500 in losses, the expected loss (the average cost per year over the long term) for each organization without pooling is $500, calculated as follows:

$$\text{Expected loss} = (.80 \times \$0) + (.20 \times \$2,500) = \$500.$$

Four years out of every five—that is, 80 percent (or .80) of the time—expected loss is $0. Over the long term, one year out of every five—that is, 20 percent (or .20) of the time—it is $2,500.

The variability in losses can be measured using standard deviation. Standard deviation is the average of the differences (deviation) between possible outcomes and the expected value of those outcomes. In this example, the standard deviation is $1,000. It is calculated as follows:

$$\text{Standard deviation} = \sqrt{.8\big(\$0 - \$500\big)^2 + .2\big(\$2,500 - \$500\big)^2} = \$1,000.$$

Suppose Galston and Atwell agree to evenly split any losses that the two may incur. That is, they agree to share losses equally, each paying half their combined average loss. This constitutes a pool, because Galston and Atwell are pooling their resources to collectively pay for losses that may occur.

Exhibit 2-2 lists the four possible outcomes that result from this arrangement and shows how pooling will affect the distribution of losses for each. The second column shows the probability that a given outcome will occur. Because Galston's losses are independent of Atwell's, the probability that neither organization will have an accident is simply the probability that Galston will not have an accident multiplied by the probability that Atwell will not have an accident. Therefore, the probability of the first listed outcome is .8 × .8 = 0.64. The greater the probability, the more likely an outcome will occur.

EXHIBIT 2-2

Probability Distribution of Losses Paid by Each Organization (Galston and Atwell) With Pooling

	Possible Outcomes	Probability	Total Losses	Losses Paid by Each Organization (Average Loss)
1.	Neither Atwell nor Galston has an accident.	(.8)(.8) = .64	$ 0	$ 0
2.	Atwell has an accident, but Galston does not.	(.2)(.8) = .16	$2,500	$1,250
3.	Galston has an accident, but Atwell does not.	(.2)(.8) = .16	$2,500	$1,250
4.	Both Atwell and Galston have an accident.	(.2)(.2) = .04	$5,000	$2,500

The probability that Atwell will have an accident but Galston will not equals .2 × .8 = .16. The probability that Galston will have an accident but Atwell will not is also .16. Therefore, the probability that only one of the organizations will have an accident equals .16 + .16 = .32. The probability of the fourth outcome (both have an accident) is .2 × .2 = .04.

This example demonstrates that pooling does not change accident frequency or severity, but does change the probability distribution of losses facing each organization. The probability that Galston will pay losses equal to $2,500 is reduced from .20 to .04. This is because Galston will not need to pay $2,500 unless both Galston and Atwell experience an accident. Given that their accidents are independent, or uncorrelated, the probability that both Galston and Atwell will have an accident is lower than the probability that only Galston, or only Atwell, will have an accident.

Although the probability that either organization will face a $2,500 loss is reduced, the probability that neither organization will have a loss is also reduced from .80 to .64. Even if Galston does not have an accident, Atwell might have one, and vice versa.

Although both Atwell's risk and Galston's risk are reduced by pooling, each organization's expected loss is unchanged. It still equals $500, based on calculations shown in Exhibit 2-3.

EXHIBIT 2-3

Expected Losses Paid by Each Organization (Galston and Atwell) With Pooling

(a)	(b)	(a) × (b)
Losses by Each Organization (Average Loss)	Probability	
$ 0	.64	$ 0
$1,250	.16	$200
$1,250	.16	$200
$2,500	.04	$100
Total	**1.00**	**$500**

Pooling reduces each organization's risk but does not change each organization's expected accident cost.

Because the pooling arrangement reduces the probabilities of the extreme outcomes, the standard deviation of expected losses paid by both Galston and Atwell is reduced. Recall that, without pooling, the standard deviation of losses in this example is $1,000. With pooling, the standard deviation of losses declines to $707, calculated as follows:

Standard deviation =

$$\sqrt{.64 \times (\$0 - \$500)^2 + .32 \times (\$1,250 - \$500)^2 + .04 \times (\$2,500 - \$500)^2} = \$707.$$

In summary, pooling does not change either organization's expected loss but makes both of their actual losses more consistent and less variable. Pooling, therefore, ultimately reduces each organization's risk.

Adding organizations to the pool further reduces risk for each participant. To illustrate, suppose that Calloway, who has the same probability distribution for losses as Atwell and Galston, joins the pool. At year's end, each organization will pay one-third of their collective total losses (the average loss). The addition of a third organization whose losses are independent of the other two further reduces the probability of extreme outcomes ($0 or $2,500). For example, for Atwell to pay $2,500 in accident costs, all three organizations must have a $2,500 loss. The probability of this occurring is .2 × .2 × .2 = .008. As a consequence, the standard deviation for each organization decreases with the addition of another participant. While risk (standard deviation) decreases, each organization's expected loss remains constant at $500.

The probability distribution of each organization's accident cost will continue to change as more participants are added to the pool. Exhibit 2-4 compares the probability distribution for average losses when four or twenty participants are in the pool. Note that as the number of pool participants increases, the probability of extreme outcomes (very high average losses and very low average losses) decreases. Stated differently, the probability that average losses (the amounts paid by each participant) will be close to $500 (the expected loss) increases. Also, as the number of participants increases, the probability distribution of each organization's loss (the average loss) becomes more bell-shaped. A bell-shaped (or symmetrical) distribution is characteristic of a normal distribution, which has known characteristics that can be used to develop reliable forecasts.

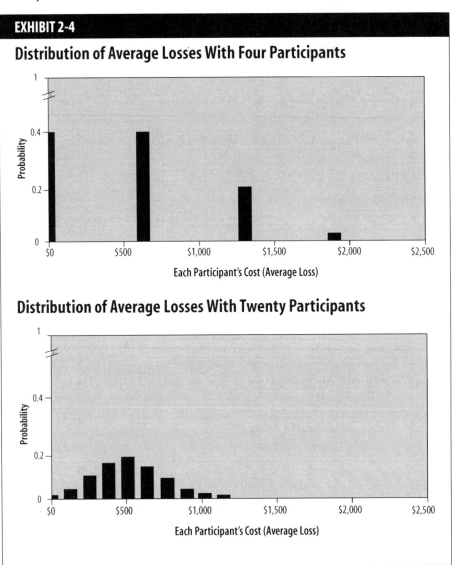

EXHIBIT 2-4

Distribution of Average Losses With Four Participants

Distribution of Average Losses With Twenty Participants

As the number of pool participants increases, the probability of extreme outcomes decreases and the loss probability distribution for each participant becomes more bell-shaped.

In summary, pooling increases the predictability of each of its participant's losses by reducing the variability of their average loss. Therefore, pooling reduces each participant's risk. As even more participants are added, the loss probability distribution becomes increasingly bell-shaped.

Although pooling does not prevent losses or transfer risk, it does reduce the amount of risk borne by each participant. The law of large numbers provides a mathematical explanation of the risk reduction that results from pooling.

How the Law of Large Numbers Explains Pooling

When the number of participants in a pool becomes very large, the standard deviation of the average losses to the pool approaches zero, rendering the risk negligible for each participant. This result reflects what is known as the law of large numbers. The **law of large numbers** is a mathematical principle stating that when the number of similar, independent exposure units increases, the relative accuracy of predictions about future outcomes based on these exposure units also increases. Though the law of large numbers can be expressed mathematically, it essentially postulates that the mean of a random sample of a population approaches the mean (expected value) of the population as a whole as the sample size increases.

When applied to a pool, the law of large numbers relies on independent (uncorrelated) losses to accurately predict expected losses. However, hazard risks are often positively correlated.

Law of large numbers
A mathematical principle stating that when the number of similar, independent exposure units increases, the relative accuracy of predictions about future outcomes based on these exposure units also increases.

How Positively Correlated Losses Affect a Pool

Positively correlated losses increase the probability that multiple pool participants will suffer simultaneous losses. For example, a natural disaster may affect only one pool participant but probably will inflict losses on many other pool participants. Conversely, positively correlated losses imply that when one pool participant incurs losses below expectations or suffers no loss, then so will other pool participants. Therefore, when losses are positively correlated, average losses are more difficult to predict.

The effect of positively correlated losses on the distribution of average losses is summarized in Exhibit 2-5, which presents two cases in which 1,000 participants are in the pool and each participant has an expected loss of $500. In one case, each participant's losses are uncorrelated; in the other, they are positively correlated. As illustrated, when losses are positively correlated, their distribution has a greater variability (higher standard deviation), which means that losses are less predictable.

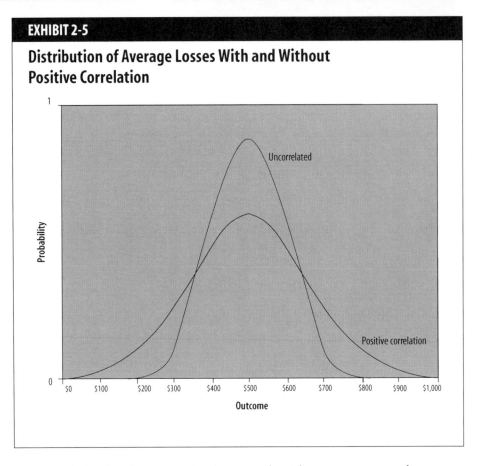

EXHIBIT 2-5

Distribution of Average Losses With and Without Positive Correlation

When losses are positively correlated, their distribution has a greater variability (higher standard deviation), making them less predictable.

Loss correlation has important implications for risk management and insurance. Positively correlated losses have the potential of causing simultaneous loss to large numbers of pool participants, thereby undermining the risk sharing principles on which pooling is based.

Insurance relies on the principles of pooling to operate. However, two key features distinguish it from pooling alone.

How Insurance Differs From Pooling

Pooling is a mechanism for sharing losses; but not for transferring risks. Insurance, although it is based on loss-sharing principles, is a risk-transfer technique that provides stronger guarantees that sufficient funds will be available in the event of a loss than does pooling alone.

Although an insurer fundamentally resembles a formal pooling mechanism, the two are distinct in the following two important ways:

1. Insurance transfers risk from the insured to the insurer in exchange for premiums, rather than simply serving as a conduit for sharing losses with others.

2. The insurer has additional financial resources from which it can fund losses, enabling it to provide a stronger guarantee that sufficient funds will be available in the event of a loss, further reducing risk.

The premiums an insurer receives should be sufficient to pay for losses, expenses, profits, and contingencies. Contingencies are often addressed by including a risk charge (or risk loading) in the premium. A **risk charge** is an amount over and above the expected loss component of the premium to compensate the insurer for taking the risk that losses may be higher than expected. The premium amount compensates the insurer for assuming the insured's risk. Insurer collection of premium eliminates the counterparty risk that is present in pooling. **Counterparty risk** is the risk that the other party to an agreement will default.

Insurers have net worth (called policyholders' surplus) available to satisfy losses that exceed premiums paid by insureds. Net worth is the excess of assets over liabilities. Excess assets may be the result of retained earnings or contributed capital. Regardless of its source, an insurer's net worth provides it with the financial strength it needs to financially endure unexpected losses that would otherwise bankrupt a pool, which has no surplus from which to draw.

Risk transfer, and the resulting financial stability, is not the only aspect of insurance that organizations seek. Many organizations also value the risk management services provided by insurers as part of the insurance product.

Risk charge
An amount over and above the expected loss component of the premium to compensate the insurer for taking the risk that losses may be higher than expected.

Counterparty risk
The risk that the other party to an agreement will default.

Insurer-Provided Risk Management Services

Many organizations rely on their insurers to provide risk management services. These same services are needed by organizations that choose to retain their hazard risk. Insurers provide risk management services because they derive an immediate benefit when their insureds' losses are prevented or reduced. Likewise, organizations benefit from these services. When organizations consider risk financing techniques other than insurance, they should consider the cost of insurer-provided risk management services as well as the expense the organization would incur to replace them. The following risk management services can be purchased independently of the insurance product from many insurers or third-party administrators:

- Risk control services
- Claim and legal services

Risk Control Services

Because they handle the losses of many different insureds, insurers develop expertise in assessing and controlling risk. This expertise is especially important when dealing with hazards that may result in employee injury as well as for high-severity losses. Insurers provide assistance both in identifying loss exposures and in recommending ways to control the associated risk of loss.

With insurance, insurers bear the cost of losses, which provides a strong financial incentive for them to identify and implement measures that control their insureds' losses. Insurers provide risk control services to organizations both to complement insurance coverage and as a separate fee-based service. Insured organizations strive to control their losses because the premium for the next coverage period may be based, in part, on current loss experience.

Claim and Legal Services

Because they handle claims made by many different policyholders, insurers are adept at claim handling. Settling claims, administering claim payments, and preventing fraud are among the specialized areas of expertise necessary to handle claims. As mentioned, under guaranteed-cost insurance, an insurer has a financial incentive to control claim costs because of its contractual obligation to pay for losses regardless of their severity. Insurers have other specialized areas of claim expertise, such as the management of medical and disability claims. In addition, insurers have knowledge of systems to report, track, and pay for claims.

Many claims, especially liability claims, require attorneys with special expertise. Insurers not only employ staff attorneys with such expertise, but they also develop a network of legal resources over a large geographic area, benefiting policyholders that have widespread operations.

With liability insurance, insurers are often viewed as a third party by the claimant and the insured. Sometimes this is advantageous in that it reduces stress on other relationships between two parties that may need to cooperate in other matters. For example, workers' compensation claims potentially create conflict between worker and employer. The conflict is usually mitigated when an insurer, rather than the employer, negotiates issues involving the claim.

In summary, insurance is an effective risk financing technique because it offers the financial certainty of risk transfer while including services that address the insured organization's need to control risks and mitigate losses. Insurance's effectiveness increases when loss exposures have certain characteristics.

CHARACTERISTICS OF AN IDEALLY INSURABLE LOSS EXPOSURE

Pooling reduces risk for individual pool participants if the pool is sufficiently large. However, pool size is just one of several characteristics insurers consider when evaluating the viability of a loss exposure for insurance. The loss exposures individual insurers choose to insure often are determined by characteristics that make some loss exposures more desirable to insure than others. Exhibit 2-6 shows the six characteristics of an ideally insurable loss exposure.

EXHIBIT 2-6

Six Characteristics of an Ideally Insurable Loss Exposure

1. Pure risk—involves pure risk, not speculative risk

2. Fortuitous losses—subject to fortuitous loss from the insured's standpoint

3. Definite and measurable—subject to losses that are definite in time, cause, and location and that are measurable

4. Homogenous—one of a large number of similar exposure units

5. Independent and not catastrophic—not subject to a loss that would simultaneously affect many other similar loss exposures; loss would not be catastrophic

6. Affordable—premiums are economically feasible

Note that these are ideal, not requisite, characteristics. Most insured loss exposures do not completely meet all of these criteria. This section outlines each of these characteristics and explains why and how they affect an insurer's willingness to provide insurance coverage.

Pure Risk

Pure risk, the first characteristic of an ideally insurable loss exposure, is a chance of loss or no loss, but no chance of gain. For example, robbery would be considered a pure risk because the robbery victim cannot possibly experience a gain as a result, even if indemnified for the loss by insurance. Such a situation creates an incentive for an insured to safeguard its loss exposures. Insurance contracts generally promise to indemnify the insured. That is, they promise to restore it to the same financial position that it was in before the loss. The pure risk associated with a loss exposure is generally insurable.

In contrast, speculative risk is generally not insurable. Speculative risk is a chance of loss, no loss, or gain. For example, plant expansion to satisfy expected product demand would constitute a speculative risk because it may result in needed production capacity or it could be an investment that cannot be used when product demand does not materialize. Speculative risk is inherent in the operation of almost all organizations. Some speculative risks are subject to risk financing techniques such as hedging, but insurance is not a risk financing technique applied to speculative risks because it is not economically feasible for an organization to insure its profits.

Fortuitous Losses

The second characteristic of an ideally insurable loss exposure is that its associated loss should be fortuitous (or accidental) from the insured's perspective. When there is no uncertainty regarding loss, no risk of loss exists. Insurance would serve no purpose in such a case. Uncertainty is absent when a loss cannot possibly happen, or when it is guaranteed to happen. By definition, a loss cannot occur when an exposure is avoided, so there is no risk of loss to transfer to an insurer.

Uncertainty also is absent when the organization has complete control over whether a loss occurs. In such a situation, chance of loss exists, but the organization faces no uncertainty. An insurer would be unwise to knowingly provide insurance against a loss that can be caused at will by the party who, in turn, will receive payment for that loss from the insurer. Otherwise, for example, an organization that owns a building that it no longer needs could profit by burning it down. Insurance policies normally exclude coverage for losses that are expected or deliberately caused by the insured.

Definite and Measurable

Ideally, whether an insured event has occurred should be obvious, and insurers should draft insurance policies that leave little doubt as to what they cover. Insurance is best suited for covering potential losses that can later be determined to have happened at a specific time. Therefore, the third characteristic of an ideally insurable loss exposure is that it be definite and measurable. Insurance typically provides coverage for a specific period, after which the insurer is not obligated to pay for the insured's losses

Establishing a definite time that a loss occurred does not often present a problem with property insurance, because most property losses involve a dramatic event that is immediately apparent. Even so, questions sometimes develop relating to property losses caused by employee theft, gradual contamination or pollution, mold damage, or other causes of loss that occur over a period of time. In liability insurance, questions often develop regarding the timing of the event that triggers coverage, because an injury may manifest many years after the accident that caused it.

Just as this characteristic requires that losses be definite in time, they also must be measurable. For example, the value of a "priceless" painting is not really determined until it is sold. The painting's insurer must establish a value that would be paid before the loss occurs. However, for most insured property, the insurer relies on insurance policy provisions to establish the method used to determine the amount the insurer will pay. Similarly, liability insurance policies contain limits of liability that allow the insurer to limit loss amounts.

Homogenous

The fourth characteristic of an ideally insurable loss exposure is that it must also be homogenous, that is, one of a large number of similar exposure units. The importance of having a large number of exposure units to improve predictability has already been discussed in the context of pooling—increasing the size of the pool decreases the risk. Embedded in the definition of the law of large numbers is the requirement that loss exposures be similar. Similar exposure units, because they are expected to respond similarly to similar causes of loss, improve loss predictability. For example, restaurants share many of the same loss characteristics and consequently have similar loss experience. Because of the diversity in loss exposures, the similarity among them is relative.

Despite the number of exposure units insured, few insurers have enough exposure units in each classification to make loss predictions entirely accurate when using only their own data. Most insurers aggregate exposure and loss data with other insurers so that expected, or average, losses for each classification can be determined. Individual insurers use expected losses (called loss costs) to set their premium rates.

Independent and Not Catastrophic

Insurance is based on the premise that only a small percentage of the loss exposures will experience a loss at any one time. Consequently, a relatively small insurance premium paid by each insured is sufficient to pay for all losses. That is, the premiums of the many go to pay the losses of the unfortunate few. However, catastrophic events have proven to overwhelm insurers' financial resources, thereby making them unable to pay claims. For example, Hurricane Andrew in 1992 is cited as the primary cause of several insurer insolvencies. The fifth characteristic of an ideally insurable loss exposure, therefore, is that the loss must be independent and not catastrophic.

The effect of a catastrophic loss is relative to the insurer's financial strength. Therefore, insurers have devised means to mitigate the financial effect of potential catastrophic losses. For example, most property insurers minimize the geographic concentration of their loss exposures by limiting the accumulated value of insured properties in a particular area. Insurers can also minimize the geographic concentration of loss exposures by purchasing reinsurance. Reinsurance enables insurers to share the risk of loss with other insurers. In addition to spreading risk geographically, insurers can spread risk among many different types of insurance. An insurer's product diversity may enable it to better withstand losses on one type of insurance while profiting from another. For example, an insurer may have an unprofitable year with its property insurance products because of a catastrophic event while it continues to earn a profit on its general liability and workers' compensation insurance products.

Affordable

The sixth and final characteristic of an ideally insurable loss exposure is that the loss must be affordable. Insurers sell insurance and organizations buy insurance only when it makes good economic sense to do so. Exposures involving high loss frequency or low loss severity often fail to meet that criterion.

High-frequency losses often are predictable enough to be funded using retention, which avoids the overhead expenses of insurance. For example, an organization that ships a large number of inexpensive packages can usually predict the total losses associated with them.

Most low-severity losses are inconsequential, so they can readily be managed with one's own resources. For example, a large organization can easily pay for a physical damage loss that occurs to one of its vehicles.

Although insurance works well for many low-frequency loss exposures, it may not be economically feasible for losses with a very low frequency, because there is no demand for protection against something that is considered highly unlikely to occur. For example, until Mount Saint Helens erupted in Washington, most people thought the possibility of a volcanic eruption was practically nonexistent in the continental United States. Many property insurance policies made no specific reference to damage originating from volcanoes, and there was no demand for insurance against volcanic eruption. Likewise, people in many areas of the U.S. where earthquakes are possible but unlikely to occur do not purchase earthquake insurance.

Loss exposures involving very high severity and very low frequency losses are often difficult to insure. The insurance market has often been able to insure such loss exposures as the marketplace has quantified the risk of loss. For example, nuclear power plant accidents that result in radioactive contamination are so infrequent that they are unpredictable. Their consequences, however, are extremely severe. Insurers, through pools, have been able to insure this loss exposure, but only through worldwide risk-sharing arrangements.

Loss exposures that satisfy many of the six characteristics of an ideally insurable loss exposure are more likely to be insured through one of the principal types of insurance than those that do not. The next section describes these types of commercial insurance.

TYPES OF INSURANCE THAT ADDRESS SPECIFIC LOSS EXPOSURES

Insurers provide insurance coverage for most, but not all, loss exposures. Risk management professionals need to understand the types of insurance available and the coverage provided by each so that they can evaluate whether their organization's risk can be effectively transferred using insurance. Exhibit 2-7 shows the principal types of commercial insurance.

Manuscript policy
An insurance policy that is developed to meet a unique coverage need; generally a one-of-a-kind policy.

Although this is an extensive list, it is by no means exhaustive. Insurers have developed insurance coverage for specific loss exposures that may not normally be insured. Many insurers are willing to customize insurance coverage to satisfy specific insurance needs through the use of manuscript policies. A **manuscript policy** is an insurance policy that is developed to meet a unique coverage need; it is generally a one-of-a-kind policy. Manuscript policies are typically used for organizations with unusual loss exposures or for loss exposures not routinely covered by insurers.

EXHIBIT 2-7

Types of Commercial Insurance

Property insurance	Environmental insurance
Business income insurance	Aircraft insurance
General liability insurance	Umbrella liability insurance
Auto insurance	Surety bonds
Workers' compensation and employers' liability insurance	Ocean marine insurance
	Inland marine insurance
Flood insurance	Crime insurance
Directors and officers liability insurance	Equipment breakdown insurance
Employment practices liability insurance	Businessowners insurance
Professional liability insurance	Difference in conditions (DIC) insurance

Property Insurance

Commercial property insurance can be loosely described as insurance on commercial buildings and their contents. That is not an entirely accurate description, however, because commercial property insurance also covers certain structures that are not buildings, such as signs and permanently installed fixtures. Moreover, it insures items of personal property other than those that are strictly contents of a building, such as property outside buildings. However, with only limited exceptions, commercial property insurance is restricted to property on (or within 100 feet of) the insured location. Therefore, most of the personal property insured is personal property located inside the building.

Commercial property insurance coverage can be provided under several coverage forms. The Building and Personal Property Coverage Form, developed by Insurance Services Office (ISO), can be used by most organizations. Some organizations require specialized coverage forms for buildings under construction, condominium association buildings, and the property of condominium unit owners. Other organizations purchase a package policy that combines property insurance and liability into a single coverage form, such as the businessowners coverage form. ISO commercial package policy also combines property insurance and liability insurance, but the property component is the Building and Personal Property Coverage Form (BPP). Depending on the nature of its loss exposures, an insured may have to purchase more than one commercial property coverage form.

Any of these coverage forms must be supplemented with a causes of loss form to express the covered causes of loss. The three fundamental causes of loss forms available are basic form, broad form, and special form. Flood and earthquake causes of loss can be added by endorsement. Exhibit 2-8 shows the covered causes of loss in the basic and broad forms.

EXHIBIT 2-8

Covered Causes of Loss in Basic and Broad Forms

Both Forms Cover:

- Fire
- Lightning
- Explosion
- Windstorm or hail
- Smoke
- Aircraft or vehicles
- Riot or civil commotion
- Vandalism
- Sprinkler leakage
- Sinkhole collapse
- Volcanic action

Broad Form Also Covers:

- Falling objects
- Weight of snow, ice, or sleet
- Water damage
- Collapse caused by certain causes of loss (provided as an additional coverage)

The Causes of Loss—Broad Form expands the number of causes of loss that are insured by the Causes of Loss—Basic Form.

The Causes of Loss—Special Form (or simply "special form"), instead of listing the causes of loss covered, states that it covers "risks of direct physical loss," subject to the exclusions and limitations expressed in the form. This type of coverage is often referred to as "all-risks" coverage. However, that phrase overstates the breadth of coverage provided.

Risk management professionals are as interested in what a policy does not cover as in what it does cover. Exclusions potentially create coverage gaps that must be addressed through other risk financing techniques. The basic form, broad form, and special form each contain exclusions that further define the coverage provided. The exclusions for the Causes of Loss—Basic Form include the following:

Ordinance or law—Ordinances or laws may require damaged or destroyed buildings to be rebuilt to current building standards. Compliance with current building codes is not covered because of this exclusion. However, the exclusion can be eliminated for an additional premium.

Earth movement—Earth movement includes earthquake, landslide, mine subsidence, and similar earth movements, but not sinkhole collapse. (Sinkhole collapse is already a covered cause of loss.) Earthquake is not a covered cause of loss under the basic form, but earthquake coverage can be added for an additional premium. When added to the policy, earthquake coverage also covers land shocks and movement resulting from volcanic eruption, which are not included in volcanic action cause of loss coverage.

Government action—Seizure or destruction of property by government action is not covered. This exclusion does not apply to the destruction of property by governmental order to stop the spread of a covered fire, in which case the policy provides coverage.

Nuclear hazard—The basic form excludes loss caused by nuclear reaction, radiation, or radioactive contamination. Loss by fire resulting from these causes is covered. Some coverage for radioactive contamination can be provided by endorsement.

Utility services—The basic form excludes loss caused by power failure or failure of other utility services if the damage causing such failure occurs away from the described premises. However, loss from a covered cause of loss resulting from power failure is covered. Coverage for off-premises service interruption caused by an insured cause of loss is available by endorsement.

War and military action—The war and military action exclusion eliminates coverage for loss caused by war, revolution, insurrection, or similar actions.

Water—Loss caused by flooding and related causes of loss is difficult to insure. Depending on location, some insureds have a much greater likelihood than others of suffering a flood loss. Moreover, the consequences of a flood can be catastrophic. Insurers, therefore, exclude flood losses from commercial property forms. The water exclusion eliminates coverage for damage caused by flood, surface water, tides, and tidal waves; mudslide or mudflow; backing up of sewers, drains, or sumps; and underground water pressing on, or flowing or seeping through, foundations, walls, doors, windows, or other openings. However, damage by fire, explosion, or sprinkler leakage caused by any of the foregoing is covered. The exclusions listed apply regardless of whether the loss event results in widespread damage.

Other exclusions—The basic form also excludes loss or damage caused by the following:

- Artificially generated electric currents. However, if a fire results, the resulting fire damage is covered.

- Rupture or bursting of water pipes unless caused by a covered cause of loss. This exclusion does not apply to sprinkler leakage.

- Leakage of water or steam from any part of an appliance or system containing water or steam (other than an automatic sprinkler system), unless caused by a covered cause of loss.

- Explosion of steam boilers, steam pipes, steam turbines, or steam engines owned by, leased to, or operated by the insured. However, if such an explosion causes a fire or a combustion explosion, the damage caused by fire or combustion explosion is covered.

- Mechanical breakdown, including rupture or bursting caused by centrifugal force.

- Loss resulting from the neglect of the insured to use all reasonable means to save and preserve property at and after the time of loss. This exclusion reinforces the insured's duty to protect covered property after a loss.

Business Income Insurance

Business income (BI) insurance covers the reduction in an organization's income when operations are interrupted by damage to property caused by a covered cause of loss. Because the severity of a business income loss correlates with the length of time required to restore the property, business income coverage is called a "time element" coverage, or "business interruption" coverage.

Insurance for most business income loss exposures can be provided under either of the following two ISO forms:

1. The Business Income (and Extra Expense) Coverage Form, which covers both business income loss and extra expense losses
2. The Business Income (Without Extra Expense) Coverage Form, which covers business income loss but covers extra expenses only to the extent that they reduce the business income loss

Business income is the sum of net profit or loss that would have been earned or incurred if operations had not been suspended plus normal operating expenses, including payroll, that continues during the suspension. For manufacturing organizations, net income includes the net sales value of production. Extra expense, in the context of extra expense coverage, is coverage for extra expenses incurred by the named insured to avoid or minimize the suspension of operations.

Organizations can purchase business income insurance as part of a property insurance package policy or as a stand-alone policy. The causes of loss covered for business income coverage can be designated by either the same causes of loss form that applies to other coverage forms or by a different causes of loss form that applies to business income coverage only.

General Liability Insurance

Commercial general liability (CGL) insurance is the most basic, and often the most important, coverage for insuring commercial general liability loss exposures. The loss exposures covered by CGL insurance are often characterized as premises, operations, products, and completed operations. With the exception of automobile loss exposures and workers' compensation obligations, CGL insurance covers the majority of liability loss exposures facing many organizations.

The principal coverage form used to provide CGL insurance is ISO Commercial General Liability Coverage Form. The two versions of this coverage form differ only with respect to what must transpire to trigger coverage. These two CGL coverage form versions are the following:

*   The occurrence coverage form covers bodily injury or property damage that occurs during the policy period, regardless of when a claim is actually made against the insured organization.

- The claims-made coverage form covers bodily injury or property damage that occurs after the retroactive date stated in the policy. The retroactive date stated in the policy can be the same as the policy inception date or can be earlier than the policy inception date, but only if a claim for the injury or damage is first made at some time during the policy period (or during an extended reporting period, if applicable).

Apart from the coverage trigger, both forms provide the same coverages, which are summarized as follows:

Coverage A—Bodily Injury and Property Damage Liability. The insurer agrees to pay on behalf of the insured those sums that the insured becomes legally obligated to pay as damages because of bodily injury or property damage covered by the policy. The insurer also agrees to defend the insured against claims or suits alleging such damages. Several exclusions define the scope of coverage. Among the most important exclusions are those applying to intended injury, injury to employees of the insured, pollution, aircraft, automobiles, watercraft, and damage to the insured's own work or products. The majority of excluded loss exposures are normally covered by other types of insurance, such as auto insurance or workers' compensation insurance. The exclusions are often used to eliminate duplicate coverage under two separate insurance policies, but the risk management professional must be familiar with the complementary coverages in all of these various insurance policies.

Coverage B—Personal and Advertising Injury Liability. The insurer agrees to pay on behalf of the insured those sums that the insured becomes legally obligated to pay as damages because of personal and advertising injury to which the insurance applies. Personal and advertising injury includes such offenses as libel, slander, false arrest, wrongful eviction, and infringement of copyright.

Coverage C—Medical Payments. Medical payments insurance covers medical expenses, irrespective of whether the insured organization is legally liable to pay them, for persons other than insureds who are injured on the insured's premises or because of the insured's operations.

Auto Insurance

ISO commercial auto coverage forms include the Business Auto Coverage Form, the Garage Coverage Form, the Truckers Coverage Form, and the Motor Carriers Coverage Form. All four coverage forms can be used to provide auto liability insurance and auto physical damage insurance. Other coverages—such as medical payments, uninsured motorists, and personal injury protection—can be added by endorsement.

The Business Auto Coverage Form is the most frequently used of the four ISO commercial auto forms. It is designed to meet the auto insurance needs of most types of organizations.

The Garage Coverage Form is designed to meet the special needs of automobile dealers. Because it is often difficult to separate the auto liability and general liability loss exposures of an auto dealer, the Garage Coverage Form insures both types of loss exposures. It also provides garagekeepers coverage, which insures damage to customers' vehicles while in the insured's care, custody, or control. The Garage Coverage Form also includes provisions for insuring the inventory of an auto dealer on a reporting or nonreporting basis.

The Truckers Coverage Form and the Motor Carrier Coverage Form are similar in that each is specifically designed for insuring the auto liability and physical damage loss exposures of individuals or organizations in the business of transporting the property of others. The Motor Carrier Coverage Form, which was introduced in 1993, is designed to accommodate changes in trucking regulation that occurred after the Truckers Coverage Form was developed in the late 1970s.

Workers' Compensation and Employers' Liability Insurance

With the exception of maritime employers, almost all employers must obtain workers' compensation insurance or qualify as a self-insurer under the applicable state workers' compensation statute. Except in the few states that require workers' compensation insurance to be purchased from the state government, most workers' compensation insurance is provided in connection with employers' liability insurance in a single policy.

The most commonly used workers' compensation and employers' liability policy is that of the National Council on Compensation Insurance (NCCI). The workers' compensation portion of the policy covers the insured's obligation for occupational injury and disease under the relevant workers' compensation law(s). Employers are typically responsible for medical expenses of injured workers without limitation and are also liable for disability payments when injured workers cannot work. Employers' level of responsibility differs by state, but employer exposure to workers' compensation losses is generally a very significant amount. The employers' liability portion of the policy covers common-law suits against the employer that arise out of employee injury or disease. By endorsement, the policy can be extended to cover obligations under other statutes, such as the U.S. Longshore and Harbor Workers' Compensation Act (LHWCA).

Flood Insurance

A commercial insured's first layer of flood coverage is often obtained through the National Flood Insurance Program (NFIP). Additional layers of flood insurance, if needed, can usually be arranged by endorsement to a commercial package policy or under a difference in conditions (DIC) policy. The main policy form that NFIP uses to provide flood insurance on commercial buildings and contents is the Standard Flood Insurance Policy—General Property Form.

The NFIP also offers a Residential Condominium Building Association Policy for insuring residential condominium buildings and contents that are owned either by the unit owners in common or by the condominium association solely.

Directors and Officers Liability Insurance

The individuals who serve as the directors and officers of a corporation can be sued for breach of their corporate duties. Such suits may be brought by stockholders or by persons outside the corporation. In recognition of this loss exposure, many corporations agree (or may even be required by law) to indemnify their directors and officers for the costs resulting from suits against them.

Directors and officers (D&O) liability policies have traditionally contained two insuring agreements. The first agreement covers the directors and officers of the insured corporation for their personal liability as directors and officers that results from a "wrongful act." The second agreement, often referred to as company reimbursement coverage, covers the sums that the insured is required or permitted by law to pay to the directors and officers as indemnification. In addition, some D&O liability policies include entity coverage, which covers the named corporation against lawsuits made directly against the corporation alleging wrongful acts covered by the policy.

Employment Practices Liability Insurance

In response to an increase in lawsuits by employees against their employers for various employment-related offenses, many organizations now purchase employment practices liability insurance. This insurance covers the insured, its directors and officers, and, often, its employees for liability arising out of various employment-related offenses alleged to have been committed against its employees. Examples of these offenses are wrongful termination, discrimination, and sexual harassment.

Professional Liability Insurance

Insurers provide professional liability insurance for people in many different professions and occupations. Those who purchase professional liability insurance include physicians, dentists, veterinarians, nurses, accountants, architects, engineers, lawyers, insurance agents and brokers, and even hair stylists and tattoo artists.

The coverage provided by a professional liability policy varies with the type of professional activity being insured. For example, a physician's professional liability policy typically covers a patient's injuries that result from a medical incident, whereas an accountant's professional liability policy typically covers all sums that the insured becomes legally obligated to pay because of errors or omissions in providing accounting services, excluding bodily injury or property damage. Virtually all professional liability policies are on a claims-made basis.

Environmental Insurance

Insurers have developed various types of environmental insurance, both first-party and third-party, to manage pollution-related loss exposures that are largely excluded by most other commercial insurance policies. The leading insurers in environmental insurance use independently developed policies. The Pollution and Remediation Legal Liability Policy is an example of a site-specific environmental impairment liability (EIL) policy. Typically, this type of policy covers the insured's liability for bodily injury and property damage resulting from pollution occurring at or emanating from the insured premises, the costs of cleaning up and removing each pollutant, and the costs of defending against claims alleging covered damages.

Aircraft Insurance

The CGL policy excludes liability for the ownership, maintenance, or use of aircraft. However, an aircraft policy can be used to provide both liability and physical damage insurance on aircraft.

Umbrella Liability Insurance

The three main purposes of a commercial umbrella liability policy are as follows:

1. To provide an additional amount of insurance when damages for which the insured is held liable exceed the per occurrence limit in an underlying liability policy
2. To pay liability claims that are not covered in full by an underlying policy because the aggregate limit in the underlying liability policy has been depleted or exhausted
3. To cover claims that are outside the scope of the coverage of underlying policies

A similar coverage is commercial excess liability insurance, which serves all but the last listed purpose. Not all insurers follow the terminology used here. An insurer that provides a true umbrella liability policy might name it "Excess Liability Policy," and an insurer whose form provides only excess liability coverage (as defined here) might call the policy its "Umbrella Excess Liability Policy."

Umbrella liability policies require that the insured maintain certain underlying coverages, up to stipulated limits of liability, during the policy term. Therefore, virtually every umbrella policy contains a schedule of underlying coverages. Requirements for underlying insurance vary by insurer.

Surety Bonds

A surety bond involves three parties: the principal, the obligee, and the surety. The principal is obligated to perform in some way for the benefit of the obligee. The surety guarantees to the obligee that the principal will fulfill the underlying obligations. In most cases, the party making the guarantee—the surety—is an insurance company that also sells property and liability insurance.

Many types of surety bonds are used in a variety of circumstances. However, all surety bonds can be divided into the following categories:

- Contract bonds guarantee the performance of public or private contracts. Common examples of contract bonds are bid bonds, performance bonds, and payment bonds.

- License and permit bonds are required by federal, state, or municipal governments as prerequisites to engaging in certain business activities. Among those parties that may need such bonds are contractors who work on public streets, plumbers, electricians, and automobile dealers.

- Court bonds are prescribed by statute and include judicial bonds and fiduciary bonds. Judicial bonds arise out of litigation and are posted by parties seeking court remedies or defending against legal actions seeking court remedies. Fiduciary bonds are filed in probate courts and courts that exercise equitable jurisdiction; they guarantee that persons whom such courts have entrusted with the care of others' property will perform their specified duties faithfully.

- Miscellaneous bonds are those that do not fit well under other commercial surety bond classifications. They often support private relationships and unique business needs. Some significant miscellaneous bonds include lost securities bonds, hazardous waste bonds, and financial guaranty bonds.

Ocean Marine Insurance

Many organizations import and export goods that are transported across oceans. In addition, organizations ship materials on inland waterways, lakes, rivers, and canals. Waterborne vessels perform many activities, such as drilling for oil and gas and helping build and maintain marine facilities. Tugboats provide essential assistance to larger vessels and move barges on waterways. Yachts are used for pleasure trips. Property and liability exposures that arise out of such activities can be insured with ocean marine insurance.

Some of the same perils that threaten property on land also threaten waterborne commerce. For example, vessels and cargoes are subject to loss by causes of loss such as fire, lightning, and windstorm. However, the hazards to waterborne shipping go well beyond those affecting land transportation. For a ship, there is the complex interaction between the wind and the water and the risk that the ship may strike rocks or shoals. Physical damage or machinery malfunction that would be minor ashore could be disastrous to a ship. For example, a hole in the side of a building may be a minor problem, while a hole in the side of a ship could very well cause its total loss. Goods shipped by water are subject to loss due to perils such as corrosion, moisture, and the pitching and rolling of ships.

Ocean marine insurance policies are classified as hull, cargo, and protection and indemnity (P&I).

Hull—A hull policy provides coverage for the hull of the ship, materials and equipment, and stores and provisions for the officers and crew. Also included are the machinery, boilers, and fuel supplies owned by the insured. A hull insurance policy also contains an important liability insurance coverage, referred to as the collision or running down clause. This covers liability for damage to other ships and their cargoes from collision involving the insured vessel.

Cargo—Cargo can be covered for specified causes of loss or on an "all-risks" basis. Protection can apply to only a single voyage or to all voyages of a particular shipper.

Protection and Indemnity (P&I)—A P&I policy provides liability coverage for damage to shore and waterway installations and bodily injury to persons, including employees and passengers, as well as cargo being carried. The P&I policy also covers the insured shipowner's or operator's liability for fines that may be imposed for violation of laws. If a ship is sunk and constitutes a hazard to navigation, the cost of raising, destroying, or removing the wreck is also covered by P&I insurance.

Inland Marine Insurance

Inland marine insurance grew out of ocean marine cargo insurance to meet new coverage needs that emerged in the early twentieth century. Today, the category covers a wide range of loss exposures whose common link is an element of transportation or communication. Examples of inland marine loss exposures are property in domestic transit, property in the custody of a bailee, mobile equipment, buildings in the course of construction, computer equipment, and cable television systems.

In many states (depending on state insurance regulations), some types of commercial inland marine insurance are nonfiled, meaning that insurers are not required to file their forms or rates with regulatory authorities. Being exempt from filing requirements allows insurers to tailor inland marine forms and rates to fit particular loss exposures that are not adequately insured under other property forms.

Crime Insurance

Commercial crime insurance covers causes of loss that are not covered in commercial property forms. These causes of loss include, but are not limited to, theft committed by employees, forgery, computer fraud, and extortion.

Crime insurance also covers two important types of property that commercial property forms exclude: money and securities. Crime insurance on money and securities covers destruction or disappearance in addition to theft.

Various advisory organizations, including the American Association of Insurance Services (AAIS), ISO, and The Surety Association of America (SSA) have developed commercial crime forms for the use of their member companies.

Equipment Breakdown Insurance

Equipment breakdown insurance (traditionally known as boiler and machinery insurance) covers loss resulting from the accidental breakdown of almost any type of equipment that operates under pressure or that controls, transmits, transforms, or uses mechanical or electrical power. Examples of such equipment are steam boilers and other pressure vessels; electrical generating and transmitting equipment; pumps, compressors, turbines, and engines; air conditioning and refrigeration systems; production machinery used in manufacturing operations; and electrically powered office equipment such as computers, telephone systems, and copiers.

Although these types of equipment are covered property under the BPP Form, the BPP covers such equipment only against the causes of loss covered by the causes of loss forms used with the BPP. The causes of loss forms exclude electrical breakdown, mechanical breakdown, and steam boiler explosion, all of which can damage the equipment and sometimes the other property around it.

Equipment breakdown coverage can fill this gap, covering physical damage to both the covered equipment and other property of the insured that results from the accidental breakdown of covered equipment. Equipment breakdown insurance can also cover loss of business income, extra expense, and other consequential losses resulting from such physical damage.

The Equipment Breakdown Coverage Form can be used either in a stand-alone equipment breakdown policy or to add equipment breakdown coverage to a commercial package policy. An alternative approach used by some insurers is to build equipment breakdown coverage into their commercial property policies by eliminating particular exclusions from those policies and adding clauses that provide equipment breakdown coverage.

Perhaps the most valuable aspect of equipment breakdown insurance is the loss control services that accompany it. Insurers have specialty engineers who perform regular inspections of the equipment. Their recommendations help the organization operate the equipment safely.

Businessowners Insurance

Many organizations are insured under businessowners policies instead of the more cumbersome type of commercial package policy that includes the various coverage parts such as commercial property, equipment breakdown, crime, inland marine, and commercial general liability. Typically, businessowners policies provide, in one form, most of the property and liability coverages needed by small to medium-sized businesses. A businessowners policy ordinarily includes building and personal property coverage, business income and extra expense coverage, selected crime and inland marine coverages, and equipment breakdown coverage. Liability coverage, like that provided by the CGL, is also included in the policy. Hired and nonowned auto liability coverage and various professional liability endorsements can be added as needed.

Difference in Conditions Insurance

Organizations purchase difference in conditions (DIC) insurance to fill in gaps left by other types of property insurance. DIC insurance was designed as a means of providing "all-risks" coverage to organizations whose property insurance provided only basic or broad causes of loss. It is still used for that purpose, but it is more often purchased to provide the following:

- Flood and earthquake coverage for loss exposures that are not covered in other property policies
- Excess limits over flood and earthquake coverages included in other property policies
- Coverage for loss exposures not covered in other property policies, such as property in transit or loss of business income resulting from theft or transit losses
- Coverage for property at overseas locations

DIC policies are a nonfiled class of inland marine insurance in most states. Therefore, insurers have great flexibility in arranging the insurance to address the specific needs or exposures of their insureds.

Despite the effectiveness of insurance in providing risk financing, it should be evaluated relative to other risk financing techniques. Consequently, the advantages of insurance usually serve to discount suggestions to consider other risk financing techniques. Likewise, the disadvantages of insurance usually serve to initiate consideration of other risk financing techniques.

ADVANTAGES AND DISADVANTAGES OF INSURANCE

All risk financing plans entail advantages and disadvantages. Insurance, because of its usefulness in risk financing, is usually the risk financing technique against which others are compared. Consequently, its advantages often are used by risk management professionals to convince an organization's management that it is the preferable risk financing technique. Likewise, the disadvantages of insurance often are cited by risk management professionals to entice an organization's management to consider alternative risk financing techniques. Risk management professionals should evaluate each of these advantages and disadvantages when considering using insurance as a risk financing technique.

Advantages of Insurance as a Risk Financing Technique

Because of its numerous advantages, insurance is often the only risk financing technique an organization considers. These advantages include the following:

- Insurance reduces financial uncertainty from accidental losses.
- Insurance provides access to claim handling services.
- Insurance offers access to risk control services.
- Insurance satisfies creditor requirements.
- Insurance satisfies legal requirements.
- Insurance satisfies business requirements.
- Insurance offers tax-deductible premiums.
- Insurance is flexible in design.
- Insurance is easy to exit.

Insurance reduces financial uncertainty that stems from accidental losses. Organizations that buy insurance have purchased the insurer's promise that they will be made whole for covered losses that occur. Therefore, the insurer's promise, regardless of whether a loss occurs, makes the insured's uncertainty tolerable. This advantage often prompts risk management professionals, and the organization's management, to select insurance as a risk financing technique because of the reduced uncertainty it provides relative to other risk financing techniques that involve a higher retention component.

Another advantage insurance provides is access to claim handling services. Insurers are adept at handling a large volume of claims, complex claims, and claims that require special expertise. Because premiums are predetermined and prepaid, insurers have a financial incentive to expeditiously handle claim costs. Risk management professionals often prefer that an insurer or third-party administrator handle claims because the claimant is usually in a relationship with the insured as a consumer or employee. Insurer claim handling services are generally considered to be impartial in settling claims.

Insurance also offers access to risk control expertise. The purchase of insurance includes the risk control services of the insurer. Risk control efforts are aimed at reducing the frequency or severity of losses or making them more predictable. Risk control services include on-site inspections of the insured organization's operations and recommendations the insured can implement to reduce exposure to accidental loss. Risk management professionals generally recognize the value and expense savings provided by the insurer's risk control services and weigh the advantages of those services when evaluating alternative insurance proposals, as well as alternative risk financing techniques.

Additionally, insurance serves to satisfy creditor requirements. Organizations frequently borrow funds to purchase real and personal property. Creditors, financial institutions and others, normally retain a financial interest in the property until the loan is repaid. The loan agreement usually requires that the organization purchase insurance and name the creditor as either a mortgagee (real property) or as a loss payee (personal property). In the event of an accidental loss, the creditor is repaid the outstanding loan amount by the insurer. This advantage of insurance allows risk management professionals to easily satisfy creditor requirements through the purchase of a properly drafted insurance policy. Satisfying creditor requirements may be more difficult if the organization uses an alternative risk financing technique.

Similarly, insurance satisfies legal requirements. Organizations are required to have insurance for their automobile liability and workers' compensation loss exposures. Most states permit organizations to self-insure these loss exposures. Where permitted, evidence of a qualified self-insurance plan satisfies legal requirements, although such plans must meet state-imposed regulations that vary by state. These requirements, such as providing financial security and paying an annual assessment, are not burdensome for a large organization, but may prove onerous for a small organization. Risk management professionals usually recognize that the advantages related to the purchase of insurance enable the organization to avoid the administrative expense of satisfying legal requirements through alternate means and possible penalties if those requirements are not met properly.

Insurance also satisfies business requirements. Organizations often enter into contracts with others that require them to purchase insurance or provide evidence of insurance. For example, a lease may require the lessee to purchase property insurance and specify the legal interests of the lessor. Similarly, a general contractor may require subcontractors to provide a certificate of insurance, a document issued by an insurer as evidence of insurance. Organizations that do not use insurance for risk financing may have to convince the parties with which they contract that the risk financing alternative used is as reliable as insurance. Risk management professionals should consider this advantage and the possible additional contractual negotiations that may be needed if an alternative risk financing technique is used.

Insurance premiums are a tax-deductible business expense. Organizations that purchase insurance reflect this expense when the premium is paid. In contrast, retained losses are deductible only when the loss is actually paid. Therefore, both insurance premiums and retained losses are allowable tax-deductible expenses that reduce taxable income but differ in the timing of those expenses. Insurance presents an advantage in that its premiums offer an immediate tax-deductible expense, whereas retained losses are often expensed over many years. Risk management professionals often prefer the regularity and consistency of insurance premium payments to unpredictable and uneven loss payments.

Another advantage of insurance is the flexibility of its design. Insurers are willing to tailor coverage to suit the needs of the insured organization. Additionally, the coverage selected can be further modified through coverage limit and deductible selection. Risk management professionals often use insurance for risk financing because it can be adapted so easily.

Finally, insurance, as a risk financing strategy, is easy to exit. For a variety of reasons, an organization may chose to switch insurers or use another risk financing technique. The contractual relationship between the insured and the insurer can be terminated at any time. At the time of policy termination, the insured has no obligation to the insurer, while the insurer is obligated to pay losses that occurred during the policy term. This advantage of most types of insurance allows risk management professionals to move their insurance program at will from one insurer to another with confidence that past insured losses will be covered by their prior insurer.

Disadvantages of Insurance as a Risk Financing Technique

Although insurance offers organizations several advantages relative to alternative risk financing techniques, it also entails disadvantages. The major disadvantages of insurance as a risk financing technique are the following:

- Insurance premiums include insurer expenses, profits, and risk charges.
- Insurance premiums diminish cash flows.
- Insurance coverage is not a complete transfer of hazard risk.
- Insurance price and availability at desired terms and conditions fluctuate.

Insurance premiums include insurer expenses, profits, and risk charges. Therefore, insureds share in insurer expenses, regardless of whether those expenses are related to services they receive. This can be a disadvantage relative to alternative risk financing techniques. For example, insurers incur marketing expenses that are passed along to the insurance purchasers. Some insurer administrative expenses are incurred to cover the cost of doing business, such as licensing fees, assessments, and bonds. Additionally, insurers offer several services, such as claim payment services and risk control services, from which the insured may not receive a direct benefit. Risk management professionals are often concerned with the size of insurer expenses. The larger this expense component is relative to claims, the greater their desire to consider alternative risk financing techniques.

Insurance premium payments also diminish cash flows, because the insured organization no longer has those funds to use for generating income. This disadvantage requires risk management professionals to use cash flow analysis to evaluate the opportunity cost associated with the advance payment requirements of insurance and weigh it against risk financing plans that involve retaining funds until loss payments are actually made to claimants.

Another disadvantage of using insurance is that its coverage is not a complete transfer of hazard risk. Organizations are often exposed to hazard risk for which there is no private insurance coverage. For example, organizations exposed to the possibility of flood-related losses usually can obtain that coverage only through a government plan, the Federal Flood Insurance Program. Also, insurance coverage is subject to exclusions and conditions that preclude or limit risk transfer. Coverage disputes, which are disagreements between the insurer and the insured organization, may result in the organization not having insurance coverage it thought it had purchased. Risk management professionals often choose insurance because it reduces uncertainty to a tolerable level. However, they should recognize that risk transfer with insurance is not absolute.

Insurance price and availability at desired terms and conditions fluctuate. Risk management professionals relying on insurance to finance risk recognize that the insurance premiums charged to the organization and insurance's availability are subject to increases and decreases caused by insurer business cycles called underwriting cycles. An **underwriting cycle** is a cyclical pattern of insurance pricing in which a soft market (low rates, relaxed underwriting, and underwriting losses for insurers) is eventually followed by a hard market (high rates, restrictive underwriting, and underwriting gains for insurers) before the pattern repeats itself. The underwriting cycle creates uncertainty in insurance pricing and insurance coverage availability that is independent of the insured's loss experience with the insurer. Many organizations have been forced to consider alternative risk financing techniques as a consequence of an underwriting cycle change and have chosen to continue using the alternate risk financing technique because underwriting cycles disrupt organizational budget planning.

Underwriting cycle
A cyclical pattern of insurance pricing in which a soft market (low rates, relaxed underwriting, and underwriting losses for insurers) is eventually followed by a hard market (high rates, restrictive underwriting, and underwriting gains for insurers) before the pattern repeats itself.

SUMMARY

Organizations that want to incorporate security and certainty in their risk financing plan usually choose insurance as its primary feature. The operation of insurance relies on pooling. A pool is an association of persons or organizations that combine their resources to economically finance recovery from accidental losses. Pooling arrangements reduce risk without transferring it. While the pooling arrangement does not change pool participants' expected cost, it makes the actual cost more consistent and less variable. Adding more participants to the pool further reduces the variability of the average loss for all participants. Additionally, as more participants are added to the pool, the loss probability distribution becomes increasingly bell-shaped.

The law of large numbers provides a mathematical explanation of risk reduction that can result from pooling. It states that when the number of similar, independent exposure units increases, the relative accuracy of predictions about future outcomes based on those exposures also increases.

Many losses are positively correlated; that is, they are not independent of one another. Pooling arrangements reduce risk for each participant, provided that losses are not perfectly positively correlated. With uncorrelated losses, there is a relatively high probability that one organization's unexpectedly high losses will be offset by other participants' unexpectedly low losses. When losses are positively correlated, the distribution of losses has a greater variability (higher standard deviation), making them less predictable.

Insurance differs from pooling in the following two important ways:

1. Insurance transfers risk from the insured to the insurer in exchange for premiums, rather than simply serving as a conduit for passing along its costs to others.

2. The insurer introduces additional financial resources, enabling the insurer to provide a stronger guarantee that sufficient funds will be available in the event of a loss, further reducing the insured's risk.

In addition to accepting an organization's risk of loss, insurers provide the organization with services in the areas of loss control, claim processing, and legal advice.

Individual insurers can choose the loss exposures they insure, a choice often guided by loss exposure characteristics. The six characteristics of an ideally insurable loss exposure are as follows:

1. Pure risk—involves pure risk, not speculative risk

2. Fortuitous losses—subject to fortuitous loss from the insured's standpoint

3. Definite and measurable—subject to losses that are definite in time, cause, and location and that are measurable

4. Homogenous—one of a large number of similar exposure units

5. Independent and not catastrophic—not subject to a loss that would simultaneously affect many other similar loss exposures; loss would not be catastrophic

6. Affordable—premiums are economically feasible

These are ideal characteristics of insurable loss exposures; they are not prerequisites used by insurers in providing insurance coverage.

Insurers provide insurance coverage for most, but not all, loss exposures. Risk management professionals need to understand the types of insurance that are available and the coverage provided by each type so that they can evaluate whether their organization's loss exposures can be effectively transferred using insurance. Insurers also create manuscript policies to meet unique needs.

All risk financing plans have advantages and disadvantages. The major advantages of insurance as a risk financing techniques are as follows:

- Insurance reduces financial uncertainty from accidental losses.
- Insurance provides access to claim handling services.
- Insurance offers access to risk control services.
- Insurance satisfies creditor requirements.
- Insurance satisfies legal requirements.
- Insurance satisfies business requirements.
- Insurance offers tax-deductible premiums.
- Insurance is flexible in design.
- Insurance is easy to exit.

The major disadvantages of insurance as a risk financing technique are as follows:

- Insurance premiums include insurer expenses, profits, and risk charges.
- Insurance premiums diminish cash flows.
- Insurance coverage is not a complete transfer of hazard risk.
- Insurance price and availability at desired terms and conditions fluctuate.

Insurance is a versatile risk financing technique and its use in an organization's risk financing plan warrants further investigation. The chapter that follows describes insurance program design.

CHAPTER NOTE

1. Discussion here is drawn from Scott E. Harrington and Gregory R. Neihaus, *Risk Management and Insurance*, 2nd ed. (New York: McGraw-Hill, 2003), pp. 54–63.

Chapter 3

Direct Your Learning

Insurance Plan Design

After learning the content of this chapter and completing the corresponding course guide assignment, you should be able to:

- Describe the importance and contents of insurance binders.

- Describe the physical construction of insurance policies.

- Summarize the effect of each of the following common policy provisions:
  - Declarations
  - Definitions
  - Insuring agreement
  - Conditions
  - Exclusions
  - Miscellaneous provisions

- Describe the types of property and liability deductibles.

- Explain how large deductible plans operate.

- Describe the role of excess liability insurance in providing an organization with adequate liability coverage limits.

- Describe the role of umbrella liability insurance in providing an organization with adequate liability coverage limits.

- Define or describe each of the Key Words and Phrases for this chapter.

Develop Your Perspective

What are the main topics covered in the chapter?

This chapter describes the preliminary insurance contract (binder) and the final insurance contract (policy) used by insurers. Risk management professionals need to know how to evaluate the insurance coverage purchased so that they know whether the organization's loss exposures are adequately insured.

Review an insurance binder.

- What information is contained in the binder?
- Why does a risk management professional need to scrutinize this information?

Why is it important to learn about these topics?

Insurance is not an absolute transfer of risk. Risk management professionals must be aware of insurance coverage provisions that stipulate the parameters within which risk is transferred, including deductibles, and coverage limits.

Examine the categories of property-casualty insurance policy provisions.

- How do the policy provisions coordinate to delineate coverage?
- In what instances might policy conditions affect whether an insurance policy responds to a loss?

How can you use what you will learn?

Analyze your organization's current liability insurance plan.

- Would a large deductible plan help your organization satisfy its risk financing goals?
- Why might the liability coverage provided by an umbrella liability policy be preferable to that provided by an excess liability policy?

Chapter 3
Insurance Plan Design

Just as an organization's risk financing program employs different techniques, its insurance plan uses a combination of insurance policies to satisfy specific risk financing needs. Relative to other risk financing techniques, insurance is an easily implemented means of addressing hazard risk. However, insurance contracts themselves are complex. A risk management professional's misinterpretation of how an insurance plan's contracts grant coverage may result in insurance coverage gaps or overlaps. Therefore, understanding the elements of an insurance plan and how they interact is crucial to determining the plan's effectiveness.

Because individual policies form the foundation of an organization's insurance plan, the risk management professional should know each of the key components of policy construction in order to devise a plan that balances insurance with an element of risk retention. The analysis of an insurance policy begins with the study of the insurance binder. An **insurance binder** (also called a binder) is a temporary oral or written agreement to provide insurance coverage until a written policy is issued.

Insurance binder
A temporary oral or written agreement to provide insurance coverage until a formal written policy is issued.

INSURANCE BINDERS

Risk management professionals generally want a binder to serve as evidence of insurance until the actual policy can be issued. The binder is not the policy itself, but rather a one- or two-page summary of the promised insurance coverages.

Insurers authorize their sales representatives to bind coverage, that is, to provide immediate insurance coverage, pending their acceptance or rejection of the insurance proposal. Coverage can be requested and granted in person or over the phone. The resulting oral binders are usually readily reduced to writing. Although a binder is only a summary of key policy information, it puts in force the entire insurance policy, including all the policy provisions. Binders are typically effective for thirty days but can be extended or reissued if the formal insurance policy has not been issued.

Because the insurer's claim representatives use the binder to settle losses until the policy is issued, risk management professionals should scrutinize the insurer's binder as carefully as they would the insurance policy itself. Many claims are settled based on the information contained in the binder alone. Binders also encapsulate much of the final policy's organization-specific information. Exhibit 3-1 shows a commercial insurance binder that many insurers have used to replace their company-specific insurance binders, applications, and claim notices.

A binder includes the following key items of information:

- Names of the insured, insurer, and producer
- Insurance coverage effective and expiration dates
- Coverages and limits information by type of insurance
- Mortgagee and loss payee information

The insurer's sales representative sends copies of the binder to the insured and the insurer. The insurer also receives the insurance application, which contains additional information the insurer uses to evaluate (underwrite) the insured organization's loss exposures.

Evaluating the insurance binder is the first step in assessing the completeness of the insurance plan. The risk management professional must also evaluate the policy issued by the insurer. Insurance policies vary in their organization or construction. Consequently, risk management professionals need the skills that will enable them to determine whether the insurance coverage granted by the insurer matches what they requested.

PHYSICAL CONSTRUCTION OF INSURANCE POLICIES

Insurance policies can be constructed in several ways and can contain one or more forms (documents). In some cases, one form, combined with a declarations page, constitutes the entire policy, while, in other cases, multiple forms are included with a declarations page to form the insurance policy.

Monoline policy
An insurance policy that covers a single type of insurance.

Package policy
An insurance policy that covers more than one type of insurance.

An insurance policy can be used for one or more types of insurance. A **monoline policy** is an insurance policy that covers a single type of insurance. For example, when an insurer provides a single policy providing only commercial general liability coverage, it is providing a monoline policy. A **package policy** is an insurance policy that covers more than one type of insurance. For example, when commercial general liability coverage and commercial property coverage are included in the same insurance policy, the policy is provided on a package policy basis. Insurers usually reduce the insurance premium for package policies because of the cost savings that result from evaluating several of an insured organization's loss exposures together rather than separately, as with a monoline policy. Because there is more than one approach to providing such coverage, a risk management professional should examine each coverage part.

EXHIBIT 3-1

ACORD Insurance Binder

ACORD®

INSURANCE BINDER

DATE (MM/DD/YYYY)

THIS BINDER IS A TEMPORARY INSURANCE CONTRACT, SUBJECT TO THE CONDITIONS SHOWN ON THE REVERSE SIDE OF THIS FORM.

AGENCY	COMPANY			BINDER #		
		EFFECTIVE			**EXPIRATION**	
	DATE	TIME		DATE	TIME	
			AM			12:01 AM
			PM			NOON

PHONE (A/C, No, Ext):	FAX (A/C, No):	THIS BINDER IS ISSUED TO EXTEND COVERAGE IN THE ABOVE NAMED COMPANY PER EXPIRING POLICY #:
CODE:	SUB CODE:	
AGENCY CUSTOMER ID:		DESCRIPTION OF OPERATIONS/VEHICLES/PROPERTY (Including Location)
INSURED		

COVERAGES

LIMITS

TYPE OF INSURANCE	COVERAGE/FORMS	DEDUCTIBLE	COINS %	AMOUNT
PROPERTY CAUSES OF LOSS ☐ BASIC ☐ BROAD ☐ SPEC				
GENERAL LIABILITY		EACH OCCURRENCE		$
☐ COMMERCIAL GENERAL LIABILITY		DAMAGE TO RENTED PREMISES		$
☐ CLAIMS MADE ☐ OCCUR		MED EXP (Any one person)		$
		PERSONAL & ADV INJURY		$
		GENERAL AGGREGATE		$
	RETRO DATE FOR CLAIMS MADE:	PRODUCTS - COMP/OP AGG		$
AUTOMOBILE LIABILITY		COMBINED SINGLE LIMIT		$
☐ ANY AUTO		BODILY INJURY (Per person)		$
☐ ALL OWNED AUTOS		BODILY INJURY (Per accident)		$
☐ SCHEDULED AUTOS		PROPERTY DAMAGE		$
☐ HIRED AUTOS		MEDICAL PAYMENTS		$
☐ NON-OWNED AUTOS		PERSONAL INJURY PROT		$
		UNINSURED MOTORIST		$
				$
AUTO PHYSICAL DAMAGE DEDUCTIBLE	☐ ALL VEHICLES ☐ SCHEDULED VEHICLES	☐ ACTUAL CASH VALUE		
☐ COLLISION:		☐ STATED AMOUNT		$
☐ OTHER THAN COL:		☐ OTHER		
GARAGE LIABILITY		AUTO ONLY - EA ACCIDENT		$
☐ ANY AUTO		OTHER THAN AUTO ONLY:		
		EACH ACCIDENT		$
		AGGREGATE		$
EXCESS LIABILITY		EACH OCCURRENCE		$
☐ UMBRELLA FORM		AGGREGATE		$
☐ OTHER THAN UMBRELLA FORM	RETRO DATE FOR CLAIMS MADE:	SELF-INSURED RETENTION		$
		☐ WC STATUTORY LIMITS		
WORKER'S COMPENSATION AND EMPLOYER'S LIABILITY		E.L. EACH ACCIDENT		$
		E.L. DISEASE - EA EMPLOYEE		$
		E.L. DISEASE - POLICY LIMIT		$
SPECIAL CONDITIONS/ OTHER COVERAGES		FEES		$
		TAXES		$
		ESTIMATED TOTAL PREMIUM		$

NAME & ADDRESS

	☐ MORTGAGEE ☐ LOSS PAYEE	☐ ADDITIONAL INSURED
	LOAN #	
	AUTHORIZED REPRESENTATIVE	

ACORD 75 (2004/09)   NOTE: IMPORTANT STATE INFORMATION ON REVERSE SIDE   © ACORD CORPORATION 1993-2004

Coverage part
One or more forms that, together, provide coverage for a type of insurance.

A **coverage part** consists of one or more forms that, together, provide coverage for a type of insurance. It may include the following components:

- Declarations page that applies only to that coverage part
- One or more coverage forms, which contain insuring agreements, exclusions, and other policy provisions
- Applicable endorsements, which modify the terms of the coverage form(s) to fit the coverage needs of the particular insured

Risk management professionals should be able to recognize the physical construction of the insurance policies they receive from insurers because construction relates to coordination of coverages the policies provide, and frequently, the premium the insurer charges.

An insurance policy also can be viewed as a collection of self-contained policies or modular policies. This distinction can help determine whether contracts are complete or whether other coverage forms also need to be evaluated.

Self-Contained Versus Modular Policies

Self-contained policy
A single document that contains all the agreements between the insured and the insurer and that forms a complete insurance policy.

A **self-contained policy** is a single document that contains all the agreements between the insured and the insurer and that forms a complete insurance policy. The single document identifies the insurer and the insured and the amounts, terms, and conditions of coverage. An **endorsement**, a document that amends an insurance policy, can be added to a policy to add, clarify, restrict, or remove coverage provided by the original insurance policy.

Endorsement
A document that amends an insurance policy.

A self-contained policy is appropriate for insuring loss exposures that are similar among many insureds. For example, the relatively uncomplicated insurance needs of many small to medium-sized businesses are typically provided in a self-contained policy (a businessowners policy). Such policies include several basic coverages automatically and allow the insured to add optional coverages as needed.

Modular policy
An insurance policy that consists of several different documents, none of which by itself forms a complete policy.

Conversely, a **modular policy** is an insurance policy that consists of several different documents, none of which by itself forms a complete policy. Modular policies are created by mixing and matching a set of components designed around one basic policy component, also known as a policy jacket. The policy jacket of a modular policy often includes common policy conditions, definitions, or other provisions that apply to all other policy components used with it.

The modular approach is commonly used in commercial insurance coverage for which the insured's loss exposures require more customization of the insurance policy. In addition to being a package policy, Insurance Services Office's (ISO) commercial package policy is a modular policy. Exhibit 3-2 shows the various components that may be included in an ISO commercial package policy. Every commercial package policy contains both common policy conditions and common declarations. If one type of insurance is included, the policy is completed by adding the necessary forms that constitute that coverage part. For example, if commercial property insurance is provided, the commercial property coverage part includes a commercial property declarations page, the necessary commercial property coverage forms, a causes of loss form, and a commercial property conditions form, in addition to the common policy conditions and common declarations. This combination of documents constitutes a monoline policy that covers one type of insurance—commercial property.

EXHIBIT 3-2

Components of ISO Commercial Package Policy (CPP)

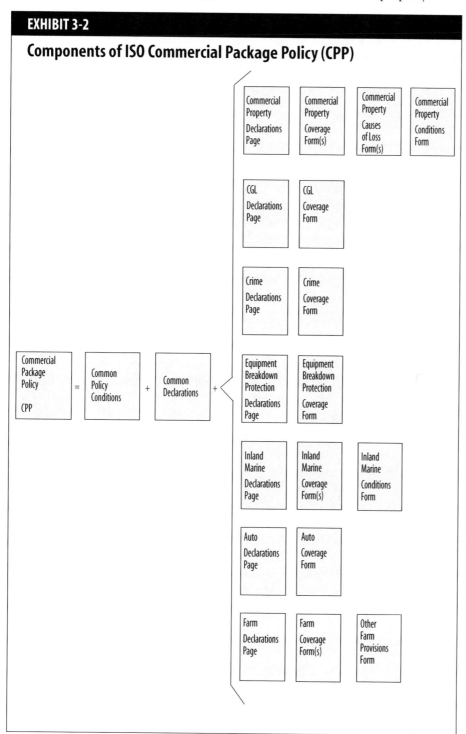

ISO commercial package policy consists of certain minimum components (the common policy conditions and common declarations), as well as declaration pages and coverage forms for each type of insurance included in the modular policy.

An advantage of the modular approach is that a single policy can include several types of insurance. The resulting combination is not a monoline policy, but a package or multi-line policy. The commercial package policy shown in Exhibit 3-2 is flexible enough to cover the majority of loss exposures most organizations face.

The various coverages shown in Exhibit 3-2 are not required to be combined in a commercial package policy. However, ISO does specify that two or more coverage parts must be included for the policy to constitute a package policy and to qualify for the package policy discount. Similar coverage could be provided with separate self-contained commercial property policies, commercial general liability policies, crime policies, and so forth. That is, the insured organization has the option of purchasing multiple, stand-alone policies or a single commercial package policy to cover the same loss exposures. However, relative to multiple self-contained policies, the modular approach to policy construction has the following advantages:

- Carefully designed and coordinated provisions in the various forms minimize the possibility of coverage gaps and overlaps that may exist when several monoline policies are used.
- Consistent terminology, definitions, and policy language make coverage interpretation easier for the insured organization.
- Fewer forms are required to meet a wide range of needs.
- Insurers often give a package discount when several coverages are included in the same policy.

The first three advantages listed are important to risk management professionals conducting policy analysis. Analyzing a single, self-contained policy is not difficult. In fact, it is probably easier for a risk management professional to analyze a single, self-contained policy than a single modular policy, because he or she must determine how the various modular forms fit together. Unfortunately, most organizations are protected by more than one self-contained policy. Analyzing multiple self-contained policies is more difficult than analyzing a single modular policy. Multiple self-contained policies often include multiple copies of related forms and endorsements, use inconsistent terminology, and have gaps and overlaps in coverage that hamper policy analysis. Well-coordinated modular policies offer risk management professionals a better framework for contract analysis than multiple self-contained policies. Insurance policy categories overlap. For example, modular policies can be either monoline or package policies. Categorizing insurance policies by type often makes it easier for the risk management professional to analyze the organization's insurance coverage.

Another approach to categorizing insurance policies is based on whether they are assembled from preprinted forms or forms that are uniquely designed for the insured organization's loss exposures. As with the other approaches to policy categorization, being able to recognize which types of forms a policy uses will enable the risk management professional to better analyze the organization's insurance policies.

Preprinted Forms

Most insurance policies are assembled from one or more preprinted forms and endorsements. Preprinted forms are ready-made forms developed for use with many different insureds. They refer to the insured in general terms ("the insured," "you," and so forth) so that they can be used to insure any organization without customization. The declarations page that is added to the preprinted forms contains the specific information about the insured (the who, what, where, and when information) that customizes the insurance policy.

Using preprinted forms eliminates the need for the insurer and its sales representative to keep a complete duplicate of each insured's entire policy in their files. They must maintain only the declarations page information, which may be stored electronically. Details of applicable coverage can be obtained by the insurer or the producer, whenever necessary, by examining copies of the preprinted forms referred to within the declarations information.

Preprinted forms can be further classified as standard forms or nonstandard forms. As their names imply, standard forms are used industry-wide, whereas nonstandard forms are not.

Standard Forms

Insurance advisory organizations, such as ISO and the American Association of Insurance Services (AAIS), have developed standard insurance forms that are available for use by individual insurers. A **standard insurance form** is a preprinted insurance form developed by an insurance advisory organization. These standard forms are usually accompanied by a portfolio of coordinated endorsements that reflect necessary state variations or that customize coverage. Because they are widely used, standard forms provide benchmarks against which nonstandard forms can be evaluated.

Standard insurance form
A preprinted insurance form developed by an insurance advisory organization.

Preprinted standard forms typically are among the easiest forms for risk management professionals to work with during policy analysis. The coverage provided by these forms is widely understood, and many of them have been subjected to litigation, which has added further clarity to their meaning. Furthermore, most risk management professionals have more experience working with preprinted standard forms than they do with most other forms.

Nonstandard Forms

Many insurers have developed their own company-specific preprinted forms, especially for high-volume types of insurance (such as businessowners) or for coverages in which an insurer specializes (such as professional liability). A **nonstandard form** is a preprinted insurance form that includes wording and/ or provisions that vary from what is used in a standard form. Such forms are nonstandard because their policy wording and content can vary from the provisions used by other insurers or from those developed by insurance advisory organizations. Many nonstandard forms contain coverage enhancements not found in standard forms.

Nonstandard form
A preprinted insurance form that includes wording and/or provisions that vary from what is used in a standard form.

Similar to preprinted standard forms, preprinted nonstandard forms typically are among the easiest for risk management professionals to work with during policy analysis. Though these forms are referred to as nonstandard, many of them are widely used by some of the largest United States insurers. While the use of nonstandard forms may not be as widespread as the use of standard forms, they are still commonly used. Therefore, risk management professionals experienced with standard forms would have less difficulty analyzing nonstandard forms.

Manuscript Forms

Manuscript form
An insurance form that is drafted according to terms negotiated between a specific insured (or group of insureds) and an insurer.

In contrast to preprinted forms, manuscript forms are customized forms developed for one specific insured or for a small group of insureds with common unique coverage needs. A **manuscript form** is an insurance form that is drafted according to terms negotiated between a specific insured (or group of insureds) and an insurer. If an insurance policy includes a manuscript form, it is often called a manuscript policy. A manuscript form can be specifically drafted or selected for a particular need, such as, for example, products liability coverage for a manufacturer of cardiac pacemakers. Usually, most manuscript forms are not individually composed but are adapted from wording previously developed and used in standard forms or other insurance policies. As a whole, a manuscript form is a unique document used for one insured, or for more than one insured in some cases. For example, a manuscript form may be developed to meet the specific needs of a particular association or group of businesses. Manuscript endorsements can also be used.

A manuscript form's wording is generally developed through negotiation between the insurer and the insured organization. When the parties develop policy language together, courts will not necessarily interpret ambiguity in the insured's favor, as they would with a standard or nonstandard form developed solely by the insurer.

Manuscript forms are the most difficult forms for risk management professionals to interpret. These forms, because they often contain unique wording or unique combinations of wording from other forms, can vary widely. Manuscript forms do not have the same history of court interpretations on which risk management professionals can rely. Consequently, the insurer, the insured organization, and courts may interpret the same manuscript form differently, thereby reducing the certainty afforded by most insurance contracts.

Related Documents

In addition to insurance policies' basic formats, several other documents can become part of the policy, either by physical attachment or by reference within the policy. Examples include the completed application for insurance, endorsements, the insurer's bylaws, the terms of relevant statutes, and other miscellaneous documents.

An insurance application is the documented request for coverage, whether the request is made orally, in writing, or over the Internet. The application contains information about the insured and the loss exposures presented to the insurer. Insurers use the information provided on the application to determine whether to accept the organization's loss exposures, as well as to price the policy. While the declarations page often contains much of the same information as the application, the insurer usually keeps the completed application to preserve the representations the insured made. Representations are statements made by the insured to obtain insurance. The application can be used, if necessary, to provide evidence if misleading or false material information was provided by the insured. In some jurisdictions, statutes explicitly require that any written application be made part of the policy for some types of insurance.

Other documents sometimes added to the insurance policy are endorsements. Any endorsement added becomes part of the insurance policy. Terms that may be used instead of endorsement include "policy change," "addition," "amendment," and "codicil." Alternatively, an endorsement may have only a descriptive title, such as Loss Payable Clause.

An endorsement may be a preprinted; computer-printed; typewritten; or handwritten line, sentence, paragraph, or set of paragraphs on a separate sheet of paper attached to other documents forming the policy. Although rare, an endorsement may also take the form of a handwritten note in the margin of a basic policy, form, or coverage part and may be dated and initialed by an insured and the insurer's authorized representative.

Endorsements often are intended to modify a basic policy form. When the endorsement provisions differ from basic policy provisions, they can raise questions about the correct interpretation of an insurance policy. The following two general rules of interpretation apply:

1. An endorsement takes precedence over any conflicting terms in the policy to which it is attached.
2. A handwritten endorsement supersedes a computer-printed or typewritten one. Handwritten alterations tend to reflect true intent more accurately than do other, preprinted policy terms.

In certain circumstances, the insurer's bylaws or the provisions of pertinent statutes are incorporated into an insurance policy. For example, the policyholders of mutual and reciprocal insurers typically have some rights and duties associated with managing the insurer's operations that are specified in the policy.

Policies providing workers' compensation insurance or auto no-fault insurance are among those that typically provide benefits specified by state statute. The relevant statutes usually are not printed in the insurance policy. Rather, they are incorporated by reference. For example, Exhibit 3-3 shows an excerpt from the standard National Council on Compensation Insurance (NCCI) Workers Compensation and Employers Liability Insurance Policy that refers to the state's workers' compensation laws.

EXHIBIT 3-3

Excerpt from the NCCI Workers Compensation and Employers Liability Insurance Policy

We Will Pay

We will pay promptly when due the benefits required of you by the workers compensation law.

. . .

Workers Compensation Law

Workers Compensation Law means the workers or workmen's compensation law and occupational disease law of each state or territory named in item 3. A. of the Information Page. Information Page refers to the declarations page of the workers' compensation policy. It includes any amendments to that law which are in effect during the policy period. It does not include any federal workers or workmen's compensation law, any federal occupational disease law or the provisions of any law that provide nonoccupational disability benefits.

Some policies include contract wording that makes specific reference to a particular law.

Insurance policies sometimes incorporate the insurer's rating manual (or the insurer's rules and rates, whether found in the manual or elsewhere) not by including the entire manual, but by referring to it in the policy language. Exhibit 3-4 shows an excerpt from ISO Commercial General Liability Coverage Form in which the premium audit provision incorporates the insurer's rules and rates.

EXHIBIT 3-4

Excerpt from the ISO Commercial General Liability Coverage Form

5.   Premium Audit

a.   We will compute all premiums for this Coverage Part in accordance with our rules and rates.

Some policies include contract wording that makes specific reference to the insurer's rules and rates.

Although the rules and rates themselves do not appear in the policy, they become, in this way, part of the policy. The applicable rules and rates usually have been approved by a state insurance regulator.

Subject to statutory or regulatory constraints, insurance policies may incorporate virtually any document. Some frequently incorporated miscellaneous documents include premium notes (promissory notes accepted by the insurer in lieu of a cash premium payment), inspection reports, and specification sheets or operating manuals relating to safety equipment or procedures.

In some situations, an insurer and the insured organization may agree that the coverage provided by a particular property or liability insurance policy is conditioned on the use of certain procedures or safety equipment. For example, a set of operating instructions or a manual of specifications can be incorporated into the policy by reference and used to define precisely and conveniently the agreed-upon procedures or equipment.

States are increasingly requiring insurers to provide a "notice to policyholders," informing them of significant changes when an insurance policy is revised. In other cases, insurers are required to furnish policyholders with documents summarizing the coverage options available to insureds and choices that must be made. However, these informational documents generally are not part of the insurance policy as such.

Any of these related documents can alter the basic forms that are included in an insurance policy. Therefore, related documents make policy analysis more difficult for risk management professionals. They add to the volume and complexity of forms that must be evaluated. As the number of related documents grows, so does the likelihood that one or more of the documents may contradict, exclude or expand provisions in the basic forms.

Understanding the construction of the organization's insurance policies is another step toward understanding the coverage provided by the insurer. The risk management professional's ability to categorize the functions of common policy provisions contributes to policy analysis. Analyzing an insurance policy is aided when the risk management professional can categorize the functions of common policy provisions.

COMMON POLICY PROVISIONS

Every insurance policy contains numerous policy provisions. A **policy provision** is any term or clause included in an insurance policy that specifies requirements or clarifies intended meaning. These contractual provisions express distinctive concepts or stipulations in the form of clauses, sentences, or paragraphs in the policy. Some policy provisions are common to almost all insurance policies, while others are unique to specific policies. Despite the wide variation in property-casualty insurance policy provisions, each of them can be placed into one of the following six categories, depending on the purpose it serves:

1. Declarations
2. Definitions
3. Insuring agreements
4. Conditions
5. Exclusions
6. Miscellaneous provisions

Insurance policies usually contain several sections (or coverages) and often a variety of headings and subheadings that do not necessarily coincide with these six categories of policy provisions. The following discussion is not intended to describe the labeled sections of an insurance policy, because not all property-casualty insurance policies include these six labeled sections.

Policy provision
Any term or clause included in an insurance policy that specifies requirements or clarifies intended meaning.

Rather, the discussion focuses on the characteristics of individual policy provisions regardless of the policy section or heading under which any specific provision is located. For example, coverage is usually granted in the insuring agreement, but may be granted in other provisions—even in a provision that is designed to perform a function other than grant coverage.

Declarations

Declarations refers to the portion of the policy that contains information declared by the insured on the insurance application, along with the insurer's declaration about provided coverage. Insurance policy declarations typically contain not only information that has been declared, but also any information unique to a particular policy.

The declarations (sometimes called the information page or declarations page) typically appear as the first page (or one of the first pages) of an insurance policy and contain the following information:

- Policy or policy number
- Policy inception and expiration dates (policy period)
- Name of the insurer
- Name of the insurance agent
- Name of the insured(s)
- Names of persons or organizations whose additional interests are covered (for example, a mortgagee, a loss payee, or an additional insured)
- Mailing address of the insured
- Physical address and description of the covered property or operations
- Numbers and edition dates of all attached forms and endorsements
- Dollar amounts of applicable policy limits
- Dollar amounts of applicable deductibles
- Premium

Exhibit 3-5 shows the declarations page for the commercial property coverage part. When more information is required for the declarations than will fit, insurers use endorsements or schedules. Schedules are often used to list the properties, equipment, or vehicles insured.

Definitions

The definitions section defines terms used throughout the entire policy or form and generally appears in the back of the policy, but may appear anywhere. Policies typically use boldface type or quotation marks to distinguish words and phrases that are defined elsewhere in the policy. Exhibit 3-6 shows an excerpt from the definitions section of ISO Garage Coverage form.

EXHIBIT 3-5

Commercial Property Declarations

COMMERCIAL PROPERTY
CP DS 00 10 00

COMMERCIAL PROPERTY COVERAGE PART
DECLARATIONS PAGE

POLICY NO. SP 0001   EFFECTIVE DATE   10 / 1 / 2005   [X] "X" If Supplemental
Declarations Is Attached

NAMED INSURED

AMR Corporation

DESCRIPTION OF PREMISES

Prem. No.	Bldg. No.	Location, Construction And Occupancy
001	001	2000 Industrial Highway, Workingtown, PA 19000
		Joisted Masonry
		Storm Door Manufacturing

COVERAGES PROVIDED   Insurance At The Described Premises Applies Only For Coverages For Which A Limit Of Insurance Is Shown

Prem. No.	Bldg. No.	Coverage	Limit Of Insurance	Covered Causes Of Loss	Coinsurance*	Rates
001	001	Building	2,000,000	Special	80%	(See Sched.)
		Your Business Personal Prop.	1,120,000	Broad	80%	
		Personal Prop. of Others	50,000	Broad	80%	
		Business Income & Extra Expense	680,000	Special	80%	

*If Extra Expense Coverage, Limits On Loss Payment

OPTIONAL COVERAGES   Applicable Only When Entries Are Made In The Schedule Below

Prem. No.	Bldg. No.	Agreed Value			Replacement Cost (X)		
		Expiration Date	Cov.	Amount	Building	Pers. Prop.	Including "Stock"
001	001	10/1/2004	Building	$2,000,000	X		

	Inflation Guard (%)		*Monthly Limit Of Indemnity (Fraction)	Maximum Period Of Indemnity (X)	*Extended Period Of Indemnity (Days)
	Bldg.	Pers. Prop.			
	3%	3%			

*Applies to Business Income Only

MORTGAGEHOLDERS

Prem. No.	Bldg. No.	Mortgageholder Name And Mailing Address
001	001	Workingtown Savings and Loan Assn.
		400 Main Street
		Workingtown, PA 19001

DEDUCTIBLE

$1,000. **Exceptions:**

FORMS APPLICABLE

To All Coverages: CP 00 10, CP 00 30, CP 00 90, CP 10 30

CP DS 00 10 00   Copyright, Insurance Services Office, Inc., 1999   Page 1 of 1   □

EXHIBIT 3-6

Definitions in ISO Garage Coverage Form

SECTION VI – DEFINITIONS

A. "Accident" includes continuous or repeated exposure to the same conditions resulting in "bodily injury" or "property damage".

B. "Auto" means a land motor vehicle, "trailer" or semitrailer.

C. "Bodily injury" means bodily injury, sickness or disease sustained by a person including death resulting from any of these.

D. "Covered pollution cost or expense" means any cost or expense arising out of:

　　1. Any request, demand, order or statutory or regulatory requirement; or

　　2. Any claim or "suit" by or on behalf of a governmental authority demanding that the "insured" or others test for, monitor, clean up, remove, contain, treat, detoxify or neutralize, or in any way respond to, or assess the effects of "pollutants".

．．．

E. "Customer's auto" means a customer's land motor vehicle, "trailer" or semitrailer. It also includes any "customer's auto" while left with you for service, repair, storage or safekeeping. Customers include your "employees", and members of their households who pay for services performed.

F. "Diminution in value" means the actual or perceived loss in market value or resale value which results from a direct and accidental "loss".

Most insurance policies contain a definitions section in which words with special meanings are defined.

Includes copyrighted material of Insurance Services Office, Inc., with its permission. Copyright, ISO Properties, Inc., 2000.

Many insurance policies refer to the insurer as "we" and the named insured as "you." Such personal pronouns are used extensively throughout these policies. "You" and "we," together with related pronouns such as "us," "our," and "your," are often defined in an untitled preamble to the policy, rather than in a definitions section.

Words and phrases defined within an insurance policy have special, defined meanings when they are used within that particular policy. Undefined words and phrases are interpreted according to the following rules of policy interpretation:

- Everyday words are given their ordinary meanings.
- Technical words are given their technical meanings.
- Words with an established legal meaning are given their legal meanings.
- Consideration is also given to the local, cultural, and trade-usage meanings of words, if applicable.

Many of the definitions that appear in insurance policies today exist because of real or perceived ambiguity associated with the use of those terms in previous insurance policies. Risk management professionals should review defined terms in order to avoid misinterpreting the meaning of a policy provision.

Insuring Agreements

An **insuring agreement** is a statement in an insurance policy that the insurer will, under certain circumstances, make a payment or provide a service. Following the declarations, and possibly preceded by a section containing definitions, the body of most insurance policies begins with an insuring agreement.

Insuring agreement
A statement in an insurance policy that the insurer will, under certain circumstances, make a payment or provide a service.

An insurance policy contains an insuring agreement for each coverage being offered. Therefore, package policies contain multiple insuring agreements. For example, the excerpt from the Business Auto Coverage Form—Insuring Agreement shown in Exhibit 3-7 contains an insuring agreement for each coverage.

The term insuring agreement most often is applied to statements that introduce a policy's coverage section. However, insuring agreement is also an entirely appropriate label for statements introducing coverage extensions, additional coverages, supplementary payments, and so forth. Even relatively obscure unlabeled statements within declarations, definitions, exclusions, or conditions can serve as insuring agreements.

Scope of Insuring Agreements

Insuring agreements can be divided into two broad categories:

1. Comprehensive, all-purpose insuring agreements describe extremely broad, unrestricted coverage that applies to virtually all causes of loss or to virtually all situations. This broad coverage is both clarified and narrowed by exclusions, definitions, and other policy provisions.
2. Limited or single-purpose insuring agreements restrict coverage to certain causes of loss or to certain situations. Exclusions, definitions, and other policy provisions serve to clarify and narrow coverage, but also may broaden the coverage.

Whether comprehensive or limited, insuring agreements state the insurer's obligations in relatively broad terms. The full scope of coverage cannot be determined without examining the rest of the policy, because the insurer's obligations are invariably clarified or modified by other policy provisions.

EXHIBIT 3-7

Business Auto Coverage Form—Insuring Agreement

SECTION II – LIABILITY COVERAGE

A. Coverage

We will pay all sums an "insured" legally must pay as damages because of "bodily injury" or "property damage" to which this insurance applies, caused by an "accident" and resulting from the ownership, maintenance or use of a covered "auto".

We will pay all sums an "insured" legally must pay as a "covered pollution cost or expense" to which this insurance applies, caused by an "accident" and resulting from the ownership, maintenance or use of covered "autos". However, we will only pay for the "covered pollution cost or expense" if there is either "bodily injury" or "property damage" to which this insurance applies that is caused by the same "accident".

We have the right and duty to defend any "insured" against a "suit" asking for such damages or a "covered pollution cost or expense". However, we have no duty to defend any "insured" against a "suit" seeking damages for "bodily injury" or "property damage" or a "covered pollution cost or expense" to which this insurance does not apply. We may investigate and settle any claim or "suit" as we consider appropriate. Our duty to defend or settle ends when the Liability Coverage Limit of Insurance has been exhausted by payment or judgments or settlements.

. . .

SECTION III – PHYSICAL DAMAGE COVERAGE

A. Coverage

1. We will pay for "loss" to a covered "auto" or its equipment under:

a. Comprehensive Coverage

From any cause of loss except:

(1) The covered "auto's" collision with another object; or

(2) The covered "auto's" overturn.

b. Specified Causes of Loss Coverage Caused by:

(1) Fire, lighting or explosion;

(2) Theft;

(3) Windstorm, hail or earthquake;

(4) Flood;

(5) Mischief of vandalism; or

(6) The sinking, burning, collision or derailment of any conveyance transporting the covered "auto".

c. Collision Coverage

Caused by:

(1) The covered "auto's" collision with another object; or

(2) The covered "auto's" overturn.

Insurance policies typically contain an insuring agreement for each coverage provided.

Insuring Agreements for Extended, Additional, or Supplemental Coverages

Many insurance policies include secondary or supplemental coverages along with the main coverage in the insuring agreement. These coverages have various labels, such as coverage extensions, additional coverages, or supplementary payments.

Generally, a coverage extension extends a portion of a basic policy coverage to apply to a type of property or loss that would not otherwise be covered. Additional coverage adds a type of coverage not otherwise provided. Supplementary payments clarify the extent of coverage for certain expenses in liability insurance. All these coverages are considered insuring agreements. However, labels for such coverages can vary by policy.

For example, commercial property policies treat coverage for collapse as an additional coverage rather than as a cause of loss. The additional coverage for collapse is provided under specific circumstances. Exhibit 3-8 shows an excerpt from the commercial property Causes of Loss—Broad Form and illustrates the limiting language used to provide additional coverage.

EXHIBIT 3-8

Insuring Agreement under Additional Coverages

C. Additional Coverages – Collapse

The term Covered Cause of Loss includes the Collapse Additional Coverage as described and limited in 1. through 5. below

1. With respect to buildings:

    a. Collapse means an abrupt falling down or caving in of a building or any part of a building with the result that the building or part of the building cannot be occupied for its intended purpose;

    b. A building or any part of a building that is in danger of falling down or caving in is not considered to be in a state of collapse;

    c. A part of a building that is standing is not considered to be in a state of collapse even if it has separated from another part of the building;

    d. A building that is standing or any part of a building that is standing is not considered to be in a state of collapse even if it shows evidence of cracking, bulging, sagging bending, leaning, settling, shrinkage or expansion.

Includes copyrighted material of Insurance Services Office, Inc., with its permission. Copyright, ISO Properties, Inc., 2001.

Additional coverages, as well as coverage extensions and supplementary payments, often serve to extend coverage, even though they are not presented as insuring agreements.

Other Provisions That Function as Insuring Agreements

Other policy provisions may also serve as insuring agreements by granting or restoring coverage otherwise excluded. These other policy provisions could be anywhere in the policy, such as in the definitions or exclusions section. Exhibit 3-9 shows an instance in which a policy term definition grants coverage.

EXHIBIT 3-9

Insuring Agreement in the Definitions Section

The insuring agreement of ISO Commercial General Liability (CGL) policy (CG 00 01 10 01) provides broad liability coverage, but this broad coverage is restricted by an auto exclusion, which reads in part as follows:

[This insurance does not apply to] "Bodily injury" or "property damage" arising out of the ownership, maintenance, use or entrustment to others of any ... "auto" ... owned or operated by or rented or loaned to any insured. Use includes operation and "loading or unloading".

The definition of "auto" reads as follows:

"Auto" means a land motor vehicle, trailer or semitrailer designed for travel on public roads, including any attached machinery or equipment. But "auto" does not include "mobile equipment".

Coverage may be granted or restored in almost any policy provision.

Includes copyrighted material of Insurance Services Office, Inc., with its permission. Copyright, ISO Properties, Inc., 2003.

The Commercial General Liability (CGL) insuring agreement is broad enough to include claims involving liability for motor vehicle accidents. The exclusion removes coverage for autos. However, the definition of auto states that mobile equipment is not an auto. The effect of the last sentence in the definition, therefore, is to grant coverage (actually, to restore coverage otherwise excluded) for liability arising out of mobile equipment (subject to other policy provisions). Exhibit 3-10 contains an example of an insuring agreement appearing as an exception to an exclusion in the exclusions section.

EXHIBIT 3-10

Insuring Agreement Appearing in the Exclusions Section

The CGL also grants liquor liability coverage for most businesses through an exception to the liquor liability exclusion. The entire exclusion, which concludes with the exception, reads as follows:

[This insurance does not apply to:] "Bodily injury" or "property damage" for which any insured may be held liable by reason of:

(1) Causing or contributing to the intoxication of any person;

(2) The furnishing of alcoholic beverages to a person under the legal drinking age or under the influence of alcohol; or

(3) Any statute, ordinance or regulation relating to the sale, gift, distribution or use of alcoholic beverages.

This exclusion applies only if you are in the business of manufacturing, distributing, selling, serving or furnishing alcoholic beverages.

Coverage can be granted indirectly, such as with an exception to an exclusion.

Includes copyrighted material of Insurance Services Office, Inc., with its permission. Copyright, ISO Properties, Inc., 2000.

Because of the exception in the final sentence of the exclusion in Exhibit 3-10, coverage applies to office parties and other liquor-related situations for businesses that are not in the alcoholic beverage business. This provision is frequently called "host liquor liability coverage," and it is, in effect, an insuring agreement.

Conditions

A policy **condition** is any provision in an insurance policy that qualifies an otherwise enforceable promise of the insurer. Some policy conditions are found in the conditions section of the policy, while others are found in the forms, endorsements, or other documents that together constitute the entire insurance policy.

Condition
Any provision in an insurance policy that qualifies an otherwise enforceable promise of the insurer.

In a policy's insuring agreement, the insurer promises to pay to the insured, to pay on the insured's behalf to defend the insured, and/or to provide various additional services. However, such promises are not unconditional. The insurer promises to pay, furnish a defense, or provide other services that are enforceable only if an insured event occurs and only if the insured has fulfilled its contractual duties as specified in the policy conditions.

Examples of common policy conditions include the insured's obligation to pay premiums, report losses promptly, provide appropriate documentation for losses, cooperate with the insurer in any legal proceedings, and refrain from jeopardizing an insurer's rights to recover from responsible third parties. If the insured does not adhere to these conditions, then the insurer may be released from any obligation to perform some or all of its otherwise enforceable promises.

Exclusions

Exclusions are policy provisions that state what the insurer does not intend to cover. The word "intend" is important: The primary function of exclusions is to clarify the coverages granted by the insurer, not to take away coverage from the insured. Specifying what the insurer does not intend to cover is a proven way of clarifying what aspects the insurer does intend to cover. Exhibit 3-11 summarizes the six purposes of exclusions in a property-liability insurance policy.

To a certain extent, all exclusions help keep premiums reasonable. Logically, a higher premium would be required to pay for the additional losses that might be covered whenever a policy is broadened by eliminating an exclusion. Any exclusion can also serve more than one purpose.

EXHIBIT 3-11

Six Purposes of Exclusions

1. Eliminate coverage for uninsurable loss exposures

   Some loss exposures (such as intentional acts) possess few if any of the ideal characteristics of an insurable loss exposure. Exclusions allow insurers to preclude coverage for these loss exposures.

2. Assist in managing moral and morale hazards

   Moral hazards are defects or weaknesses in human character that lead some people to exaggerate losses or intentionally cause them to collect insurance proceeds. Exclusions help insurers minimize these types of loss exposures.

   Morale hazards exist when the likelihood or severity of a loss is increased because a person is not as careful as the person should be in preventing losses from occurring. Some exclusions assist in managing morale hazards by making the insureds themselves bear the losses that result from their own carelessness.

3. Reduce likelihood of coverage duplications

   In some cases, two insurance policies provide coverage for the same loss. Exclusions ensure that two policies work together to provide complementary, not duplicate, coverage and that insureds are not paying duplicate premiums.

4. Eliminate coverages not needed by the typical insured

   Exclusions sometimes allow insurers to exclude coverage for loss exposures not faced by the typical insured. This means that all insureds would not have to share the costs of covering the loss exposures that relatively few insureds have.

5. Eliminate coverages requiring special treatment

   Exclusions eliminate the coverages that require substantially different insurer services from what is normally required.

6. Assist in keeping premiums reasonable

   Exclusions allow insurers to preclude insuring loss exposures that would otherwise increase costs. By keeping costs down, insurers can offer premiums that a sufficiently large number of insurance buyers consider reasonable.

Eliminate Coverage for Uninsurable Loss Exposures

Some loss exposures are deemed uninsurable by private insurers. For example, nearly all property-casualty insurance policies exclude loss exposures relating to war. Following the terrorist attacks of September 11, 2001, many insurers also began excluding certified acts of terrorism from coverage. Exhibit 3-12 shows ISO Exclusion of Certified Acts of Terrorism endorsement.

Other common exclusions of uninsurable loss exposures involve losses due to intentional acts of the insured or other nonaccidental events, nuclear radiation, earthquake, flood damage to fixed-location property, normal wear and tear, and inherent vice. Inherent vice is a quality inherent in an object that tends to destroy it, as when iron rusts, wood rots, or rubber deteriorates.

EXHIBIT 3-12

ISO Exclusion of Certified Acts of Terrorism

COMMERCIAL GENERAL LIABILITY
CG 21 73 12 02

THIS ENDORSEMENT CHANGES THE POLICY. PLEASE READ IT CAREFULLY.

EXCLUSION OF CERTIFIED ACTS OF TERRORISM

This endorsement modifies insurance provided under the following:

COMMERCIAL GENERAL LIABILITY COVERAGE PART
LIQUOR LIABILITY COVERAGE PART
OWNERS AND CONTRACTORS PROTECTIVE LIABILITY COVERAGE PART
POLLUTION LIABILITY COVERAGE PART
PRODUCTS/COMPLETED OPERATIONS LIABILITY COVERAGE PART
RAILROAD PROTECTIVE LIABILITY COVERAGE PART
UNDERGROUND STORAGE TANK POLICY

A. The following exclusion is added:

This insurance does not apply to:

TERRORISM

"Any injury or damage" arising, directly or indirectly, out of "a certified act of terrorism".

B. The following definitions are added:

1. For the purposes of this endorsement, "any injury or damage" means any injury or damage covered under any Coverage Part to which this endorsement is applicable, and includes but is not limited to "bodily injury", "property damage", "personal and advertising injury", "injury" or "environmental damage" as may be defined in any applicable Coverage Part.

2. "Certified act of terrorism" means an act that is certified by the Secretary of the Treasury, in concurrence with the Secretary of State and the Attorney General of the United States, to be an act of terrorism pursuant to the federal Terrorism Risk Insurance Act of 2002. The federal Terrorism Risk Insurance Act of 2002 sets forth the following criteria for a "certified act of terrorism":

a. The act resulted in aggregate losses in excess of $5 million; and

b. The act is a violent act or an act that is dangerous to human life, property or infrastructure and is committed by an individual or individuals acting on behalf of any foreign person or foreign interest, as part of an effort to coerce the civilian population of the United States or to influence the policy or affect the conduct of the United States Government by coercion.

CG 21 73 12 02   © ISO Properties, Inc., 2002   Page 1 of 1   □

Each of those excluded loss exposures fails to sufficiently possess at least one of the ideal characteristics of an insurable loss exposure. War, terrorism, and nuclear loss exposures involve an incalculable catastrophe potential. Inherent vice and similar loss exposures are not accidental or fortuitous in nature but are predictable, expected, and, in varying degrees, controllable by the insured.

Assist in Managing Moral and Morale Hazards

Both moral and morale hazards are behavioral problems. Exclusions help to induce appropriate behavior by the insureds. Exclusions can help manage moral hazards to the extent that they eliminate coverage for the insured's intentional acts that are essentially uninsurable. Exhibit 3-13 shows an excerpt from ISO Commercial General Liability Coverage Form, which contains such an exclusion.

EXHIBIT 3-13

Excerpt from ISO Commercial General Liability Coverage Form— Managing Moral Hazards

2. Exclusions

    This insurance does not apply to:

    a. Expected Or Intended Injury

        "Bodily injury" or "property damage" expected or intended from the standpoint of the insured. This exclusion does not apply to "bodily injury" resulting from the use of reasonable force to protect persons or property.

Includes copyrighted material of Insurance Services Office, Inc., with its permission. Copyright, ISO Properties, Inc., 2000.

Expected or intended injury exclusions eliminate coverage for losses that arise from moral hazards.

This exclusion eliminates coverage for intentionally harmful results. Other conditions and miscellaneous provisions make it difficult to exaggerate losses successfully.

Some exclusions assist in managing morale hazards by making the insureds themselves bear the losses that result from their own carelessness. Exhibit 3-14 shows an excerpt from the Commercial Property Causes of Loss—Broad Form, which excludes coverage for damage to the insured organization's property caused by owned or operated vehicles.

Reduce the Likelihood of Coverage Duplications

Having two insurance policies provide coverage for the same loss is usually unnecessary and wasteful. It is unnecessary because coverage under one policy is all that is needed to indemnify the insured (unless policy restrictions or limits of insurance preclude full recovery). It is wasteful because, at least in theory, each policy providing coverage for certain types of losses includes a related premium charge (which is admittedly negligible in some cases).

EXHIBIT 3-14

Excerpt from ISO Commercial Property Causes of Loss—Broad Form—Managing Morale Hazards—Exclusions Assisting in Managing Morale Hazards

A.   Covered Causes of Loss

When Broad is shown in the Declarations, Covered Causes of Loss means the following:

. . .

6.   Aircraft or Vehicles, meaning only physical contact of an aircraft, a spacecraft, a self-propelled missile, a vehicle or an object thrown up by a vehicle with the described property or with the building or structure containing the described property. This cause of loss includes loss or damage by objects falling from aircraft.

We will not pay for loss or damage caused by or resulting from vehicles you own or which are operated in the course of your business.

Includes copyrighted material of Insurance Services Office, Inc., with its permission. Copyright, ISO Properties, Inc., 2001.

Insurance policies usually contain exclusions for losses caused by the insured's carelessness, a morale hazard.

Eliminate Coverages Not Needed by the Typical Insured

Insurance coverages are designed to address the needs of most organizations rather than those of a few. Consequently, uncommon loss exposures should be excluded, because they should be specifically insured by those relatively few insured organizations that have them. For example, ISO Commercial Liability Coverage Form excludes aircraft and watercraft liability because most insured organizations do not have that loss exposure. Exhibit 3-15 shows an excerpt from ISO Commercial General Liability Coverage Form that contains an aircraft, auto, and watercraft exclusion. Auto is excluded because it is more appropriately insured by a coverage form dedicated to that loss exposure.

EXHIBIT 3-15

Excerpt from ISO Commercial General Liability Coverage Form—Exclusions Eliminating Coverages Not Needed by the Typical Insured

2.   Exclusions

This insurance does not apply to:

. . .

g.   Aircraft, Auto Or Watercraft

"Bodily injury" or "property damage" arising out of the ownership, maintenance, use or entrustment to others of any aircraft, "auto" or watercraft owned or operated by or rented or loaned to any insured. Use includes operation and "loading or unloading".

Includes copyrighted material of Insurance Services Office, Inc., with its permission. Copyright, ISO Properties, Inc., 2003.

Insurance policies usually contain exclusions for uncommon loss exposures.

Organizations that need coverage for these relatively uncommon loss exposures should purchase it separately. Including this coverage and thereby requiring all insureds to share the costs of covering the substantial loss exposures of relatively few insureds would be inequitable.

Eliminate Coverages Requiring Special Treatment

Coverage that necessitates special treatment may require special rating or underwriting, risk control, or reinsurance treatment that is substantially different from what is normally required for the policy containing the exclusion. For example, many commercial general liability policies exclude the professional liability loss exposure. However, coverage for specific types of professional liability can be added to a CGL policy by endorsement. Similarly, many property policies exclude coverage for property on exhibition at a convention or trade fair because property on exhibit is especially vulnerable to loss by theft and other causes of loss.

Assist in Keeping Premiums Reasonable

All exclusions assist in keeping premiums reasonable to some extent. However, it is the primary purpose of some exclusions, and it is the only purpose of others. Exhibit 3-16 contains an example from ISO Business Auto Coverage Form.

EXHIBIT 3-16

Excerpt From ISO Business Auto Coverage Form

B.   Exclusions

. . .

3.   We will not pay for "loss" caused by or resulting from any of the following unless caused by other "loss" that is covered by this insurance:

a.   Wear and tear, freezing, mechanical or electrical breakdown.

b.   Blowouts, punctures or other road damage to tires.

Includes copyrighted material of Insurance Services Office, Inc., with its permission. Copyright, ISO Properties, Inc., 2000.

Some exclusions focus on keeping premiums reasonable by eliminating coverage for losses that result from wear and tear or that occur because of poor maintenance.

Organizations usually budget for predictable expenses. Many losses are therefore more economically handled through retention than insurance. For example, most organizations would be unwilling to pay for tire damage coverage when the cost of this coverage would be high compared to the cost of a new tire or a tire repair. Other, minor and predictable losses are consequently excluded by insurance policies because the insurer and the insured organization would effectively be "trading dollars" with the insurer, adding costs to the transaction in the form of insurer expenses and profit.

Miscellaneous Provisions

Miscellaneous provisions are policy provisions that do not fit into the other five categories of common policy provisions. Insurance policies often contain provisions that deal with the relationship between the insured and the insurer, or they may help to establish working procedures for implementing coverage. However, such provisions do not have the force of conditions. Consequently, if the insured does not follow the procedures specified in the miscellaneous provisions, the insurer may still be required to fulfill its contractual promises.

One example of a miscellaneous provision is a valuation provision that sets standards for measuring losses under the policy. Some miscellaneous provisions are unique to particular types of insurers, as in the following examples:

- A policy issued by a mutual insurer is likely to describe each insured's right to vote in the election of the board of directors.
- A policy issued by a reciprocal insurer is likely to specify the attorney-in-fact's authority to implement its powers on the insured's behalf.

Although it generally represents only a dollar figure entry on the declarations page of an insurance policy, the deductible directly affects the amount of the insured organization's recovery, if any, from an insurer.

DEDUCTIBLES

Deductibles support the economical operation of insurance. A **deductible** is the amount that must be retained by the insured before the insured can recover from the insurer. Insurance is generally used to transfer only those financial consequences that the insured cannot afford to retain. Deductibles allow the insured organization to obtain the risk transfer it needs while retaining those losses it can safely absorb.

Deductible
The amount that must be retained by the insured before the insured can recover from the insurer.

Insurance can be purchased with no or small deductibles, but the insured organization pays a higher premium as a consequence. The cost of insurer-paid claims, regardless of their size, is an expense that insurers pass along to insureds as part of the insurance premium. Consequently, no or small deductible insurance policies are costly from both the insured's and the insurer's perspective. The insured organization with no or low deductible would be better off financially in the long run by directly paying those losses it can afford to retain.

Insurers charge a lower premium when the insured accepts a higher deductible. Insured organizations evaluate deductibles relative to the amount of premium savings that the deductible provides, as well as the likelihood of loss under the deductible. Additionally, the insured organization must be able to fund those losses that occur within the deductible. For example, an insured organization with a $1,000 property deductible that is considering a $10,000 property deductible would need a substantial premium savings and confidence in its estimate of the losses that may occur during the policy term. Consequently, choosing a deductible is a subjective decision, despite the abundance of past loss data that may be at the organization's disposal.

Deductibles are usually found in property insurance policies, but organizations can purchase liability insurance policies with deductibles as well. Deductibles are usually specified dollar amounts, but not always. Various types of property and liability deductibles may be included in an insurance plan.

Property Deductibles

Insurance policies usually do not specify the type of deductible, but rather describe the operation of the deductible that applies to the particular policy. Property deductibles, however, can be categorized as follows:

- Flat, or straight, deductible
- Disappearing, or franchise, deductible
- Percentage deductible
- Aggregate annual deductible

Flat, or straight, deductible
A deductible stated in a dollar amount.

A **flat**, or **straight**, **deductible** is a deductible stated in a dollar amount. Deductibles usually apply per occurrence regardless of the number of items of covered property that are damaged. For example, if the insured organization suffers a wind loss to three buildings, then the deductible amount would be subtracted from the total amount of loss. The insurer, in this instance, would net the deductible from the amount payable to the insured organization. The insurance coverage specified in the policy is diminished by the amount of the deductible. For example, coverage for a structure insured for $500,000 with a $5,000 deductible would provide only $495,000 in indemnification should a total loss occur. Losses that do not exceed the deductible are not paid by the insurer.

Disappearing, or franchise, deductible
A deductible that decreases in amount as the amount of loss increases, and disappears entirely after a specified amount of loss is surpassed.

A **disappearing**, or **franchise**, **deductible** is a deductible that decreases in amount as the amount of loss increases, and disappears entirely after a specified amount of loss is surpassed. For example, the insured organization may choose a $5,000 disappearing deductible that is reduced for losses that exceed $5,000 and that does not apply for losses that surpass $25,000. Disappearing deductibles disappear when the insured organization incurs a significant loss, thereby allowing the policy to pay the entire amount.

Percentage deductible
A deductible that is stated as a specified percentage.

A **percentage deductible** is a deductible that is stated as a specified percentage. Some percentage deductibles are a specified percentage of the loss, while other percentage deductibles are a specified percentage of the amount of insurance on the affected property or a specified percentage of the value of the affected property. For example, ISO offers two earthquake endorsements. Among the differences in these endorsements, one has a deductible that applies as a percentage of the amount of insurance, while the other has a deductible that applies as a percentage of the property's value.

Aggregate annual deductible
A deductible that limits the total amount of losses retained during a year.

An **aggregate annual deductible** is a deductible that limits the total amount of losses retained during a year. After the aggregate annual deductible has been met, the insurer provides first-dollar coverage on all subsequent losses. Aggregate annual deductibles are also used in liability policies that contain deductibles.

Liability Deductibles

Risk management professionals are accustomed to property insurance deductibles, but the use of liability insurance deductibles is not as routine. As mentioned previously, selecting a deductible amount and weighing the premium savings provided by the insurer relative to the possible retained losses is subjective. However, risk management professionals are more likely to retain a share of property losses than liability losses because a liability loss has more intangible elements. Unlike property claims, one occurrence under a liability insurance policy may result in multiple liability claims, and those claims, and their deductibles, can aggregate to substantial amounts.

Unlike property deductible provisions that must be read to be categorized, most liability deductibles are clearly specified. The most frequently used liability deductibles are as follows:

- Per claim deductible
- Per accident/occurrence deductible
- Waiting period deductible

A **per claim deductible** is a deductible that applies to all damages sustained by any one person or organization as a result of one occurrence. Therefore, if five people make claims against the insured organization for bodily injury or property damage incurred in one occurrence, a per claim deductible will apply separately to each person's claim.

Per claim deductible
A deductible that applies to all damages sustained by any one person or organization as a result of one occurrence.

A **per accident/occurrence deductible** is a deductible that applies only once to the total of all claims paid arising out of one accident or occurrence. For example, only one deductible would apply to the previous example in which five people incurred bodily injury or property damage under a liability policy with a per accident/occurrence deductible instead of the deductible applying to each claim.

Per accident/occurrence deductible
A deductible that applies only once to the total of all claims paid arising out of one accident or occurrence.

The operation of a liability deductible differs from that of a property deductible. Under the terms of a typical liability deducible endorsement, the insurer pays the entire amount of the liability claim and is then reimbursed by the insured organization for the deductible amount. The amount of liability coverage is in excess of the liability deductible. That is, unlike a property deductible, a liability deductible does not diminish the amount of coverage provided by the insurer. For example, an insurer that provides a $300,000 liability coverage limit with a $50,000 liability deductible would respond to claims up to $350,000, but would expect reimbursement from the insured organization for $50,000. Given the same deductible amount, a claim for $100,000 would also require a $50,000 reimbursement by the insured, whereas claims below the $50,000 deductible would be paid for by the insurer but reimbursed in their entirety by the insured organization.

A **waiting period deductible** is a deductible that is specified in time. Workers' compensation disability benefits are payable to disabled employees only after a waiting period that usually ranges from three to seven days after the injury. In most states, disability benefits are retroactive to the date of the injury if the injured employee is unable to work for a specified period, which can be as short as five days or as long as six weeks, depending on the applicable statute.

Waiting period deductible
A deductible that is specified in time.

Some organizations want to lower their cost of risk by assuming significant retention amounts within an insurance plan. These large deductible plans are treated separately from insurance plans with typical deductible amounts.

LARGE DEDUCTIBLE PLANS

Large deductible plan
An insurance policy with a per occurrence or per accident deductible of $100,000 or more.

A **large deductible plan** is an insurance policy with a per occurrence or per accident deductible of $100,000 or more. Such plans are used for workers' compensation, automobile liability, or general liability. Large deductible plans are similar to the previously discussed deductibles that are used for both property and liability insurance coverages. Technically, any insurance deductible plan constitutes a hybrid plan. However, large deductible plans involve considerably more retention than do ordinary deductibles, and therefore truly constitute a risk financing plan that has many of the characteristics of self-insurance.

Purpose and Operation of Large Deductible Plans

Organizations use large deductible plans to lower their cost of risk. Large deductible plans enable the organization to pay a reduced insurance premium while retaining losses below the deductible level. The organization transfers the financial consequences for losses that are above the deductible to the insurer. As losses occur, the insurer settles each claim and then periodically bills the insured organization for the amount of the loss and claim-handling expense up to the deductible level. Consequently, large deductible plans enable organizations to defer cash outflows for accidental losses. Large deductible plans are a form of risk retention; that is, the assumption of hazard risk that could be otherwise transferred to an insurer. Organizations that choose large deductible plans usually make a commitment to controlling losses they would otherwise retain. Exhibit 3-17 shows the operation of a large deductible plan. The insured organization usually must provide the insurer with a form of financial security, such as a letter of credit, to guarantee payment of covered losses up to the deductible level.

Under a large deductible plan, the insured organization retains losses below the deductible and, up to the policy limit, transfers to the insurer that portion of any loss that exceeds the deductible.

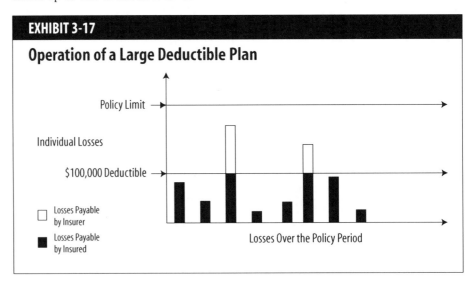

EXHIBIT 3-17

Operation of a Large Deductible Plan

A large deductible is similar to a self-insured retention (SIR). Both a large deductible and a SIR require the insured organization to retain a relatively large amount of loss. A key difference is that, with a SIR, the insured organization is responsible for adjusting and paying its own losses up to the SIR amount. Organizations with SIRs frequently outsource these tasks to an independent claim adjusting organization and pay a fee for that service. Under a large deductible plan, the insurer adjusts and pays all claims for loss, even those below the deductible level, and seeks reimbursement from the insured. In effect, the insurer is guaranteeing the payment of all claims.

Therefore, a large deductible plan gives the insurer direct control over individual claims that start out small but have the potential to exceed the deductible level. To compensate for a lack of control over individual self-insured claims, a policy with a SIR usually requires strict reporting to the insurer of any claims that have the potential to exceed the amount of the SIR.

Large deductible plans are used for workers' compensation, auto liability, and general liability policies. In a large deductible plan applicable to these coverages, the workers' compensation deductible can apply on a per person and/or a per accident basis, whereas the auto liability deductible usually applies on a per accident basis and the general liability deductible on a per occurrence basis. The plan can also include an aggregate deductible, which caps total deductible payments over a period of time (usually one year). Exhibit 3-18 shows an example of a large deductible plan for an organization's workers' compensation loss exposure. The example illustrates how large deductible plans can be tailored to meet the insured organization's loss expectations and financial ability to retain accidental losses.

Under a large deductible plan, the amount that the insurer incurs to adjust losses, including legal defense costs, can be inside or outside the deductible. If they are inside, or included, the insurer adds them to the amount of the loss for the purpose of determining the total amount that is subject to the deductible. If they are outside, they are not added to the amount of the loss for the purpose of determining the amount subject to the deductible and are usually prorated between the insured and the insurer based on the size of the loss.

Advantages and Disadvantages of Large Deductible Plans

An organization's motive for adopting a large deductible plan is to reduce its cost of risk. Even though most of the premium reduction is offset because the organization must pay for its losses under the deductible, reducing the premium reduces costs for the following two main reasons:

1. States impose various charges, such as premium taxes and residual market loadings. A **residual market loading** is an amount charged to make up for losses in a state-sponsored plan to insure high-risk exposures, such as an assigned risk plan for auto insurance. A residual market loading is calculated based on a percentage of premium.

2. An insurance premium includes charges for the insurer's overhead costs and profit.

Residual market loading
An amount charged to make up for losses in a state-sponsored plan to insure high-risk exposures, such as an assigned risk plan for auto insurance.

EXHIBIT 3-18

Example of a Large Deductible Plan for an Organization's Workers' Compensation Loss Exposure

Assume that a large deductible plan applied to workers' compensation incorporates the following:

- A deductible of $100,000 for each injured person
- A deductible of $250,000 per accident, regardless of the number of persons injured
- An annual aggregate deductible of $350,000

Assume six employees are injured in a single year, with four employees injured in a single accident. The table below shows the cost of the losses for each employee.

Accident No.	Employee No.	Amount of Loss	Amount Payable Under Deductible
1	1	$150,000	$100,000
1	2	85,000	85,000
1	3	70,000	65,000
1	4	10,000	0
2	5	50,000	50,000
3	6	60,000	50,000
		$425,000	$350,000

Under this large deductible plan, the insured organization would reimburse the insurer $100,000 for Employee 1 (subject to the per person deductible) and a total of $250,000 for Employee 1 through Employee 4 because they were involved in a single accident. In addition, the insured organization would reimburse the insurer for an additional $100,000 for Employee 5 and Employee 6 together, with the annual aggregate deductible capped at $350,000.

Large deductible plans can be tailored to meet the insured organization's expectations of future losses.

A large deductible plan dramatically reduces the cost of risk compared with other insurance plans by avoiding a substantial amount of premium taxes, residual market loadings, and insurer overhead and profit charges.[1]

Another advantage of a large deductible plan is that it allows the insured organization to benefit from the cash flow available on the reserves (funds set aside) for retained losses. The insured organization reimburses the insurer as it pays losses under the deductible. Workers' compensation, auto liability, and general liability losses are usually paid over several years after they are incurred, so the insured organization can retain its funds until claims are actually paid, thereby enhancing the insured organization's cash flow.

As with any risk financing plan with a retention component, losses under a large deductible plan may be higher than expected, lowering an organization's net income and cash flow. By keeping its per occurrence (or accident) and annual aggregate deductibles at a prudent level, an organization can manage its uncertainty about the cost of its retained losses.

As mentioned, some organizations use SIR or self-insurance as part of their risk financing plan, rather than using a deductible or a large deductible plan. Excess liability insurance and umbrella liability are used by organizations to address high severity losses.

EXCESS LIABILITY INSURANCE

Excess liability insurance provides insurance coverage for losses that exceed the limits of underlying insurance coverage or a retention amount. The retention amount may be a large deductible or a SIR (self-insurance). Insurers selling excess liability insurance policies generally use nonstandard forms, so the coverage provided by excess liability insurance policies varies by insurer.

Excess liability insurance
Insurance coverage for losses that exceed the limits of underlying insurance coverage or a retention amount.

Excess liability insurance policies may provide the same coverage as that of the underlying insurance policies, but not always. While an excess liability insurance policy is rarely broader in coverage than the underlying policies, many insurers use excess liability insurance coverage forms that restrict coverage. For example, an excess liability insurance policy may expressly exclude products recall coverage, even though it is being provided by the underlying general liability insurance policy. Exhibit 3-19 shows that excess liability is above an organization's underlying insurance, because it applies after the underlying insurance has been exhausted.

EXHIBIT 3-19

Excess Liability Insurance Applies After Underlying Insurance

Excess Liability Insurance		
General Liability Insurance	Auto Liability Insurance	Workers' Compensation Insurance

Excess liability insurance provides additional liability insurance coverage beyond that provided by the insured organization's underlying liability insurance policies.

Although excess liability policy provisions vary among insurers, they generally perform the following two basic functions:

1. Providing additional liability limits above the each occurrence/accident limits of the insured's underlying liability policies
2. Taking the place of the underlying liability insurance when underlying aggregate liability limits have been exhausted

An excess liability policy above an underlying liability policy may take any of the following three basic forms:

1. A following-form subject to the same provisions as the underlying liability policy
2. A self-contained policy subject to its own provisions
3. A combination of the two types

When excess liability insurance is above a self-insured retention instead of an underlying liability policy, the following two types of excess liability insurance are commonly used:

1. Specific excess liability insurance
2. Aggregate excess liability insurance

Following-Form Excess Liability Policies

Following-form excess liability policy
Excess liability insurance that covers a liability loss that exceeds the underlying policy limits only if the underlying insurance covers the loss.

A **following-form excess liability policy** covers a liability loss that exceeds the underlying policy limits only if the underlying insurance covers the loss. As an illustration, assume that an insured organization has an underlying liability policy with a per occurrence limit of $1 million and a following-form excess liability policy with a per occurrence limit of $1 million. If a claimant obtains a judgment of $1,250,000 against the insured organization for bodily injury that the underlying liability policy covers, the underlying liability policy would pay its per occurrence limit of $1 million, and the excess liability policy would pay the remaining $250,000.

Although many excess liability policies are called following-form policies, most contain endorsements that limit coverage. For example, an excess liability policy might follow the provisions of the underlying liability policies only to the extent that they do not conflict with the provisions of the excess liability policy. The result is that the excess liability policy may cover less than the underlying liability policy covers.

Self-Contained Excess Liability Policies

Self-contained excess liability policy
Excess liability insurance policy that is subject to its own provisions only, so coverage applies only to the extent described in the policy.

A **self-contained excess liability policy** is subject to its own provisions only, so coverage applies only to the extent described in the policy. The policy does not depend on the provisions of the underlying policies for determining the scope of the coverage (with one exception, noted subsequently). Because self-contained excess liability policies are independent of the underlying liability policies, coverage gaps between the excess and underlying liability policies can occur.

Combination excess liability policy
An excess liability insurance policy that combines the following-form and self-contained approaches by incorporating the provisions of the underlying policy and then modifying those provisions with additional conditions or exclusions in the excess policy.

A self-contained excess policy applies to a loss that exceeds the underlying limits only if the loss is also covered under the provisions of the excess policy. For example, the excess policy may not cover injury within the products-completed operations hazard, even though the underlying policy does cover this hazard. In such a case, the excess liability policy would not pay for a products liability loss, even though the loss was covered by the underlying policy and exceeded the per occurrence limit of the underlying policy.

Combination Excess Liability Policies

A **combination excess liability policy** combines the following-form and self-contained approaches by incorporating the provisions of the underlying policy and then modifying those provisions with additional conditions or exclusions in the excess policy. One type of combination form is an excess liability policy that provides the broader coverages typically found in an umbrella liability policy, but without any obligation to drop down (provide primary coverage) when a claim is excluded by the primary policy but covered by the excess liability policy. Because many insurance professionals do not distinguish between excess and umbrella policies, insureds may not be aware that combination excess policies provide a narrower grant of coverage than umbrella policies.

Specific and Aggregate (or Stop Loss) Excess Liability Insurance

Specific excess liability insurance and aggregate excess liability insurance are designed to be used with self-insured retentions. A **specific excess liability insurance policy** is an excess liability policy that requires the insured organization to retain a stipulated amount of liability loss from the first dollar for all losses resulting from a single occurrence or accident. The excess liability insurer pays losses above the per occurrence/accident retention, subject to the policy limit. For example, if the specific excess liability policy required a retention of $100,000 per occurrence, the excess liability insurer would pay for all losses resulting from a single occurrence in excess of $100,000 up to the policy limit.

> **Specific excess liability insurance policy**
> An excess liability policy that requires the insured organization to retain a stipulated amount of liability loss from the first dollar for all losses resulting from a single occurrence or accident.

An **aggregate**, or **stop loss, excess liability insurance policy** is an excess liability policy that requires the insured organization to retain a specified amount of liability loss from the first dollar during a specified period, usually one year. The total amount of losses to be retained during a period of time is called an aggregate retention. The excess liability insurer then pays for, up to the policy limit, all losses for that period that exceed the aggregate retention.

> **Aggregate**, or **stop loss, excess liability insurance policy**
> An excess liability policy that requires the insured organization to retain a specified amount of liability loss from the first dollar during a specified period, usually one year.

Some policies combine the specific and aggregate excess approaches. Such policies provide the insured organization with the benefits of both approaches. For example, an insured organization may incur several moderate losses during a policy period, none of which exceeds the per occurrence or per accident retention. Under a specific excess liability policy, the insured organization would not be able to collect any insurance proceeds. With a combined specific/aggregate excess policy, however, if the total of losses for the policy period exceeded the aggregate retention, the insured organization could collect insurance proceeds for the amount of loss in excess of the aggregate retention. Exhibit 3-20 shows how specific excess and aggregate excess liability insurance may be combined in an organization's insurance plan.

While excess liability insurance policies apply to only one underlying insurance policy, umbrella liability insurance policies may provide excess coverage for more than one type of liability insurance policy. The following section describes the other features of umbrella liability insurance that make it distinctive from excess liability insurance policies.

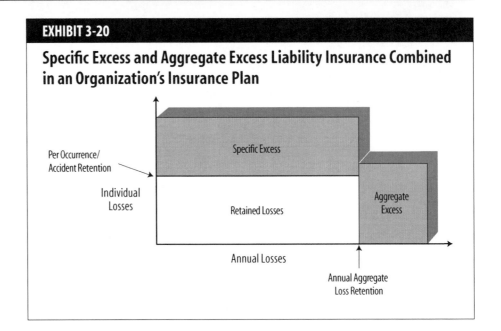

EXHIBIT 3-20

Specific Excess and Aggregate Excess Liability Insurance Combined in an Organization's Insurance Plan

Specific and aggregate excess liability insurance policies are designed to be used with an organization's SIR.

UMBRELLA LIABILITY INSURANCE

Umbrella liability insurance policy

Excess liability insurance that provides coverage above underlying policies but also offers coverage not available in the underlying policies subject to a self-insured retention (retained limit).

An **umbrella liability insurance policy** provides coverage above underlying policies but also offers coverage not available in the underlying policies subject to a self-insured retention (SIR), which is a retained limit. Coverage provided by the umbrella liability insurance policy and not available in the underlying policies is said to drop down over the self-insured retention. An umbrella policy also usually drops down over the aggregate limits of the underlying policies. Unlike excess liability insurance that provides excess coverage for only one underlying insurance policy, an umbrella liability insurance policy may provide excess coverage for more than one type of liability insurance policy, such as general liability, auto liability, and employers' liability.

Basic Functions of Umbrella Liability Policies

Although umbrella liability policy provisions vary among insurers, they generally perform three basic functions. Like an ordinary excess liability policy, they do the following:

1. Provide additional limits above the per occurrence limits of the insured's underlying liability policies

2. Take the place of the underlying liability insurance when underlying aggregate limits are exhausted

In addition, they do the following:

3. Cover some claims that the insured organization's underlying liability policies do not cover

The second and third functions are frequently referred to as drop-down coverage. **Drop-down coverage** is an umbrella liability policy provision stating that it will provide primary insurance coverage should the underlying liability limits be exhausted or if the underlying liability insurance does not cover some liability claims.

Self-Insured Retention

The claims not covered by the insured's underlying policies are subject to a SIR. The retention normally does not apply in the following circumstances:

- When paying the excess amount of a loss that the underlying liability policy covers
- When dropping down to pay a loss because the underlying policy's aggregate liability limit has been exhausted

Self-insured retentions vary in amount, from as low as $500 for small organizations to $1 million or more for large organizations. Many policies do not apply the self-insured retention to defense costs.

Exclusions Omitted From an Umbrella Liability Policy

Insurers omit some underlying policy exclusions from an umbrella liability policy to broaden the coverage. For example, an umbrella liability policy often has no exclusion of liability assumed under contract. If the insured organization becomes legally obligated to pay damages because of a hold-harmless agreement under circumstances that the underlying liability policy excludes but the umbrella liability policy does not, the insured organization's contractual liability will be covered by the umbrella liability policy. If the insured organization's underlying liability insurance does not cover the contractual liability, the umbrella liability policy provides drop-down coverage, subject to a SIR.

Other underlying policy exclusions that are frequently omitted from umbrella liability policies to provide coverage that is broader than the underlying policies include the following:

- The liquor liability exclusion of a general liability policy
- The employers' liability insurance exclusion of accidents occurring outside the United States or Canada
- The employers' liability insurance exclusion of injury to persons subject to the Federal Employers' Liability Act, the Jones Act, and similar laws permitting employees to sue their employers
- The employers' liability insurance exclusion of injury to persons knowingly employed in violation of law

Drop-down coverage
An umbrella liability policy provision stating that it will provide primary insurance coverage should the underlying liability limits be exhausted or if the underlying liability insurance does not cover some liability claims.

Umbrella Liability Policy Exclusions Less Restrictive Than the Underlying Coverage

Sometimes the umbrella liability policy provides broader coverage than the underlying liability policy by providing less restrictive exclusions. Consequently, the underlying liability policy may exclude coverage in an instance in which the umbrella liability policy will respond.

Umbrella Liability Policy Exclusions More Restrictive Than the Underlying Coverage

Because they provide drop-down coverage for claims not covered by the underlying insurance, umbrella liability policies are usually thought of as being broader than the underlying liability policies in all respects. However, most umbrella liability policies contain some exclusions that are broader than those in the underlying policies. Therefore, these umbrella exclusions restrict coverage to a greater extent than do the exclusions in the underlying policies. To accomplish this effect, the insurer may use modified versions of exclusions found in underlying policies or may add exclusions that have no counterparts in underlying policies. A common example of an underlying policy exclusion that is modified in the umbrella to restrict coverage even further is the pollution exclusion.

STRUCTURING A LIABILITY INSURANCE PROGRAM

Risk management professionals may structure a liability insurance program by purchasing a combination of excess and umbrella liability insurance policies. Liability insurance is usually purchased in layers, with the underlying (or primary) insurance providing the first layer. Insurers vary in the amount of liability limits they are willing to sell to an organization. Consequently, the risk management professional must evaluate the adequacy of each underlying layer and determine how much additional excess or umbrella liability coverage needs to be purchased. The risk management professional may find that the organization's liability insurance needs can best be met with both excess and umbrella liability insurance. Because excess liability is often sold in layers, the risk management professional may have to purchase several excess liability policies for certain liability loss exposures for which the organization has a significant loss exposure. Exhibit 3-21 shows a multilayered liability insurance program.

The organization's liability insurance program shown in Exhibit 3-21 illustrates several approaches an organization may use to obtain the liability coverage limits it needs. An umbrella liability policy provides liability coverage above the limits of liability provided by the underlying policies for the most frequently affected loss exposures: general liability, auto liability, and employers' liability. Because the limits of liability provided by the umbrella liability policy are insufficient, three excess liability policies were purchased.

Note that the organization purchased a **buffer layer**, an excess liability policy that fills the gap between an underlying insurance policy and the umbrella liability policy. To achieve sufficient liability limits for aircraft liability and directors' and officers' liability loss exposures, excess liability policies were purchased for each. Also note that the umbrella liability policy contains drop-down coverage, which provides coverage for liability loss exposures not otherwise insured.

Buffer layer
An excess liability policy that fills the gap between an underlying insurance policy and the umbrella liability policy.

EXHIBIT 3-21

Multilayered Liability Insurance Program

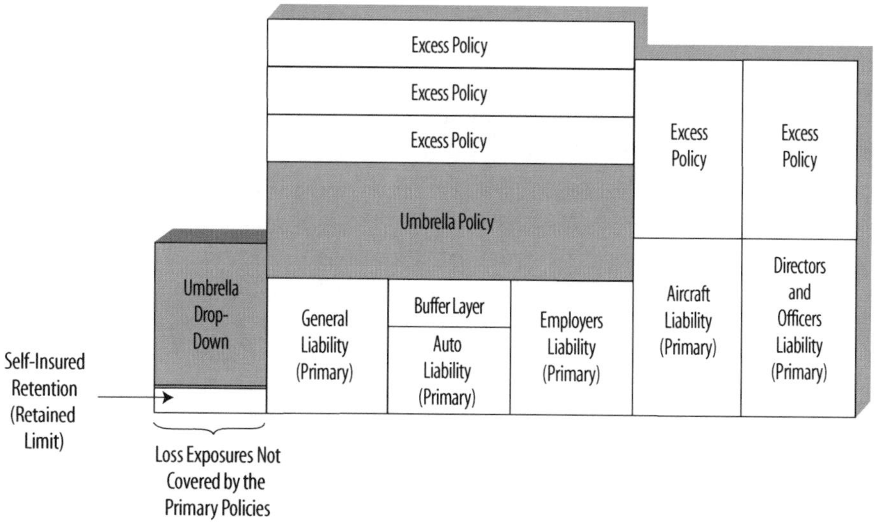

A liability insurance program may be structured using a combination of excess and umbrella liability insurance policies.

CASE STUDIES IN INSURANCE PLAN DESIGN

The following case studies illustrate the application of insurance plans to specific situations. The plans outlined are realistic for the circumstances shown, but are not necessarily the only appropriate options.

Coastal Warehouse Company

Coastal Warehouse Company (CWC) is located in a coastal town in the Southeastern U.S. CWC is a public warehouse, that is, it stores goods for others. Its facility consists of two separate warehouses. Most of the goods at CWC are stored pending delivery. For example, the local retail furniture store chain stores furniture at CWC until it is sold. In general, there is significant turnover of goods. However, CWC also provides long-term storage of financial records. CWC's risk management professional has arranged a fairly comprehensive insurance plan for CWC's loss exposures. However, its property insurance excludes losses due to flood. Additionally, CWC's insurer has excluded losses due to wind. Because of CWC's proximity to the coast, it is subject to hurricanes. Hurricanes can cause flooding in the form of storm surge, as well as extensive wind damage.

CWC's risk management professional responds to this coverage gap in its property insurance needs. CWC purchases a $500,000 building coverage policy for each of its warehouses. This is the maximum amount available under the National Flood Insurance Program (NFIP). CWC purchases a $50,000 contents coverage policy for each building (the NFIP maximum is $500,000 per structure) to cover its own property stored in each building. Customer property is insured through a warehouse operators legal liability policy. CWC's buildings are valued at $750,000 each. Consequently, CWC purchases $250,000 in excess flood insurance from a commercial insurer. CWC purchases $1.5 million in windstorm coverage from the state's wind and hail association. (The maximum amount of coverage this state's wind and hail association will provide is $2.5 million for each structure.) The association is financially backed by all the insurers selling property insurance in the state. Because CWC's risk management professional was aware of the gaps in property coverage and opportunities in the insurance marketplace to fill those gaps, CWC's insurance plan now protects the organization from the financial consequences of hurricane-related losses.

Baby Products Manufacturing Company

Baby Products Manufacturing Company (BPMC) designs and manufactures cribs, high chairs, strollers, and playpens that are sold by national retailers. Despite potential cost-of-risk savings that may be obtained through other types of risk financing plans, BPMC's management is most comfortable using insurance. However, BPMC's exclusive reliance on insurance presents its risk management professional with a dilemma. BPMC has a history of products liability losses that have made purchasing a commercial general liability (CGL) insurance policy very expensive. In the past, some insurers have suggested that BPMC purchase a CGL policy that excludes products liability coverage and retain its product liability losses. This approach was unacceptable to BPMC's management.

In an attempt to address this situation, BPMC's risk management professional purchases a CGL insurance policy with a $100,000 deductible that is applicable only to products liability coverage. The CGL provides a $1 million per occurrence limit and a $2 million products/completed operations aggregate limit. BPMC's risk management professional also directs the CGL policy to contain an endorsement that excludes designated products. The designated products include BPMC's discontinued Stroller Classic, which still generates liability claims. Consequently, BPMC retains all losses from this discontinued product.

Relative to what BPMC believes is its potential exposure to liability losses, this amount of coverage is insufficient. Consequently, BPMC's risk management professional purchases $5 million in excess liability coverage. BPMC's risk management professional has negotiated excess liability coverage that will cover losses that arise from its discontinued products as well.

SUMMARY

Organizations that rely on insurance as a means of financing risk need to be assured that insurance policies purchased actually address their insurance needs. Therefore, risk management professionals should understand insurance policy construction and provisions to assess the coverage the insurer provides.

The contractual relationship between an insurer and the insured organization is often initiated by the issuance of an insurance binder. An insurance binder is a temporary oral or written agreement to provide insurance coverage until a formal written policy is issued. The binder is a one- or two-page summary of the provided insurance coverages. Risk management professionals should scrutinize the insurer's binder as carefully as they would examine the insurance policy that is ultimately issued, because the binder is relied on by the insurer's claim representatives in settling losses.

Insurance policies are physically constructed in several ways. An understanding of the approaches to policy construction enables the risk management professional to more accurately evaluate the completeness of the insurance coverage received. A monoline policy is an insurance policy that covers a single type of insurance. A package policy is an insurance policy that covers more than one type of insurance. A coverage part consists of one or more forms that, together, provide coverage for a type of insurance. An insurance plan may consist of any or all of these policy types. Risk management professionals should be able to recognize the physical construction of the insurance policies they receive from insurers because construction relates to the coordination of coverages the policies provide and the premium the insurer charges.

Another way of categorizing the construction of an insurance policy is to determine whether it contains self-contained policies or modular policies. Risk management professionals need to be able to make this distinction to determine whether the contract they are reviewing is complete or whether other coverage forms need to be evaluated as well. A self-contained policy is a single document that contains all the agreements between the insured and the insurer and that forms a complete insurance policy. A modular policy is an insurance policy that consists of several different documents, none of which by itself forms a complete policy.

Another approach to categorizing insurance policies is to determine whether they are assembled from preprinted forms or from forms that are uniquely designed for the insured organization's loss exposures. Preprinted forms are ready-made forms developed for use with many different insureds. Preprinted forms can be further classified as standard forms or nonstandard forms. As their names imply, standard forms are used industry-wide, whereas nonstandard forms are not. In contrast to preprinted forms, manuscript forms are custom forms developed for one specific insured or for a small group of insureds that have common unique coverage needs. A manuscript form is an insurance form that is drafted according to terms negotiated between a specific insured (or group of insureds) and an insurer. Because nonstandard and manuscript forms are not standard forms, the risk management professional may need to devote more time to analyzing them than if a standard form was used.

Understanding the construction of the organization's insurance policies is another step toward understanding the coverage provided by the insurer. The risk management professional should be able to read the organization's insurance policies and determine the coverage they provide. Reading, and therefore analyzing, an insurance policy is aided when the risk management professional can categorize the functions of common policy provisions. The six categories of property-liability insurance policy provisions are the following:

1. Declarations
2. Definitions
3. Insuring agreements
4. Conditions
5. Exclusions
6. Miscellaneous provisions

The declarations contain information that has been declared and information that is unique to that particular policy. The definitions section defines terms used throughout the policy. The insuring agreement is a statement in an insurance policy that the insurer will, under certain circumstances, make payment or provide a service. Conditions are any provision that qualifies an otherwise enforceable promise of the insurer. Exclusions specify what the insurance does not cover. Miscellaneous provisions are policy provisions that do not fit into the other five categories of common policy provisions.

Although it generally represents only a dollar figure entry on the declarations page of an insurance policy, the deductible directly affects the amount that the insured organization recovers, if any, from an insurer. A deductible is the amount that must be retained by the insured before the insured can recover from the insurer. Insurance can be purchased with no or small deductibles, but the insured organization pays a more expensive premium as a consequence. Deductibles are usually found in property insurance, but organizations can purchase liability insurance policies with deductibles as well.

Some organizations want to lower their cost of risk by assuming significant retention amounts within an insurance plan. Large deductible plans are treated separately from insurance plans with typical deductible amounts. Large deductible plans enable the organization to pay a reduced insurance premium while retaining losses below the deductible level. As losses occur, the insurer settles each claim, then periodically bills the insured organization for the amount of the loss and the claim-handling expense up to the deductible level.

Some organizations use self-insured retention (SIR) or self-insurance as part of their risk financing plan rather than a deductible or a large deductible plan. However, SIR (that is, significant retentions) is not practical for most organizations if the retention is unlimited. Excess liability insurance and umbrella liability insurance are used by organizations to address high-severity losses. Excess and umbrella liability insurance provide coverage for losses that exceed the limits of underlying insurance coverage or a retention amount. The retention amount may be a large deductible or a SIR.

While excess liability insurance policies apply to only one underlying insurance policy, an umbrella liability insurance policy may provide excess coverage for more than one type of liability insurance policy, such as general liability, auto liability, and employers' liability. An umbrella liability insurance policy provides coverage above underlying policies but also offers coverage not available in the underlying policies subject to a SIR. Coverage provided by the umbrella liability insurance policy and not available in the underlying policies is said to drop down over the self-insured retention. An umbrella policy also usually drops down over the aggregate limits of the underlying policies.

Risk management professionals may structure a liability insurance program by purchasing a combination of excess and umbrella liability insurance policies. Liability insurance is usually purchased in layers, with the underlying (or primary) insurance providing the first layer. Insurers vary in the amount of liability limits that they are willing to sell to an organization. Consequently, the risk management professional must evaluate the adequacy of each underlying liability limit and determine how much additional excess or umbrella liability coverage must be purchased. The risk management professional may find that the organization's liability insurance needs can best be met with both excess and umbrella liability insurance. Because excess liability is often sold in layers, the risk management professional may have to purchase several excess liability policies for certain liability loss exposures for which the organization believes that it has a significant loss exposure.

In addition to understanding how the various types of insurance coverage interact to form a complete insurance plan, the risk management professional must also master techniques for forecasting the expected losses that the insurance will cover. The next chapter discusses these techniques and how they can be used to further evaluate risk financing plans.

CHAPTER NOTE

1.   Several states have taken steps to impose premium taxes and residual market loadings on the retained-loss portion of large deductible plans.

Chapter 4

Direct Your Learning

Forecasting Accidental Losses and Risk Financing Needs

After learning the content of this chapter and completing the corresponding course guide assignment, you should be able to:

■ Describe the steps in forecasting expected losses.

■ Explain how to forecast the probable variation from expected losses.

■ Explain how loss forecasts can be used to estimate cash flow needs.

■ Explain how loss forecasts can be used to:

- Budget for retained losses

- Evaluate alternative retention levels

- Evaluate insurer premium charges

- Update accounting reserves for retained losses

■ Given a case, forecast expected losses and estimate the net present value of cash flow needs.

■ Define or describe each of the Key Words and Phrases for this chapter.

Develop Your Perspective

What are the main topics covered in the chapter?

Financing the risk of accidental loss would be a relatively simple task if the frequency, severity, and timing of those losses were known in advance. To provide their organizations with a degree of certainty about unpredictable losses, risk management professionals use loss forecasting and cash flow analysis to anticipate their organization's risk financing needs.

Identify the three-part process of forecasting accidental losses.

- What are the four steps in forecasting expected losses?
- Which cash flows must be discounted back to present-day dollars to make an accurate estimate of cash flow needs?

Why is it important to learn about these topics?

Risk management professionals need to understand their organization's expected losses in order to select an appropriate risk financing plan. Loss forecasting and cash flow analysis enable the risk management professional to model the organization's retention when evaluating proposed risk financing plans.

Consider why losses may need to be limited to a specified amount for analysis purposes.

- Explain how insurance advisory organization-developed increased limit factor tables are used in loss forecasting.
- Explain how increased limit factor tables can be used to evaluate the reasonableness of the premium being charged the insured organization.

How can you use what you will learn?

Analyze your organization's past losses.

- How much should your organization budget for retained losses under its existing risk financing plan?
- Would your organization be better off financially with a higher or lower retention?

Chapter 4

Forecasting Accidental Losses and Risk Financing Needs

Forecasting accidental losses is fundamental to the quantitative evaluation and comparison of risk financing plans and to the determination of related cash flow needs. The accidental loss forecasting process is especially important to the assessment of risk financing plans that involve some loss retention. It consists of the following three parts:

1. Part 1—Forecasting expected losses
2. Part 2—Forecasting probable variation from expected losses
3. Part 3—Estimating cash flow needs

Part 1 entails calculating an estimate of the expected (or average) losses for the coming year based on past data. Part 2 involves probability distributions and probability intervals that are used to estimate the probable variation from expected losses. Part 3 incorporates a method for estimating the timing of loss payments.

Forecasting accidental losses involves organizing past loss data and using statistical techniques to analyze them. This complex process is illustrated in the following case study, which uses a single set of facts involving a hypothetical company, the Tarnton Company (Tarnton). Tarnton's risk management professional uses forecasting to evaluate its current risk financing plan in order to determine what changes, if any, should be made in the future.

THE TARNTON COMPANY CASE STUDY

The Tarnton Company manufactures denim pants and jackets. Its operations include dyeing cloth, cutting the cloth to size, and sewing the cut cloth to create finished goods. In 20X5, Tarnton had $64.2 million in sales. It expects sales for 20X6 to increase to $70 million. Because Tarnton is planning to increase the number of its retail outlets during 20X6, it expects its annual sales to grow to $75 million in 20X7. Tarnton has a broad range of loss exposures, but its risk management professional (and this case study) focuses on the organization's general liability loss exposures.

General liability loss exposures arise out of premises and operations, products liability, and completed operations. General liability insurance is the most basic, and the most important, coverage for insuring the owners and operators of businesses against losses from lawsuits filed by members of the general public, because it covers many of the loss exposures common to most businesses.

Tarnton's general liability coverage has a $1 million per occurrence limit. The Insurance Services Office (ISO) general liability policy defines an occurrence as an accident, including continuous or repeated exposure to substantially the same general harmful conditions. Although several claims (and claimants) may result from an occurrence, the occurrence limit is the most an insurer will pay. For example, Tarnton could have used a contaminated clothing dye that caused a reaction in hundreds of customers. This could result in hundreds of claims, but is only one occurrence.

General liability insurance is sold with an annual aggregate limit, which further limits the dollar amount of losses an insurer will pay in a year. Most general liability insurance polices include an annual aggregate limit for products liability loss exposures and another annual aggregate limit for all other losses paid under the policy. For simplicity's sake, this case study does not consider annual aggregate limits.

Tarnton's general liability insurance policy has a $50,000 per occurrence deductible. This means that Tarnton's insurer will expect reimbursement from Tarnton for payments it makes up to $50,000. A per claim liability deductible likely would result in a greater retention amount because of the possibility that multiple claims (and claimants) may arise from a single occurrence. Ordinarily, most organizations do not purchase general liability insurance with a liability deductible. Instead, they purchase a general liability policy that pays all claims without any financial participation from the insured.

Tarnton's general liability insurance premium for 20X7 is estimated at $220,000. This estimated premium is based on Tarnton's estimated sales. When actual sales for 20X7 are known, Tarnton's insurer will adjust the premium accordingly. However, Tarnton's premium is not the only expense related to this insurance policy. Tarnton's risk management professional must also consider the amount Tarnton will retain because of its $50,000 liability deductible.

Tarnton's management has asked its risk management professional to answer the following four questions regarding its general liability insurance:

1. How much should Tarnton budget in 20X7 for retained general liability losses? A basic loss forecast (Part 1) provides the amount, on average, that Tarnton must pay for losses that fall wholly or partially within its liability deductible, but actual losses in any one year may be considerably higher or lower. A good estimate of the fluctuations above the average (Part 2) provides information allowing Tarnton to consider budgeting some amount above the expected average rate for retained losses.

2. Would Tarnton fare better financially with a $100,000 liability deductible instead of a $50,000 liability deductible? By estimating the additional losses that would be retained under a $100,000 liability deductible, Tarnton can determine whether the premium reduction resulting from the higher liability deductible is a sufficient financial incentive to assume greater risk of loss.

3. Is Tarnton's insurer charging a reasonable premium for the $50,001 to $1 million layer? Tarnton can estimate the insurer's average expected losses and other costs in the layer from $50,001 to $1 million and compare them with the estimated $220,000 premium for that layer.

4. Are Tarnton's accounting reserves for losses in prior years reasonable? Tarnton's accounting reserves for retained losses represent a liability, and the reserves should be adjusted each year using the latest information on past losses.

The remainder of this chapter explores how Tarnton's risk management professional would answer these questions.

PART 1: FORECASTING EXPECTED LOSSES

Preparing a forecast of expected losses (dollar amounts) requires Tarnton's risk management professional to complete the following four steps:

1. Collect and organize past data
2. Limit individual losses
3. Apply loss development and trend factors to the data
4. Forecast losses

These four steps are shown in Exhibit 4-1.

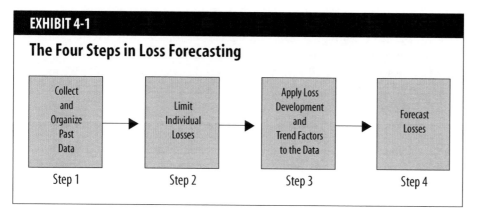

EXHIBIT 4-1

The Four Steps in Loss Forecasting

Step 1 — Collect and Organize Past Data → Step 2 — Limit Individual Losses → Step 3 — Apply Loss Development and Trend Factors to the Data → Step 4 — Forecast Losses

Step 1: Collect and Organize Past Data

Tarnton's risk management professional first must collect past loss and exposure data and organize them for further analysis. Ideally, a minimum of five years of past loss and exposure data are needed to make an accurate forecast; many organizations collect as much as ten years of data.

Loss Data

Paid losses
Losses that have been paid to, or on behalf of, insureds during a given period.

Loss reserves
A liability on an insurer's balance sheet that shows the estimated amount that will be required to settle claims that have occurred but have not yet been paid.

Loss adjustment expense reserves
Estimates of the future cost of defending and settling claims for losses that have already occurred.

Incurred losses
The sum of paid losses, loss reserves, and loss adjustment expense reserves.

Loss data required for forecasts of expected losses include paid losses, loss reserves, and loss adjustment expense reserves, which, together, determine incurred losses. **Paid losses** are losses that have been paid to, or on behalf of, insureds during a given period. **Loss reserves** are a liability on an insurer's balance sheet that shows the estimated amount that will be required to settle claims that have occurred but have not yet been paid. **Loss adjustment expense reserves** are estimates of the future cost of defending and settling claims for losses that have already occurred. Loss adjustment expense reserve data may be collected separately but included in loss reserves for analysis purposes because they are derived from the claims that constitute the loss reserves. **Incurred losses** are the sum of paid losses, loss reserves, and loss adjustment expense reserves, as shown in the following formula:

Incurred losses = Paid losses + Loss reserves + Loss adjustment expense reserves.

Paid losses, loss reserves, loss adjustment expense reserves, and incurred losses usually are accumulated on an accident-year basis, that is, that they are related to all accidents that occur in a twelve-month period. As loss payments are made during the accident year, paid losses increase and reserves decrease equally. Therefore, incurred losses are unchanged. However, incurred losses do change when a reserve is amended because of additional information about a claim or because a new claim is reported. An accident year's accounts can be kept open for many years until all of that year's losses are paid.

Exhibit 4-2 shows data on twenty-six past losses for Tarnton. (To minimize the number of calculations for this chapter, the number of losses has been kept low; however, a credible forecast requires a larger number of past losses.) Loss reserves and loss adjustment expenses have been combined, as they often are, into the reserves column. The paid losses and loss reserves sum to equal the incurred losses shown in the third column.

Loss development
The increase or decrease of incurred losses over time.

Loss payout pattern
A listing of incurred loss payments over time.

For all accident years, Tarnton's loss data are evaluated as of 6/30/X6, six months after the end of year 20X5. It is also necessary, however, to collect loss data as of several previous annual evaluation dates (6/30/X5, 6/30/X4, 6/30/X3, and 6/30/X2), because Tarnton's paid losses and loss reserves change over time. An analysis of the previous evaluations allows Tarnton to track past loss development and payout patterns. **Loss development** is the increase or decrease of incurred losses over time. A **loss payout pattern** is a listing of incurred loss payments over time. A subsequent section of this chapter shows how Tarnton's risk management professional could forecast its loss development and payout patterns based on past data.

For large claims, such as those over $100,000, Tarnton's risk management professional should obtain specific information on the cause and circumstances of loss so that risk control techniques can be used to mitigate similar future losses. Tarnton had one very significant loss of $1,239,000 in 20X2.

EXHIBIT 4-2

General Liability Loss Data for Tarnton as of 6/30/20X6

Accident Year	Paid Losses	Loss Reserves	Incurred Losses
20X1	$ 17,000	$ 4,000	$ 21,000
	30,000	4,000	34,000
	21,000	7,000	28,000
	4,600	1,400	6,000
	142,000	58,000	200,000
Total	$ 214,600	$ 74,400	$ 289,000
20X2	$ 24,000	$ 5,000	$ 29,000
	2,000	1,000	3,000
	760,000	479,000	1,239,000
	15,000	10,000	25,000
	5,000	4,000	9,000
	4,000	4,000	8,000
	28,000	6,000	34,000
Total	$ 838,000	$509,000	$1,347,000
20X3	$ 15,000	$ 7,000	$ 22,000
	14,000	9,000	23,000
	3,000	8,000	11,000
	6,000	2,000	8,000
	32,000	51,000	83,000
	13,000	14,000	27,000
Total	$ 83,000	$ 91,000	$ 174,000
20X4	$ 9,000	$ 19,000	$ 28,000
	15,000	12,000	27,000
	8,000	8,000	16,000
	13,000	52,000	65,000
Total	$ 45,000	$ 91,000	$ 136,000
20X5	$ 4,000	$ 15,000	$ 19,000
	3,000	15,000	18,000
	6,000	9,000	15,000
	7,000	11,750	18,750
Total	$ 20,000	$ 50,750	$ 70,750

Collecting and organizing data, such as the data presented here, is the first step in loss forecasting.

Exposure Data

Exposure data must be collected by type of coverage for each past year and projected for the coming year (20X7 in this case). An **exposure unit** is a fundamental measure of an exposure that correlates the possibility of a loss with its likely amount. The exposure unit for general liability insurance can be, for example, annual sales (in thousands of dollars), building square footage, units (apartments), admissions (theaters), or another measure of public liability. For a manufacturer such as Tarnton, the exposure unit is sales. Similarly, number of vehicles or miles driven is commonly used for commercial automobile liability insurance; payroll or the number of employees for workers' compensation insurance, and so forth.

Tarnton obtained the historical and projected exposure data from organizational records and internal forecasts. Exhibit 4-3 shows how the past and projected exposure data for Tarnton are organized.

EXHIBIT 4-3

Past and Projected Exposure Data for Tarnton

Accident Year	Sales
20X1	$47,421,000
20X2	$50,020,000
20X3	$55,169,000
20X4	$58,921,000
20X5	$64,282,000
20X6	$70,000,000 (Projected)
20X7	$75,000,000 (Projected)

Step 2: Limit Individual Losses

Once loss data have been collected, the size of the individual losses must be limited, as necessary. Limiting losses involves capping them at a specific dollar amount. For example, constructing a loss payout pattern that limits losses to $50,000 means losses of $50,000 or less are listed at their actual amount and individual losses of more than $50,000 are reduced to a value of $50,000.

Risk management professionals will limit losses to match the layer being forecast. Limiting losses, as Tarnton's risk management professional has done in Exhibit 4-4, also stabilizes losses. That is, Tarnton's losses do not vary significantly from year to year when losses that exceed $50,000 are capped.

Exhibit 4-5 shows how limiting individual losses enables Tarnton's risk management professional to focus on the layer of losses that have sufficient frequency to be predictable and therefore retainable. Losses in the $50,001 to $1 million layer are less frequent and more severe than the $0 to $50,000 layer. Consequently, the higher loss layer is less predictable and more suited for risk transfer.

EXHIBIT 4-4

General Liability Loss Data Limited to $50,000 for Tarnton as of 6/30/20X6

Accident Year	Total Losses 6/30/X6	Losses Limited to $50,000
20X1	$ 21,000	$ 21,000
	34,000	34,000
	28,000	28,000
	6,000	6,000
	200,000	50,000
Total	$ 289,000	$ 139,000
20X2	$ 29,000	$ 29,000
	3,000	3,000
	1,239,000	50,000
	25,000	25,000
	9,000	9,000
	8,000	8,000
	34,000	34,000
Total	$1,347,000	$ 158,000
20X3	$ 22,000	$ 22,000
	23,000	23,000
	11,000	11,000
	8,000	8,000
	83,000	50,000
	27,000	27,000
Total	$ 174,000	$ 141,000
20X4	$ 28,000	$ 28,000
	27,000	27,000
	16,000	16,000
	65,000	50,000
Total	$ 136,000	$ 121,000
20X5	$ 19,000	$ 19,000
	18,000	18,000
	15,000	15,000
	18,750	18,750
Total	$ 70,750	$ 70,750

Loss data are limited to match the layer being forecast.

Tarnton's risk management professional may be able to use industry-wide loss data, if available, to supplement its own loss data in the $50,001 to $1 million layer. However, Tarnton's risk management professional is more likely to use increased limit factor tables developed by insurance advisory organizations. **Increased limit factor tables** are tables used by insurers to price layers of

Increased limit factor tables
Tables used by insurers to price layers of coverage in excess of the insurer's base limit.

coverage in excess of the insurer's base limit. For example, a primary insurer's base limit for general liability policies may be $100,000 per occurrence and $200,000 aggregate (denoted as $100/$200), but those base limits can be increased in increments (for example, $200/$200, $100/$300, $1,000/$3,000, and so forth) by applying an increased limit factor to the premium developed for the base limit. Increased limit factor tables are actuarially developed and based on considerable industry-wide loss data, making them a sound foundation for forecasting losses.

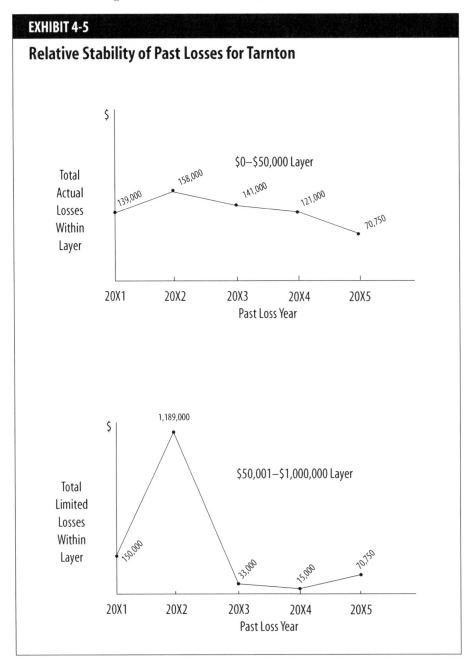

EXHIBIT 4-5

Relative Stability of Past Losses for Tarnton

High loss frequency in lower layers results in stability.

It is difficult to determine the level at which to limit losses in order to produce past losses that are stable and therefore credible enough for loss forecasting purposes. Although mathematical formulas can be used for this, judgment usually helps determine the appropriate level. One way to make this determination is to limit past losses at various levels, such as $25,000, $50,000, and $100,000, and then to analyze the past losses under each limit (retention level) to identify a limit at which past total losses are fairly stable from year to year. This is the approach that Tarnton used to select the $50,000 liability deductible it currently uses.

Step 3: Apply Loss Development and Trend Factors to the Data

Trend factors are percentages that are applied to current dollar amounts that restate dollar amounts for the forecasted year. These factors reflect changes that occur over time, such as inflation, regulatory changes, and legal rulings. Applying trend factors to data allows the risk management professional make all the data comparable by nullifying external factors. **Loss development factors** are percentages applied to aggregate past losses for each year in order to add an amount for the possibility of both late-reported claims and a future increase in the incurred amount for reported claims. Loss development factors ordinarily are used to forecast liability losses, which tend to exhibit patterns of late claim reporting and underreserving. Because property losses ordinarily are reported and paid quickly, loss development factors usually are not used for a property loss forecast.

Loss Development

Loss development presents an obstacle to accurately forecasting losses. Unlike other historical data, such as Tarnton's historical sales data for 20X1 through 20X5, past loss data are subject to change long after the end of the accident year. Earlier accident years such as 20X1 probably are less subject to development than more recent accident years, such as 20X5. Tarnton's risk management professional may reasonably conclude that the total incurred loss amount for 20X1 shown in Exhibit 4-2 is the ultimate loss for that year.

The graph in Exhibit 4-6 shows loss development for a single policy year, assuming no further development sixty-six months after the beginning of the policy year. Certainty regarding the value of ultimate losses incurred increases over time. To estimate ultimate losses (final actual losses), ultimate loss development factors are applied to past incurred losses for each year. An **ultimate loss development factor** is a numeric factor that is applied to the most recent estimate of incurred loss for a specific accident year to estimate the ultimate incurred loss value for that year. The factors applied bear an inverse relationship to the age of each accident year because most loss development occurs early in the life of a claim.

Trend factors
Percentages that are applied to current dollar amounts that restate dollar amounts for the forecasted year.

Loss development factors
Percentages applied to aggregate past losses for each year in order to add an amount for the possibility of both late-reported claims and a future increase in the incurred amount for reported claims.

Ultimate loss development factor
A numeric factor that is applied to the most recent estimate of incurred loss for a specific accident year to estimate the ultimate incurred loss value for that year.

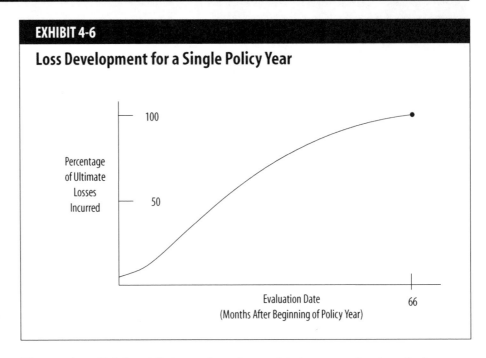

EXHIBIT 4-6

Loss Development for a Single Policy Year

Percentage of Ultimate Losses Incurred

100

50

Evaluation Date
(Months After Beginning of Policy Year)

66

The exhibit assumes that ultimate losses incurred are known sixty-six months following policy inception.

The graph in Exhibit 4-7 shows the relationship between the size of a loss development factor and the evaluation date for a single accident year. A loss development factor for an accident year that is evaluated sixty-six months after the beginning of that accident year is much smaller than a loss development factor for an accident year evaluated only eighteen months after the beginning of the accident year. Loss development factors become smaller over time because most loss development has occurred.

This relationship is represented in Exhibit 4-8, which shows loss development factors for general liability calculated from an insurer's past losses and used by its national accounts department. Loss development, and consequently loss development factors, vary by type of loss exposure. Some categories of losses settle more quickly than others. Dividing general liability losses into such categories helps Tarnton's risk management professional focus risk control efforts.

Loss development factors can be used to help estimate the ultimate value of a group of claims. For example, the loss development factor of 3.75 for bodily injury liability claims evaluated eighteen months after the beginning of an accident year means that the ultimate value of those claims will, on the average, be 3.75 times their incurred value at eighteen months. Therefore, the projected ultimate value for bodily injury liability claims for which $100,000 has been paid during the first eighteen months after the beginning of the accident year and for which the reserve for future payments at the eighteen-month evaluation is $250,000 (a total incurred amount of $350,000) is $350,000 × 3.75, or $1,312,500. Similarly, if the total incurred claims are valued at $1,450,000 sixty-six months after the beginning of the policy year, then the projected ultimate value of the claims should, according to Exhibit 4-8, be equal to $1,450,000 × 1.20, or $1,740,000.

EXHIBIT 4-7

Relationship Between Size of Loss Development Factor and the Evaluation Date

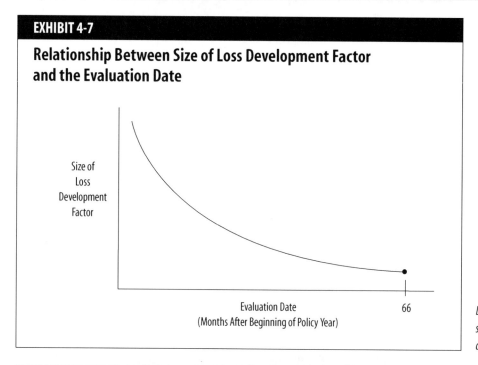

Size of
Loss
Development
Factor

Evaluation Date
(Months After Beginning of Policy Year)

66

Loss development factors become smaller over time because most loss development has occurred.

EXHIBIT 4-8

Typical Loss Development Factors—General Liability

Evaluation Date (Months After Beginning of Policy Year)	Bodily Injury Liability	Products Liability
18	3.75	4.52
30	2.10	2.27
42	1.48	1.49
54	1.30	1.34
66	1.20	1.21
78	1.12	1.14
90	1.07	1.08

Loss development, and consequently loss development factors, vary by type of loss exposure. Some categories of losses settle more quickly than others.

Loss development factors are used to estimate the development of an entire group of losses, as opposed to an individual loss. Some loss development factors apply only to open claims, others to open and closed claims together. Unless otherwise specified, this chapter discusses development of open claims.

Whether a loss develops depends on its circumstances. For example, if the parties to a settlement agree on the amount of a loss that is reflected in the current reserve amount for the loss, then it would not be appropriate to apply a loss development factor to that loss. Other individual losses from the same year may develop much more or much less than indicated by the relevant loss development factor. Loss development factors reflect the average development for an entire group of losses, including an amount for unreported losses, and therefore should be applied only to total aggregate losses for each past year.

Loss development factors are available from several insurance advisory organizations and trade organizations. They must relate to the body of past data to which they will be applied. For example, when projecting losses for a clothing manufacturer such as Tarnton, the loss development factors for general liability from Exhibit 4-8 can be used if Tarnton's exposure is similar to other manufacturers whose data were used to generate the general liability loss development factors. Even then, the loss reserves may not have been similarly set. Therefore, someone who is familiar with the loss exposure should determine the factor's applicability to Tarnton.

Loss development factors can be calculated from an organization's own past loss data if a sufficiently large number of past losses exists. This approach is preferable to using industry-wide factors, because it calculates loss development factors from the same data to which those factors are applied. Exhibits 4-9 through 4-12 show how loss development factors are calculated based on past loss data and how they are applied to the most recent evaluation of prior loss years.

Exhibit 4-4 shows total incurred losses limited to $50,000 per loss as of 6/30/X6. The total losses for each year are shown in Exhibit 4-9, with the columns representing different evaluation dates in months from the beginning of the accident year and the rows representing accident years.

Exhibit 4-9 shows Tarnton's past losses from a perspective of a 6/30/X6 evaluation. The $139,000 represents the 6/30/X6 evaluation of the 20X1 accident year, which takes place sixty-six months after the beginning of that year. The 6/30/X6 evaluation of the 20X2 accident year is $158,000, which occurs fifty-four months after the beginning of that accident year. The other numbers in the diagonal are the 6/30/X6 evaluation of their respective accident years. Such tables of dollar amounts or development factors for losses often are called loss triangles because, when tabulated, the projected dollar amounts fall on the diagonal, or the hypotenuse, of a triangle.

As mentioned, it is useful to collect loss data as of 6/30/X5, 6/30/X4, 6/30/X3, and 6/30/X2. The 6/30/X5 evaluation of the 20X1 accident year is fifty-four months after the beginning of that year, the 6/30/X4 evaluation of the 20X1 accident year is forty-two months after the beginning of that year, and so forth. Loss data from previous evaluations, as summarized in Exhibit 4-9, can be used to construct the loss triangle in the upper portion of Exhibit 4-10. Changes in periodic loss evaluations can be converted to loss development factors, which can be used to estimate ultimate loss amounts.

EXHIBIT 4-9

General Liability (Losses Limited to $50,000 for All Evaluation Dates) for Tarnton

Months From the Beginning of the Accident Year

Accident Year	18	30	42	54	66
20X1	$63,551	$100,410	$120,492	$134,951	$139,000
20X2	72,238	119,915	146,296	$158,000	
20X3	71,069	113,710	$141,000		
20X4	73,780	$121,000			
20X5	$70,750				

Total Incurred Losses

Loss triangles show past losses from the perspective of a particular evaluation date.

EXHIBIT 4-10

Calculation of General Liability Period-to-Period Loss Development Factors for Tarnton

Months From the Beginning of the Accident Year

Accident Year	18–30	31–42	43–54	55–66
20X1	1.58	1.20	1.12	1.03
20X2	1.66	1.22	1.08	
20X3	1.60	1.24		
20X4	1.64			
Average	1.62	1.22	1.10	1.03

54 months to ultimate	$1.03 =$	1.03 *
42 months to ultimate	$1.10 \times 1.03 =$	1.13
30 months to ultimate	$1.22 \times 1.10 \times 1.03 =$	1.38
18 months to ultimate	$1.62 \times 1.22 \times 1.10 \times 1.03 =$	2.24

* Rounded

Changes in periodic loss evaluations can be converted to loss development factors, which can be used to estimate ultimate loss amounts.

Note that total incurred losses for each year tends to increase or develop over time. This development is caused by late-reported claims and increases in the values assigned to reported claims.

Total losses are assumed to be fully developed for each year after sixty-six months. This assumption probably would not be true for many liability loss exposures, such as general liability, workers' compensation, and medical malpractice. These claims generate periodic payments that extend over long periods. Nevertheless, for 20X1, because no further development is expected beyond sixty-six months, $139,000 is the estimated ultimate amount of losses to be paid. To estimate the ultimate amount of losses for each of the other years, one must calculate twelve-month loss development factors for each past year, as shown in Exhibit 4-10.

The top part of Exhibit 4-10 shows the calculation of twelve-month loss development factors. For example, the eighteen-to-thirty-month factor of 1.58 for year 20X1 is the thirty-month evaluation ($100,410) divided by the eighteen-month evaluation ($63,551) for year 20X1. The other twelve-month loss development factors are similarly calculated. The individual twelve-month loss development factors for each past year are averaged to forecast twelve-month loss development factors. For example, the twelve-month loss development factors for eighteen to thirty months for the 20X1 through 20X4 past accident years are averaged to determine a forecast factor of 1.62 for that period. Sometimes, one or more of the past twelve-month loss development factors may need to be eliminated from the calculation of the average if, in the judgment of the analyst, the factors are inconsistent with other twelve-month loss development factors. Using judgment is important when deciding which factors to eliminate.

As discussed, each year is assumed to be fully developed at sixty-six months; the estimated ultimate amount that will be paid for each accident year is reflected in the loss figure evaluated at sixty-six months. Therefore, the twelve-month loss development factors from sixty-six months onward are equal to 1.00, because no further loss development is expected. The bottom part of Exhibit 4-10 shows the loss development factor used to estimate ultimate losses at each evaluation date. For example, if total incurred losses are evaluated as of thirty months after the beginning of the policy year, the factor used to estimate ultimate losses is 1.38. Each factor at the bottom of Exhibit 4-10 is calculated by multiplying the forecasted or average factors for each interim period. For example, the factor for thirty months to ultimate (or sixty-six months) is estimated by multiplying the average twelve-month loss development factor for thirty to forty-two months (1.22) by the average factor for forty-two to fifty-four months (1.10) and multiplying the total (1.342) by the average factor for fifty-four to sixty-six months (1.03). That is, $1.22 \times 1.10 \times 1.03 = 1.38226$, which rounds to 1.38, as shown on the second line from the bottom of Exhibit 4-10.

Exhibit 4-11 shows how the factors calculated in Exhibit 4-10 are used to estimate Tarnton's ultimate incurred losses for each of the past accident years. To estimate the ultimate incurred losses for each year, total incurred losses for each past accident year are taken from Exhibit 4-9, and the loss development factors calculated at the bottom of Exhibit 4-10 are applied to the total incurred losses.

EXHIBIT 4-11

Estimate of Ultimate Incurred General Liability Losses (Limited to $50,000) for Tarnton

Accident Year	Evaluation Date (Months)	Total Incurred Losses	Loss Development Factor	Estimated Ultimate Incurred Losses
20X1	66	$139,000	1.00	$139,000
20X2	54	158,000	1.03	162,740
20X3	42	141,000	1.13	159,330
20X4	30	121,000	1.38	166,980
20X5	18	70,750	2.24	158,480

Estimated ultimate incurred losses are determined by multiplying the appropriate loss development factor by the amount of total incurred losses.

The estimated ultimate incurred losses in the second column of Exhibit 4-12 are an estimate of the total amount that Tarnton eventually will pay for each past year once all the losses are finally settled. Those losses are limited to $50,000.

EXHIBIT 4-12

Estimated Ultimate Incurred General Liability Losses (Limited to $50,000 and Adjusted for Inflation to the Year 20X7)

Accident Year	Estimated Ultimate Incurred Losses	Trend Factor to 20X7	Adjusted Total Incurred Losses
20X1	$139,000	1.66	$230,740
20X2	162,740	1.60	260,384
20X3	159,330	1.55	246,962
20X4	166,980	1.50	250,470
20X5	158,480	1.44	228,211

Adjusted total incurred losses are estimated ultimate losses multiplied by an appropriate trend factor.

Under actual, rather than hypothetical, conditions, the information in Exhibits 4-9 and 4-10 should be updated annually. For the 6/30/X7 evaluation date, another diagonal row of figures would be added and the loss development factors recalculated. Those updated loss development factors would then be applied to the incurred losses as of 6/30/X7 to update the estimated ultimate incurred losses for each past year as shown in Exhibit 4-12. At any point in time, the ultimate incurred losses are an estimate of the final amount to be paid for each year, based on the available past information. If the payment, reserving, or reporting patterns of losses change, then the estimated ultimate incurred losses will reflect that change.

Tarnton could use the information in Exhibits 4-2 and 4-9 through 4-12 to update the accounting reserves for retained losses from past accident years (assuming it retained $50,000 per loss for each of the past policy years). For Tarnton's financial statements to accurately reflect the eventual cost of retained losses, accounting reserves should equal the difference between the estimated ultimate retained losses for each past year and the paid amounts for each past year. For each individual loss, the paid amounts in Exhibit 4-2 should be limited to the retention limit of $50,000. For the year 20X2, Tarnton's accounting reserves should equal the difference between the estimated ultimate incurred losses of $163,000 (rounded) (Exhibit 4-12) and the paid amounts of $128,000 (Exhibit 4-2), or $35,000. (The $128,000 of payments to date is taken from the first column of Exhibit 4-2, with each loss to $50,000 and all payments and estimated ultimate incurred losses rounded to the nearest $1,000.)

Tarnton's accounting reserves for retained losses should be reviewed every time the information in Exhibits 4-10 through 4-12 is updated, which is usually annually. For each future period, Tarnton's losses may develop more or less than expected, requiring future adjustments to the accounting reserve estimates. For example, when the information in Exhibit 4-12 is updated as of 6/30/X7, estimated ultimate incurred losses may be higher because of higher than expected loss development, requiring Tarnton to make an adjustment to the accounting reserves for past retained losses.

In most cases, the analysis is not as straightforward as just illustrated, simply because loss exposures change over time. For example, if Tarnton sells a hazardous operation and no longer has the associated loss exposure, then past exposures and losses from that operation should be deleted from its database. Conversely, if Tarnton acquires a hazardous operation, then any available past losses and exposures from that operation should be added to its database. Changing insurers or claim administrators during the past period also may influence Tarnton's loss development. Any resulting differences will be reflected in the loss development patterns observed for different past loss years.

Adjustments must be made to Tarnton's past loss figures when changes to exposures, insurers, and claim administration, and so forth, occur. If the loss development pattern for a particular year is highly unusual, data from that year should be excluded from Tarnton's analysis. Estimating future loss development based on past loss development is an acquired skill; Tarnton's analyst must use experience and good judgment when calculating and applying loss development factors.

Loss Trend Factors

As mentioned, loss trend factors reflect price level changes over time. Exhibits 4-12 and 4-13 show Tarnton's estimated ultimate incurred losses (the second column in Exhibit 4-12) and exposure amounts (sales in the fourth column of Exhibit 4-13) adjusted for inflation to the year 20X7. Note that different trend factors are used for Tarnton's losses and exposures.

EXHIBIT 4-13

Past Exposure Information Adjusted for Inflation to the Year 20X7 for Tarnton

Accident Year	Actual Sales (000)	Trend Factor to 20X7	Adjusted Sales (000)
20X1	$47,421	1.59	$75,399
20X2	50,020	1.47	73,529
20X3	55,169	1.36	75,030
20X4	58,921	1.26	74,240
20X5	64,282	1.17	75,210

Projected exposure (sales for year 20X7) is $75,000,000.

Adjusted sales are calculated by multiplying actual sales by the appropriate trend factor to reflect inflation.

Step 4: Forecast Losses

Forecasting Tarnton's losses for the next accident year entails comparing the adjusted total loss for each past year (Exhibit 4-12) to the adjusted exposure for each past year (Exhibit 4-13) and forecasting Tarnton's losses per unit of exposure. Then, by using the forecasted exposure amount, Tarnton's total losses may be estimated for 20X7.

Compare Past Losses to Past Exposures

Column 2 of Exhibit 4-14 shows Tarnton's adjusted total incurred losses for each past accident year from Exhibit 4-12. Those losses are limited to $50,000 and are adjusted for loss development and trended for price level changes to the year 20X7. Column 3 shows adjusted sales from Exhibit 4-13. Column 4 is losses per $1,000 of sales, which is calculated by dividing Column 2 by Column 3. The next step for Tarnton's risk management professional is to forecast losses per $1,000 of sales for the year 20X7.

EXHIBIT 4-14

Calculation of General Liability Losses per $1,000 of Sales for Tarnton (All Losses in 20X7 Constant Dollars and Limited to $50,000)

Accident Year	Adjusted Total Incurred Losses	Adjusted Sales	Losses per $1,000 of Sales
20X1	$230,740	$75,399	$3.06
20X2	260,384	73,529	3.54
20X3	246,962	75,030	3.29
20X4	250,470	74,240	3.37
20X5	228,211	75,210	3.03
		Average	$3.26

Column 4 of Exhibit 4-14 shows that losses per $1,000 of sales (adjusted for price level changes) have been fairly steady. Therefore, it is probably appropriate for Tarnton to use the average of all the figures in that column when forecasting the losses per $1,000 of sales for the year 20X7.

Sometimes, using a statistical measure other than the average of all past years is appropriate. For example, if one of the past years includes an abnormally high figure, then this figure should probably be excluded before the average is calculated. Alternatively, one may decide that the more recent years should be weighed more heavily in the calculation than the more distant years, assuming that the more recent years are better predictors of the future. In such situations, one could assign weights in the form of percentages that total 100 percent, such as those shown in Column 3 of Exhibit 4-15, to each year's loss experience. In the example, the most recent year (20X5) receives three times as much weight as the most distant year (20X1). Tarnton's past losses per $1,000 of sales are multiplied by the assigned weights, and the results are summed to forecast the Tarnton's losses per $1,000 of sales for 20X7.

EXHIBIT 4-15

Forecasted General Liability Losses per $1,000 of Sales for Tarnton (Based on Assigned Weights)

(1) Accident Year	(2) Losses per $1,000 of Sales	(3) Assigned Weights	(4) Forecasted General Liability Losses (Col. 2 × Col. 3)
20X1	$3.06	10%	$0.31
20X2	3.54	10	0.35
20X3	3.29	20	0.66
20X4	3.37	30	1.01
20X5	3.03	30	0.91
Total		100%	$3.24

Tarnton's risk management professional has assigned higher weights to the years that, in his judgment, more accurately indicate what will occur in the future.

If an upward or downward trend is detected in the losses per $1,000 of sales for successive past years, trend analysis techniques, including time series analysis and regression analysis, could be used to obtain a more accurate forecast. Also, if a successful risk control program is in place, a case could be made for adjusting the forecast downward, because such a program will likely prevent or reduce future losses.

Estimate Exposures

As mentioned, estimated 20X7 sales will depend on Tarnton's sales forecast. It should be noted that if a large increase in sales is projected, forecasted losses will be correspondingly higher. In Exhibits 4-13 and 4-14, projected sales (in thousands of dollars) were $75 million similar to previous years (adjusted for price level changes to 20X7 dollars).

Calculate Expected Losses

Tarnton projects its sales for year 20X7 to be $75 million, or 75,000 units of sales at $1,000 each. Exhibit 4-14 shows how Tarnton's risk management professional has calculated its average losses to be $3.26 per $1,000 of sales. If sales total $75 million, then expected losses are $245,000 ($3.26 × 75,000, rounded). That projected loss figure is for losses limited to $50,000 and, therefore, applies only to the deductible layer for Tarnton. The loss figure represents the long-run average expected losses and does not indicate the variability around the average in any one year.

Use Increased Limit Factor Tables

Increased limit factor tables can be used to evaluate liability deductible alternatives and the reasonableness of the premium being charged for layers of coverage. Insurance advisory organizations develop increased limit factors from aggregated insurer data, because few insurers would have sufficient claims in high-limit layers to make conclusive loss forecasts. Tarnton's management wants its current $50,000 liability deductible evaluated relative to a $100,000 liability deductible. Management also wants to determine whether the $220,000 proposed premium is reasonable for the $50,001 to $1 million layer.

The increased limit factors shown in Exhibit 4-16 were developed to increase liability limits from the basic liability limit ($25,000) to higher liability limits. Consequently, the increased limit factor for $25,000 is 1.00. If Tarnton wanted liability coverage limits of $100,000, the premium developed for the basic coverage limit, such as $5,000, would be increased by a factor of 1.55, or $7,750. The implication is that a premium surcharge of 55 percent (a factor of 1.55) is sufficient to pay for those losses that lie between the basic coverage limit of $25,000 and the increased limit of $100,000.

Tarnton's risk management professional can use the increased limit factor table shown in Exhibit 4-16 to forecast losses within specific layers. The increased limit factors from $50,000 to $100,000 and from $50,000 to $1,000,000 can be calculated from the data in Exhibit 4-16. That calculation uses the increased limit factors at each limit as follows:

$50,000 to $100,000 = 1.55 ÷ 1.20 = 1.29.

$50,000 to $1,000,000 = 2.50 ÷ 1.20 = 2.08.

EXHIBIT 4-16

General Liability Increased Limit Factor Table

Loss Limit	Increased Limit Factor
$ 25,000	1.00
50,000	1.20
100,000	1.55
200,000	1.80
500,000	2.20
1,000,000	2.50

Insurance advisory organizations develop increased limit factors from aggregated insurer data because few insurers would have sufficient claims in high limit layers to make conclusive loss forecasts.

Tarnton can now estimate the total losses under both the $100,000 deductible and the $1 million limit, as shown in Exhibit 4-17. The average expected losses for the layer from $50,000 to $1 million is calculated by determining the difference in the forecast losses at the $50,000 and $1 million limits, or $265,000.

EXHIBIT 4-17

Tarnton's Forecasted Losses at Various Loss Limits Using Increased Limit Factors

Limit	Increased Limits Factor	Forecasted Losses*
$ 50,000	N/A	$245,000
100,000	1.29	316,000
1,000,000	2.08	510,000

*Rounded to the nearest $1,000

Increased limit factors can be used to forecast losses between specific loss limits.

PART 2: FORECASTING PROBABLE VARIATION FROM EXPECTED LOSS

The loss forecasts to be developed in Part 2 provide information on the probability of alternative loss outcomes around a long-term average or expected amount. Tarnton's retained losses for 20X7 will almost surely not equal the calculated $245,000. They will be higher or lower, and indeed may be considerably higher or lower. To estimate the probability of alternative total loss outcomes, Tarnton analyzes its loss frequency and severity separately. These analyses yield the following three types of probability distributions:

1. A frequency probability distribution
2. A severity probability distribution
3. A total loss probability distribution

A **frequency probability distribution** is a representation that shows the probability of various numbers of losses over a certain period, such as a calendar year. A **severity probability distribution** is a representation that shows the probability of various sizes of each individual loss. The **total loss probability distribution** is a representation that shows the probability of particular total loss outcomes for a given period, such as a calendar year, and is constructed by combining the frequency and severity probability distributions.

To measure the effectiveness of various risk control techniques, it is important to understand all three types of probability distributions. Effective risk control techniques should reduce actual loss frequency and severity compared to the probable loss frequency and severity indicated in the probability distribution. For example, risk control can reduce the frequency of loss (loss prevention), the severity of loss (loss reduction), or both. Increasing the size of a liability deductible will not affect the frequency distribution of retained losses, but will change both the severity and total loss distributions of retained losses.

The next section shows how to construct the frequency, severity, and total loss probability distributions for Tarnton for losses limited to $50,000. Probability intervals, which determine the extent to which forecast losses can vary from average losses, are then discussed.

Frequency probability distribution
A representation that shows the probability of various numbers of losses over a certain period, such as a calendar year.

Severity probability distribution
A representation that shows the probability of various sizes of each individual loss.

Total probability distribution
A representation that shows the probability of total loss outcomes for a given period, such as a calendar year, and is constructed by combining the frequency and severity probability distributions.

Frequency Probability Distribution

Tarnton experienced a total of twenty-six losses in years 20X1 through 20X5. A frequency distribution of these losses is shown in Exhibit 4-18.

EXHIBIT 4-18	
Frequency Distribution of Losses for Tarnton	
Year	**Frequency**
20X1	5
20X2	7
20X3	6
20X4	4
20X5	4
Total	26

A frequency distribution shows the frequency of losses over time.

Because losses are evaluated as of 6/30/X6, it is likely that some claims were unreported, especially for more recent years. Based on the past patterns of claim reporting, Tarnton can assume that two more claims will be reported for each of the 20X4 and 20X5 years. The frequency for the years 20X4 and 20X5 becomes six. The total frequency over the five-year period becomes thirty, for an average of six losses per year. The actual frequency of losses in any one year varies from the average of six, with a low of four and a high of seven.

The past frequency observations can be grouped together to develop a frequency probability distribution, as shown in Exhibit 4-19. Note that the sum of the probabilities of the various outcomes is 100 percent, or 1.00. The bottom part of Exhibit 4-19 is a bar chart that shows the relative probability of various outcomes. The numbers along the horizontal axis show the various frequency amounts, and the numbers on the vertical axis show the probabilities of each individual frequency amount. The total probability indicated by the bars on the chart is 100 percent.

EXHIBIT 4-19

Frequency Probability Distribution for Tarnton

Frequency	Number of Outcomes	Probability
5	1	.20
6	3	.60
7	1	.20

Because there are five years of historical loss data, each year is given a 20 percent weight. Three of the five years had six claims. Consequently, six claims are given a 60 percent weight.

Tarnton's mean (or average) claim frequency per year is six, which is determined by dividing the total of thirty losses over the five-year period by five. The average claim frequency also can be calculated from a frequency distribution and is called the expected value of that distribution. **Expected value** is the weighted average of all of the possible outcomes of a probability distribution. The expected value is calculated by multiplying each possible outcome by its probability and summing the results. Exhibit 4-20 shows the calculation of Tarnton's mean frequency based on the frequency probability distribution shown in Exhibit 4-19. Note that the calculation produces the same average frequency of six computed in Exhibit 4-19.

Expected value
The weighted average of all of the possible outcomes of a probability distribution.

EXHIBIT 4-20

Calculation of Mean Frequency for Tarnton

Frequency	Probability	Frequency × Probability
5	.20	1.0
6	.60	3.6
7	.20	1.4
Mean Frequency		6.0

The mean frequency is loss frequency weighted by each frequency's probability.

In the frequency distribution in Exhibit 4-19, other frequency outcomes, such as three and nine, were not observed. Such outcomes certainly are possible and probably would occur if the sample were based on a large number of past years.

The bar chart in Exhibit 4-19 suggests the shape of a curve that shows the probability of loss frequencies. Exhibit 4-21 shows the curve superimposed on the bar chart. This curve indicates that loss frequency is positively skewed, that is, loss frequencies are concentrated at low-frequency levels to the left of the curve. As with all probability distributions, the total area underlying the curve equals 100 percent because it shows the probability of all possible frequency outcomes.

EXHIBIT 4-21

Frequency Probability Distribution Showing All Possible Outcomes for Tarnton

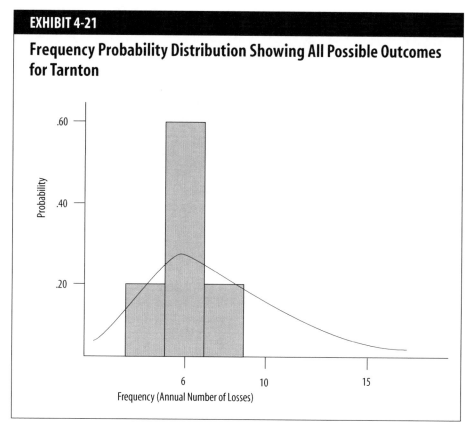

Severity Probability Distribution

A severity probability distribution is calculated similarly to a frequency probability distribution but is based on the size of individual losses rather than on annual frequency figures. For example, assume that Tarnton's total incurred losses, limited to $50,000 and adjusted for inflation, fall within the severity ranges shown in Exhibit 4-22. A bar chart can be constructed from this severity distribution, as shown in Exhibit 4-23.

A loss severity probability distribution is calculated similarly to a frequency distribution, but is based on the size of individual losses rather than on annual frequency figures.

EXHIBIT 4-22

Severity Ranges for Tarnton

Severity Range	Number of Outcomes	Probability
$ 10,000 – 29,999	6	.23
30,000 – 44,999	6	.23
45,000 – 49,999	5	.19
50,000 and up	9	.35
Total	26	1.00

EXHIBIT 4-23

Loss Severity Probability Distribution for Tarnton

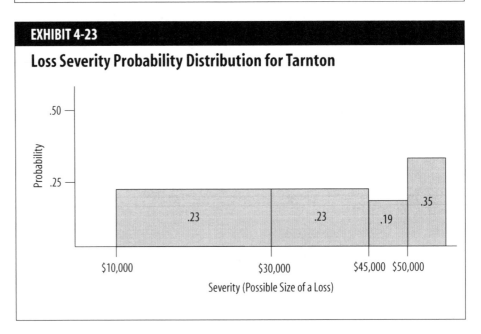

A severity probability distribution can be depicted as a bar chart. Amounts above $50,000 trail off, reflecting the $50,000 and up severity range.

As with the previously constructed frequency distribution, past losses are insufficient to accurately represent the probability of loss at all of the different loss outcomes. The bar chart in Exhibit 4-23 suggests the shape of a curve that shows the probability of various loss severities that could be derived with additional observations. Exhibit 4-24 shows that curve superimposed on the bar chart.

EXHIBIT 4-24

Loss Severity Probability Distribution Showing All Possible Outcomes for Tarnton

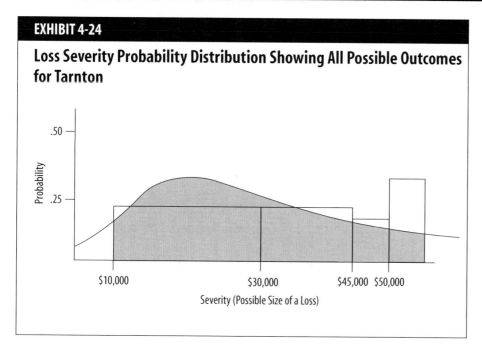

Just as with the frequency distribution, the mean or average severity can be calculated. To do so, the average severity outcome in each range is multiplied by the probability of the losses falling within that range. Exhibit 4-25 shows the calculation of Tarnton's mean or average severity. (All losses greater than $50,000 are limited to $50,000.)

EXHIBIT 4-25

Calculation of Mean Severity for Tarnton

Severity Range	Mean Severity	Probability	Mean Severity × Probability
$10,000 – 29,999	$20,000	.23	$ 4,600
30,000 – 44,999	37,500	.23	8,625
45,000 – 49,999	47,500	.19	9,025
50,000 and over	50,000	.35	17,500
Total		1.00	$39,750

Mean severity for the loss distribution is calculated by multiplying the probability for each severity range by the midpoint for each severity range.

Total Loss Probability Distribution

The total loss probability distribution is the probability distribution for total losses over a given period, generally a calendar year. The mean of the total loss probability distribution can be determined easily. The mean of the frequency distribution multiplied by the mean of the severity distribution produces the mean of the total loss distribution. For Tarnton, the mean frequency is six, and the mean severity is $39,750. Multiplying those two amounts gives the mean or average of total losses for that year of $239,000 (rounded to the nearest $1,000). (Note that this figure is reasonably close to the previous estimate of $245,000, which was calculated in a more precise manner by trending and developing losses and then relating them to exposures.) The mean of the total loss distribution is equivalent to the expected or average total losses calculated in Part 1 of the basic loss forecast.

For any given year, Tarnton's frequency may vary from six, and Tarnton's average severity may vary from $39,750. For example, one year may have only four losses, equal to $20,000, $18,750, $6,000, and $12,000. Average severity for that year is $14,188, and total losses are the sum of the individual losses, or $56,750. On the other hand, several large losses may occur in a year that would total much more than the mean or long-run average total losses. The range of possible total losses for a given period is represented by the total loss probability distribution. Exhibit 4-26 shows Tarnton's total loss probability distribution, constructed from the frequency and severity probability distributions. Computer software is used to construct these frequency and severity probability distributions. Included in Exhibit 4-26 is a probability interval, which is discussed next.

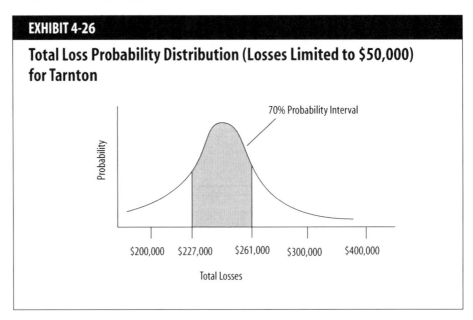

EXHIBIT 4-26

Total Loss Probability Distribution (Losses Limited to $50,000) for Tarnton

There is a 70 percent probability that Tarnton's 20X7 losses will fall between $227,000 and $261,000.

Probability Intervals

To determine the extent to which actual losses are likely to vary from the long-term average total losses, actuaries calculate probability intervals using the total loss probability distribution. A probability interval is a representation that shows the probability of outcomes falling within certain ranges of a probability distribution. The probability interval is determined by the area underneath a probability distribution curve. For example, assume that there is a 70 percent chance that Tarnton's total losses will fall between $227,000 and $261,000 (Exhibit 4-26). There is a 30 percent chance that losses will fall outside that range. Therefore, in seven out of every ten years (70 percent of the time), total losses are expected to fall between $227,000 and $261,000, which is the 70 percent probability interval.

PART 3: ESTIMATING CASH FLOW NEEDS

For financial management purposes, an organization must forecast not only the estimated total cost of a risk financing plan, but also the expected timing of cash payments for the plan's related expenses, including insurance premiums, retained losses, and loss adjustment expenses. Projecting cash outflows allows the organization to have cash available when needed.

Future cash payments for losses, premiums, and other expenses can be discounted back to present-day dollars through a technique known as net present value analysis. This analysis shows how many dollars would have to be invested at the time of the analysis, assuming a certain return on the investment, to meet future cash outflows. Net present value analysis compares the true cost of risk financing plans, because the cost of each is adjusted for differences in cash flow timing.

The first step of the net present value analysis is to define a loss payout pattern. A loss payout pattern is a representation that shows the ultimate payout for the incurred losses expected to be paid. Exhibit 4-27 shows a hypothetical loss payout pattern for accident year 20X7. For accident year 20X7, 25 percent of the incurred losses are expected to be paid during that same year, and an additional 25 percent are expected to be paid in the year 20X8. It ultimately takes five years for all of the losses incurred in accident year 20X7 to be paid.

EXHIBIT 4-27

Example of a Loss Payout Pattern

| | Years in Which Losses Are Paid | | | | |
Accident Year	20X7	20X8	20X9	20Y0	20Y1
20X7	25%	25%	20%	20%	10%

Loss payout patterns are used to estimate the timing of loss payouts, and consequently forecast cash flow needs.

The remainder of this section describes how to estimate Tarnton's future cash needs to meet loss payments. In addition, net present value analysis will be used to show how much money Tarnton must set aside today to meet future cash needs.

Estimates of Loss Payout Patterns

Loss payout patterns can be projected based on Tarnton's past payout patterns, industry data, or a combination of the two. Many insurance advisory organizations publish statistics on loss payout patterns for individual types of insurance. In many cases, using both industry statistics and the organization's past payout patterns can be helpful in projecting loss payout patterns.

The Tarnton example demonstrates how loss payout patterns can be estimated using past data. The paid losses shown in Exhibit 4-2 for each accident year must first be limited to $50,000 and then compared with the estimated ultimate incurred losses in Exhibit 4-12. Exhibit 4-28 shows the resulting past percentages for Tarnton's loss payout pattern.

EXHIBIT 4-28

Past Loss Payout Pattern for Tarnton

Accident Year	Months After Beginning of Accident Year	Paid Losses (Limited to $50,000)	Estimated Ultimate Incurred Losses	Cumulative Percentage Paid
20X1	66	$122,600	$139,000	88%
20X2	54	128,000	162,740	79
20X3	42	83,000	159,330	52
20X4	30	45,000	166,980	27
20X5	18	20,000	158,480	13

Cumulative percentages paid can be used to estimate the percentage of estimated ultimate incurred losses that will be paid as of each future year for the forecasted losses.

The cumulative percentages paid in the far right column of Exhibit 4-28 can be used to estimate the percentage of estimated ultimate incurred losses that will be paid as of each future year for the forecasted losses for the 20X7 year shown in Exhibit 4-29. For example, the $22,050 shown as the current amount paid for the period with the midpoint at twelve months after the beginning of the policy year is 9 percent of the $245,000 estimated total loss amount. The last column of Exhibit 4-29 (cumulative amount paid) accumulates the period payments in the "current amount paid" column. Note that it will take Tarnton more than sixty-six months to pay out the estimated total loss amount of $245,000. This analysis assumes that the remaining loss payments from sixty-six months to ultimate will be paid in the sixty-sixth month.

A negative paid loss amount, such as for the period with the midpoint at sixty months, although somewhat unusual, may result from payout factors developed using past loss data, which may have included large recoveries from others, favorable investment results on reserved funds for structured loss settlements, or other offsets to losses. Structured loss settlements are periodic and guaranteed payments made for damages and paid over a specified period.

EXHIBIT 4-29

Projected Cumulative Loss Payout Pattern for Year 20X7 for Tarnton

Months After Beginning of Accident Year	Cumulative Percentage Paid	Current Amount Paid	Cumulative Amount Paid
12	9%	$22,050	$ 22,050
18	13	9,800	31,850
24	20	17,150	49,000
30	27	17,150	66,150
36	40	31,850	98,000
42	52	29,400	127,400
48	66	34,300	161,700
54	79	31,850	193,550
60	78	−2,450	191,100
66	88	24,500	215,600
After 66 Months	100	29,400	245,000

Cumulative amounts paid can be estimated using cumulative percentages paid.

If, for budgetary reasons, Tarnton wants to estimate the amount to be paid at the end of each budgeting or fiscal year (twelve, twenty-four, thirty-six, and so on, months after the beginning of each year), then the figures in Exhibit 4-29 could be used to estimate the percentage paid at each of those points.

Tarnton's estimated payout pattern is for losses limited to $50,000. The higher the limit used in constructing the payout pattern from a given number of losses, the less credible the pattern, because very large loss payments can distort the results by inflating the projected cumulative amount paid. (Even in the example, a $50,000 loss payment would significantly affect the present value of Tarnton's future loss payments.)

Usefulness of Present Value Analysis

When budgeting for the cost of retained losses, an organization may want to use an amount based on the present value of the projected retained losses to reflect the interest that the budgeted funds will earn until losses are paid. The preceding present value analysis covered only the average expected total losses. If a conservative budget figure is desired for losses, present value analysis can be done at the upper end of the 90 percent probability interval or at some other level above the average.

Present value analysis is useful when evaluating alternative retention levels. The higher the retention level, the more cash flow is required, which, in turn, increases potential investment income. As mentioned, one must be careful when evaluating the loss payout at a high retention level, because a large past loss paid out all at once can distort the calculated loss payout pattern.

Insurers generally do not explicitly recognize the value of the cash flow when calculating their premiums. In many cases, they assume that any investment income earned on cash flow serves as a cushion against adverse loss experience. Nevertheless, present value analysis is useful to the risk management professional in evaluating the reasonableness of the insurer's premium charge, because he or she can determine the insurer's expected earnings on premium payments.

The accounting reserves placed on past retained losses could be evaluated on a present value basis. It often makes sense, however, for Tarnton to be conservative and leave these reserves at their gross values to provide a cushion against possible future loss development. Present value analysis is important when comparing risk financing plans. The total cash payout of various plans can be compared on a present value basis in order for Tarnton to choose the plan with the lowest present value cost.

Net Present Value Analysis Applied to Loss Payouts

Given that retained losses will, on average, equal $245,000, and given the loss payout pattern in the second column of Exhibit 4-29, Tarnton's management can use present value analysis to estimate the amount of cash that must be set aside now to pay for those future losses.

Tarnton must first determine the value of the cash flows over time (also known as the time value of money). For example, assume that Tarnton is able to earn 12 percent per year on the cash flows generated by retaining losses. Present value factors, using a rate of 12 percent, can be applied to the loss payout to determine the amount of cash that must currently be set aside. This is shown in Exhibit 4-30, which uses the payout pattern shown in the second column of Exhibit 4-29 (cumulative percentage paid), but assumes that the losses paid after sixty months are all paid out during the year 20Y2. (Note that just the amount paid in each year is used in Exhibit 4-30 and that the previous exhibits showed cumulative amounts.) The present value factors in Exhibit 4-30 are calculated using the midpoint of each year, the date on which all payments for that year are assumed to be made.

As illustrated in Exhibit 4-30, the present value of $245,000 in retained losses is equal to $169,552, which is the sum of the six annual present values for years 20X7 through 20Y2. Therefore, $169,552 would need to be set aside now to pay the retained losses over the future periods.

Note that the cash flows shown in Exhibit 4-30 relate solely to the 20X7 policy year. However, total cash flow needs for a given year actually would be based on the accumulation of loss payments from several past policy years.

EXHIBIT 4-30

Calculation of Present Value of Periodic Loss Payments for Tarnton

	Year					
	20X7	20X8	20X9	20Y0	20Y1	20Y2
Amount Paid	$22,050	$26,950	$49,000	$63,700	$29,400	$53,900
Present Value Factor at 12%	0.943	0.842	0.752	0.671	0.600	0.535
	$20,793	$22,692	$36,848	$42,743	$17,640	$28,836

Total Net Present Value = $169,552.

The net present value calculations shown match the expected periodic loss payments to determine the amount presently required to pay future losses.

The sources of the figures in Exhibit 4-30 merit some explanation. The first figure in the "amount paid" row, $22,050, is the total of Tarnton's claim payments made during the policy year in which the claim arose. Therefore, on average, these claims were made six months before the end of the policy year and should be discounted for a period of six months or at an annualized rate of one-half of the assumed annual discount rate—here, 6 percent instead of the posited 12 percent. Discounted at 6 percent, $22,050 equals $20,793 ($22,050 × 0.943).

Just as this $22,050 is discounted for six months to account for the assumption that payments are made at the midpoint of the year in which the claim arose, so the present value factors for discounting these periodic claim payments must be adjusted to account for the assumption that all claim payments are made at the midpoint of the policy year in which they occur. This results in a six-month lag in valuation dates. Payments made during subsequent twelve-month periods must therefore be discounted for eighteen, thirty, forty-two, fifty-four, and sixty-six months, respectively. This discounting can be achieved by using annual discount rates for one, two, three, four, and five periods (years), respectively—and by the further discounting of the results for an additional one-half period.

Therefore, the 12 percent present value factors for 20X8 through 20Y2 shown in Exhibit 4-30 are products of (a) the discount factor for one, two, three, four, and five periods times (b) the constant 12 percent discount factor for an additional six months (0.943).

For example, the 12 percent present value factor for the second twelve-month period in Exhibit 4-30, 0.842, is 0.893 times the constant of 0.943.

The figures in the "amount paid" row of Exhibit 4-30 also take into account the six-month lag in the valuation of claim payments.

The second twelve-month amount paid, $26,950, is the sum of the current payments made at eighteen and twenty-four months (from Exhibit 4-29,

$9,800 and $17,150, respectively). Similarly, the current payments for the third twelve-month period, for 20X9 in Exhibit 4-30, give the sum of the current payments for thirty and thirty-six months, $17,150 and $31,850, respectively, totaling $49,000. These payments, which total $245,000 from 20X7 through 20Y2, have a present value of $169,552.

Once cash flow needs have been estimated using these techniques, the risk management professional can then use the forecasts as a valuable planning tool.

USING THE INFORMATION PROVIDED BY LOSS FORECASTS

Tarnton's risk management professional can use the information generated by a loss forecast both to plan for the future and to evaluate what has occurred in the past. Analyzing the projected losses helps to do the following:

- Budget for retained losses
- Evaluate alternative retention levels
- Evaluate insurer premium charges
- Update accounting reserves for retained losses that occurred in the past

Exhibit 4-31 shows some of the information that can be gleaned from Tarnton's loss forecast when it is combined with a hypothetical probability distribution. Information on average expected losses and various probability intervals is shown separately for losses under the policy limit of $1 million retained losses under the $50,000 deductible, and insured losses in the layer from $50,000 to $1 million. On average, $510,000 in total general liability losses are expected to fall under the $1 million policy for the year 20X7, with $245,000 expected to fall below the $50,000 deductible and $265,000 expected to fall within the insured portion, or the layer from $50,000 to $1 million. Those expected loss figures are derived from the previously explained basic loss forecast (see Exhibit 4-17).

Three probability intervals and their corresponding loss ranges are shown in Exhibit 4-31: 50 percent, 70 percent, and 90 percent. For each probability level, the loss ranges for retained losses are narrower than those for the total losses subject to a limit of $1 million, confirming that losses under the deductible are more predictable than total losses. The loss ranges for insured losses are wider than for total losses and retained losses, indicating that the insurer's losses are less predictable than Tarnton's.

The following calculations depend on having past data that are both considerable in quantity and relevant and the assumption that the future will essentially be like the past. The quantity of data needed to produce credible probability intervals is appreciably greater than the quantity needed for credibly estimating a mean.

EXHIBIT 4-31

General Liability for Tarnton
Policy Limit = $1,000,000 – Projected Losses for Year 20X7

Total Losses Subject to a Policy Limit of $1,000,000
Average Expected Losses = $510,000.

Probability Intervals

50%	$498,000 – $529,000
70%	487,000 – 540,000
90%	473,000 – 554,000

Total Retained Losses Under a $50,000 Deductible
Average Expected Losses = $245,000.

Probability Intervals

50%	$232,000 – $256,000
70%	227,000 – 261,000
90%	222,000 – 266,000

Total Insured Losses in the Layer From $50,000 to $1,000,000
Average Expected Losses = $265,000.

Probability Intervals

50%	$223,000 – $303,000
70%	153,000 – 373,000
90%	0 – 610,000

Probability distributions can be used to determine the likelihood of a range of expected losses.

Budget for Retained Losses

The information in Exhibit 4-31 can be used when Tarnton budgets an amount for retained losses. The amount to be budgeted depends on Tarnton's degree of financial conservatism. For example, Tarnton may want to budget only for the average expected losses of $245,000. However, retained losses probably will exceed that figure. To be sure that enough is budgeted, Tarnton may want to budget an amount equal to the highest end of the 90 percent probability interval, or $266,000. Because the severity probability distribution is positively skewed, which implies that the mean of the distribution is greater than the mode, larger losses are less likely to occur than smaller losses. The severity of those losses, however, can have a far greater financial consequence. (Recall that the mean of a distribution is its arithmetic average; the median is the midpoint, halfway between the highest and lowest values in the distribution; and the mode is the value that occurs most frequently in a distribution.) Many would argue that, to achieve conservatism, the budgeted amount should equal or exceed the greater of the mode, median, or mean loss amount.

Evaluate Alternative Retention Levels

The information in the upper part of Exhibit 4-32 can be generated for total retained losses under a $100,000 deductible. The increase in the expected losses from the $50,000 deductible to the $100,000 deductible ($316,000 minus $245,000, or $71,000) can be compared to the premium savings. More importantly, the increased risk at the various probability intervals must be considered. For example, the highest end of the 90 percent probability interval increases from $266,000 to $356,000. Therefore, when deciding to retain more of the exposure, Tarnton must consider both the expected loss amount and the possibility of additional retained losses. The lower part of Exhibit 4-32 depicts the 90 percent probability interval for retained losses under the $100,000 deductible.

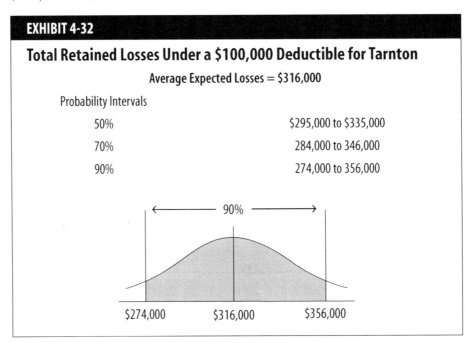

EXHIBIT 4-32

Total Retained Losses Under a $100,000 Deductible for Tarnton

Average Expected Losses = $316,000

Probability Intervals

50%	$295,000 to $335,000
70%	284,000 to 346,000
90%	274,000 to 356,000

$274,000 $316,000 $356,000

Probability intervals depict the range of losses that might aggregate for a particular deductible amount.

Evaluate Insurer Premium Charges

As discussed previously, loss estimates can help determine the reasonableness of an insurer's premium charge. In Exhibit 4-31, the expected average losses to be covered by the premium can be calculated by subtracting the total retained losses with a $50,000 deductible from the total average expected losses ($510,000 – $245,000 = $265,000). Insurer expenses must be added to that figure before comparing it with the quoted premium charge for Tarnton of $220,000. Also, Tarnton's insured losses are subject to much more variability than the retained losses. Therefore, the insurer will build in a risk charge to cover any contingencies. The insurer will be able to earn investment income on the $220,000 premium (paid in advance) until losses are paid, which can take years. Considering this, the $220,000 premium charge appears reasonable, assuming that the increased limits factors used in the analysis also are reasonable.

Update Accounting Reserves for Retained Losses

The previous discussion of past loss development showed how its analysis can be used to update accounting reserves for incurred retained losses from past years. Exhibit 4-12 illustrates how that analysis showed the expected, or average, ultimate value of losses to be paid for each year. If necessary, probability intervals can be constructed around those amounts in order to set more conservative accounting reserves.

SUMMARY

Organizations can use accidental loss forecasting to evaluate risk financing alternatives, especially risk financing plans that involve some loss retention. This accidental loss forecasting process consists of the following three parts:

1. Part 1—Forecasting expected losses
2. Part 2—Forecasting probable variation from expected losses
3. Part 3—Estimating cash flow needs

Forecasting expected losses (Part 1) is a four-step process that requires the risk management professional to collect and organize past data, limit individual losses, apply loss development and trend factors to the data, and forecast losses.

Forecasts of probable variation from expected loss (Part 2) are needed because organizations need to anticipate higher or lower loss amounts than those forecast in Part 1. Loss frequency and loss severity distributions can be used to determine the total loss probability distribution, which shows the range of possible total losses.

Past frequency and severity should be analyzed separately to estimate the probability of alternative total loss outcomes. From that information, the following three types of probability distributions can be constructed:

1. Frequency probability distribution
2. Severity probability distribution
3. Total loss probability distribution

To determine the extent to which actual losses are likely to vary from the long-term average total losses, actuaries calculate probability intervals using the total loss probability distribution. A probability interval shows the probability of outcomes falling within certain ranges.

Estimates of cash flow (Part 3) allow an organization to have cash available when needed. Future case payments for losses, premiums, and other expenses can be discounted back to preset-day dollars through net present value analysis. The first step in this analysis is to define the payout pattern, which is a representation that shows the ultimate payout for the incurred losses expected to be paid. Loss payout patterns can be projected based on an organization's own past payout patterns, industry data, or a combination of the two. Cumulative percentages paid can be used to estimate the percentage of estimated ultimate incurred losses that will be paid as of each future year for the forecasted losses. Cumulative amounts paid can be estimated using cumulative percentages paid. Present value analysis is useful when evaluating alternative retention levels. The higher the retention level, the more cash flow is required, which, in turn, increases potential investment income. An organization can use present value analysis to estimate the amount of cash that must be set aside immediately to pay for those future losses.

Risk managers must be sure that sufficient funds are budgeted to pay for retained losses and must evaluate alternative retention levels in light of the probability of additional retained losses. Loss estimates can help determine the reasonableness of an insurer's premium charge. Analysis of past loss development can be used to update accounting reserves for incurred retained losses from past years.

For financial management purposes, an organization must forecast not only the estimated total cost of a risk financing plan but also the expected timing of cash payments for the plan's related expenses, including insurance premiums, retained losses, and loss adjustment expenses. Projecting cash outflow is important so that the organization can have cash available when needed. If an organization has a large number of past losses, it can project loss payout patterns based on its own past payout patterns, industry data, or a combination of the two.

Present value analysis is useful when evaluating alternative retention levels. The higher the retention level, the greater the amount of cash flow involved. Therefore, there is a greater potential amount of investment income. Present value analysis is also useful in evaluating alternative risk financing plans.

Often, the results of an analysis of an organization's accidental loss forecasts reveal that self-insurance is the best risk financing plan available. This is frequently the case when forecasts are reasonably accurate, because self-insurance involves retaining accidental losses. Therefore, the risk management professional should understand how self-insurance can contribute to the organization's overall risk financing strategy.

Chapter 5

Direct Your Learning

Self-Insurance Plans

After learning the content of this chapter and completing the corresponding course guide assignment, you should be able to:

- Describe the purpose and operation of self-insurance plans.
- Describe the two types of self-insurance plans.
- Describe the administration of individual self-insurance plans.
- Describe the advantages and disadvantages of self-insurance plans.
- Given a case, justify a self-insurance plan that can meet an organization's risk financing needs.
- Define or describe each of the Key Words and Phrases for this chapter.

Develop Your Perspective

What are the main topics covered in the chapter?

This chapter examines an approach to retaining losses called self-insurance. Self-insurance is a misnomer because it is insurance in name only. Self-insurance is actually a formalized retention program that anticipates that losses will occur and formulates a plan to fund them.

Identify the approaches to funding self-insurance plans.

- What usually prevents organizations from using pre-loss funding as the sole means to finance risk?

- Would you consider post-loss funding an acceptable strategy for financing risk, or consider it only as a last resort?

Why is it important to learn about these topics?

Self-insurance allows organizations to reduce their cost of risk, but also involves the possibility that losses, and consequently the cost of risk, will be higher than they would have been had insurance been purchased.

Consider the advantages and disadvantages of self-insurance plans based on their relative importance to your organization.

- Which one of the advantages of self-insurance plans would most likely cause your organization to consider forgoing insurance and use self-insurance?

- Which one of the disadvantages of self-insurance would most likely cause your organization enough concern that it would continue to use insurance?

How can you use what you will learn?

Analyze your organization's loss exposures that are best suited for a self-insurance plan.

- Do the states in which your organization operates permit self-insurance plans?

- Is your company willing to assume the task of administering a self-insurance plan?

Chapter 5
Self-Insurance Plans

Some organizations are able to forecast their accidental losses with enough accuracy to determine whether they can be retained through a formalized plan to fund possible losses in lieu of insurance. This practice is known as self-insurance. The term self-insurance is often used informally to include any loss amount an organization retains, such as the retained portion of losses under deductible plans, retrospective rating plans, captive insurance plans, pools, and finite risk plans, as well as retentions for unanticipated losses (also called retention by default, or simply "going bare"). However, self-insurance is actually a distinct risk financing plan. Formal self-insurance plans, such as those discussed in this chapter, require organizations to have sufficient financial resources and risk tolerance to retain potentially significant losses. Therefore, organizations with self-insurance plans have usually embraced risk control as part of their corporate culture. In order to recommend self-insurance as a viable risk financing alternative, the risk management professional must understand its advantages and disadvantages relative to insurance, as well as the associated administrative tasks it requires.

PURPOSE AND OPERATION OF SELF-INSURANCE PLANS

The purpose of a self-insurance plan is to enable an organization to lower its long-term cost of risk by allowing it to pay for its own losses without incurring the transaction costs associated with insurance. **Self-insurance** is a form of retention under which an organization records its losses and maintains a formal system to pay for them. Self-insurance can be contrasted with **informal retention**, which is a form of retention by which an organization pays for its losses with its cash flow and/or current (liquid) assets but does not anticipate losses and, consequently, does not involve formal payment procedures or methods for recording losses.

Self-insurance is best applied to losses that are of both high frequency and low severity. Such losses are somewhat predictable in total over a defined time period, such as one year. (Losses that are both low frequency and low severity are easily self-insured; however, they are usually retained informally, thus eliminating the associated administrative costs.) High-severity losses

Self-insurance
A form of retention under which an organization records its losses and maintains a formal system to pay for them.

Informal retention
A form of retention by which an organization pays for its losses with its cash flow and/or current (liquid) assets but does not anticipate losses and, consequently, does not involve formal payment procedures or methods for recording losses.

are unsuitable for self-insurance because they are typically low frequency and therefore are relatively unpredictable, as well as too large to retain. Some organizations also self-insure medium-severity losses, although the resulting financial effect can be unpredictable, depending on their frequency.

A self-insurance plan is usually coupled with the purchase of excess liability insurance to cover severe losses. Excess liability insurance limits the organization's exposure to loss to an acceptable level and limits the accumulation of losses. Low-frequency and high-severity losses are often addressed by insurance or other risk transfer plans. Exhibit 5-1 shows how a self-insurance plan and excess liability insurance may address an organization's loss exposures relative to the frequency and severity of potential losses.

Self-insurance is usually combined with a risk transfer plan, such as excess liability insurance. Self-insurance is best applied to high-frequency, low-severity losses, which are more predictable in total. A hybrid or transfer plan is best applied to low-frequency, high-severity losses, which are less predictable in total.

EXHIBIT 5-1

Self-Insurance Combined With Other Excess Liability Insurance

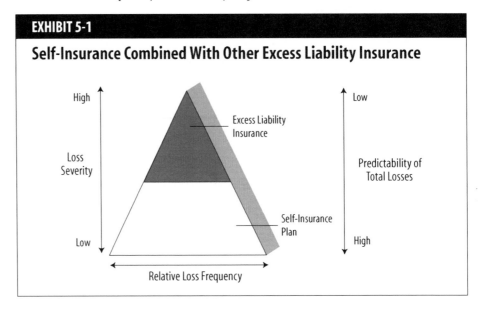

Self-insurance is most appropriate for organizations that are committed to risk control, are able to tolerate risk retention, and are willing to devote capital and resources to the program's financing and administration. Many organizations begin to consider self-insurance when their annual minimum insurance premium exceeds $500,000 for any one type of insurance coverage. More specific guidelines exist to help organizations determine whether their annual minimum premium is sufficient to make self-insurance an economically feasible alternative.

Self-insurance is particularly well-suited for financing losses that can be budgeted and paid out over time, because the self-insured organization saves money that it would otherwise pay toward premiums in the meantime. For this reason, workers' compensation, general liability, and automobile liability loss exposures are often self-insured. One source estimates that 6,000 U.S. organizations use self-insurance plans for their workers' compensation loss exposures.[1] Other loss exposures that are often self-insured include auto physical damage and professional liability, as well as flood and earthquake, for which there is a limited insurance market. Organizations can also use self-insurance to administer healthcare benefits.

Self-Insured Healthcare Benefits

Since the passage of the Employee Retirement Income Security Act (ERISA), organizations have been allowed to self-insure healthcare benefits instead of purchasing healthcare insurance. Self-insured health plans (also called employer-based health plans) are the means through which over 50 million U.S. employees receive healthcare benefits[2]

As with self-insurance plans for property-casualty loss exposures, self-insured healthcare plans are formal retention plans designed to fund and administer healthcare benefits. Most self-insured healthcare benefit plans require employees to contribute funds to offset the plan's cost. These plans also involve using a third-party administrator and purchasing excess insurance.

Organizations considering self-insurance must weigh its cash flow benefits against its tax ramifications. Self-insured organizations must recognize losses when they are incurred and establish a liability for them. Self-insured losses are not a tax-deductible expense until they are actually paid. Organizations that purchase insurance from an insurer, however, may treat the insurance premium as a tax-deductible expense regardless of when, or if, losses are incurred.

TYPES OF SELF-INSURANCE PLANS

Self-insurance plans can be implemented for one organization (individual self-insurance plans), or for more than one organization (group self-insurance plans). Individual self-insurance plans can be used to address a number of loss exposures, whereas group self-insurance plans can be used only to address workers' compensation loss exposures and healthcare benefits. Types of self-insurance plans and the loss exposures to which each can apply are shown in Exhibit 5-2.

EXHIBIT 5-2

Types of Self-Insurance Plans and Applicable Loss Exposures

Individual Self-Insurance Plans	Group Self-Insurance Plans
• Workers' compensation	• Workers' compensation
• Auto liability	• Healthcare benefits
• General liability	
• Auto physical damage	
• Professional liability	
• Earthquake	
• Flood	
• Healthcare benefits	

Individual Self-Insurance Plans

Individual self-insurance plan
A retention plan that involves only one organization.

An **individual self-insurance plan** is a retention plan that involves only one organization. Any organization can self-insure its loss exposures, provided that the state (or states) in which it operates permits self-insurance plans and that it satisfies any applicable regulatory requirements. Generally, only workers' compensation, auto liability, and general liability self-insurance plans are subject to state regulatory control.

Group Self-Insurance Plans

Group self-insurance plan
An organization of several similar employers that have formed a not-for-profit association or corporation to which they pay premiums to manage self-insurance of their workers' compensation and healthcare benefits loss exposures.

A **group self-insurance plan** is an organization of several similar employers that have formed a not-for-profit association or corporation to which they pay premiums to manage self-insurance of their workers' compensation and healthcare benefits loss exposures. Unlike individual self-insurance plans, which can be used with several types of loss exposures, group self-insurance plans can be used only for workers' compensation loss exposures and healthcare benefits. Exhibit 5-3 lists the states that allow individual and/or group workers' compensation self-insurance.

A group self-insurance plan operates like an insurer in that it pools the loss exposures of its members. The plan's administrator issues member agreements, collects premiums, and manages claims. The administrator also purchases excess liability insurance (or excess of loss reinsurance, described in a subsequent chapter), and makes required state regulatory filings.

A group self-insurance plan can benefit an organization that is too small to self-insure its loss exposures on its own. Savings are achieved through economies of scale in administration, claim handling, and the purchase of excess liability insurance (or reinsurance).

ADMINISTRATION OF INDIVIDUAL SELF-INSURANCE PLANS

A self-insurance plan requires funding, keeping records of claims, adjusting claims, and reserving losses. It also entails managing litigation; making regulatory filings; paying taxes, assessments, and fees; and maintaining excess liability insurance. These administration activities can be time consuming, especially for an organization that is self-insured in several states. The self-insured organization can perform these activities itself or hire another organization to perform them on its behalf.

Funding

The reserves for self-insured loss payments can be funded or unfunded. If they are unfunded, the self-insured organization pays for losses out of its cash flow or available current (liquid) assets. If they are funded, the reserves are backed by an internal fund that is recorded as an asset on the organization's balance sheet. This fund is used by the organization to pay for its retained losses as

EXHIBIT 5-3

States Allowing Individual and/or Group Workers' Compensation Self-Insurance Plans

State	Individual Allowed	Group Allowed	State	Individual Allowed	Group Allowed
Alabama	X	X	Missouri	X	X
Alaska	X		Montana	X	X
Arizona	X	X	Nebraska	X	
Arkansas	X	X	Nevada	X	X
California	X	X	New Hampshire	X	X
Colorado	X	X	New Jersey	X	X[1]
Connecticut	X	X	New Mexico	X	X
Delaware	X	X	New York	X	X
District of Columbia	X		North Carolina	X	X
Florida	X	X	North Dakota[2]		
Georgia	X	X	Ohio	X	
Hawaii	X	X	Oklahoma	X	X
Idaho	X		Oregon	X	X
Illinois	X	X	Pennsylvania	X	X
Indiana	X		Rhode Island	X	X
Iowa	X	X	South Carolina	X	X
Kansas	X	X	South Dakota	X	
Kentucky	X	X	Tennessee	X	X
Louisiana	X	X	Texas	X	
Maine	X	X	Utah	X	
Maryland	X	X	Vermont	X	X
Massachusetts	X	X	Virginia	X	X
Michigan	X	X	Washington	X	X[3]
Minnesota	X	X	West Virginia	X	
Mississippi	X	X	Wisconsin	X	
			Wyoming[2]		

[1] Municipalities, school boards, hospitals, and community colleges only.

[2] Self-insurance not permitted.

[3] School districts and public or not-for-profit hospitals only.

Source: www.irmi.com/Expert/Articles/2001Fuge08.aspx (accessed March 18, 2006).

they become due. An organization that maintains an internal fund incurs an opportunity cost, because the cash is tied up in relatively liquid assets. However, investment earnings from the internal funds may be sufficient to offset the cost of administering the self-insurance plan.

Recordkeeping

A self-insured organization must track its self-insured claims with a recordkeeping system that produces information that would be found in an insurer's loss report. The information contained in this system should include claims identified by number and type, as well as the amount paid and reserved for each claim. The system also can contribute to the organization's risk control program by compiling information on the cause of each loss.

Claim Settlement

A self-insured organization must devote considerable resources to claim settlement. As with insurance, claims must be investigated, evaluated, negotiated, and paid. Also, the self-insured organization may wish to pursue legal action against parties responsible for a loss. These claim settlement activities require a staff with specialized knowledge and skills.

Third-party administrator (TPA)
An organization that settles claims on another organization's behalf.

Some self-insured organizations create an in-house department to settle claims. This can require a significant commitment of organizational resources, depending on the organization's work and its geographic diversity. Others hire a **third-party administrator (TPA)**, which is an organization that settles claims on another organization's behalf. TPAs usually settle claims, keep claim records, and perform statistical analyses. An arrangement in which a TPA is hired to settle claims is sometimes called an administrative services only (ASO) plan.

Whether in-house or from a TPA, a claim representative must determine which property is damaged, who is liable for the loss, and how much money should be paid. While investigating and evaluating a claim, a claim representative must obtain and verify information, then compare it with other sources. For example, a claim representative may do any of the following:

- Investigate an accident scene
- Verify a claimant's statement of salary with the claimant's employer
- Compare a claimant's statement of the circumstances surrounding an accident with a police report's

When new information contradicts previously known information, a claim representative reexamines all of the information and investigates further to resolve the conflict or to determine which information is most credible. To determine the value of a loss, a claim representative usually consults numerous sources of information, such as valuation guides and records of prior claims with similar characteristics. To negotiate a claim settlement, the claim representative must have a thorough grasp of all the associated facts and communicate effectively.

Loss Reserves

Claim reporting does not always result in the immediate payment or denial of a claim. Like insurers, self-insurers must recognize potential claim payments as a liability on their financial statements in the form of loss reserves. Loss reserves are estimates of the amounts to be paid in the future for losses that occurred in the past.

Claim representatives play a vital role in establishing a self-insurer's loss reserves. After the claim representative receives a claim notice, obtains initial information, and verifies that the self-insurance plan covers the loss, the claim representative establishes a reserve for the loss. Loss reserving is straightforward for most property claims in which the claim representative can readily establish that loss has occurred and can estimate its amount. However, liability claims involve the estimation of bodily injury and property damage loss, and consequently are more difficult to accurately estimate.

The accuracy of a loss reserve's estimate has significant implications for the self-insured organization. An overestimation of loss reserves results in an understatement of net income. Conversely, an understatement of loss reserves results in an overstatement of net income. Therefore, an unethical organization could manipulate its loss reserve amounts in order to minimize the volatility of its financial results over time (a practice known as earnings smoothing). Generally accepted accounting principles (GAAP) state that a loss reserve must be established if the following two conditions are met:

1. The loss occurred before the date of the financial statements.
2. The amount that will be paid on the loss can be reasonably estimated.[3]

Sometimes losses have occurred so recently that the self-insurer is not informed of them yet. In other instances, the bodily injury or property damage is latent and, consequently, the injured party has yet to discover it or pursue a claim. **Incurred but not reported (IBNR) losses** are losses that have occurred but have not yet been reported to the insurer. A self-insured organization should include reserves for its retained IBNR losses if they can be reasonably estimated. A self-insured organization with a large volume of losses per year usually can reasonably estimate its retained IBNR loss liability.

Incurred but not reported (IBNR) losses
Losses that have occurred but have not yet been reported to the insurer.

The preceding financial accounting rules help to prevent a self-insured organization from using self-insured loss reserves to "smooth" its earnings. For example, under GAAP, a self-insured organization cannot post loss reserves as a liability on its balance sheet and as an expense on its income statement if the losses have not yet occurred. If the organization were able to do this, it could later use those reserves and prematurely charged expenses to offset a year of higher-than-normal self-insured losses.

Loss reserving requires a great deal of careful analysis. Reserving for an individual claim is not a one-time activity. The loss reserve must be constantly evaluated and reevaluated as new information about the claim becomes available until the claim is settled.

Litigation Management

Litigation management involves controlling the cost of legal expenses for claims that are litigated. Activities involved in litigation management include evaluating and selecting defense lawyers, supervising them during litigation, and keeping records of their costs. It also involves auditing legal bills and evaluating alternative fee-billing strategies.

Another important aspect of litigation management involves the cost-effective resolution of claim disputes. A self-insured organization should set guidelines for the conditions under which it settles claims in order to avoid continuing litigation. The organization should also set guidelines for using alternative dispute resolution (ADR) techniques, such as mediation and arbitration. Insurers, TPAs, and large self-insured organizations often employ litigation managers who oversee the litigation management process.

Regulatory Filings

To self-insure workers' compensation and/or auto liability loss exposures, an organization must qualify as a self-insurer separately in, and make periodic filings with, each state in which it seeks to self-insure such loss exposures. Because each state has its own unique set of requirements for organizations to qualify as self-insurers, organizations that operate in several states can face complex challenges. These requirements specify items such as financial security filing fees, taxes, assessments, excess liability insurance and periodic reports.

As a result of these varying regulatory requirements, an organization may self-insure its workers' compensation and/or auto liability loss exposures only in some of the states in which it operates. Consequently, self-insurance may be practical for certain loss exposures in certain states and not in others. Exhibit 5-4 illustrates some of these regulatory filing requirements by comparing the workers' compensation self-insurance qualifications of South Carolina and Pennsylvania.

Taxes, Assessments, and Fees

Most states require self-insurance plans to pay taxes, assessments, and fees, but each state has its own approach to determine the amounts owed. For example, some states require self-insured organizations to pay a percentage of their workers' compensation losses. Other states impose a tax based on a percentage of what the organization would have paid to an insurer in premium.

This cost component of a self-insurance plan is generally lower than that of insurance, because the state's charges are not levied against the self-insured organization's administrative and risk control expenses. An insurance plan includes these expenses in its premium. The premium for insurance also includes a residual market loading that is passed along to the insured organization. Self-insured organizations do, however, pay a residual market loading as part of the premium for excess liability insurance.

EXHIBIT 5-4

Comparison of Workers' Compensation Self-Insurance Qualifications

	South Carolina	Pennsylvania
Security	Determined individually subject to a minimum of $250,000. A surety bond or letter of credit is acceptable.	Surety bond, letter of credit, or government securities held in trust are acceptable. Amount determined individually, but no less than the applicant's total greatest annual incurred losses in Pennsylvania during the latest three policy years.
Filing Fee	$250 per self-insurer plus $100 per subsidiary.	$500 initially, $100 at renewal.
Taxes, Assessments, and Fees	2.5% of total cost. Second injury fund contribution also required.	Annual assessments for various funds, including second injury fund.
Excess Insurance Requirements	Specific excess required—minimum self-insured; amount determined by the commission.	Specific and aggregate excess may be required.
Term	Continuous.	One year.

International Risk Management Institute, Inc., *Risk Financing: A Guide to Insurance Cash Flow* (Dallas: International Risk Management Institute), pp. C-57–C-61.

Excess Liability Insurance

Many states require a self-insurer to purchase excess liability insurance. Some states specify the conditions under which such a purchase must be made. In other states, the agency responsible for self-insurance reviews each applicant and decides whether to require excess liability insurance. If excess liability insurance is required, specifications must be determined and bids obtained from various insurers. Finally, the excess liability insurance program must be reviewed periodically to ensure that it continues to meet the organization's needs.

ADVANTAGES AND DISADVANTAGES OF SELF-INSURANCE PLANS

As with any risk financing plan, using a self-insurance plan involves advantages and disadvantages. Some advantages and disadvantages mirror those associated with other retention plans, while others are unique to self-insurance plans.

Advantages

Self-insurance provides several advantages to an organization when compared with insurance. The major advantages of self-insurance plans are as follows:

- Control over claims
- Risk control

- Long-term cost savings
- Cash flow benefits

One major advantage of self-insurance is that it allows an organization to exercise direct control over claim settlement. (This advantage also exists with other retention plans.) The self-insured organization can select its own panel of defense attorneys and set specific guidelines for settling its claims. For example, the organization can determine the amount of effort it will invest in defending, rather than settling, a claim. The ability to set guidelines for settlement offers could be particularly important to an organization whose claims could affect its reputation, such as those involving allegations that it negligently manufactured a product, for instance.

Claims can be minimized or eliminated through risk control. Self-insurance's emphasis on risk control is another of its advantages. When an organization directly pays the cost of its own losses, it has an incentive to prevent and reduce them because, by doing so, it saves the associated loss payments and the expense of settling the claims. Also, the organization avoids having to devote resources in the aftermath of a loss, such as spending time to tend to workers' injuries or repairing damage. Furthermore, loss prevention efforts help the organization avoid possible major disruptions in its operations, such as those caused by a plant's total shutdown after an explosion.

Self-insurance's long-run costs tend to be lower than the cost of risk transfer. This advantage of self-insurance allows an organization to save money because it does not have to contribute to an insurer's overhead costs and profits, which are included in the expense component of an insurance premium. A self-insured organization also does not have to pay an insurer's risk charge and is not subject to premium taxes and residual market loadings. However, self-insurance is subject to various other taxes, assessments, and fees.

An organization that self-insures can gain an advantage from the cash flow generated by retained losses that are paid over a time period. Present value analysis can be used to measure this advantage of self-insurance and should be applied to all the costs of a self-insurance plan, not just paid losses. This analysis allows the present value cost of a self-insurance plan to be compared with the present value cost of other plans that involve retaining low- to medium-severity losses, such as a large deductible plan, a retrospective rating plan, or a captive insurance plan. Present value analysis can also be used to compare the cost of self-insurance and insurance.

Disadvantages

Self-insurance also has disadvantages when compared with insurance. The major disadvantages of self-insurance include the following:

- Uncertainty of retained loss outcomes
- Administrative requirements

- Deferral of tax deductions
- Contractual requirements

One major disadvantage of self-insurance is the associated uncertainty of retained loss outcomes, which can negatively affect an organization's earnings, net worth, and cash flow. When an organization decides to finance losses by self-insuring rather than transferring them using insurance, it faces the possibility that self-insured losses will be much more frequent or severe than initially expected. Therefore, an organization should limit its self-insured loss retention to a level at which it is comfortable with the uncertainty of the retained loss outcomes.

A self-insured loss retention can apply on a per occurrence or per accident basis, an aggregate stop-loss basis, or a combination of the two. With a per occurrence or per accident basis, a limit applies to the amount that the self-insured organization will pay for each loss occurrence or accident, regardless of the number of claims that arise from a single occurrence or accident. On an aggregate stop-loss, a limit applies to the amount that the self-insured organization will pay in total for all loss occurrences or accidents that take place during a specified period.

The administrative requirements self-insurance imposes on an organization constitute another of its disadvantages. Claims must be recorded, adjusted, and reserved; litigation must be managed; regulatory filings must be made with the states (depending on the type of loss exposure); and taxes, assessments, and fees must be paid (depending on the type of loss exposure). These services are normally provided by an insurer under an insured plan.

All risk retention and transfer expenses are tax-deductible. However, the value of the tax-deductible expense varies depending on when it is paid. Because of the time value of money, organizations derive a greater economic benefit by taking tax benefits sooner rather than later.

Under a self-insurance plan, an organization is allowed a tax deduction only as losses are paid out rather than as they are incurred. Depending on the type of loss exposure involved, losses may not be paid out until several years after they are incurred. Therefore, tax deductions are delayed under a self-insurance plan when compared with the timing of tax deductions under many other types of risk financing plans. An organization is not allowed to deduct its self-insured loss reserves, which are estimates of loss amounts that have occurred but will not be paid until future years.

This deferral of tax deductions is another disadvantage of self-insurance. By contrast, insurance allows an organization to take a tax deduction in the year in which the premium is paid. This disadvantage of self-insurance is more significant for liability losses than for property losses, which tend to be paid soon after they occur.

Measuring the Disadvantage of Taking a Tax Deduction on Losses as They Are Paid Rather Than as They Are Incurred

Present value analysis can be used to measure the cash flow disadvantage of taking a tax deduction on self-insured losses as they are paid rather than as they are incurred. Take the case of a large manufacturer that self-insures its workers' compensation loss exposure. Assume that this organization has thousands of workers' compensation claims each year. When workers are injured on the job (losses are incurred), they do not immediately receive payment for the full amount of their losses. Instead, the self-insured manufacturer pays lost wages and other expenses over time—usually over many years. In addition, the self-insured manufacturer usually pays lump-sum settlements for loss of limb and other specified injuries many years after an injury occurs. Therefore, workers' compensation losses are usually paid out over a long period. The self-insured organization must estimate future payments by setting reserves for each loss soon after it occurs and can take a tax deduction only as the losses are paid rather than as they are incurred. This is a disadvantage that can be measured using present value analysis.

Assume that the manufacturer incurs $1 million in retained workers' compensation losses in Year 1 and that the losses are paid out as shown over Year 1 through Year 5.

	Year 1	Year 2	Year 3	Year 4	Year 5	Total
Incurred Losses	$1,000,000					
Percent Paid	25%	25%	20%	15%	15%	
Amount Paid	$250,000	$250,000	$200,000	$150,000	$150,000	$1,000,000
Loss Reserve	$750,000	$500,000	$300,000	$150,000	$0	

Even though $1 million in losses is incurred in Year 1, only $250,000 is paid to claimants in Year 1. Therefore, the manufacturer establishes a reserve for future loss payments (loss reserve) of $750,000 at the end of Year 1. (This example assumes that the manufacturer can accurately determine its reserves for incurred losses at the end of Year 1.) This reserve is reduced as losses are paid out in Year 2 through Year 5.

Assume that the manufacturer has an annual after-tax cost of capital of 10 percent. Therefore, it values any after-tax deferred cash outflow benefits at 10 percent yearly because it can invest the additional cash back into its business and, therefore, avoid raising additional capital. Further, assume that the manufacturer is in a 30 percent marginal tax bracket.

The present value of the disadvantage to the manufacturer of taking a tax deduction as the $1 million in losses is paid in Year 1 through Year 5 rather than taking the tax deduction on the $1 million in incurred losses in Year 1 is calculated as follows: (To simplify the analysis, assume that the tax savings occurs at the end of each year.)

Tax Deduction for Losses as They Are Incurred

	Year 1
Incurred Losses	$1,000,000
Savings in Taxes (30%)	$300,000
Present Value Factor (10%)	0.9091
Present Value of the Tax Savings	$272,730

Tax Deduction for Losses as They Are Paid

	Year 1	Year 2	Year 3	Year 4	Year 5	Total
Paid Losses	$250,000	$250,000	$200,000	$150,000	$150,000	$1,000,000
Savings in Taxes (30%)	$75,000	$75,000	$60,000	$45,000	$45,000	$300,000
Present Value Factor (10%)	0.9091	0.8264	0.7513	0.6830	0.6209	
Present Value of the Tax Savings	$68,183	$61,980	$45,078	$30,735	$27,941	$233,917

Note that under each option, the manufacturer saves $300,000 in income taxes ($1 million in losses × 30 percent marginal tax rate). However, the tax savings occur at different times, depending on whether the manufacturer can deduct its losses as they are incurred or as they are paid.

The calculations show that $272,730 is the present value of the tax savings if the manufacturer takes a tax deduction for the incurred losses at the end of Year 1. By contrast, the manufacturer will have $233,917 as the present value of the tax savings if it takes a tax deduction as it pays losses in Year 1 through Year 5. The difference between the two numbers is the present value disadvantage to the manufacturer of taking a deduction as losses are paid rather than incurred.

$272,730	Present value advantage of deducting losses as incurred
− $233,917	Present value advantage of deducting losses as paid
$ 38,813	Present value disadvantage of deducting losses as paid rather than as incurred

General business contracts often require one party to purchase insurance for another party's benefit. Sometimes an organization finds it difficult to use its self-insurance plan for this purpose, which is another disadvantage of self-insurance. For example, if an organization leases a building, it may be required to name the landlord as an additional insured under a general liability insurance policy that covers liability arising from the building's occupancy. The landlord may not accept the tenant's self-insurance plan and, instead, may insist that the tenant purchase a general liability insurance policy for this purpose.

CASE STUDIES IN SELF-INSURANCE PLANS

The following case studies illustrate the application of self-insurance plans to specific situations. The self-insurance plans outlined are realistic for the circumstances shown, but are not necessarily the only appropriate options.

Carpentry Contractor Company

Carpentry Contractor Company (CCC) is a subcontractor for several regional home builders that construct 150 to 200 houses on a single tract of land. CCC's employees completely frame a home and then move to the next one. Its management believes wholeheartedly in risk control, whose good loss results have generally been reflected in CCC's workers' compensation premium. However, CCC's management thinks that it is paying too much for this coverage and that its insurer will never be able to completely recognize CCC's risk control efforts because it operates in a hazardous industry. Consequently, CCC's risk management professional has been asked to present a recommendation to management about self-insurance.

The risk management professional believes that CCC's commitment to risk control will significantly contribute to the success of its self-insurance program. Reduced losses will directly and immediately translate into cost savings. The causality of losses and increased costs can be used by management to motivate workers to adhere to work safety rules to prevent on-the-job injuries and to respond quickly to those injuries that do occur so that losses are mitigated. CCC's management has observed that most risk control activities aimed at reducing construction-related injuries deal with worker behavior. It is therefore willing to implement safety programs that provide employees with incentives for following risk control procedures. Since these safety and incentive programs have been implemented, CCC has developed a culture in which employee safety is paramount.

Metal Products Manufacturing Company

Metal Products Manufacturing Company (MPMC) has been producing garden tools for 100 years. While some of its manufacturing methods are somewhat outdated by today's standards, MPMC makes sturdy steel tools and charges a top price for them. MPMC's risk management professional is stunned when MPMC's insurance broker tells her that its insurance renewal will include a 175-percent increase in its workers' compensation premium. The risk management professional had expected a price increase because insurance prices had been steadily increasing, but not one that large. MPMC's insurance broker explains that the insurance marketplace is in one of its pricing cycles in which insurance is expensive, if available at all.

MPMC's risk management professional presents a solid case to management that self-insurance will insulate it from these insurance pricing cycles. She explains that self-insurance plan costs will rise when underlying costs rise, primarily MPMC's losses, but that overall costs can be limited through the purchase of specific and aggregate excess liability insurance. Because specific and aggregate excess liability insurance is subject to insurance pricing cycles, its cost and availability are likely to fluctuate in accordance with the insurance marketplace. Therefore, MPMC's management needs to be prepared for the possibility it may have to absorb a greater retention in the future.

Lastly, MPMC's risk management professional emphasizes that a self-insurance plan is a long-term commitment, and that MPMC would not be exiting and entering the primary insurance market depending on future changes in insurance pricing cycles. Most states require self-insurers to post security in the form of letters of credit, bonds, or a combination of both that must remain in place until all losses under the self-insured plan are paid. Consequently, abandoning the self-insurance plan will not necessarily enable MPMC to eliminate the costs of administering the self-insurance plan.

MPMC's management commits to the self-insurance plan because of the long-term cost savings and the belief that its cost can be controlled. Therefore, in the long-run, a self-insurance plan will help minimize the fluctuation that MPMC's previous insurance plan produced.

SUMMARY

Self-insurance lowers the long-term cost of risk by allowing an organization to pay for its own losses without the transaction costs associated with insurance. Self-insurance is a form of retention under which an organization records its losses and maintains a formal system to pay for them. A self-insurance plan is usually coupled with the purchase of excess insurance (risk transfer) to cover severe losses, as well as to limit the accumulation of losses.

Self-insurance is best practiced by organizations that have a tolerance for risk retention and a willingness to devote capital and resources to financing and administering a self-insurance program. It is best applied to losses that are of both low severity and high frequency.

Because self-insurance involves certain overhead costs and other expenses as well as the assumption of risk of loss, an organization should have the financial resources and a sufficient amount of loss exposures for self-insurance to be economically feasible. These economic considerations should be balanced with the accounting disadvantage that self-insured organizations must recognize losses when they are incurred and establish a liability for them without counting them as a tax-deductible expense until they are actually paid.

Self-insurance is particularly well-suited for financing losses that are paid out over a specified time period. This provides a cash flow benefit to the self-insured organization. Consequently, workers' compensation, general liability, and automobile liability loss exposures are often self-insured.

Self-insurance plans can be implemented for one organization (individual self-insurance) or for more than one organization (group self-insurance plans). Individual self-insurance plans involve a single organization. Group self-insurance involves several similar employers that have formed a not-for-profit association or corporation to which they pay premiums to manage self-insurance of their workers' compensation or healthcare benefits loss exposures.

The administration of a self-insurance plan involves activities such as funding, recordkeeping, claim adjusting, loss reserving, litigation management, making regulatory filings, and maintaining excess insurance. To self-insure workers' compensation and/or automobile liability in most states, an organization must qualify as a self-insurer. This can be complex and time consuming, because each state has its own unique set of requirements.

A self-insurance plan has many advantages and disadvantages that are similar to those of all retention plans. However, some are unique to self-insurance. The major advantages of using self-insurance plans include the following:

- Control over claims
- Risk control
- Long-term savings
- Cash flow benefits

The major disadvantages of using self-insurance plans include the following:

- Uncertainty of retained loss outcomes
- Administrative requirements
- Deferral of tax deductions
- Contractual requirements

A properly designed and managed self-insurance plan can help an organization meet its risk financing goals. Another type of financing plan organizations consider is the retrospective rating plan, which combines the elements of risk retention found in self-insurance with components of risk transfer.

CHAPTER NOTES

1. Self-Insurance Institute of America, www.siia.org/public/articles/index. cfm?Cat=25 (accessed February 27, 2006).

2. Self-Insurance Institute of America, www.siia.org/public/articles/index. cfm?Cat=24 (accessed February 27, 2006).

3. Financial Accounting Standards Board, Statement of Financial Accounting Standards No. 5, "Accounting for Contingencies" (Norwalk, Conn.: FASB, March 1975), p. 6. Available online at www.fasb.org/pdf/fas5.pdf, p. 6 (accessed February 27, 2006).

Direct Your Learning

Retrospective Rating Plans

After learning the content of this chapter and completing the corresponding course guide assignment, you should be able to:

■ Describe the purpose and operation of retrospective rating plans.

■ Given a case, calculate the premium for a retrospective rating plan.

■ Describe the types of retrospective rating plans.

■ Describe the administration of retrospective rating plans.

■ Describe the advantages and disadvantages of retrospective rating plans.

■ Given a case, justify a retrospective rating plan that can meet an organization's risk financing needs.

■ Define or describe each of the Key Words and Phrases for this chapter.

Develop Your Perspective

What are the main topics covered in the chapter?

This chapter examines an alternative approach to pricing guaranteed-cost insurance plans. Retrospective rating plans use the insured organization's current losses as the primary component in determining the current policy premium. Consequently, retrospective rating plans are considered to be a cost-plus approach to financing losses.

Identify the components of the retrospective rating insurance premium formula.

- What is the effect of using paid losses instead of incurred loses in determining converted losses?

- What is the effect of having a minimum premium and a maximum premium relatively close in amount?

Why is it important to learn about these topics?

One way organizations can reduce their long-term cost of risk is by retaining more risk. Retrospective rating plans can serve as a stepping-stone from a guaranteed-cost insurance plan to a risk financing plan that may provide the organization with a lower cost of risk.

Review the advantages and disadvantages of retrospective rating plans based on their relative importance to your organization.

- How would your organization be motivated to improve its risk control efforts if improvement in its loss experience were reflected in its insurance costs?

- Why would your organization be willing to deal with the stacking of letters of credit that are often involved in using paid loss retrospective rating plans?

How can you use what you will learn?

Enter your organization's annual workers' compensation losses into the retrospective rating insurance premium formula.

- What minimum and maximum premiums are most practical for your organization?

- Would your organization be able to tolerate the uncertainty that is possible with a retrospective rating plan?

Chapter 6
Retrospective Rating Plans

Organizations that want more risk retention while still keeping an insurance program often consider using a retrospective rating plan. A **retrospective rating plan** is a hybrid risk financing plan in which an organization buys insurance subject to a rating formula that adjusts the premium after the end of the policy period based on the insured organization's actual losses during the policy period. Retrospective rating plans provide an alternative means for pricing insurance. Rather than using industry-wide loss experience to determine premiums, a retrospective rating plan uses the insured organization's own losses from the current policy period to price the current policy period. To the extent that the insured organization is effectively paying for its own losses through the retrospective rating plan premium, the retrospective rating plan is a risk retention plan. To the extent that the insurer assumes the insured organization's losses above specified monetary limits, the retrospective rating plan is a risk transfer plan.

Because a retrospective rating plan contains elements of both risk retention and risk transfer, it is considered a hybrid risk financing plan. Unlike guaranteed-cost insurance program pricing, retrospective rating plans respond almost immediately to changes in the organization's loss experience, regardless of whether the loss experience improves or deteriorates.

Understanding the retrospective rating premium formula is central to obtaining the benefits of this pricing approach. Once the insured organization and the insurer mutually agree to a formula, it is then used with either incurred or paid losses to determine the premium. The decision to use paid losses instead of incurred losses is another instance in which the insured organization and the insurer must agree. Although retrospective rating plans are insurance plans, the insured organization assumes some administrative responsibilities with a retrospective rating plan that are not inherent in guaranteed-cost insurance. As with all risk financing plans, the organization and its risk management professional must weigh the advantages with the disadvantages presented by retrospective rating plans to determine whether the plan is suited for the organization.

Retrospective rating plan
A hybrid risk financing plan in which an organization buys insurance subject to a rating formula that adjusts the premium after the end of the policy period based on the insured organization's actual losses during the policy period.

PURPOSE AND OPERATION OF RETROSPECTIVE RATING PLANS

The purpose of a retrospective rating plan is to adjust the premium for guaranteed-cost insurance to reflect the insured organization's current losses. Because the retrospective premium reflects losses incurred during the policy period, the retrospective rating plan provides an incentive to the insured organization to use risk control and thereby reduce losses. To the extent that the insured controls losses, it is rewarded through lower premiums.

Because a retrospective rating plan is an optional pricing plan applied to insurance, the risk management professional needs to know the types of losses covered by the plan and how the retrospective rating insurance premium is determined.

Types of Losses Covered

Organizations commonly use retrospective rating plans for losses arising from their liability loss exposures that are covered by workers' compensation, auto liability, and general liability insurance policies. Organizations can also use retrospective rating plans for auto physical damage, crime, and glass loss exposures. A single retrospective rating plan can be used for more than one type of loss exposure. For example, workers' compensation, auto liability, and general liability are commonly combined under a single retrospective rating plan.

In general, organizations use retrospective rating plans to finance their low- to medium-severity losses.[1] These types of losses usually have a high frequency and are therefore somewhat predictable in total. Exhibit 6-1 shows the characteristics of losses usually covered by retrospective rating plans.

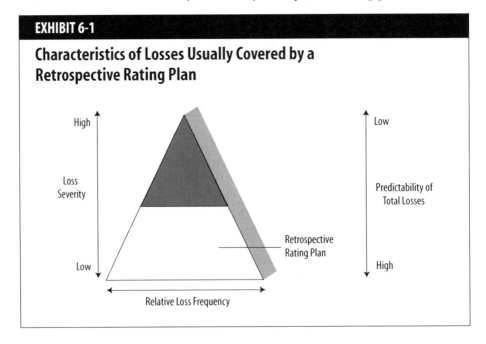

EXHIBIT 6-1

Characteristics of Losses Usually Covered by a Retrospective Rating Plan

Insurers generally use retrospective rating plans developed by the National Council on Compensation Insurance (NCCI) for workers' compensation and by the Insurance Services Office (ISO) for coverages other than workers' compensation. Both organizations have developed eligibility rules, pricing procedures, and retrospective rating premium endorsements that are filed with and authorized for use by the state insurance departments. When a retrospective rating plan is used, the insurer attaches the appropriate retrospective rating premium endorsement to the policy. If multiple insurance policies are subject to the same insurance plan, then a retrospective rating premium endorsement is attached to each.

Premium Determination

As with any insurance plan, the insured organization under a retrospective rating plan pays a premium to the insurer. The insurer uses the premium to reimburse claimants for losses and to pay other expenses such as premium taxes, residual market loadings, loss adjustment costs, and legal defense fees. The premium also includes an amount to cover the insurer's overhead and profit.

Under a guaranteed-cost insurance plan, the premium for the policy period does not vary with the insured's losses that occur during the policy period. Therefore, guaranteed-cost insurance is a risk transfer technique. In contrast, under a retrospective rating plan, the insured organization pays a deposit premium at the beginning of the policy period, and the insurer (using a rating formula agreed on in advance of the policy period) adjusts the premium after the end of the policy period to include a portion of the insured organization's covered losses that occurred during the policy period. Because the premium is adjusted upward or downward based directly on a portion of covered losses, the insured organization is, in effect, retaining a portion of its own losses.

Retrospective rating plan rating is frequently confused with experience rating, because both take the insured organization's loss experience into consideration. **Experience rating** is a rating plan that adjusts the premium for the current policy period to recognize the loss experience of the insured organization during *past* policy periods. In contrast, retrospective rating plans adjust the premium for the current policy period to recognize the insured's loss experience during the *current* policy period. The insured organization's past loss experience is not completely ignored in the retrospective rating plan, because past loss experience is reflected in the standard premium. However, past lost experience is less important relative to current losses.

The adjusted premium under a retrospective rating plan is subject to a maximum amount and a minimum amount agreed to in the policy. The **maximum premium** is the most an insured organization is required to pay under a retrospective rating plan, regardless of the amount of incurred losses. By agreeing to limit the amount by which the premium can be adjusted upward based on covered losses, the insurer accepts the risk that total losses during the policy period could exceed a maximum amount. The adjusted

Experience rating
A rating plan that adjusts the premium for the current policy period to recognize the loss experience of the insured organization during *past* policy periods.

Maximum premium
The most an insured organization is required to pay under a retrospective rating plan, regardless of the amount of incurred losses.

Minimum premium
The least an insured organization is required to pay under a retrospective rating plan, regardless of the amount of incurred losses.

premium is also often subject to a minimum amount, called a minimum premium. The **minimum premium** is the least an insured organization is required to pay under a retrospective rating plan, regardless of the amount of incurred losses. For example, the maximum and minimum premiums for a retrospective rating plan might be $1,000,000 and, $200,000 respectively. If during the policy period the insured organization experiences a total of $1,400,000 in losses subject to the policy's loss limit, the premium is limited to the maximum premium of $1,000,000. If the insured organization experiences no losses during the policy period, the minimum premium of $200,000 still applies.

Provided the insured organization has a sufficiently large enough premium, the retrospective rating plan can be designed to cap losses and thereby minimize the insured organization's retention by using a loss limit. **Loss limit** is the level at which each individual accident or occurrence is limited for the purpose of calculating a retrospective rating insurance premium. The use of a loss limit is another optional factor in a retrospective rating plan. When used, the amount and its cost are negotiated between the insurer and the insured organization. For example, if the loss limit under a retrospective rating plan is $100,000 per occurrence, only the first $100,000 of each covered loss occurrence is included in the retrospective rating insurance premium. The amount of each loss occurrence that exceeds $100,000 and that is less than the policy limit is transferred to the insurer. Exhibit 6-2 shows the relationship between retained and transferred losses under a retrospective rating plan.

Loss limit
The level at which each individual accident or occurrence is limited for the purpose of calculating a retrospective rating insurance premium.

Under a retrospective rating plan, a loss limit caps the amount of individual losses included in the determination of the retrospective rating premium. The most the insured organization must pay under a retrospective rating insurance plan is specified as the maximum premium.

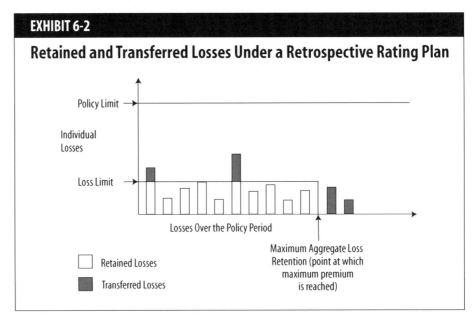

EXHIBIT 6-2

Retained and Transferred Losses Under a Retrospective Rating Plan

The premium under a retrospective rating plan includes costs other than retained losses, such as insurer overhead and profits, residual market loadings, and premium taxes. The retrospective rating plan premium also includes a risk transfer premium that compensates the insurer for accepting the risk that either or both of the following might occur:

- An individual loss will fall between the loss limit and the policy limit. (The premium component that covers this risk is called an excess loss premium.)
- The total of losses subject to the loss limit during the policy period will exceed the aggregate amount that causes the retrospective rating plan premium to reach the maximum premium. (The premium component that covers this risk is called an insurance charge.)

The purpose of the risk transfer portion of a retrospective rating plan premium is to compensate the insurer for limiting the amount of an insured's covered losses included in the retrospective rating insurance premium adjustments. Exhibit 6-3 shows the relationship between losses and premium for a typical retrospective rating plan. Note that the premium is limited by both the maximum and minimum premiums.

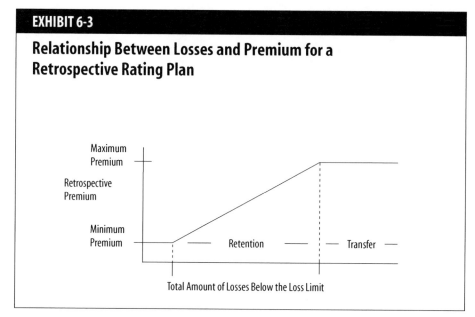

EXHIBIT 6-3

Relationship Between Losses and Premium for a Retrospective Rating Plan

The retrospective rating insurance premium increases as losses increase. However, the premium cannot be less than the minimum premium or more than the maximum premium.

To summarize, the premium for a retrospective rating plan includes a portion of the insured organization's covered losses during the policy period and is subject to maximum and minimum amounts. Therefore, a retrospective rating plan allows an insured organization to effectively retain a portion of its losses. If an insured organization incurs higher-than-average losses during a policy period, the final adjusted premium under a retrospective rating plan is higher than the premium that the insured organization would pay under a guaranteed-cost insurance plan to cover the same losses. The opposite is true if losses are lower than average. When used, the loss limit softens the impact of large individual losses on the insured organization. The portion of losses not retained is transferred to the insurer, which is compensated through risk transfer premium charges (the excess loss premium and the insurance charge) that are built into the retrospective rating plan premium. The retrospective rating plan premium also includes charges for other components, such as residual market loadings, premium taxes, and insurer overhead and profit.

Risk management professionals must also understand how the premium components of the plan interact. The retrospective rating plan premium formula specifies the relationship among these premium components.

CALCULATION OF RETROSPECTIVE RATING PLAN INSURANCE PREMIUMS

A retrospective rating insurance premium is calculated using a formula whose factors are agreed upon by the insurer and the insured organization. The retrospective rating plan premium can be expressed as a mathematical formula called the retrospective rating insurance premium formula.

Retrospective Rating Insurance Premium Formula

Retrospective rating insurance premium formula
(Basic premium + Converted losses + Excess loss premium) × Tax multiplier.

The formula for calculating premium, or the **retrospective rating insurance premium formula**, is as follows:

$$\text{Retrospective rating plan premium}^* = \left(\text{Basic premium} + \text{Converted losses} + \text{Excess loss premium} \right) \times \text{Tax multiplier.}$$

*Subject to maximum and minimum amounts

To understand the retrospective rating insurance premium formula, each of its components should be analyzed separately.

Standard Premium

Standard premium
A premium that is calculated by using state insurance department-authorized rating classifications, applying them to an insured organization's estimated exposures for the policy period, and allowing for various adjustments.

An underlying component of the retrospective rating insurance formula is the standard premium. **Standard premium** is a premium that is calculated by using state insurance department-authorized rating classifications, applying them to an insured organization's estimated exposures for the policy period, and allowing for various adjustments. Standard premium is the amount the insured organization would pay for insurance coverage under a guaranteed-cost insurance plan. The standard premium reflects a combination of industry-wide loss experience for a class of organizations (exposure rating), and the insured organization's actual loss experience (experience rating). The calculation of standard premium is as follows:

$$\text{Manual premium} = \frac{\text{Exposure units}}{\text{Exposure base}} \times \text{Manual rate.}$$

$$\text{Standard premium} = \text{Manual premium} \times \text{Experience modification factor.}$$

The manual rate (the exposure rating component) is developed from industry-wide exposure data. For a guaranteed-cost insurance plan, a premium discount to the standard premium may be available, depending on the size of insured organization's premium. Insurers provide a premium discount because the relative cost of servicing the policy does not increase proportionately with the size of the premium. Some of the components of the retrospective premium formula are based on an insured's standard premium without an allowance for the premium discount.

At the beginning of the policy period, the standard premium is estimated based on an insured organization's estimated exposures for the period. The standard premium is adjusted after the end of the policy period based on the insured organization's actual exposures for the period. Therefore, if an insured organization's exposures, such as sales, turn out to be greater than estimated at the beginning of the policy period, its standard premium is adjusted upward.

Basic Premium

The **basic premium** is a component of the retrospective rating insurance premium formula that covers insurer acquisition expenses, administrative costs, overhead, and profit, as well as the insurance charge. The **insurance charge** (mentioned previously) is a component of the basic premium that provides the insurer with premium to compensate it for the risk that the calculated retrospective rating insurance premium may be higher than the maximum premium or lower than the minimum premium. The insurance charge reflects both of these possibilities.

The basic premium is expressed as a percentage of the insured organization's standard premium. Therefore, when the standard premium is adjusted after the end of the policy period based on actual exposures, the dollar amount of the basic premium automatically adjusts as well.

Converted Losses

Converted losses is a component of the retrospective rating insurance premium formula that is the product of incurred losses and an applicable loss conversion factor. A **loss conversion factor** is a factor applied to incurred losses so that the converted losses reflect loss adjustment expenses. For example, if an insured organization had annual incurred losses of \$500,000 and its retrospective rating premium formula contained a loss conversion factor of 1.25, the converted losses would be \$625,000 (\$500,000 × 1.25). The formula for converted losses is as follows:

$$\text{Converted losses} = \text{Loss conversion factor} \times \text{Incurred losses}.$$

A high loss conversion factor implies that the insurer expects that the losses will be costly to settle. Consequently, a retrospective rating plan with a high loss conversion factor is more expensive for the insured organization than one with a lower loss conversion factor.

The losses included in the determination of converted losses are those below the loss limit applicable to individual losses. The losses include allocated loss adjustment expenses but not unallocated loss adjustment expenses.

Basic premium
A component of the retrospective rating insurance premium formula that covers insurer acquisition expenses, administrative costs, overhead, and profit, as well as the insurance charge.

Insurance charge
A component of the basic premium that provides the insurer with premium to compensate it for the risk that the calculated retrospective rating insurance premium may be higher than the maximum premium or lower than the minimum premium.

Converted losses
A component of the retrospective rating insurance premium formula that is the product of incurred losses and an applicable loss conversion factor.

Loss conversion factor
A factor applied to incurred losses so that the converted losses reflect loss adjustment expenses.

Excess Loss Premium

The **excess loss premium** is a component of the retrospective rating insurance premium formula that compensates the insurer for the risk that an individual loss will exceed the loss limit. For example, assume that the loss limit is $250,000 per occurrence and that the policy limit is $1 million per occurrence. The excess loss premium compensates the insurer for the risk that losses will fall in the layer between $250,000 and $1 million per occurrence.

The excess loss premium is the product of the standard premium and the excess loss premium factor. The formula for the excess loss premium is as follows:

Excess loss premium = Standard premium × Excess loss premium factor.

For example, if the standard premium is $600,000 and the excess loss premium is 15 percent, the excess loss premium is $90,000 ($600,000 × 15 percent). When the standard premium is adjusted after the end of the policy period based on actual exposures, the dollar amount of the excess loss premium automatically adjusts as well.

The excess loss premium factor, and consequently the excess loss premium amount, varies with the amount of the loss limit. In the preceding example, the excess loss premium factor would be higher if the loss limit were $100,000 per occurrence rather than $250,000 per occurrence, because the insurer's risk of loss would be greater.

Tax Multiplier

The **tax multiplier** is a component of the retrospective rating insurance premium formula that covers the insurer's cost for state premium taxes, licenses fees, insurance organization assessments, and residual market loadings that the insurer must pay on all collected premiums. The tax multiplier is expressed as a factor that, when multiplied by the other premium components, adds a specified percentage to them. For example, if the amount to be added is 4 percent, the tax multiplier is 1.04.

Maximum and Minimum Premiums

Maximum and minimum premiums are expressed as a percentage of the standard premium. For example, an insured organization and the insurer may agree to a 150 percent maximum premium and a 50 percent minimum premium. If the standard premium is $900,000, the maximum premium is $1,350,000 ($900,000 × 1.50), and the minimum premium is $450,000 ($900,000 × 0.50). When the standard premium is adjusted after the end of the policy period based on actual exposures, the dollar amounts of the maximum and minimum premiums automatically adjust as well.

Premium Adjustments

Under a retrospective rating plan, insurers generally require the insured organization to pay a deposit premium at the beginning of the policy term that is subsequently adjusted when exposures and losses are known. The deposit premium is usually equal to the standard premium. Some insurers permit the insured organization to pay the deposit premium in installments throughout the policy period. In some cases, the insurer allows the insured organization to pay the standard premium over a period that extends beyond the policy period.

As discussed, the initial standard premium for the retrospective rating plan is based on estimated exposures. Sometime after the end of the policy period, the insurer adjusts the standard premium based on actual exposures for the policy period. At about the same time, the insurer applies the retrospective rating insurance premium formula to the adjusted standard premium, considering the insured organization's incurred losses (paid and reserved losses) for the policy period. The result is an adjusted retrospective rating plan premium that also accounts for what the insured organization has already paid in premium.

In subsequent periods, usually annually, further adjustments are made to the retrospective rating plan premium by applying the retrospective rating insurance premium formula to subsequent evaluations of incurred losses that occurred during the policy period. If the evaluation of incurred losses for the policy period shows an increase in cumulative incurred losses from one adjustment to the next, an additional premium is due. If the evaluation shows that cumulative incurred losses for the policy period have decreased, premium is returned to the insured organization. This series of premium adjustments, which can go on for several years after the policy period, continues until all retained losses are paid or until the insurer and the insured organization agree that no further retrospective rating premium adjustments are required. Therefore, a retrospective rating plan premium for a single policy period usually is not finalized until many years after the policy period.

Exhibit 6-4 illustrates the relationship between incurred losses and premium adjustments for an incurred loss retrospective rating plan. The standard premium is paid during the policy period and, in this example, is adjusted at two evaluation points, Evaluation Point #1 and Evaluation Point #2. Because this example assumes that the cumulative incurred losses at Evaluation Point #1 were less than those anticipated by the standard premium, a return premium is due to the insured organization at Evaluation Point #1. This example assumes that, at Evaluation Point #2, cumulative incurred losses further increased, so the insured organization pays an additional premium. Although Exhibit 6-4 shows only two evaluation points, usually there are many subsequent evaluation points, each of which cause corresponding adjustments to the cumulative premium.

EXHIBIT 6-4

Relationship Between Incurred Losses and Premium Adjustments for an Incurred Loss Retrospective Rating Plan

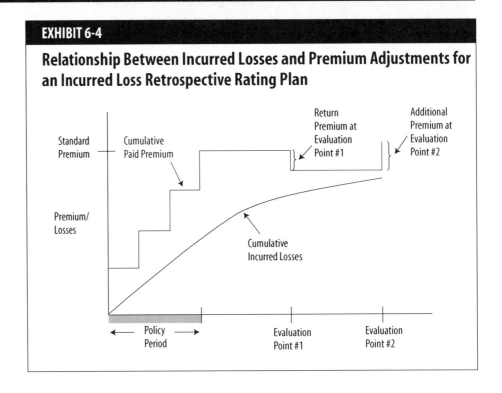

Retrospective Rating Plan Insurance Premium Calculation Case Study

Assume that Canston Manufacturing Company (Canston) has the following cost factors for its incurred loss retrospective rating plan:

Policy limit	$1,000,000 per occurrence
Standard premium	$700,000
Premium discount	$50,000
Basic premium	20% of standard premium
Loss conversion factor	1.10
Loss limit	$500,000 per occurrence
Excess loss premium factor	5%
Tax multiplier	1.04
Maximum premium	150% of standard premium
Minimum premium	40% of standard premium

Analysis:

- The standard premium of $700,000 minus the premium discount of $50,000 ($650,000) is the amount that Canston would pay for a guaranteed-cost insurance plan.

- The basic premium is 20 percent of standard premium, or $140,000. (The basic premium includes an insurance charge.)

- The excess loss premium factor is 5 percent of the standard premium, or an excess loss premium of $35,000.

- The maximum premium is 150 percent of standard premium, or $1,050,000, and the minimum premium is 40 percent of standard premium, or $280,000.

- Using the retrospective rating insurance premium formula, the retrospective rating plan premium is calculated as follows:

$$\text{Retrospective rating plan premium} = \left(\text{Basic premium} + \text{Converted losses} + \text{Excess loss premium} \right) \times \text{Tax multiplier.}$$

$$= [\$140,000 + (\text{Losses} \times 1.10) + \$35,000] \times 1.04.$$

Using the preceding formula, the retrospective rating plan premium is calculated to equal each of the following amounts at various incurred loss amounts:

Incurred Losses	Premium	
$ 50,000	$ 280,000	Minimum Premium Applies
100,000	296,400	
200,000	410,800	
300,000	525,200	
400,000	639,600	
500,000	754,000	
600,000	868,400	
700,000	982,800	
800,000	1,050,000	Maximum Premium Applies

Losses of $50,000 or less cause the minimum premium to apply, whereas losses of $800,000 or more cause the maximum premium to apply.

Canston pays the standard premium of $700,000 as a deposit during the policy period. The premium is adjusted upward or downward as incurred losses for the policy period are evaluated at subsequent annual intervals. For example, if at the first evaluation date Canston's incurred losses are $600,000, then an additional premium of $168,400 is due ($868,400 – $700,000).

Because a portion of the premium includes the insured organization's covered losses, the insured organization should periodically audit the insurer's claim-handling, loss-payment, and loss-reserving practices. Often, a broker or a risk management consultant performs this audit function on the insured organization's behalf.

TYPES OF RETROSPECTIVE RATING PLANS

Retrospective rating plans allow insured organizations to retain monies to serve other business needs that would otherwise be spent on insurance premiums. Some insurers allow insured organizations even greater cash flow flexibility by using a paid loss retrospective rating plan instead of an incurred loss retrospective rating plan.

Incurred Loss Retrospective Rating Plan

Incurred loss retrospective rating plan

A retrospective rating plan in which the insured organization pays a deposit premium during the policy period; after the end of the policy period, the insurer adjusts the premium based on the insured organization's actual incurred losses.

An **incurred loss retrospective rating plan** is a retrospective rating plan in which the insured organization pays a deposit premium during the policy period; after the end of the policy period, the insurer adjusts the premium based on the insured organization's actual incurred losses. An incurred loss retrospective rating plan is the type of retrospective rating plan generally offered by insurers. Incurred losses are the sum of paid losses, reserved losses, and loss adjustment expense reserves. Under an incurred loss retrospective rating plan, the insured organization pays the insurer a premium based on incurred losses, even though those losses may not be paid to a claimant until much later. Because it pays premium when losses are incurred rather than when they are paid, the insured organization does not receive the cash flow available on its loss reserves, which the insurer holds.

Exhibit 6-5 shows the relationship between losses and premium payments for an incurred loss retrospective rating plan. Note that the premium payments track the incurred losses rather than the paid losses, providing less cash flow benefit to the insured organization than would be case if premium payments tracked paid losses.

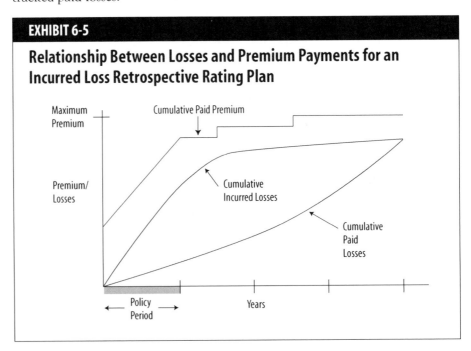

EXHIBIT 6-5

Relationship Between Losses and Premium Payments for an Incurred Loss Retrospective Rating Plan

Paid Loss Retrospective Rating Plan

A **paid loss retrospective rating plan** is a retrospective rating plan in which the insured organization pays a deposit premium at the beginning of the policy period and reimburses the insurer for its losses as the insurer pays for them and in which the total amount paid is subject to the minimum and maximum premiums. For most liability losses, the insurer's loss payments are made over a period of several years after the losses occur. Therefore, the insured organization benefits from the cash flow available on the funds it retains rather than paying them to the insurer. Relative to an incurred loss retrospective rating plan, the insurer generally requires a smaller deposit premium, thereby further enhancing the insured organization's cash flow. The insured organization must provide the insurer with security, such as a letter of credit, to guarantee future premium payments on losses that have occurred but have not yet been paid by the insurer. The need to provide acceptable forms of security is one of the factors that make paid loss retrospective rating plans more complex to administer than guaranteed-cost insurance.

Exhibit 6-6 shows the relationship between losses and premium payments for a paid loss retrospective rating plan. Note that the cumulative paid premium tracks the cumulative paid losses rather than the cumulative incurred losses, providing a sizable cash flow benefit to the insured organization because premium is not fully paid until several years after the policy period. Just as with any retrospective rating plan, the paid loss amounts are subject to a loss limit and a maximum premium, so a paid loss retrospective rating plan also has an element of risk transfer.

Paid loss retrospective rating plan
A retrospective rating plan in which the insured organization pays a deposit premium at the beginning of the policy period and reimburses the insurer for its losses as the insurer pays for them and in which the total amount paid is subject to the minimum and maximum premiums.

EXHIBIT 6-6

Relationship Between Losses and Premium Payments for a Paid Loss Retrospective Rating Plan

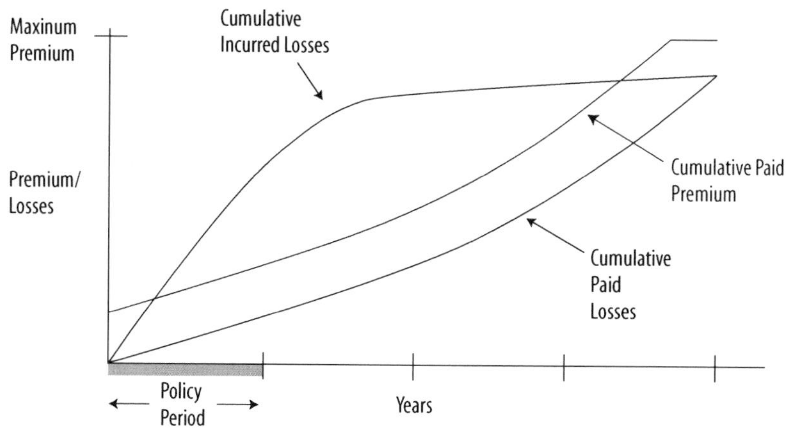

Comparison of Paid Loss With Incurred Loss Retrospective Rating Plans

Given the previous discussion of paid loss and incurred loss retrospective rating plans, it would seem that an insured would always favor a paid loss over an incurred loss retrospective rating plan. With both plans, the insured organization pays for the insurer's estimated expenses, but with the paid loss plan the insured organization pays premium only as its retained losses are paid rather than incurred, benefiting from the cash flow on retained funds. Under an incurred loss plan, even being able to take a tax deduction on the premium based on incurred rather than paid losses does not compensate for the disadvantage of not benefiting from the cash flow on the insurer's loss reserves.

However, under a paid loss retrospective rating plan, an insurer usually adds an amount to the basic premium to compensate itself for not having use of the cash flow on the loss reserves. Therefore, an insured organization should not automatically choose a paid loss plan over an incurred loss plan, because the decision depends on the relationship between the amount that the insurer adds to the basic premium and the value of the cash flow benefit to the insured.

For example, assume Parne Manufacturing (Parne) is trying to decide between an incurred loss retrospective rating plan and a paid loss retrospective rating plan with the following cost factors:

	Incurred Loss Retrospective Insurance Plan	Paid Loss Retrospective Insurance Plan
Policy limit	$1,000,000 per occurrence	Same
Standard premium	$700,000	Same
Basic premium	20% of standard premium	28% of standard premium
Loss conversion factor	1.10	Same
Loss limit	$500,000 per occurrence	Same
Excess loss premium factor	5%	Same
Tax multiplier	1.04	Same
Maximum premium	150% of standard premium	158% of standard premium
Minimum premium	40% of standard premium	Same

Note that the difference between the two plans is the charge for the basic premium, which is higher under the paid loss plan. The maximum premium is also adjusted upward to account for the influence of the higher basic premium as part of the retrospective rating insurance premium formula. This higher charge for the basic premium is meant to compensate the insurer for its loss of use of cash flow on the loss reserves under the paid loss retrospective rating plan.

Present value analysis should be used to compare the paid loss and incurred loss plans. The cash flow benefit from paying premium as the losses are paid under the paid loss plan may or may not offset the additional amount loaded into the basic premium.

An additional factor to consider when choosing between a paid loss and an incurred loss retrospective rating plan is the additional administrative tasks associated with a paid loss retrospective plan. The next section describes these tasks, as well as other administrative responsibilities of the insured organization under a retrospective rating insurance plan.

ADMINISTRATION OF RETROSPECTIVE RATING PLANS

Retrospective rating plans require the insured organization to perform only a moderate amount of administration. Because they are based on insurance, the insurer, rather than the insured organization, is responsible for many of the administrative tasks, such as adjusting losses, making necessary filings with the state regulatory authorities, and paying applicable premium taxes and residual market loadings. The insured organization's responsibility is limited to making premium payments and arranging for any required security (collateral), such as letters of credit, to guarantee future loss payments under a paid loss retrospective rating plan.

Collateral Requirements

Paid loss retrospective rating plans enable the insured organization to retain funds until the insurer has actually paid the claimant. For many types of losses, particularly workers' compensation, for which some benefits are paid periodically over time, the contractual relationship between the insured organization and the insurer can last many years beyond the policy expiration. Consequently, insurers require the insured organization to provide collateral to guarantee that future premium adjustments will be paid. Examples of acceptable forms of collateral include letters of credit, certificates of deposit, or first rights to an escrow account.

Maintaining collateral can be expensive and time consuming for the insured organization. For example, banks charge a fee for providing a letter of credit, even if the credit promised is never accessed. The cost of the letter of credit is relative to the credit worthiness of the insured organization and the bank's expectation that it will be used. Letters of credit need to be periodically renewed, particularly for long-term commitments typical of the obligations the insured organization assumes under a retrospective rating plan. As the insured organization uses retrospective rating plans over a period of years, the risk management professional needs to keep track of a letter of credit for each policy term. Consequently, maintaining a retrospective rating plan involves expenses and administrative work that are not present when guaranteed-cost insurance is used.

Financial Accounting Issues

For financial accounting purposes, an organization must recognize its retained losses as they are incurred. Therefore, it follows that an organization using a retrospective rating plan should recognize any future premium payments that are due based on current retained losses that have been incurred. These payments must be posted as a liability on the organization's balance sheet and charged as an expense on its income statement.

For example, assume that an organization pays a deposit premium for an incurred loss retrospective rating plan and discovers at the end of the policy period that its incurred losses are much higher than expected. When it prepares its next set of financial statements, the organization should recognize the additional premium that is due at the next adjustment by using the retrospective rating plan premium formula and applying it to the incurred losses. The higher-than-expected incurred losses create an obligation (liability) on the insured organization's part.

With a paid loss retrospective rating plan, premium payments are based on paid rather than incurred losses. However, for financial accounting purposes, the insured organization must calculate what the premium would be at any time if incurred losses rather than paid losses were used. The difference between the amount of premium using incurred losses and the amount currently paid should be recognized as a liability on the organization's balance sheet and as an expense on its income statement.

With either type of retrospective rating plan, an organization may need to recognize an amount for incurred but not reported (IBNR) retained losses. If an IBNR amount can be estimated with reasonable accuracy, then the organization should use it when applying the retrospective rating insurance premium formula to its losses. The insured organization should include any additional premium resulting from IBNR losses as a liability on its balance sheet and as an expense on its income statement.

Tax Treatment

An important tax issue for risk financing is the timing of expense deductions from an organization's taxable income. In general, under a retrospective rating plan, an organization can take a tax deduction on premiums when they are paid. Therefore, an incurred loss retrospective rating plan, in effect, allows an organization to deduct its reserves for the retained portion of its losses, because premiums are paid based on incurred losses. This favorable timing of the tax deduction helps offset some of the cash flow disadvantage of paying premium based on incurred rather than paid losses. A paid loss retrospective rating plan does not allow an organization to deduct funds set aside for retained losses because, in general, premiums are paid, and therefore deductible for tax purposes, only when losses are paid.

Exit Strategy

As with guaranteed-cost insurance, an insured organization can terminate a retrospective rating plan at any time, although a financial penalty may apply if the insurance policy is cancelled before its normal termination date. Because the final retrospective rating plan premium is subject to adjustment, particularly with a paid loss retrospective rating plan, terminating a retrospective rating plan is more cumbersome than terminating a guaranteed-cost insurance plan.

Because retrospective rating plans are insurance plans, they are easy to administer relative to other risk financing plans. The extent to which retrospective rating plans are not considered an administrative burden should be weighed along with the advantage and disadvantage of retrospective rating plans.

ADVANTAGES AND DISADVANTAGES OF RETROSPECTIVE RATING PLANS

Because they are hybrid risk financing plans, retrospective rating plans have many of the advantages and disadvantages of both retention and transfer. The degree to which these advantages and disadvantages apply to a specific retrospective rating plan depends on the plan's design—that is, the degree of retention versus the degree of transfer built into the plan.

Advantages

One advantage of retention is that its long-run cost tends to be lower than the cost of transfer. By retaining a portion of losses under a retrospective rating plan, rather than transferring all losses under a guaranteed-cost insurance plan, an organization can save certain expenses. One significant expense saved is insurer risk charges, which are extra charges that an insurer includes as part of its guaranteed-cost premium to cover the chance that losses will be higher than expected. In addition, savings result from the cash flow gained by retaining losses under a paid loss retrospective rating plan.

Retrospective rating plans also encourage risk control. With a retrospective rating plan, an organization that is able to reduce its losses quickly realizes a premium savings compared with what it would pay under a guaranteed-cost insurance plan. This direct link between losses and premium is a major incentive for an insured organization to control its losses.

If designed properly, a retrospective rating plan also provides many of the advantages of risk transfer. If the loss limit and the maximum premium are set to reduce the uncertainty of the insured organization's retrospective rating plan premium adjustments to a level it can tolerate, then the insured organization benefits from the relative stability that the retrospective rating plan provides in earnings, net worth, and cash flow. A retrospective rating plan that covers more than one type of loss exposure provides stability through diversification by allowing the insured organization to retain losses from different types of loss exposures under a single plan.

Disadvantages

If a retrospective rating plan is not properly designed, it can make financial planning difficult for the insured organization. For example, if the loss limit and maximum premium are set at a high level, the insured organization may not be able to tolerate the uncertainty created by the possibility of upward premium adjustments that reduce its earnings, net worth, and cash flow.

If the insurer sets unrealistically high reserves for the retained portion of losses, the insured organization would pay a premium based on inflated loss reserve figures, resulting in a loss of cash flow, an additional disadvantage with a retrospective rating plan. Under this scenario, the premium would eventually be adjusted downward as losses are paid, because the inflated loss reserves would be eliminated. In the meantime, however, the insurer would have use of the insured organization's funds.

An objection raised to retrospective rating plans is that an insurer may not diligently adjust losses when it knows the insured organization is retaining them, resulting in loss payments that are higher than necessary. However, insurers contend that they adjust claims similarly regardless of the type of plan and that the claim representative for a specific loss typically has no knowledge of the type of plan involved.

Another disadvantage of retrospective rating plans is that the losses that the insured organization ultimately retains are initially paid to the insurer as a premium. Because the insured organization pays them as "premium," the losses must be increased so that the insurer can pay premium taxes and residual market loadings. Premium taxes and residual market loadings add expenses to retrospective rating plans that do not exist with every risk financing plan.

Ultimately, each organization must weigh these advantages and disadvantages when deciding whether a retrospective rating plan is the most appropriate means to finance risk. The organization in the following case study focuses on factors important to it and chooses to use a retrospective rating plan.

CASE STUDY IN RETROSPECTIVE RATING PLAN DESIGN

The following case study illustrates the application of a retrospective rating plan to a specific situation. The proposed plans outlined are realistic for the circumstances shown, but are not necessarily the only retrospective options appropriate for the hypothetical organization. Two caveats should be kept in mind when reading these cases. First, retrospective rating plan design is a function of insurance marketplace conditions and is influenced by who is assisting the risk management professional in developing the program. Second, retrospective rating plan design is usually based on an in-depth analysis of the insured organization's historical loss experience and financial condition, as well as such subjective factors as senior management's risk aversion.

Etchley Manufacturing (Etchley) makes high-end bedding—sheets, bedspreads, and comforters, which it sells primarily to the major hotel chains. Last year, Etchley sold its subsidiary that manufactured baby cribs. Although other economic factors contributed to the sale, one key factor was the lawsuits brought against Etchley for design defects that resulted in bodily injury to children. Etchley's management structured the terms of the subsidiary's sale so that any future lawsuits would be the responsibility of its new owners.

Etchley's management is concerned that its adverse past loss experience will be part of its loss experience for several more years and has asked its risk management professional to investigate alternatives to its guaranteed-cost insurance plan that may meet its risk financing goals. Because Etchley's management is relatively risk-averse, the risk management professional decides to compare Etchley's current insurance plan with a retrospective rating plan.

Etchley's risk management professional identifies the following four steps in evaluating retrospective rating plans relative to its guaranteed-cost insurance plan:

1. *Determine which coverages to include in the retrospective rating plan.* Etchley's risk management professional immediately identifies its workers' compensation loss exposure, because its associated losses are relatively stable. Etchley's risk management professional also considers including its general liability loss exposure. Management is most concerned about this loss exposure, and it also offers the potential of a significant premium cost savings. If the retrospective rating plan is effective in reducing Etchley's cost of risk, the risk management professional may consider additional loss exposures in the future. However, the risk management professional recognizes that retrospective rating plans are usually used with workers' compensation, and that retrospective rating plans that combine loss exposures beyond workers' compensation, auto liability, and general liability are uncommon.

2. *Determine the limit to which the retrospective rating plan will apply.* The retrospective rating plan can apply to the total policy limit or a lesser amount. For example, Etchley may have a $1 million limit for its general liability coverage but may choose to apply the retrospective rating plan to a $250,000 limit. Selecting a lower limit to which to apply the retrospective rating plan is not an option with retrospective rating plans that apply to worker's compensation. Workers' compensation coverage is provided without coverage limits because state statutes specify benefits. Etchley's risk management professional decides to apply the retrospective rating plan to the total coverage limit of its general liability coverage, or $1 million.

3. *Determine the loss limitation, if any.* Etchley's standard premium is large enough to permit a loss limitation. Etchley's risk management professional decides that purchasing a loss limit is prudent because it mitigates the losses included in the retrospective rating plan formula and, consequently, the final retrospective rating plan premium. Etchley's risk management professional considers three loss limitations that apply on a per accident basis: $200,000, $300,000, and $250,000.

4. *Determine the maximum and minimum premiums.* Etchley's risk management professional wants several maximum and minimum premium combinations to evaluate with various expected loss scenarios to present to management. A high maximum premium and a high minimum premium should result in a relatively low basic premium because of the smaller insurance charge that results. Conversely, a low maximum premium and a low minimum premium should result in a relatively high basic premium.

Etchley's insurer will likely want a maximum premium that is large enough to cover expected losses as well as some cushion in case losses are greater than expected. Etchley's risk management professional is unwilling to select a high maximum premium because Etchley's management is risk-averse and already concerned about rising insurance costs. Maximum premium factors generally range from 100 percent (a factor of 1.00) to 150 percent (a factor of 1.50).

Selecting a minimum premium is not as cumbersome, because the insurer simply charges more for the lower minimum. Some insurers allow insured organizations to purchase a retrospective rating plan with a minimum that covers the product of the basic premium and the tax multiplier. Minimum premium factors generally range from 60 percent (a factor of 0.60) to 25 percent (a factor of 0.25).

Etchley's risk management professional researches Etchley's options and develops a proposal. Exhibit 6-7 compares the three proposed retrospective rating plan alternatives.

Etchley's risk management professional can now present four options to management. Etchley's guaranteed cost insurance premium is determined to be $1.2 million. The other options shown in Exhibit 6-7 need to be considered relative to management's expectation for losses.

Etchley's management should evaluate these options while considering its past loss experience. Exhibit 6-7 shows what Etchley's premiums would be for three levels of losses—$600,000, $800,000, and $1,000,000. If, for example, Etchley's management could predict that its losses would be $600,000 or less, then the retrospective rating plan with the $300,000 loss limitation would be the most economical choice. However, the uncertainty of ultimate losses makes plan selection challenging.

EXHIBIT 6-7

Comparison of Etchley's Retrospective Rating Plan Alternatives

Loss limitation	$200,000 each accident	$300,000 each accident	$250,000 each accident
Plan factors:			
Basic	0.375	0.325	0.360
Tax multiplier	1.090	1.090	1.085
Loss conversion factor	1.110	1.120	1.090
Maximum premium	1.500	1.814	1.500
Minimum premium	Basic x tax	0.35425	0.500
Estimated premiums:			
Excess loss premiums	$25,000	$15,000	$22,500
Standard premiums	$1,200,000	$1,200,000	$1,200,000
Estimated program cost			
Minimum premium	**$490,500**	**$425,100**	**$600,000**
@ $600,000 losses	$1,243,690	$1,173,930	$1,202,723
@ $800,000 losses	$1,485,670	$1,418,090	$1,439,253
@ $1,000,000 losses	$1,727,650	$1,662,250	$1,675,783
Maximum premium	**$1,800,000**	**$2,176,800**	**$1,800,000**
Other factors	Pay-in: 12 monthly payments @ $103,453	Pay-in: 12 monthly payments @ $97,715	Pay-in: 12 monthly payments @ $100,068

SUMMARY

Retrospective rating plans provide an alternative means for pricing guaranteed-cost insurance coverage. Because a retrospective rating plan contains elements of risk retention and risk transfer, it is considered a hybrid risk financing plan. Unlike guaranteed-cost insurance program pricing, retrospective rating plans respond almost immediately to improvements, as well as deterioration, in the insured organization's loss experience.

A retrospective rating plan is a hybrid risk financing plan in which an organization buys insurance subject to a rating plan that adjusts the premium after the end of the policy period based on a portion of the insured organization's actual losses during the policy period. The purpose of a retrospective rating plan is to adjust the premium for guaranteed-cost insurance to reflect the insured organization's current losses. Organizations commonly use retrospective rating plans for losses arising from their liability loss exposures that are covered by workers' compensation, auto liability, and general liability insurance policies. Organizations can also use retrospective rating insurance plans to finance auto physical damage, crime, and glass losses. A single retrospective rating plan can be used for more than one type of loss exposure.

The adjusted premium under a retrospective rating plan is subject to a maximum amount and a minimum amount. The maximum premium is the most an insured organization will be required to pay under a retrospective rating plan regardless of the amount of incurred losses. The minimum premium is the amount charged the insured organization under a retrospective rating plan even if no losses occur. Provided the insured organization has a sufficiently large premium, the retrospective rating plan can be designed to cap losses and thereby minimize the insured organization's retention by using a loss limit. Loss limit is the level at which each individual accident or occurrence is limited for the purpose of calculating a retrospective rating insurance premium.

The formula for calculating premium (the retrospective rating plan premium formula) is as follows:

$$\text{Retrospective rating plan premium*} = \left(\text{Basic premium} + \text{Converted losses} + \text{Excess loss premium} \right) \times \text{Tax multiplier.}$$

*Subject to maximum and minimum amounts

An underlying component of the retrospective rating plan formula is standard premium. Standard premium is calculated by using state insurance department-authorized rating classifications, applying them to an insured organization's estimated exposures for the policy period, and allowing for various adjustments. The basic premium is a component of the retrospective rating insurance premium formula that covers insurer acquisition expenses, administrative costs, overhead, and profit, as well as the insurance charge. The insurance charge is a component of the basic premium that compensates the insurer for the risk that the calculated retrospective rating insurance premium may be higher than the maximum premium or lower than the minimum premium. Converted losses is a component of the retrospective rating insurance premium formula that is the product of incurred losses and an applicable loss conversion factor. A loss conversion factor is a factor that is applied to incurred losses so that the converted losses reflect loss settlement expenses. The excess loss premium is a component of the retrospective rating insurance premium formula that compensates the insurer for the risk that an individual loss will exceed the loss limit. The tax multiplier is a component of the retrospective rating insurance premium formula that covers the insurer's cost for state premium taxes, license fees, insurance advisory organization charges, and residual market loadings that the insurer must pay on all collected premiums.

An incurred loss retrospective rating plan is the type of retrospective rating plan generally offered by insurers. With it, the insured organization pays a deposit premium during the policy period; after the end of the policy period, the insurer adjusts the premium based on the insured organization's actual incurred losses. With paid loss retrospective rating plan, the insured organization pays a deposit premium at the beginning of the policy period and reimburses the insurer for its losses as the insurer pays for them and in which the total amount paid is subject to the minimum and maximum premiums. An insured organization should not automatically choose a paid loss plan over an incurred loss plan because the decision depends on the relationship between the amount that the insurer adds to the basic premium and the value of the cash flow benefit to the insured. Present value analysis should be used to compare the paid loss and incurred loss plans.

Retrospective rating plans require the insured organization to perform only a moderate amount of administration. The insured organization's responsibility is limited to making premium payments and arranging for any required security, such as letters of credit to guarantee future loss payments under a paid loss retrospective rating plan. Consequently, insurers require the insured organization to provide collateral to guarantee that future premium adjustments will be paid.

For financial accounting purposes, an organization must recognize its retained losses as they are incurred. Therefore, it follows that an organization that uses a retrospective rating plan should recognize any future premium payments that will be due based on current retained losses that have been incurred. These amounts must be posted as a liability on the organization's balance sheet and charged as an expense on its income statement.

Risk management professionals should weigh the advantages and disadvantages of retrospective rating plans when considering the composition of their organization's insurance program. Another key component of the relationship between an insurer and an insured organization is the insurer's reinsurance provisions. Understanding how reinsurance affects an insurer's coverage is crucial to the decision to use insurance to finance risk.

CHAPTER NOTE

1. For workers' compensation, a retrospective rating plan also covers high-severity losses because a workers' compensation policy covers statutory benefits, which are theoretically unlimited in amount.

Chapter 7

Direct Your Learning

Reinsurance and Its Importance to a Risk Financing Program

After learning the content of this chapter and completing the corresponding course guide assignment, you should be able to:

- Describe the purpose of reinsurance.
- Describe the six functions of reinsurance.
- Describe treaty reinsurance and facultative reinsurance.
- Describe the three sources of reinsurance.
- Describe the following types of pro rata reinsurance and their uses:
  - Quota share reinsurance
  - Surplus share reinsurance
- Given a case, determine how the primary insurer and the reinsurer would share the amount of insurance, the premium, and covered losses under quota share and surplus share treaties.
- Describe the following types of excess of loss reinsurance:
  - Per risk excess of loss reinsurance
  - Catastrophe excess of loss reinsurance
  - Per policy excess of loss reinsurance
  - Per occurrence excess of loss reinsurance
  - Aggregate excess of loss reinsurance
- Given a case, determine how the primary insurer and the reinsurer would share losses under per risk excess of loss, catastrophe excess of loss, per policy excess of loss, per occurrence excess of loss, and aggregate excess of loss treaties.
- Describe the characteristics of finite risk reinsurance.
- Explain the reinsurance concerns of risk management professionals.
- Given a case, identify how an organization may benefit from their insurer's use of reinsurance or the use of reinsurance with its captive insurer.
- Define or describe each of the Key Words and Phrases for this chapter.

Develop Your Perspective

What are the main topics covered in the chapter?

This chapter describes how reinsurance operates to finance risk. Reinsurance can be thought of in general terms as "insurance for insurers." However, reinsurance enables insurers to achieve specific functions. This chapter focuses on these functions and how they are fulfilled by various types of reinsurance.

Rank the functions of reinsurance in importance to your organization.

- How does the insurer's large-line capacity support your organization's insurance program?

- Describe a situation in which your organization's captive insurer may benefit from the advice (underwriting guidance) of a reinsurer.

Why is it important to learn about these topics?

Reinsurance enables insurers to share risk with others.

Consider the types of reinsurance.

- What type of reinsurance transaction would most likely be used by a captive insurer?

How can you use what you will learn?

Evaluate your organization's use, if any, of reinsurance.

- Has your organization ever requested a cut-through endorsement?

- Does your organization participate in a pool?

Chapter 7
Reinsurance and Its Importance to a Risk Financing Program

Every insured organization depends on the financial stability of its commercial insurers. Because commercial insurers usually rely on reinsurance to mitigate the potentially adverse effects of a single large loss or a number of smaller losses, any disruption to an insurer's reinsurance network, such as the bankruptcy of a major reinsurer, can, in turn, threaten an organization's risk financing program. Risk management professionals may not be fully familiar with their commercial insurer's reinsurance program. However, because reinsurance is essentially "insurance for insurers," they do need to be aware of reinsurance's importance as a financial safeguard to insurers. The risk management professional should first understand the concepts underlying the operation of reinsurance in order to assess how reinsurance marketing systems, reinsurance functions, and reinsurance types affect the organization's insurer.

REINSURANCE DEFINED

Reinsurance is the transfer of insurance risk from one insurer to another through a contractual agreement under which one insurer (the **reinsurer**) agrees, in return for a **reinsurance premium**, to indemnify another insurer (the **primary insurer**) for some or all of the financial consequences of certain loss exposures covered by the primary insurer's policies.[1] Reinsurance is commonly referred to as "insurance for insurers."

This text uses the term primary insurer. However, the primary insurer may also be referred to as the ceding company, the cedent, the reinsured, or the direct insurer. An insurer can also be both a primary insurer and a reinsurer.

Insurance risk is uncertainty about the adequacy of insurance premiums to pay losses. The reinsurer typically does not assume all of the primary insurer's insurance risk. The reinsurance agreement usually requires the primary insurer to retain part of its original liability. The retention can be expressed as a percentage of the original amount of insurance or as a dollar amount of loss. The reinsurance agreement does not alter the terms of the underlying (original) insurance policies or the primary insurer's obligations to honor them.

Reinsurance
The transfer of insurance risk from one insurer to another through a contractual agreement under which one insurer (the reinsurer) agrees, in return for a reinsurance premium, to indemnify another insurer (the primary insurer) for some or all of the financial consequences of certain loss exposures covered by the primary insurer's policies.

Reinsurer
The insurer that assumes all or part of the insurance risk from the primary insurer.

Reinsurance premium
The consideration paid by the primary insurer to the reinsurer for assuming some or all of the primary insurer's insurance risk.

Primary insurer
The insurer that transfers or cedes all or part of the insurance risk it has assumed to another insurer.

Insurance risk
Uncertainty about the adequacy of insurance premiums to pay losses.

The reinsurance agreement specifies the terms under which the reinsurance is provided. For example, the reinsurance agreement may state that the reinsurer must pay a percentage of all the primary insurer's losses for loss exposures subject to the agreement or must reimburse the primary insurer for losses that exceed a specified amount. Additionally, the reinsurance agreement identifies the policy, group of policies, or other categories of insurance that are included in the agreement.

Reinsurers may transfer part of the liability they have accepted in reinsurance agreements to other reinsurers. Such an agreement is called a retrocession. A **retrocession** is a reinsurance agreement whereby one reinsurer (the retrocedent) transfers all or part of the reinsurance risk it has assumed or will assume to another reinsurer (the retrocessionaire).

Retrocession
A reinsurance agreement whereby one reinsurer (the retrocedent) transfers all or part of the reinsurance risk it has assumed or will assume to another reinsurer (the retrocessionaire).

Retrocession is similar to reinsurance except for the parties involved in the agreement. This text discusses reinsurance in the context of a primary insurer-reinsurer relationship, but this discussion applies equally to retrocessions.

REINSURANCE FUNCTIONS

Reinsurance performs six principal functions for primary insurers. A primary insurer may use several different reinsurance agreements to achieve these functions. This section discusses each of the following functions separately:

1. Increase large line capacity
2. Provide catastrophe protection
3. Stabilize loss experience
4. Provide surplus relief
5. Facilitate withdrawal from a market segment
6. Provide underwriting guidance

Increase Large Line Capacity

Line
The maximum amount of insurance or limit of liability that an insurer will accept on a single loss exposure.

The maximum amount of insurance or limit of liability that an insurer will accept on a single loss exposure is called the insurer's **line**. This line is influenced by the following:

- The maximum amount of insurance or limit of liability allowed by insurance regulations. Insurance regulations prohibit an insurer from retaining (after reinsurance, usually stated as net of reinsurance) more than 10 percent of its policyholders' surplus (net worth) on any one loss exposure.
- The size of a potential loss or losses an insurer can safely retain without impairing its earnings or policyholders' surplus.
- The specific characteristics of a particular loss exposure. For example, for some insurers, the line may vary depending on property attributes such as construction, occupancy, loss prevention features, and loss reduction features.
- The amount, types, and cost of available reinsurance.

Large line capacity is an insurer's ability to provide larger amounts of insurance for property loss exposures, or higher limits of liability for liability loss exposures, than it is otherwise willing to provide.

Reinsurers provide primary insurers with large line capacity by accepting liability for loss exposures that the primary insurer is unwilling or unable to retain. This function of reinsurance allows insurers with *limited* large line capacity to participate more fully in the insurance marketplace. For example, a primary insurer may want to compete for homeowner policies in markets in which the value of the homes exceeds the amount the primary insurer feels comfortable retaining. Reinsurance allows the primary insurer to increase its market share while limiting the financial consequences of potential losses.

Provide Catastrophe Protection

Primary insurers use reinsurance to protect themselves from the financial consequences of a single catastrophic event causing multiple losses. Potential catastrophic causes of loss include fire, windstorm (hurricane, tornado, and other wind damage), and earthquakes. Other catastrophes, such as industrial explosions, airplane crashes, or product recalls, could result in significant property and liability losses. Unless appropriate reinsurance is in place, catastrophes could greatly reduce insurer earnings or even threaten insurer solvency. Purchasing reinsurance for catastrophe protection is one way that primary insurers stabilize their loss experience.

Stabilize Loss Experience

Loss experience typically fluctuates from year to year, creating variability in insurer financial results. Volatile loss experience may do the following:

- Affect the stock value of a publicly traded insurer[2]
- Alter an insurer's financial rating by independent rating agencies
- Cause abrupt changes in the approaches the insurer takes in managing the underwriting, claim, and marketing departments
- Undermine the confidence of the sales force (especially independent agents who can place their customers with other insurers)
- Possibly lead to insolvency

Therefore, insurers prefer to have stable loss experience. Using reinsurance can help maintain stability. Reinsurance can be arranged to stabilize the loss experience of a type of insurance (for example, commercial auto), a class of business (for example, truckers), or all the insurance that a primary insurer sells. A primary insurer can stabilize loss experience by obtaining reinsurance to do any, or all, of the following:

- Limit its liability for a single loss exposure
- Limit its liability for several loss exposures affected by a common event
- Limit its liability for loss exposures that aggregate claims over time

Large line capacity
An insurer's ability to provide larger amounts of insurance for property loss exposures, or higher limits of liability for liability loss exposures, than it is otherwise willing to provide.

Stabilizing loss experience is a major function of reinsurance because it aids financial planning and supports growth. It also may encourage capital investment, because investors are more likely to invest in companies with stable financial results. Exhibit 7-1 shows how reinsurance can stabilize a primary insurer's loss experience.

EXHIBIT 7-1

Stabilization of Annual Loss Experience for a Primary Insurer With a $20 Million Retention

(1)	(2)	(3)	(4)
	Actual	**Amount**	**Stabilized**
Time Period	**Losses**	**Reinsured**	**Loss Level**
(Year)	**($000)**	**($000)**	**($000)**
1	15,000	—	15,000
2	35,000	15,000	20,000
3	13,000	—	13,000
4	25,000	5,000	20,000
5	40,000	20,000	20,000
6	37,000	17,000	20,000
7	16,500	—	16,500
8	9,250	—	9,250
9	18,000	—	18,000
10	10,750	—	10,750
Total	$219,500	$57,000	$162,500

The total actual losses are $219.5 million, or an average of $21.95 million each period. If a reinsurance agreement were in place to cap losses to $20 million, the primary insurer's loss experience would be limited to the amounts shown in the stabilized loss level column. The broken line that fluctuates dramatically in the graph below represents actual losses, the dotted line represents stabilized losses, and the horizontal line represents average losses.

Graph of Hypothetical Loss Data

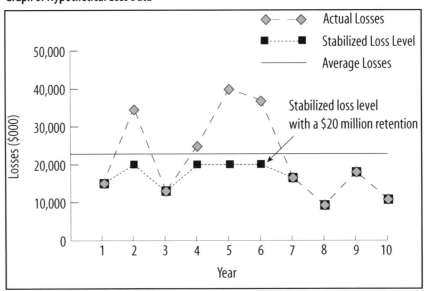

Provide Surplus Relief

During periods of rapid growth, insurers may struggle to meet the policyholders' surplus requirements imposed by insurance regulators. **Policyholders' surplus** is an insurer's net worth as reported on the financial statement prescribed by state insurance regulators. The value of the policyholders' surplus is the amount by which assets exceed liabilities and represents the financial resource the primary insurer can draw on to pay unexpected losses. Policyholders' surplus is also called surplus to policyholders or simply surplus. State insurance regulators expect an insurer's ratio of net written premiums to policyholders' surplus not to exceed 3 to 1 ($3 in net written premiums for every $1 in policyholders' surplus).[3] **Net written premiums** are the gross premiums charged to policyholders minus the premiums ceded to reinsurers plus reinsurance premiums assumed. The ratio of net written premiums to policyholders' surplus is called the **capacity ratio** (also called the leverage ratio).

From an insurance regulator's perspective, if an insurer's capacity ratio reaches or exceeds 3 to 1, the insurer is selling more insurance than is prudent relative to the size of its net worth. Although the net written premiums should be sufficient to satisfy those liabilities, they may not be.

Insurers that are growing rapidly may have difficulty maintaining a desirable capacity ratio because of how they must account for their expenses to acquire new policies. State insurance regulation mandates that, for accounting purposes, such expenses be recognized at the time a new policy is sold. Aggravating this situation is the requirement that insurers are required to recognize premiums as revenue only as they are earned over the policy's life. Immediately recognizing expenses combined with gradually recognizing revenue causes an insurer's policyholders' surplus to decrease and the capacity ratio to increase.

Some reinsurance agreements facilitate premium growth by allowing the primary insurer to deduct a ceding commission on premiums ceded to the reinsurer. The **ceding commission** is an amount paid by the reinsurer to the primary insurer to cover part or all of a primary insurer's policy acquisition expenses. The ceding commission immediately offsets the primary insurer's policy acquisition expenses for the reinsured policies and often includes a profit provision, or an additional commission, if the reinsurance ceded is profitable.

This function of reinsurance is called **surplus relief** because the ceding commission replenishes the primary insurer's policyholders' surplus. Consequently, the surplus relief facilitates the primary insurer's premium growth and the increase in policyholders' surplus lowers its capacity ratio.

Policyholders' surplus
An insurer's net worth as reported on the financial statement prescribed by state insurance regulators.

Net written premiums
The gross premiums charged to policyholders minus the premiums ceded to reinsurers plus reinsurance premiums assumed.

Capacity ratio
The ratio of net written premiums to policyholders' surplus.

Ceding commission
An amount paid by the reinsurer to the primary insurer to cover part or all of a primary insurer's policy acquisition expenses.

Surplus relief
A replenishment of policyholders' surplus provided by the ceding commission paid to the primary insurer by the reinsurer.

Facilitate Withdrawal From a Market Segment

A market segment may be a particular class of business, a geographic area, or a type of insurance. A primary insurer may want to withdraw from a market segment that is unprofitable, is undesirable, or does not fit into its strategic plan. When withdrawing from a market segment, the primary insurer has the following options:

- Stop selling new insurance policies and continue in-force insurance until all policies expire (often referred to as "run-off")
- Cancel all policies (if insurance regulations permit), and refund the unearned premiums to insureds
- Withdraw from the market segment by purchasing portfolio reinsurance

Portfolio reinsurance
A reinsurance agreement that reinsures the loss exposures of an entire type of insurance, class of business, or geographic area.

Portfolio reinsurance reinsures the loss exposures of an entire type of insurance, class of business, or geographic area. Such groupings of loss exposures are often called portfolios. Portfolio reinsurance is a way to facilitate withdrawal from a market segment. It is an exception to the general rule that reinsurers do not accept all of the liability for specified loss exposures of an insurer. In portfolio reinsurance, the reinsurer accepts all the liability for certain loss exposures covered under the primary insurer's policies. However, the primary insurer must continue to fulfill its obligations to its insureds. For example, the primary insurer may decide to use portfolio reinsurance to withdraw from the errors and omissions insurance market. In this situation, the reinsurer typically agrees to indemnify the primary insurer for all losses incurred as of, and following, the date of the portfolio reinsurance agreement. However, the primary insurer continues to pay claims to (or on behalf of) its insureds who are covered by the underlying insurance.

Portfolio reinsurance can be expensive, particularly if the portfolio has been unprofitable and is expected to incur additional losses for the reinsurer. In many states, portfolio reinsurance must be approved by the state insurance department.

Novation
An agreement under which one insurer or reinsurer is substituted for another.

Sometimes a primary insurer wants to completely eliminate the liabilities it has assumed under the insurance policies it has issued. This can be accomplished through a novation. A **novation** is an agreement under which one insurer or reinsurer is substituted for another. A novation is not considered portfolio reinsurance because the substitute insurer assumes the direct obligations to insureds covered by the underlying insurance. Usually, either state insurance regulators' approval or the insured's approval is required to effect a novation.

Provide Underwriting Guidance

Reinsurers work with a wide variety of insurers in many different circumstances. Consequently, reinsurers accumulate a great deal of underwriting expertise. A reinsurer's understanding of insurance operations and the insurance industry can assist other insurers, particularly inexperienced primary insurers entering into new markets and offering new products. For example, one medium-sized insurer reinsured 95 percent of its umbrella liability coverage over a period of years and relied heavily on the reinsurer for technical assistance in underwriting and pricing its policies. Without such technical assistance, certain primary insurers would find it difficult to generate underwriting profits from coverages with which they have limited expertise.

REINSURANCE TRANSACTIONS

The two types of reinsurance transactions are treaty and facultative. In **treaty reinsurance**, the agreement covers an entire class or portfolio of loss exposures and provides that the primary insurer's individual loss exposures that fall within the treaty are automatically reinsured. Treaty reinsurance is also called obligatory reinsurance. The reinsurance agreement is typically called the treaty.

In **facultative reinsurance**, the reinsurer underwrites each loss exposure separately. The primary insurer chooses which loss exposures to submit to the reinsurer, and the reinsurer can accept or reject any loss exposures submitted. Facultative reinsurance is also called nonobligatory reinsurance. This section discusses each type of reinsurance transaction.

Treaty Reinsurance

In treaty reinsurance, the reinsurer agrees in advance to reinsure all the loss exposures that fall within the treaty. Although some treaties allow the reinsurer limited discretion in reinsuring individual loss exposures, most treaties require that all loss exposures within the treaty's terms be reinsured.

Primary insurers usually use treaty reinsurance as the foundation of their reinsurance programs. Treaty reinsurance provides primary insurers with the certainty needed to formulate underwriting policy and develop underwriting guidelines. Primary insurers work with reinsurance intermediaries (or with reinsurers directly) to develop comprehensive reinsurance programs that address the primary insurers' varied needs. The reinsurance programs that satisfy those needs often include several reinsurance agreements and the participation of several reinsurers.

Treaty reinsurance agreements are tailored to fit the primary insurer's individual requirements. The price and terms of each reinsurance treaty are individually negotiated.

Treaty reinsurance agreements are usually designed to address a primary insurer's need to reinsure many loss exposures over a period of time. Although the reinsurance agreement's term may be for only one year, the relationship between the primary insurer and the reinsurer often spans many years. A primary insurer's management usually finds that a long-term relationship with a reinsurer enables the primary insurer to consistently fulfill its producers' requests to place insurance with them.

Treaty reinsurance
A reinsurance agreement that covers an entire class or portfolio of loss exposures and provides that the primary insurer's individual loss exposures that fall within the treaty are automatically reinsured.

Facultative reinsurance
Reinsurance of individual loss exposures in which the primary insurer chooses which loss exposures to submit to the reinsurer, and the reinsurer can accept or reject any loss exposures submitted.

Most, but not all, treaty reinsurance agreements *require* the primary insurer to cede all eligible loss exposures to the reinsurer. Primary insurers usually make treaty reinsurance agreements so their underwriters do not have to exercise discretion in using reinsurance. If treaty reinsurance agreements permitted primary insurers to choose which loss exposures they ceded to the reinsurer, the reinsurer would be exposed to adverse selection. **Adverse selection** occurs when the primary insurer decides to reinsure those loss exposures that have an increased probability of loss because the retention of those loss exposures is undesirable.

> **Adverse selection**
> The decision to reinsure those loss exposures that have an increased probability of loss because the retention of those loss exposures is undesirable.

Because treaty reinsurers are obligated to accept ceded loss exposures once the reinsurance agreement is in place, reinsurers usually want to know about the integrity and experience of the primary insurer's management and the degree to which the primary insurer's published underwriting guidelines represent its actual underwriting practices.

Facultative Reinsurance

In facultative reinsurance, the primary insurer negotiates a separate reinsurance agreement for each loss exposure it wants to reinsure. The primary insurer is not obligated to purchase reinsurance, and the reinsurer is not obligated to reinsure loss exposures submitted to it. A facultative reinsurance agreement is written for a specified period and cannot be canceled by either party unless contractual obligations, such as payment of premiums, are not met.

> **Facultative certificate of reinsurance**
> An agreement that defines the terms of the facultative reinsurance coverage on a specific loss exposure.

The reinsurer issues a facultative certificate of insurance that is attached to the primary insurer's copy of the policy being reinsured. The **facultative certificate of reinsurance** is an agreement that defines the terms of the facultative reinsurance coverage on a specific loss exposure.

Facultative reinsurance serves the following four functions:

1. Facultative reinsurance can provide large line capacity for loss exposures that exceed the limits of treaty reinsurance agreements.
2. Facultative reinsurance can reduce the primary insurer's exposure in a given geographic area. For example, a marine underwriter may be considering underwriting numerous shiploads of cargo that are stored in the same warehouse and that belong to different insureds. The underwriter could use facultative reinsurance for some of those loss exposures, thereby reducing the primary insurer's overall exposure to loss.
3. Facultative reinsurance can insure a loss exposure with atypical hazard characteristics and thereby maintain the favorable loss experience of the primary insurer's treaty reinsurance and any associated profit-sharing arrangements. Maintaining favorable treaty loss experience is important because the reinsurer has underwritten and priced the treaty with certain expectations. A loss exposure that is inconsistent with the primary insurer's typical portfolio of insurance policies may cause excessive losses and lead to the treaty's termination or a price increase.

The treaty reinsurer is usually willing for the primary insurer to remove high-hazard loss exposures from the treaty by using facultative reinsurance. These facultative placements of atypical loss exposures also benefit the treaty reinsurer. For example, an insured under a commercial property policy may request coverage for an expensive fine arts collection that the primary insurer and its treaty reinsurer would not ordinarily want to cover. Facultative reinsurance of the fine arts collection would eliminate the underwriting concern by removing this loss exposure from the treaty. Often, the treaty reinsurer's own facultative reinsurance department provides this reinsurance. The facultative reinsurer knows that adverse selection occurs in facultative reinsurance. Consequently, the loss exposures submitted for reinsurance are likely to have an increased probability of loss. Therefore, facultative reinsurance is usually priced to reflect the likelihood of adverse selection.

4. Facultative reinsurance can insure particular classes of loss exposures that are excluded under treaty reinsurance.

Primary insurers purchase facultative reinsurance mainly to reinsure loss exposures that they do not typically insure or on exposures with high levels of underwriting risk. Consequently, primary insurers use facultative reinsurance for fewer of their loss exposures than they use for treaty insurance. Primary insurers that find they are increasingly using facultative reinsurance may want to review the adequacy of their treaty reinsurance.

The expense of placing facultative reinsurance can be high for both the primary insurer and the reinsurer. In negotiating facultative reinsurance, the primary insurer must provide extensive information about each loss exposure. Consequently, administrative costs are relatively high because the primary insurer must devote a significant amount of time to complete each cession and to notify the reinsurer of any endorsement, loss notice, or policy cancellation. Likewise, the reinsurer must underwrite and price each facultative submission.

REINSURANCE SOURCES

Reinsurance can be purchased from three sources: professional reinsurers; reinsurance departments of primary insurers; and reinsurance pools, syndicates, and associations.

Professional Reinsurers

A **professional reinsurer** is an insurer whose primary business purpose is serving other insurers' reinsurance needs. As do primary insurers, professional reinsurers interact with other insurers either directly or through intermediaries.

A **direct writing reinsurer** is a reinsurer whose employees deal directly with primary insurers. These reinsurers do not necessarily obtain all their business directly from primary insurers. Most direct writing reinsurers in the United

Professional reinsurer
An insurer whose primary business purpose is serving other insurers' reinsurance needs.

Direct writing reinsurer
A professional reinsurer whose employees deal directly with primary insurers.

States have broadened their marketing system by also soliciting reinsurance business through reinsurance intermediaries.

Reinsurance intermediary
A broker who negotiates reinsurance agreements between the primary insurer and one or more reinsurers.

A **reinsurance intermediary** is a broker who negotiates reinsurance agreements between the primary insurer and one or more reinsurers. Reinsurance intermediaries work with primary insurers to develop reinsurance programs that are then placed with reinsurers. A reinsurance intermediary generally represents the primary insurer and receives a brokerage commission—almost always from the reinsurer—for placing the reinsurance and performing other necessary services. These services may include disbursing reinsurance premiums among participating reinsurers and collecting loss amounts owed to the insurer.

The variety of professional reinsurers leads to differences in how those reinsurers are used and what they can offer. However, the following are some broad generalizations about professional reinsurers:

- Primary insurers dealing with direct writing reinsurers often use fewer reinsurers in their reinsurance program.

- Reinsurance intermediaries often use more than one reinsurer to develop the reinsurance program for a primary insurer.

- Reinsurance intermediaries can often help secure high coverage limits and catastrophe coverage.

- Reinsurance intermediaries usually have access to various reinsurance solutions from both domestic and international markets.

- Reinsurance intermediaries can usually obtain reinsurance under favorable terms and at a competitive price because they can determine prevailing market conditions and work repeatedly in this market with many primary insurers.

Regardless of their approach to marketing reinsurance, professional reinsurers extensively evaluate the primary insurer before entering into a reinsurance agreement. A treaty reinsurer underwrites the primary insurer as well as the loss exposures being ceded. In evaluating the primary insurer, the reinsurer gathers information about the primary insurer's financial strength by analyzing the primary insurer's financial statements or by using information developed by a financial rating service. Other information about the primary insurer may be obtained from state insurance department bulletins and the trade press. Just as the reinsurer should evaluate the primary insurer, the primary insurer should evaluate the reinsurer's claim-paying ability, reputation, and management competence before entering into the reinsurance agreement.

Reinsurers also consider the primary insurer's experience, reputation, and management. The reinsurer relies on the integrity of the primary insurer's management, and a relationship of trust must underlie any reinsurance agreement. Whether it involves a one-time facultative agreement or an ongoing treaty agreement, the relationship between the primary insurer and the reinsurer is considered to be one of "utmost good faith." This is because each party is obligated to and relies on the other for full disclosure of material facts about the subject of the agreement. It would be considered a breach of this duty of utmost good faith if the primary insurer withheld material facts relevant to the reinsurer's underwriting decision, intentionally underestimated prior losses, or failed to disclose hazardous conditions affecting loss exposures.

Reinsurance Departments of Primary Insurers

Another source of reinsurance is through the reinsurance departments of primary insurers. Some primary insurers also serve as reinsurers and provide treaty and facultative reinsurance. A primary insurer's reinsurance operations are usually separate from its primary insurance operations so that information from other insurers remains confidential.

A primary insurer may offer reinsurance to affiliated insurers, regardless of whether it offers reinsurance to unaffiliated insurers. Many primary insurers are groups of commonly owned insurance companies, and intragroup reinsurance agreements are used to balance the financial results of all insurers in the group. The use of intragroup reinsurance agreements does not preclude using professional reinsurers.

Reinsurance Pools, Syndicates, and Associations

Reinsurance also may be obtained through **reinsurance pools**, **syndicates**, and **associations**, which are groups of insurers that share the loss exposures of the group, usually through reinsurance.

Reinsurance pools, syndicates, and associations
Groups of insurers that share the loss exposures of the group, usually through reinsurance.

Some reinsurance pools, syndicates, and associations were formed by insurers whose reinsurance needs were not adequately met in the regular marketplace. Other reinsurance pools were formed to provide specialized insurance requiring underwriting and claim expertise that individual insurers did not have. Reinsurance intermediaries have also formed reinsurance pools to provide reinsurance to their clients.

A reinsurance pool, syndicate, or association may offer reinsurance only to its member companies. Alternatively, it may also accept loss exposures from nonmember companies. Some reinsurance pools restrict their operations to narrowly defined classes of business, while others reinsure most types of insurance.

REINSURANCE TYPES

Treaty and facultative reinsurance can also be subcategorized based on whether the liability for losses is shared proportionally (pro rata) or nonproportionally (excess of loss). Exhibit 7-2 shows the types of reinsurance and their relationships.

EXHIBIT 7-2

Types of Reinsurance

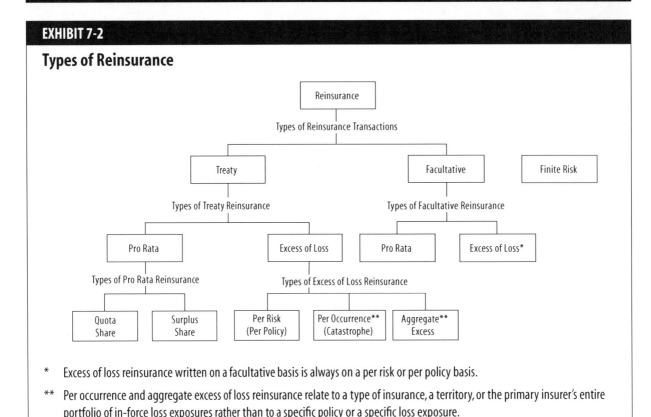

*   Excess of loss reinsurance written on a facultative basis is always on a per risk or per policy basis.

**   Per occurrence and aggregate excess of loss reinsurance relate to a type of insurance, a territory, or the primary insurer's entire portfolio of in-force loss exposures rather than to a specific policy or a specific loss exposure.

Reinsurance agreements are negotiated between a primary insurer and reinsurer. In many respects, each agreement is unique and its terms reflect the primary insurer's needs and the willingness of reinsurers in the marketplace to meet those needs. A primary insurer often uses several reinsurance agreements, which, when viewed together, constitute the primary insurer's reinsurance program.

Pro Rata Reinsurance

Pro rata reinsurance
A type of reinsurance in which the primary insurer and reinsurer proportionately share the amounts of insurance, policy premiums, and losses (including loss adjustment expenses).

Pro rata reinsurance is a type of reinsurance in which the primary insurer and reinsurer proportionately share the amounts of insurance, policy premiums, and losses (including loss adjustment expenses). Pro rata reinsurance is usually identified as one of two types: quota share or surplus share. For example, if the primary insurer shares 60 percent of the liability for each loss exposure with the reinsurer, then the reinsurer would be entitled to 60 percent of the policy premiums and would be responsible for 60 percent of each loss.

With pro rata reinsurance, the primary insurer cedes a portion of the original insurance premiums to the reinsurer as a reinsurance premium. The reinsurer usually pays the primary insurer a ceding commission for the loss exposures ceded. The ceding commission reimburses the primary insurer for policy acquisition expenses incurred when the underlying policies were sold. In addition to policy acquisition expenses, insurers incur **loss adjustment expenses**,

Loss adjustment expenses
Expenses incurred by an insurer to settle claims.

which are expenses incurred by an insurer required to settle claims. Loss adjustment expenses that can be related to a specific loss are usually shared proportionately by the primary insurer and the reinsurer.

The amount of the ceding commission paid to the primary insurer is usually negotiated. The primary insurer remits the reinsurance premium to the reinsurer net of the ceding commission. The ceding commission is referred to as a **flat commission**, which is a fixed percentage of the ceded premiums.

The reinsurance agreement may also include an additional commission, called a profit-sharing commission. A **profit-sharing commission** is a ceding commission that is contingent on the reinsurer realizing a predetermined percentage of excess profit on ceded loss exposures. The profit-sharing commission percentage is applied to the reinsurer's excess profits; that is, the profits remaining after losses, expenses, and the reinsurer's minimum margin for profit are deducted. Profit commission is also called contingent commission because its payment is contingent on the reinsurance agreement's profitability.

Sometimes, as an alternative to the flat commission and profit-sharing commission, the reinsurance agreement may contain a sliding scale commission. A **sliding scale commission** (in reinsurance) is a ceding commission based on a formula that adjusts the commission according to the profitability of the reinsurance agreement.

Quota Share Reinsurance

Quota share reinsurance is a type of pro rata reinsurance in which the primary insurer and the reinsurer share the amounts of insurance, policy premiums, and losses (including loss adjustment expenses) using a fixed percentage. For example, an insurer may arrange a reinsurance treaty in which it retains 45 percent of policy premiums, coverage limits, and losses while reinsuring the remaining amount. Because the reinsurer accepts 55 percent of the liability for each loss exposure subject to the treaty, such a treaty would be called a "55 percent quota share treaty." Quota share reinsurance can be used with both property insurance and liability insurance, but is more frequently used in property insurance.

Most reinsurance agreements specify a maximum dollar limit above which responsibility for additional coverage limits or losses reverts to the primary insurer (or is covered by another reinsurer). With a pro rata reinsurance agreement, that maximum dollar amount is stated in terms of the coverage limits of each policy subject to the treaty. For example, a primary insurer and a reinsurer may share amounts of insurance, policy premiums, and losses on a 45 percent and 55 percent basis respectively, subject to a $1 million maximum coverage amount for each policy.

In addition to a maximum coverage amount limitation, some pro rata reinsurance agreements include a per occurrence limit, which restricts the primary insurer's reinsurance recovery for losses originating from a single occurrence. This per occurrence limit may be stated as an aggregate dollar amount or as a loss ratio cap. **Loss ratio** is the ratio of incurred losses and

Flat commission
A ceding commission that is a fixed percentage of the ceded premiums.

Profit-sharing commission
A ceding commission that is contingent on the reinsurer realizing a predetermined percentage of excess profit on ceded loss exposures.

Sliding scale commission
(in reinsurance)
A ceding commission based on a formula that adjusts the commission according to the profitability of the reinsurance agreement.

Quota share reinsurance
A type of pro rata reinsurance in which the primary insurer and the reinsurer share the amounts of insurance, policy premiums, and losses (including loss adjustment expenses) using a fixed percentage.

Loss ratio
The ratio of incurred losses and loss adjustment expenses to earned premiums.

loss adjustment expenses to earned premiums. The per occurrence limit diminishes the usefulness of pro rata reinsurance in protecting the primary insurer from the effects of catastrophic events. Primary insurers exposed to catastrophic losses usually include catastrophe excess of loss reinsurance, described subsequently in this chapter, in their reinsurance programs.

EXHIBIT 7-3

Quota Share Reinsurance Example

Brookgreen Insurance Company has a quota share treaty with Cypress Reinsurer. The treaty has a $250,000 limit, a retention of 25 percent, and a cession of 75 percent. The following three policies are issued by Brookgreen Insurance Company and are subject to the pro rata treaty with Cypress Reinsurer.

- Policy A insures Building A for $25,000 for a premium of $400, with one loss of $8,000.
- Policy B insures Building B for $100,000 for a premium of $1,000, with one loss of $10,000.
- Policy C insures Building C for $150,000 for a premium of $1,500, with one loss of $60,000.

Division of Insurance, Premiums, and Losses Under Quota Share Treaty

	Brookgreen Insurance Retention (25%)	Cypress Reinsurance Cession (75%)	Total
Policy A			
Amounts of insurance	$6,250	$18,750	$25,000
Premiums	100	300	400
Losses	2,000	6,000	8,000
Policy B			
Amounts of insurance	$25,000	$75,000	$100,000
Premiums	250	750	1,000
Losses	2,500	7,500	10,000
Policy C			
Amounts of insurance	$37,500	$112,500	$150,000
Premiums	375	1,125	1,500
Losses	15,000	45,000	60,000

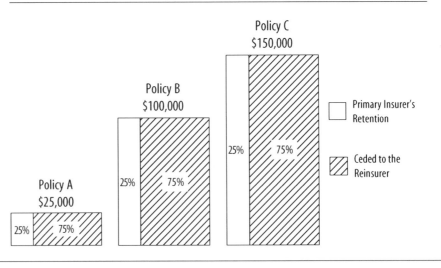

Quota share reinsurance agreements specify a fixed percentage that is applied to amounts of insurance, premiums, and losses.

Exhibit 7-3 shows how the amounts of insurance, policy premiums, and losses would be shared between a primary insurer and a reinsurer for three policies subject to their quota share treaty. These same examples are repeated in the subsequent discussion of surplus share reinsurance.

The following observations can be made about quota share reinsurance:

- As the retention and cession amounts are each a fixed percentage, the dollar amount of the retention and the dollar amount of the cession change as the amount of insurance changes. On policies with higher amounts of insurance, the primary insurer will have a higher dollar retention.

- Because the primary insurer cedes a fixed percentage under a quota share treaty, even policies with low amounts of insurance that the primary insurer could most likely safely retain are reinsured.

- Quota share treaties are straightforward to administer because of the fixed percentage used in sharing premiums and losses. The primary insurer can combine premium and loss amounts and quickly determine the amount owed to the reinsurer in premiums and the amount owed by the reinsurer in losses.

- Because the primary insurer and the reinsurer share liability for every loss exposure subject to a quota share treaty, the reinsurer is usually not subject to adverse selection. The loss ratio for the reinsurer is the same as that of the primary insurer for the ceded loss exposures.

A **variable quota share treaty** is a quota share reinsurance treaty in which the cession percentage retention varies based on specified predetermined criteria such as the amount of insurance needed. A variable quota share treaty has the advantage of enabling the primary insurer to retain a larger proportion of the small loss exposures that are within its financial capability to absorb, while maintaining a safer and smaller retention on larger loss exposures.

Variable quota share treaty
A quota share reinsurance treaty in which the cession percentage retention varies based on specified predetermined criteria such as the amount of insurance needed.

Surplus Share Reinsurance

Surplus share reinsurance is a type of pro rata reinsurance in which the policies covered are those whose amount of insurance exceeds a stipulated dollar amount, or line. When the amount of insurance exceeds the line, the reinsurer assumes the surplus share of the amount of insurance (the difference between the amount of insurance and the primary insurer's line). Surplus share reinsurance is typically used only with property insurance.

Surplus share reinsurance
A type of pro rata reinsurance in which the policies covered are those whose amount of insurance exceeds a stipulated dollar amount, or line.

The primary insurer and the reinsurer share the policy premiums and losses proportionately. The primary insurer's share of the policy premiums and losses is that proportion that the line bears to the total amount of insurance (the line plus the amount of insurance ceded). The reinsurer's share of the premiums and losses is the proportion that the amount ceded bears to the total. For example, if the line is $50,000 and the amount ceded is $200,000, the primary insurer would receive 20 percent ($50,000 ÷ $250,000) of the policy premium and pay 20 percent of all losses, and the reinsurer would receive 80 percent ($200,000 ÷ $250,000) of the policy premium and pay 80 percent of all losses. Exhibit 7-4 shows how an insurer and a reinsurer would share policy premiums, coverage limits, and losses under a surplus share treaty for the same three policies shown in Exhibit 7-3.

EXHIBIT 7-4

Surplus Share Reinsurance Example

Brookgreen Insurance Company has a surplus share treaty with Cypress Reinsurer and retains a line of $25,000. The treaty contains nine lines and provides for a maximum cession of $225,000. Therefore, the retention and reinsurance provide Brookgreen with the ability to issue policies with amounts of insurance as high as $250,000. The following three policies are issued by Brookgreen Insurance Company and are subject to the surplus share treaty with Cypress Reinsurer.

- Policy A insures Building A for $25,000 for a premium of $400, with one loss of $8,000.
- Policy B insures Building B for $100,000 for a premium of $1,000, with one loss of $10,000.
- Policy C insures Building C for $150,000 for a premium of $1,500, with one loss of $60,000.

Division of Insurance, Premiums, and Losses Under Surplus Share Treaty

	Brookgreen Insurance Retention	Cypress Reinsurance Cession	Total
Policy A			
Amounts of insurance	$25,000 (100%)	$0 (0%)	$25,000
Premiums	400	0	400
Losses	8,000	0	8,000
Policy B			
Amounts of insurance	$25,000 (25%)	$75,000 (75%)	$100,000
Premiums	250	750	1,000
Losses	2,500	7,500	10,000
Policy C			
Amounts of insurance	$25,000 (16.67%)	$125,000 (83.33%)	$150,000
Premiums	250	1,250	1,500
Losses	10,000	50,000	60,000

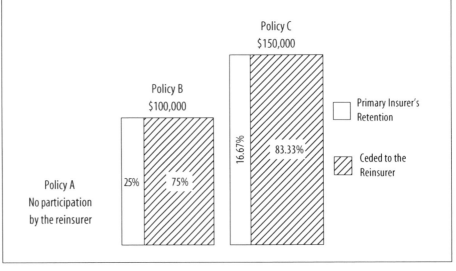

Surplus share reinsurance agreements use stipulated dollar amounts to determine if the treaty applies, and, if it does, the percentage that is applied to the amounts of insurance, premiums, and losses.

The reinsurance limit—the total limit or capacity—of a surplus share treaty is expressed in multiples of the primary insurer's line. A primary insurer with a nine-line surplus share treaty has the capacity under the treaty to insure loss exposures with amounts of insurance that exceed its retention by a multiple of nine. For example, if the line is $300,000 for a nine-line surplus share treaty, the primary insurer has a total underwriting capacity of $3 million, calculated as the $300,000 line, plus nine multiplied by the $300,000 line. In addition to being expressed as a number of lines, the reinsurance limit of a surplus share treaty can also be expressed as an amount of insurance the reinsurer is willing to provide, such as $2.7 million in the preceding example ($300,000 multiplied by nine lines).

The following observations can be made about surplus share reinsurance:

- The surplus share treaty does not cover policies with amounts of insurance that are less than the primary insurer's line. Many primary insurers use surplus share reinsurance instead of quota share reinsurance so that they do not have to cede any part of the liability for loss exposures that can be safely retained.

- The amount of insurance for a large number of loss exposures may be too small to be ceded to the treaty but, in the aggregate, may cause the primary insurer to incur significant losses that are not reinsured. For example, many homeowners policies in the same region that do not exceed the primary insurer's line could incur extensive losses from a single occurrence, such as a hurricane.

- Because the percentage of policy premiums and losses varies for each loss exposure ceded, surplus share treaties are more costly to administer than quota share treaties. Primary insurers must keep records and, in many cases, periodically provide the reinsurer with a **bordereau**, which is a report the primary insurer provides periodically to the reinsurer that contains a detailed listing of premiums and losses reinsured under the treaty.

- Surplus share treaties usually provide surplus relief to the primary insurer because the reinsurer usually pays a reinsurance commission for those policies ceded. Because loss exposures with amounts of insurance that are less than the primary insurer's line are not reinsured, a surplus share treaty typically provides the primary insurer with less surplus relief than does a quota share treaty.

Bordereau
A report the primary insurer provides periodically to the reinsurer that contains a detailed listing of premiums and losses reinsured under the treaty.

Unlike the simplified example shown in Exhibit 7-4, many surplus share treaties allow the primary insurer to increase its line from a minimum amount to a maximum amount, depending on the potential loss severity of the exposed limit. For example, Brookgreen Insurance Company's surplus share treaty may allow the company to increase its line on a "superior" loss exposure from $25,000 to $50,000. In this case, the nine-line surplus share treaty would give Brookgreen Insurance Company the large line capacity to insure loss exposures with amounts of insurance as large as $500,000; calculated as the $50,000 line, plus nine multiplied by the $50,000 line. The primary insurer's ability to vary its line also allows it to retain some loss exposures it may otherwise be required to cede. The flexibility provided by the reinsurer in the surplus share treaty is usually communicated to the primary insurer's underwriters through a line guide, or line authorization guide. The **line guide** is a document that provides the minimum and maximum line a primary insurer can retain on a loss exposure.

Line guide
A document that provides the minimum and maximum line a primary insurer can retain on a loss exposure.

When the total underwriting capacity of the primary insurer's surplus share treaty is insufficient to meet its large line capacity needs, the primary insurer can arrange for additional surplus share reinsurance from another reinsurer. When a primary insurer arranges more than one surplus share treaty, the surplus share treaty that applies immediately above the primary insurer's line is referred to as the first surplus. Other surplus share treaties are referred to in the order that they provide additional large line capacity, such as second or third surplus treaties.

Surplus share reinsurance is most useful to commercial insurers who want to adjust their retention amount based on attributes of loss exposure. Risk management professionals, and their insurance or reinsurance subsidiary, would likely not use surplus share reinsurance unless it insured or reinsured third-party business. For example, an organization may have several insurance subsidiaries, one of which sold only personal auto and homeowners insurance to its employees, but now provides insurance to others who are not related by employment to the organization.

Excess of Loss Reinsurance

Excess of loss reinsurance, also called nonproportional reinsurance, is a type of reinsurance in which the primary insurer is indemnified for losses that exceed a specified dollar amount. The following are the five types of excess of loss reinsurance:

Excess of loss reinsurance
A type of reinsurance in which the primary insurer is indemnified for losses that exceed a specified dollar amount.

1. Per risk excess of loss
2. Catastrophe excess of loss
3. Per policy excess of loss
4. Per occurrence excess of loss
5. Aggregate excess of loss

The different types of excess of loss reinsurance usually each have a specific use. Per risk excess of loss reinsurance and catastrophe excess of loss reinsurance are generally used with property loss exposures. Per policy excess of loss reinsurance and per occurrence excess of loss reinsurance are generally used with liability loss exposures. Aggregate excess of loss reinsurance is used for both property and liability loss exposures.

The common characteristic of all types of excess of loss reinsurance is that the reinsurer responds to a loss only when the loss amount exceeds the **attachment point**, which is the dollar amount above which the reinsurer responds to losses. The primary insurer fully retains losses that are less than

Attachment point
The dollar amount above which the reinsurer responds to losses.

the attachment point. The reinsurer sometimes requires the primary insurer to also retain responsibility for a percentage of the losses that exceed the attachment point. Excess of loss reinsurance can be visualized as a layer, or a series of layers, of reinsurance sitting above the primary insurer's retention. Exhibit 7-5 illustrates how excess of loss reinsurance can be layered.

EXHIBIT 7-5

How Excess of Loss Reinsurance Is Layered

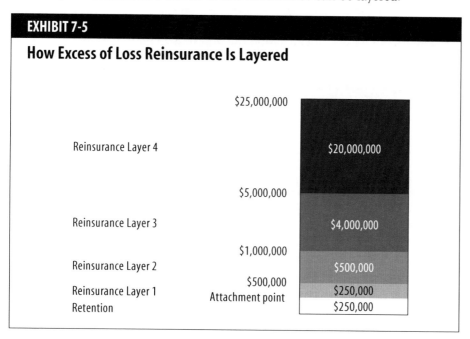

Excess of loss reinsurance is often purchased in layers. A reinsurer responds only when the amount of loss is large enough to affect its layer.

An excess of loss reinsurer's obligation to indemnify the primary insurer for losses depends on the amount of the loss and the layer of coverage that the reinsurer provides. The reinsurer providing the first layer of excess of loss reinsurance shown in Exhibit 7-5 would indemnify the primary insurer for losses that exceed $250,000 (the attachment point) up to total incurred losses of $500,000. This reinsurer describes its position in the primary insurer's excess of loss reinsurance program as being "$250,000 in excess of (denoted as 'xs') $250,000." The reinsurer in the second layer of the excess of loss reinsurance program would indemnify the primary insurer for losses that exceed $500,000 up to total incurred losses of $1 million, or "$500,000 xs $500,000." Losses that exceed the capacity of the primary insurer's excess of loss reinsurance remain the primary insurer's responsibility unless otherwise reinsured. In Exhibit 7-5, loss amounts in excess of $25 million are the primary insurer's responsibility.

Unlike pro rata reinsurance, in which the reinsurance pricing follows that of the primary insurer's pricing, excess of loss reinsurance premiums are negotiated based on the likelihood that losses will exceed the attachment point. The reinsurance premium for excess of loss reinsurance is usually stated as a percentage (often called a rate) of the policy premium charged by the primary insurer (often called the **subject premium**, which is the premium the primary insurer charges on its underlying policies and to which a rate is applied to determine the reinsurance premium). Therefore, unlike quota share

Subject premium
The premium the primary insurer charges on its underlying policies and to which a rate is applied to determine the reinsurance premium.

and surplus share reinsurance, in which the reinsurer receives a proportional share of the underlying premium, the excess of loss reinsurer receives a nonproportional share of the premium.

Generally, reinsurers do not pay ceding commissions under excess of loss reinsurance agreements. However, the reinsurer may reward the primary insurer for favorable loss experience by paying a profit commission or by reducing the rate used in calculating the reinsurance premium.

Working cover
An excess of loss reinsurance agreement with a low attachment point.

The primary insurer's attachment point is usually set at a level so that claims that are frequent enough to be expected are retained. However, an excess of loss reinsurance agreement may have a low attachment point with the expectation that the primary insurer's volume of losses will be significant. An excess of loss reinsurance agreement with a low attachment point is known as a **working cover**. A working cover enables the primary insurer to spread its losses over several years. The primary insurer and the reinsurer anticipate that profitable years will offset unprofitable ones. Primary insurers selling a type of insurance with which they have little expertise may choose to purchase a working cover until they better understand the frequency and severity of losses that the portfolio for that particular type of insurance produces. Reinsurers typically require a working cover to contain an occurrence limitation of two or three times the reinsurance limit. This requirement prevents the working cover from being exposed to catastrophic events such as a hurricane.

Co-participation provision
A provision in a reinsurance agreement that requires the primary insurer to retain a specified percentage of the losses that exceed its attachment point.

As previously mentioned, excess of loss reinsurance agreements sometimes contain a **co-participation provision**, which is a provision in a reinsurance agreement that requires the primary insurer to retain a specified percentage of the losses that exceed its attachment point. The purpose of this provision is to provide the primary insurer with a financial incentive to efficiently manage losses that exceed the attachment point. A co-participation provision is usually denoted by specifying a percentage before the position of its layer. For example, if the fourth layer in Exhibit 7-5 had a 5 percent co-participation provision, that layer would be specified as "95% of $20,000,000 xs $5,000,000."

In addition to indemnifying losses in a layer of coverage, the reinsurer's obligation may also extend to payment of loss adjustment expenses. Loss adjustment expenses are often a substantial insurer expense, especially for insurance for liability loss exposures. Therefore, excess of loss reinsurance agreements are usually very specific regarding how loss adjustment expenses attributable to specific losses are handled. In rare circumstances, they may be excluded from the reinsurance agreement, but the following are the two most common approaches to handling loss adjustment expenses:

1. Prorate the loss adjustment expenses between the primary insurer and the reinsurer based on the same percentage share that each is responsible for the loss. This approach is commonly referred to as *pro rata in addition*.
2. Add the loss adjustment expenses to the amount of the loss when applying the attachment point of the excess of loss reinsurance agreement. This approach is commonly referred to as loss adjustment expense *included in the limit*.

If loss adjustment expenses are prorated, the primary insurer pays all the loss adjustment expenses when the loss amount does not exceed the attachment point. If loss adjustment expenses are added to the loss amount, the reinsurer may have to pay a claim in which the loss amount alone does not exceed the attachment point. Primary insurers and reinsurers usually assess the potential for loss adjustment expenses independent of the actual loss potential when negotiating the excess of loss reinsurance agreement. Commonly, reinsurance agreements provide that loss adjustment expenses are prorated for property insurance and most types of liability insurance. However, excess of loss reinsurance covering liability insurance that usually involves substantial litigation often specifies that loss adjustment expenses are added to the amount of the loss when applying the attachment point. For instance, medical malpractice insurance often involves substantial loss adjustment expenses in the form of legal fees even if the claim can be settled with a nominal loss payment or no payment at all.

Per Risk Excess of Loss Reinsurance

Per risk excess of loss reinsurance covers property insurance and applies separately to *each loss* occurring to *each risk*. Per risk excess of loss is often referred to as property per risk excess of loss. The primary insurer usually determines what constitutes one risk (loss exposure). Exhibit 7-6 indicates how a reinsurer would respond if the primary insurer defined three separate buildings under a per risk excess of loss reinsurance agreement as three separate risks. In this example, a tornado damaged all three buildings in one occurrence. Because each building is a risk, the attachment point and reinsurance limit apply separately to each. The attachment point and reinsurance limit are stated as a dollar amount of loss.

Per risk excess of loss reinsurance
A type of excess of loss reinsurance that covers property insurance and that applies separately to each loss occurring to each risk.

EXHIBIT 7-6

Example of Per Risk Excess of Loss Reinsurance Applying $950,000 xs $50,000

Building Number	Loss Amount	Primary Insurer's Retention	Reinsurer's Payment
1	$ 500,000	$ 50,000	$ 450,000
2	350,000	50,000	300,000
3	700,000	50,000	650,000
Total	$1,550,000	$150,000	$1,400,000

Per risk excess of loss reinsurance agreements apply separately to each loss occurring to each risk. Consequently, the insurer's aggregate retention may be significant.

Per occurrence limits are commonly included with per risk excess of loss reinsurance agreements. A per occurrence limit restricts the amount that the reinsurer pays as the result of a single occurrence affecting multiple risks. Had a per occurrence limit of $1 million been imposed in the example in Exhibit 7-6, the reinsurer would have been responsible for only $1 million of losses (instead of $1.4 million) because the three losses arose out of the same occurrence (the tornado). Catastrophe excess of loss reinsurance, discussed next, is usually purchased in conjunction with per risk excess of loss reinsurance to protect the primary insurer from one occurrence affecting multiple risks.

Catastrophe Excess of Loss Reinsurance

Catastrophe excess of loss reinsurance

A type of excess of loss reinsurance that protects the primary insurer from an accumulation of retained losses that arise from a single catastrophic event.

Catastrophe excess of loss reinsurance is a type of excess of loss reinsurance that protects the primary insurer from an accumulation of retained losses that arise from a single catastrophic event. It may be purchased to protect the primary insurer and its reinsurers on a combined basis but is more frequently purchased to protect the primary insurer on a net basis after all other reinsurance recoveries are made. Examples of catastrophic events include tornadoes, hurricanes, and earthquakes. Such events, especially major hurricanes, can result in losses totaling billions of dollars.

As with per risk excess of loss reinsurance, the attachment point and reinsurance limit for catastrophe excess of loss reinsurance are stated as a dollar amount of loss. The attachment point is subject to negotiation, but it is usually set high enough so that it would be exceeded only if the aggregation of losses from a catastrophe would impair a primary insurer's policyholders' surplus. Additionally, losses exceeding the attachment point are usually subject to a co-participation provision.

Loss occurrence clause

A reinsurance agreement clause that defines the scope of a catastrophic occurrence for the purposes of the agreement.

Because the attachment point and reinsurance limit apply separately to each catastrophe occurring during a policy period, the catastrophe excess of loss reinsurance agreement defines the scope of a catastrophic occurrence through a loss occurrence clause (sometimes called an hours clause). A **loss occurrence clause** is a reinsurance agreement clause that defines the scope of a catastrophic occurrence for the purposes of the agreement. The loss occurrence clause specifies a period, in hours, during which the primary insurer's losses arising out of the same catastrophic occurrence can be aggregated and applied to the attachment point and reinsurance limits of the catastrophe excess of loss reinsurance agreement. Such clauses usually specify a period of 72 consecutive hours (three days) for hurricane losses and 168 consecutive hours (seven days) for earthquake losses. When making a claim against the catastrophe excess of loss reinsurance agreement, the primary insurer can usually choose the date and time when the period of consecutive hours commences in order to maximize the amount of recovery under the agreement.

Exhibit 7-7 provides an example of the operation of a loss occurrence clause in a catastrophe excess of loss reinsurance agreement and shows how a primary insurer can select the period of coverage to its advantage. In this example, the primary insurer sustains $8 million in losses from a hurricane over a four-day period. The primary insurer has a $6 million xs $1 million catastrophe excess of loss reinsurance treaty with a loss occurrence clause that stipulates a period of seventy-two consecutive hours for a hurricane. In this simplified example, selecting the specific hour of the day that coverage begins is not an issue, and no co-participation provision applies. Given the distribution of losses over the four days, the primary insurer should elect to start the seventy-two-hour period on the second day to maximize its reinsurance recovery.

Payments from the reinsurer to the primary insurer for catastrophe losses reduce the reinsurance coverage limits available to respond to future losses. Catastrophe excess of loss reinsurance agreements often include a provision that requires the primary insurer to pay an additional premium to reinstate the limits of the agreement after a loss. This provision allows the reinsurer to obtain additional premiums and gives the primary insurer confidence that sufficient limits are available should another catastrophe occur during the reinsurance agreement's term.

EXHIBIT 7-7

Example of the Operation of a Loss Occurrence Clause in a Catastrophe Excess of Loss Reinsurance Agreement

Day	Losses	Period of Coverage Providing Maximum Recovery
1	$1,000,000	
2	1,000,000	
3	2,000,000	← $7,000,000
4	4,000,000	
Total	$8,000,000	

The total losses that could potentially be applied to the reinsurance agreement are $7 million if the seventy-two-hour period starts on the second day, as opposed to $4 million if the period had started on the first day.

Primary insurers and their reinsurers usually do not anticipate that the catastrophe excess of loss reinsurance will be triggered every year. Catastrophe protection is purchased for the unlikely, but possible, event that may cause unstable operating results or that cannot be absorbed by the primary insurer's policyholders' surplus. A primary insurer's need for catastrophe reinsurance and the amount purchased depends on its catastrophe loss exposures.

Catastrophe Excess of Loss Reinsurance Example

Brookgreen Insurance Company (Brookgreen) decides to sell earthquake coverage in southern California but wants to limit its losses to approximately $1 million from any one earthquake. Brookgreen conducted a study and estimated that its maximum loss from any one earthquake, given its spread of earthquake loss exposures in southern California, would be $10 million. Brookgreen purchases catastrophe excess of loss reinsurance of 95 percent of $9,250,000 xs $750,000. If Brookgreen were to sustain a $10 million loss from an earthquake, it would retain $1,212,500 and the reinsurer would pay $8,787,500. These figures are calculated as follows:

Step 1—Determination of the loss amount exceeding the attachment point

Amount exceeding the attachment point	=	Amount of loss (subject to the reinsurance limit)	−	Retention
	=	$10,000,000	−	$750,000
	=	$9,250,000.		

Step 2—Determination of the co-participation

Amount of co-participation	=	Amount exceeding the attachment point	×	Co-participation percentage
	=	$9,250,000	×	0.05
	=	$462,500.		

Step 3—Determination of the amount of loss owed by the reinsurer

Amount owed by the reinsurer	=	Amount exceeding the attachment point	−	Amount of co-participation
	=	$9,250,000	−	$462,500
	=	$8,787,500.		

Step 4—Determination of the amount retained by Brookgreen

Amount retained by Brookgreen	=	Retention	+	Amount of co-participation
	=	$750,000	+	$462,500
	=	$1,212,500.		

Per policy excess of loss reinsurance

A type of excess of loss reinsurance that applies the attachment point and the reinsurance limit separately to each insurance policy issued by the primary insurer regardless of the number of losses occurring under each policy.

Per Policy Excess of Loss Reinsurance

Per policy excess of loss reinsurance is a type of excess of loss reinsurance that applies the attachment point and the reinsurance limit separately to each insurance policy issued by the primary insurer regardless of the number of losses occurring under each policy. Exhibit 7-8 provides an example of how a reinsurer would respond under a $900,000 xs $100,000 per policy excess of loss treaty. In this example, three separate general liability policies issued by the same primary insurer incur losses from *separate events*.

EXHIBIT 7-8

Example of Per Policy Excess of Loss Reinsurance Applying $900,000 xs $100,000

Primary Insurer has a $900,000 xs $100,000 per policy excess of loss treaty. The table below shows three policies for which Primary Insurer is indemnified by Reinsurer because the amount of loss arising out of each of the policies exceeds Primary Insurer's attachment point.

Policy	Loss Amount	Primary Insurer's Retention	Reinsurer's Payment
1	$ 300,000	$ 100,000	$ 200,000
2	500,000	100,000	400,000
3	600,000	100,000	500,000
Total	$1,400,000	$300,000	$1,100,000

Per policy excess of loss reinsurance agreements apply separately to each policy. Consequently, when many policies are affected by a loss, the insurer's aggregate retention may be significant.

Per Occurrence Excess of Loss Reinsurance

Per occurrence excess of loss reinsurance is a type of excess of loss reinsurance that applies the attachment point and the reinsurance limit to the total losses arising *from a single event* affecting one or more of the primary insurer's policies. Per occurrence excess of loss reinsurance is usually used for liability insurance. Exhibit 7-9 provides an example of how a per occurrence excess of loss treaty applies to the three policies used in Exhibit 7-8. In Exhibit 7-9, a $100,000 attachment point applies to the total losses of the policies covering the same event, and there is a $4.9 million reinsurance limit. A per occurrence excess of loss treaty covering liability insurance usually has an attachment point that is less than the highest liability policy limit offered by the primary insurer.

Per occurrence excess of loss reinsurance
A type of excess of loss reinsurance that applies the attachment point and reinsurance limit to the total losses arising from a single event affecting one or more of the primary insurer's policies.

EXHIBIT 7-9

Example of Per Occurrence Excess of Loss Reinsurance Applying $4,900,000 xs $100,000

Primary Insurer has a $4,900,000 xs $100,000 per occurrence excess of loss treaty. The table below shows how losses are accumulated to determine if the attachment point has been exceeded. Primary Insurer is indemnified by Reinsurer because the total amount of the loss arising out of all three policies exceeds Primary Insurer's attachment point.

Policy	Loss Amount		Primary Insurer's Retention		Reinsurer's Payment
1	$ 300,000				
2	500,000				
3	600,000				
Total	$1,400,000	=	$100,000	+	$1,300,000

Per occurrence excess of loss reinsurance agreements are usually designed so that the amount of loss that triggers it must be substantial.

Aggregate Excess of Loss Reinsurance

Aggregate excess of loss reinsurance is a type of excess of loss reinsurance that covers aggregated losses that exceed the attachment point and that occur over a stated period, usually one year. Aggregate excess of loss reinsurance can be used for property or liability insurance. The attachment point in an aggregate excess of loss treaty can be stated as a dollar amount of loss or as a loss ratio. When the attachment point is stated as a loss ratio, the treaty is called stop loss reinsurance. With stop loss reinsurance, the primary insurer's retention may be a loss ratio of 90 percent, and the reinsurer would indemnify losses up to a loss ratio of 120 percent. The reinsurance agreement in this instance would specify the attachment point and reinsurance limit as "30% xs 90% loss ratio." The primary insurer retains responsibility for losses above a loss ratio of 120 percent.

Aggregate excess of loss treaties are less common and can be more expensive than the other types of excess of loss reinsurance. When used, the treaty usually specifies an attachment point and reinsurance limit that does not result in the primary insurer earning a profit on the reinsured policies when the policies were unprofitable overall. Most aggregate excess of loss treaties also contain a co-participation provision of 5 to 10 percent to provide the primary insurer with an incentive to efficiently handle claims that exceed the attachment point.

Aggregate excess of loss reinsurance
A type of excess of loss reinsurance that covers aggregated losses that exceed the attachment point and that occur over a stated period, usually one year.

Aggregate Excess of Loss Reinsurance Example

Brookgreen Insurance Company (Brookgreen) offers liability insurance to a tavern. This general liability policy has an occurrence limit of $1 million and a general aggregate limit (capping the number of per occurrence dollars the insurer will pay during the policy period) of $2 million.

Brookgreen purchases facultative per occurrence excess of loss reinsurance for this policy in excess of $500,000. This insurance protects Brookgreen against any loss above $500,000 but would not respond to any loss below $500,000. If the tavern suffered three separate losses of $450,000 each, Brookgreen would not recover from the reinsurer even though the total of all losses under the policy during the policy period exceeded $500,000.

Because of concern about aggregation of losses from this and similar loss exposures, Brookgreen decides to purchase a $7 million xs $3 million aggregate excess of loss treaty that is applicable to all of its liability insurance. This treaty further stabilizes losses by indemnifying Brookgreen for accumulations of losses exceeding $3 million. For example, Brookgreen insures a cosmetics manufacturer whose wrinkle cream causes an increase in susceptibility to skin cancer. Brookgreen settles a class action suit brought by customers who used the product for $15 million. Brookgreen's net loss is $8 million (the $3 million retention plus $5 million loss amount that exceeds the $7 million limit).

Because of the stabilizing effect of aggregate excess of loss reinsurance on a primary insurer's loss ratio, it may be argued that it is the only type of reinsurance needed. However, aggregate excess of loss reinsurance has limited availability. When used, the aggregate excess of loss reinsurer usually expects to pay losses only after the primary insurer has been reimbursed under its other reinsurance agreements.

A catastrophe excess of loss reinsurance agreement, discussed previously, protects only against catastrophe losses (loss severity). An aggregate excess of loss reinsurance agreement provides the reinsured with broader protection because it includes catastrophes and unforeseen accumulations of noncatastrophic losses during a specified period (addressing both loss severity and loss frequency).

Finite Risk Reinsurance

Finite risk reinsurance is a nontraditional type of reinsurance in which the reinsurer's liability is limited and anticipated investment income is expressly acknowledged as an underwriting component. Because this type of reinsurance transfers a limited amount of risk to the reinsurer with the objective of improving the primary insurer's financial result, it is often called financial reinsurance.

Finite risk reinsurance can be arranged to protect a primary insurer against a combination of a traditionally insurable loss exposure (for example, building loss caused by an explosion) and a traditionally uninsurable loss exposure (for example, possibility of loss due to economic variables such as product demand and market competition). Finite risk reinsurance can effectively handle extremely large and unusual loss exposures, such as catastrophic losses resulting from an oil rig explosion or an earthquake.

A finite risk reinsurance agreement typically has a multi-year term—for example, three to five years—so it spreads risk as well as losses over several years, subject to an aggregate limit for the agreement's entire term. The primary insurer can rely on long-term protection, and the reinsurer can rely on a continual flow of premiums. Finite risk reinsurance provides the primary insurer with a predictable reinsurance cost over the coverage period. Consequently, both the primary insurer and the reinsurer tend to be flexible in negotiating pricing and terms.

Finite risk reinsurance premiums can be a substantial percentage— for example, 70 percent—of the reinsurance limit. This relationship between premium and reinsurance limit reduces the reinsurer's potential underwriting loss to a level that is much lower than the potential underwriting loss typically associated with traditional types of reinsurance.

Generally, finite risk reinsurance is designed to cover high severity losses. The reinsurer commonly shares profits with the primary insurer when it has favorable loss experience or has generated income by investing the prepaid premium. This profit-sharing income can compensate the primary insurer for the higher-than-usual premium for finite risk reinsurance. The reinsurer does not assess any additional premium even if its losses exceed the premium.

Finite risk reinsurance
A nontraditional type of reinsurance in which the reinsurer's liability is limited and anticipated investment income is expressly acknowledged as an underwriting component.

REINSURANCE CONCERNS OF RISK MANAGEMENT PROFESSIONALS

Normally, a risk management professional is not involved with negotiating reinsurance contracts. Typically, only insurers and reinsurers enter into reinsurance contracts. However, situations exist in which a risk management professional would deal directly with a reinsurer, such as the following:

- A reinsurer takes the place of an insurer as a result of a portfolio reinsurance arrangement.
- A reinsurer takes the place of an insurer through a cut-through endorsement added to an insurance policy.
- An organization establishes a subsidiary that insures or reinsures the organization's loss exposures.
- An organization purchases reinsurance for a pool of which it is a member.
- A reinsurer or several reinsurers team up with an insurer or several insurers to provide coverage.

Portfolio Reinsurance Arrangements

Described previously as a means through which an insurer could transfer all of the liability of specified loss exposures, portfolio reinsurance is commonly used by insurers who are withdrawing from a type of insurance or market segment. Portfolio reinsurance is not a legal substitution of one insurer for another. However, after the portfolio reinsurance transaction, the original insurer only provides services while all losses are paid by another insurer.

A risk management professional whose insurance plan has been reinsured through a portfolio reinsurance arrangement should learn the details of the transaction in order to ascertain that the insured organization's coverage is maintained and that the reinsurer is at least as financially sound as the retiring insurer. Portfolio reinsurance arrangements usually satisfy an immediate need of the insurer and pay minimal regard to the underlying insureds. Consequently, most risk management professionals would likely reconsider an insurance placement that is included as part of a portfolio reinsurance transaction and change insurers either immediately or at the expiration of the policy period.

Cut-Through Endorsements

The usefulness of insurance depends on the financial solvency of the insurer. Consequently, when the insured organization or its lenders become concerned about the insurer's financial solvency (evidenced by the insurer's financial rating) the organization may change insurers or seek additional security from the insurer. One means of accomplishing this is through the addition of a cut-through endorsement to the organizations insurance policy.

A **cut-through endorsement** (also called an assumption certificate) is an endorsement attached to an insurance policy that gives the insured a direct cause of action against the reinsurer for the reinsured amount of a loss if the primary insurer become insolvent. Therefore, an insured's or a third party's right of recovery from an insurer "cuts through" directly to the reinsurer.

The insured is not a party to the reinsurance agreement and, without the endorsement, has no right to recover directly from the reinsurer. Normally, the insured organization needs no such right because the solvent primary insurer fulfills its obligation under the underlying policy and is indemnified by the reinsurer to the extent specified in the reinsurance treaty. However, the liquidator of an insolvent primary insurer is not able to treat insurance claimants any differently than any other creditor of the primary insurer in satisfying unmet obligations. The cut-through endorsement provides the insured with direct rights against the reinsurer, bypassing the primary insurer's insolvency proceedings.

A cut-through endorsement is usually requested when the primary insurer does not satisfy the financial standards established by the insured organization's lender. The endorsement can take many forms, depending on the needs of the parties and the applicable state law. Typically, the cut-through endorsement states that reinsurance proceeds will be paid directly to the payee in the event that the primary insurer is unable to pay a loss. The payee may be the insured organization, the lender, or both. The reinsurer will respond to the insured organization and the lender, as their interests may appear, up to the limit of the reinsurance treaty.

The insolvent primary insurer's liquidator sometimes contests the enforcement of the cut-through endorsement because it reduces available funds that can be directed to other creditors. In some instances, reinsurers have been forced to pay claims twice—once on behalf of the insured under the terms of the cut-through endorsement, and again to the liquidator of the insolvent primary insurer.

Reinsurers prefer to avoid cut-through endorsements because of the administrative expenses involved in tracking them and the potential for third-party liability. However, reinsurers usually will accommodate an insurer's requests for cut-through endorsements because it is in both the insurer's and reinsurer's best interests to retain the insured organization's business.

Cut-through endorsement
An endorsement attached to an insurance policy that gives the insured a direct cause of action against the reinsurer for the reinsured amount of a loss if the primary insurer become insolvent.

Reinsurance Through a Subsidiary

Many organizations form subsidiaries called captive insurers (discussed subsequently) as a risk financing technique. However, captive insurers often rely on reinsurance as the primary means to transfer risk from the organization's economic family. Captive insurers can directly insure the organization's loss exposures, or can operate as a reinsurer for the commercial insurer that provides the organization primary insurance.

Reinsuring a Pool

Risk management representatives of pool participants often serve on governing committees of the pool and as informal advisors to the pool's management. Consequently, they must be concerned with the pool's reinsurer's financial strength, integrity, and operating efficiency, which all affect the pool's reliability, and, consequentially, the solidity and effectiveness of the organization's risk financing program.

Pools often purchase excess of loss reinsurance to provide large-line capacity to their insureds and to stabilize their net underwriting results. Although this excess of loss reinsurance is usually purchased on a treaty basis, it is sometimes purchased on a facultative basis.

Reinsurers can help the management of a pool by providing underwriting expertise. In many cases, reinsurers assist a pool in underwriting unrelated third-party business (business not related to its owners).

Cooperation Between Insurers and Reinsurers to Provide Capacity

Insurers and reinsurers sometimes cooperate to provide the capacity an insured requires. In these situations, the insured's coverage needs are often divided into layers to which insurers and reinsurers both subscribe. For example, insurers and reinsurers jointly participated to fulfill the property coverage needs of the owners of the World Trade Center in New York City.

REINSURANCE CASE STUDIES

The following case studies illustrate the application of reinsurance programs to specific situations. The programs outlined are realistic for the circumstances shown, but are not necessarily the only options that are appropriate for the given scenario.

Property Management Company

Property Management Company (PMC) operates twenty shopping malls and is developing five others. Because of the property values involved, PMC has a significant property insurance program. It also carries considerable debt in the form of bank loans used to finance the construction and operation of its shopping malls. Recently, the bank that owns the mortgage on one of its shopping malls reacted to a drop in the financial rating of the property's insurer by asking PMC to replace the insurer with another. Although PMC is willing to do so, its risk management professional does not want to shop the property independently of the others, or shop for replacement insurance in the current, high-priced insurance market.

PMC's insurance broker suggests that the insurer's recent financial downturn was not a sign of its impending insolvency and believes that the insurer has recognized and corrected its problem and should soon rebound financially. To appease the bank, PMC's insurance broker suggests that the insurer obtain a cut-through endorsement for the policy. The cut-through endorsement will allow PMC (and its mortgagee) to be indemnified for losses directly should the insurer become insolvent.

Although the insurer's reinsurer is reluctant to provide the cut-through endorsement, it does so. The reinsurer decides that the administrative expenses associated with the cut-through endorsement are minor relative to the need for the primary insurer to retain the account.

Amusement Park Company

Amusement Park Company (APC) operates five amusement parks in the U.S. Despite the superior engineering and design of its amusement rides, accidents still happen. Consequently, APC needs a liability insurance program that will protect it from the financial consequences of bodily injury and property damage claims.

APC's insurance broker believes it unlikely that a loss from a single occurrence will exceed $100 million. This belief is based on the number of park guests who can ride on any one attraction and on court testimony by economists on the current financial value of a human life. Additionally, $100 million in liability limits is the most the insurance broker believes he can obtain.

To provide the liability insurance capacity APC requires, the insurance broker devises a liability insurance plan that relies on underlying insurance and excess liability insurance. The excess liability insurance is provided by both primary insurers and reinsurers. As mentioned previously, most insurers can, and do, operate as insurers and reinsurers. Likewise, insurers that operate primarily as reinsurers can, and sometimes do, participate in the insurance marketplace as primary insurers.

An excess liability program such as the one used in this case requires more insurance capacity than one insurer is likely willing to provide. Therefore, it is divided into layers, as shown in Exhibit 7-10. This allows for optimal use of available insurance capacity. Sometimes, insurer underwriting guidelines (insurer-specific procedure manuals) limit per-layer participation. With multiple layers, an insurer may be able to participate in multiple layers and, therefore, have a larger aggregate participation.

The lower layers of the excess liability program experience more loss frequency than the higher ones, because only the largest losses affect the higher layers. Typically, the limits become larger in the higher layers to reflect this lower loss frequency and higher loss severity.

EXHIBIT 7-10

Amusement Park Company's Liability Insurance Program

Layer	Layer Amount
1	$0 to $4 million
2	$4,000,001 to $6 million
3	$6,000,001 to $8 million
4	$8,000,001 to $10 million
5	$10,000,001 to $15 million
6	$15,000,001 to $20 million
7	$20,000,001 to $25 million
8	$25,000,001 to $50 million
9	$50,000,001 to $75 million
10	$75,000,001 to $100 million

Transit Company

Transit Company (TC) is a common carrier that ships property for others. TC owns and operates a large fleet of vehicles. Insuring the long-haul trucking in which TC specializes is not always profitable for insurers. Consequently, TC's insurance costs vary from year to year, even though its losses are relatively stable. TC's management wants greater stability in its cost of risk.

TC's risk management professional believes that TC can accomplish this by forming an insurance subsidiary that insures only TC's loss exposures. To stabilize its losses, the insurance subsidiary purchases $4 million xs $1 million per occurrence excess of loss reinsurance. This amount of liability insurance satisfies the financial responsibility requirements specified in the Motor Carrier Act of 1980 for carriers of hazardous substances. Additionally, TC's insurance subsidiary purchases a $15 million xs $5 million aggregate excess of loss reinsurance policy. With these reinsurance agreements in place, TC's insurance subsidiary retains up to $1 million on each loss. If losses aggregate in excess of $5 million, the aggregate excess of loss reinsurer will respond.

SUMMARY

Reinsurance is the transfer of insurance risk from one insurer to another through a contractual agreement under which the reinsurer agrees, in return for a reinsurance premium, to indemnify the primary insurer for some or all of the financial consequences of certain loss exposures covered by the primary insurer's policies. Reinsurance performs the following six principal functions for primary insurers:

1. *Increase large line capacity.* Allows the primary insurer to provide larger amounts of insurance than it would otherwise be willing or able to do.

2. *Provide catastrophe protection.* Protects the primary insurer from the financial consequences of a single catastrophic event that causes multiple losses.

3. *Stabilize loss experience.* Stabilizes the primary insurer's loss experience by limiting the primary insurer's liability for loss exposures.

4. *Provide surplus relief.* Replenishes policyholders' surplus.

5. *Facilitate withdrawal from a market segment.* Allows the primary insurer to use portfolio reinsurance to withdraw from a market segment without canceling all of the policies in that segment.

6. *Provide underwriting guidance.* Enables the primary insurer to benefit from the reinsurer's expertise, which is particularly useful to inexperienced primary insurers.

Treaty reinsurance agreements provide coverage for an entire class or portfolio of loss exposures and involve an ongoing relationship between the primary insurer and the reinsurer. Treaty reinsurance agreements are usually obligatory; loss exposures must be ceded to and accepted by the reinsurer. Facultative reinsurance agreements insure individual loss exposures. Under a facultative agreement, the reinsurer is usually not obligated to accept the loss exposure submitted by the primary insurer.

A direct writing reinsurer deals directly with primary insurers. Alternatively, reinsurers may deal with primary insurers through reinsurance intermediaries. In either case, there must be a relationship of trust and utmost good faith between primary insurer and reinsurer. Some primary insurers also serve as reinsurers, either only to affiliates, or to both affiliates and unaffiliated insurers. Reinsurance pools, syndicates, and associations are groups of insurers that share the loss exposures of the group.

Reinsurance transactions are of two types: treaty or facultative. Treaty reinsurance is reinsurance for certain types of loss exposures under a prearranged reinsurance agreement called a treaty. In facultative reinsurance, the primary insurer negotiates a separate reinsurance agreement for each loss exposure it wants to reinsure.

Reinsurance agreements can be categorized as either pro rata (proportional) or excess of loss (nonproportional) reinsurance. Pro rata reinsurance involves the proportional sharing of amounts of insurance, policy premiums, and losses (including loss adjustment expenses) between the primary insurer and the reinsurer. Excess of loss reinsurance requires the reinsurer to indemnify the primary insurer for losses that exceed the primary insurer's retention. Pro rata reinsurance and excess of loss reinsurance are available on a facultative or treaty basis, and are used with both property and liability insurance. However, specific types of pro rata reinsurance and excess of loss reinsurance are usually used with either property or liability insurance.

With quota share reinsurance, the primary insurer and reinsurer share policy premiums, amounts of insurance, and losses using a fixed percentage. Surplus share reinsurance covers only those policies whose amount of insurance exceeds a stipulated dollar amount, or line. The primary insurer and the reinsurer then share policy premiums and losses proportionally according to the amount of the primary insurer's line and the total amount of insurance. Quota share reinsurance and surplus share reinsurance can be used for property or liability insurance. However, surplus share reinsurance is typically only used with property insurance.

Per risk excess of loss and catastrophe excess of loss reinsurance are generally used with property insurance. Per policy excess of loss and per occurrence excess of loss reinsurance are generally used with liability insurance. Aggregate excess of loss reinsurance is usually used for property insurance but can be used for liability insurance as well. The distinguishing characteristic among these types of excess of loss reinsurance is how losses are treated (individually or cumulatively) in determining whether the attachment point has been exceeded.

Finite risk reinsurance is an additional, nontraditional type of reinsurance that can be arranged to protect a primary insurer against large and unusual loss exposures. Although finite risk reinsurance premiums are typically higher than for other forms of reinsurance, the finite risk reinsurer commonly shares profits with the primary insurer when it has favorable loss experience or has generated income by investing the prepaid premium.

A risk management professional might deal directly with a reinsurer in the following situations:

- A reinsurer takes the place of an insurer through a portfolio reinsurance arrangement.
- A reinsurer takes the place of an insurer through a cut-through endorsement added to an insurance policy.
- An organization forms a subsidiary to spread risk through reinsurance.
- An organization relies on pools that in turn purchase reinsurance.
- A reinsurer or several reinsurers team up with an insurer or several insurers to provide coverage.

Reinsurance is an essential element of the insurer's financial security, and consequently, the organizations that insurers insure. Because reinsurance can affect the availability and affordability of primary insurance as well as other aspects of a risk financing plan, risk management professionals should understand how reinsurance operates. Reinsurance also is often a key component of a captive insurance plan, another tool a risk management professional can use to manage an organization's risks.

CHAPTER NOTES

1. The Reinsurance Association of America (RAA), through its *Glossary of Terms*, has brought clarity to the use of many reinsurance terms. Many of the definitions of terms in this text were adapted from the RAA glossary. The Web site for the RAA is at www.raanet.org (accessed January 13, 2004).

2. Insurers that are publicly traded are usually referred to as "stock insurers" to differentiate them from "mutual insurers," which are owned by their policyholders.

3. Insurers writing more volatile types of insurance, such as medical malpractice, may strive to keep their ratio of net written premiums to policyholders' surplus at a ratio of 2 to 1 or less.

Direct Your Learning

Captive Insurance Plans

After learning the content of this chapter and completing the corresponding course guide assignment, you should be able to:

- Describe the purpose and characteristics of captive insurance plans.

- Describe the types of captive insurance plans available.

- Describe the advantages and disadvantages of using a captive insurance plan.

- Explain how captive insurance plans operate.

- Define or describe each of the Key Words and Phrases for this chapter.

Develop Your Perspective

What are the main topics covered in the chapter?

This chapter examines captive insurance plans, what they are specifically, the different types of plans available, the advantages and disadvantages of using them, and how they operate.

Review the types of captive insurance plans.

- Has your organization researched using a particular type of captive insurance plan?

- Who at your organization determines whether to consider a captive insurance plan?

Why is it important to learn about these topics?

Captive insurance plans offer many advantages commercial insurance or retention do not, such as lower cost of risk, improved cash flow, and access to insurance otherwise not available. The risk management professional must also consider several disadvantages in conjunction with these advantages to determine whether a captive insurance plan is appropriate for the organization.

Consider the advantages and disadvantages of captive insurance plans.

- What advantages does a captive insurance plan have compared to your organization's current risk financing techniques?

- What disadvantages does a captive insurance plan have compared to your organization's current risk financing techniques?

How can you use what you will learn?

Evaluate the effectiveness of your organization's use of insurance and retention relative to captive insurance plans.

- How well do the strategies of using insurance and retention meet your organization's objectives?

- Identify loss exposures that your organization could more effectively address with a captive insurance plan than with its current strategies of insurance and retention.

Chapter 8
Captive Insurance Plans

Organizations that are willing to retain a significant share of their own losses in exchange for greater flexibility often form their own insurer to address their risk financing needs. This once novel approach to handling hazard risk, called a captive insurance plan, is now a relatively common way for organizations to reduce their overall cost of risk.

A risk management professional's decision to use a captive insurance plan is the result of a process that considers the advantages and disadvantages of using such a plan relative to other risk financing alternatives. Understanding the purpose and operation of captive insurance plans forms the foundation of this assessment.

PURPOSE AND CHARACTERISTICS OF CAPTIVE INSURANCE PLANS

A **captive insurer** is a subsidiary formed to insure the loss exposures of its parent company (or companies) and affiliates whose primary purpose usually is to reduce the parent's cost of risk. The captive insurer's relationship with its parent is just like any other insurer's. A captive insurer collects premiums, issues policies, and pays covered losses (both first-party and third-party losses). Exhibit 8-1 illustrates the relationship between a captive insurer and its parent.

Captive insurer
A subsidiary formed to insure the loss exposures of its parent company (or companies) and affiliates whose primary purpose usually is to reduce the parent's cost of risk.

EXHIBIT 8-1

The Relationship of a Captive Insurer to Its Parent(s) (Insured)

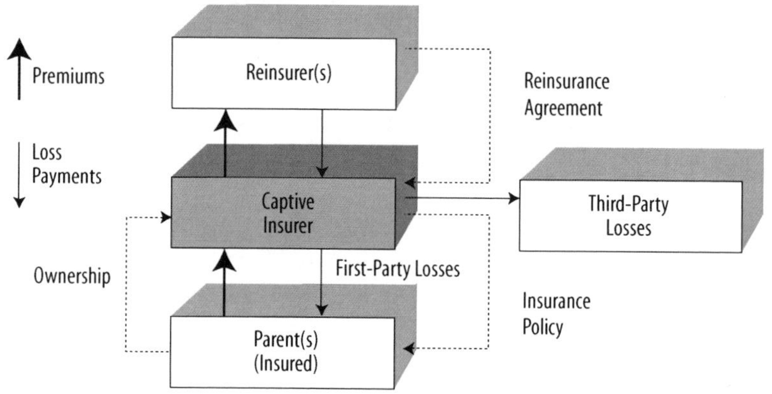

Most captive insurers purchase reinsurance, usually on an excess of loss basis, to transfer some of their loss exposures to another insurer. Reinsurance provides a captive insurer with many of the benefits previously discussed, including the ability to cover large losses.

Retaining and Transferring Losses

Captive insurers often retain losses up to a certain point and then transfer them beyond that point. Exhibit 8-2 illustrates the retained and transferred losses under a hypothetical captive insurance plan in which the captive insurer issues policies and purchases both per occurrence and annual aggregate excess of loss reinsurance. (Aggregate excess of loss reinsurance is usually difficult to obtain, even in a soft market, so most captive insurers don't purchase it.) The net retention of the captive for each occurrence is the amount below the per occurrence attachment point of the reinsurance. This is similar in concept to a loss limit under a retrospective rating plan. If the captive insurer can purchase annual aggregate excess reinsurance, then its annual retained losses are capped at an annual maximum amount. This is similar in concept to a maximum premium under a retrospective rating plan.

EXHIBIT 8-2

Retained and Transferred Losses Under a Hypothetical Captive Insurance Plan

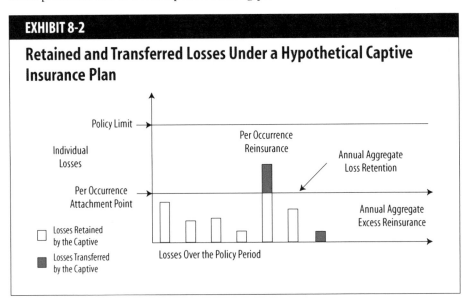

Combining a Captive Insurance Plan With Transfer and Hybrid Risk Financing Plans

A risk financing program that includes a captive insurance plan usually combines the captive insurance plan with a hybrid or transfer plan. As with a retrospective rating plan, the captive insurance plan generally is used for the first layer of losses, where there is a relatively high loss frequency and low-to-medium loss severity, with a transfer or a hybrid plan above it that covers the higher-severity losses.

For example, assume that an organization establishes a captive insurer to cover its general liability loss exposures. The captive insurer issues an insurance policy with a limit of $1 million per occurrence to its parent organization. Further, assume that the captive insurer purchases excess of loss reinsurance of $750,000 excess of $250,000 per occurrence.

Excess insurance may be above the $1 million layer of loss covered by the captive insurer. Exhibit 8-3 shows how the organization could combine excess insurance with the captive insurance plan just described.

EXHIBIT 8-3

Captive Insurance Plan Combined With Excess Insurance

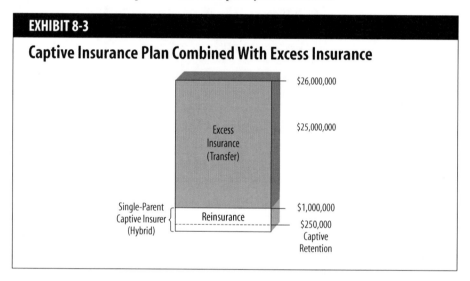

The organization purchases excess insurance on a guaranteed-cost basis with a limit of $25 million per occurrence to sit directly above the $1 million per occurrence layer of loss covered by the captive insurer. Therefore, the total limit of insurance available to the organization per occurrence is $26 million.

The organization, in effect, retains the first $250,000 per occurrence because its captive insurer retains $250,000 per occurrence, net of reinsurance. The portion of each covered loss that exceeds $250,000 per occurrence up to the policy limit of $1 million per occurrence is transferred to reinsurers through the organization's captive insurer.

To transfer risk, an organization might purchase excess insurance instead of purchasing reinsurance through its captive. For example, with the captive insurance plan just described, the organization might decide to purchase insurance for $750,000 per occurrence excess of $250,000 per occurrence rather than have the captive purchase reinsurance for the same layer of loss. In this case, the captive would issue a policy with a limit of $250,000 per occurrence rather than $1 million per occurrence. Exhibit 8-4 shows this alternative.

EXHIBIT 8-4

Purchasing Excess Insurance Instead of Reinsuring a Captive Insurer

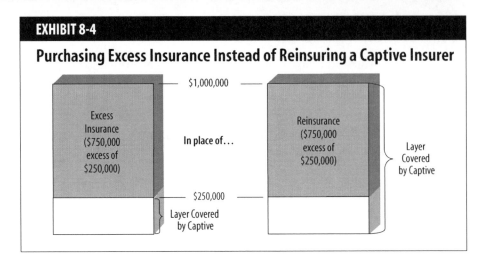

As described previously, the characteristics of a captive insurer normally involve both retention and transfer. Therefore, captive insurance often is a hybrid risk financing plan. The severity of the losses covered by a captive insurer, because losses are partially retained, is typically low to moderate. Further, because a captive insurer acts as any other insurer does, the losses are funded. Because the captive owner/parent is ultimately responsible for expenses, such as claim administration, loss control and underwriting, the administrative requirements of a captive insurance plan are substantial. Exhibit 8-5 summarizes the general characteristics of a common captive insurance plan.

EXHIBIT 8-5

General Characteristics of a Common Captive Insurance Plan

Retention/ Transfer	Severity of Losses	Funded/ Unfunded	Administrative Requirements
Hybrid (usually)	Low to medium	Usually funded	High

Several of these general characteristics change from one type of captive insurance plan to another.

TYPES OF CAPTIVE INSURANCE PLANS

Each type of captive insurance plan has unique features that address situations faced by an owner/insured(s). Captive insurance plan types include the following:

- Single parent (or pure) captive
- Group captive
- Risk retention group
- Agency captive
- Rent-a-captive
- Protected cell company

Single-Parent (or Pure) Captive

A **single-parent captive**, or **pure captive**, is a captive insurer owned by one company that insures all or part of the loss exposures of that company. Because a captive is an insurer, it requires an investment of capital by its parent(s), as well as expenditures to manage the company and to pay accounting, auditing, legal, and underwriting expenses. For a captive insurer to be economically viable, it has to insure loss exposures that generate substantial premium revenues to cover these expenditures. Consequently, single-parent captive insurers generally require a minimum annual premium of $2 million.[1]

A single-parent captive is a hybrid risk financing plan because, from its parent's point of view, a single-parent captive usually combines elements of retention and transfer. Because a single-parent captive covers its parent's losses and is part of the same economic family as its parent, losses retained by the captive are, in effect, retained by its parent. For the same reasons, losses transferred by the captive insurer (for example, through reinsurance or some other means) are, in effect, transferred by its parent. Some single-parent captive insurers who do not purchase reinsurance retain all of their losses and therefore should not be considered a hybrid plan.

Group Captive

A **group captive** is a captive insurer owned by a group of companies, usually operating similar businesses, rather than a single parent. A group captive is similar to a mutual insurer except that the insureds (owners) under a group captive exercise significantly more control over the management of the company than do the insureds under a typical commercial insurer.

An **association captive** is a group captive that is sponsored by an association. Many organizations consider the opportunity to obtain insurance through an association captive as one of the benefits of being a member of the association. For example, an association of paint manufacturers might sponsor a captive insurer for the benefit of its members.

A group captive (or an association captive) is considered a hybrid or a transfer plan, depending on its design. If each member (insured) of a group captive retains a portion of its own losses within the captive and shares the balance of its losses with other members, then the group captive is considered a hybrid plan. If each member shares all of its losses with the other members, then the group captive is considered a transfer plan.

Risk Retention Group

A **risk retention group** is a group captive formed under the requirements of the U.S. Liability Risk Retention Act of 1986 to provide liability coverage (except personal insurance, employers' liability, and workers' compensation). To form a risk retention group, all of its owners must be from the same industry and must be insured by the risk retention group. Conversely, all

Single-parent captive, or **pure captive**
A captive insurer owned by one company that insures all or part of the loss exposures of that company.

Group captive
A captive insurer owned by a group of companies, usually operating similar businesses, rather than a single parent.

Association captive
A group captive that is sponsored by an association.

Risk retention group
A group captive formed under the requirements of the U.S. Liability Risk Retention Act of 1986 to provide liability coverage (except personal insurance, employers' liability, and workers' compensation).

insureds must be owners. A major benefit of a risk retention group is that it needs to be licensed in only one state in order to provide liability coverage to group members anywhere in the United States. The Act supersedes state law that requires an insurer to be licensed in every state in which it sells insurance, thereby saving the risk retention group the expense of complying with regulations in each of the fifty states.

Agency Captive

Agency captive
A type of group captive that is owned by insurance agents or brokers rather than by the organizations insured.

An **agency captive** is a type of group captive that is owned by insurance agents or brokers rather than by the organizations insured. Agency captives are often formed in response to hard markets to insure select accounts for which there is a limited or nonexistent market. An agency may place a single line of insurance for heterogeneous businesses (such as workers' compensation for all commercial insureds) in the captive or multiple lines for homogeneous businesses (such as businessowners policies for retail stores). An agency captive provides a way for agents or brokers to assume a portion of risk and, in turn, generate underwriting and investment income.

Rent-a-Captive

Rent-a-captive
An arrangement in which an organization rents capital from a captive insurer, to which it pays premium and receives reimbursement for its losses.

A **rent-a-captive** is an arrangement in which an organization rents capital from a captive insurer, to which it pays premium and receives reimbursement for its losses. The organization also receives credit for underwriting profits and investment income. Consequently, the organization benefits from using a captive insurer but is not required to invest its own capital. Each insured keeps its own premium and loss account, so no risk shifting or distribution occurs among the members of a rent-a-captive. With some types of rent-a-captives, the insured organization must purchase nonvoting preferred stock and receives dividends on the stock equal to its underwriting profit and the investment income earned on its unearned premiums and loss reserves. If a plan does not involve the purchase of nonvoting preferred stock, then the rent-a-captive organization returns underwriting profit and investment income through some other means, such as policyholder dividends. The rent-a-captive organization charges a fee for its services. Rent-a-captives provide a means for an organization to form a captive insurer quickly without tying up capital.

Protected Cell Company

Protected cell company (PCC)
A group captive in which each participant pays premiums and receives reimbursement for its losses from, as well as credit for, underwriting profits and investment income, similar to a rent-a-captive.

A **protected cell company (PCC)** is a group captive in which each participant pays premiums and receives reimbursement for its losses from, as well as credit for, underwriting profits and investment income, similar to a rent-a-captive. With a PCC, each participant is assured that other participants will not be able to access its capital and surplus in the event the other participants become insolvent. Each participant is also assured that third-party creditors cannot access its assets. This protection does not necessarily exist with a rent-a-captive structure, which involves the purchase of preferred stock by participants.

ADVANTAGES AND DISADVANTAGES OF USING A CAPTIVE INSURANCE PLAN

Because it is usually a hybrid risk financing plan, a single-parent captive insurance plan has many of the advantages and disadvantages of both retention and transfer. The degree to which these advantages and disadvantages apply to a specific single-parent captive insurance plan depends on the design of the plan—that is, the amount of retention versus transfer built into the plan. The same is true of a group captive.

Advantages of Using a Captive Insurance Plan

There are many reasons to use a captive insurance plan, particularly when compared with other risk financing plans. The following are some of the more prominent advantages to forming or joining a captive insurer:

- Reducing the cost of risk
- Benefiting from cash flow
- Obtaining insurance not otherwise available
- Having direct access to reinsurers
- Negotiating with insurers
- Centralizing loss retention
- Obtaining potential cash flow advantages on income taxes
- Controlling losses
- Obtaining rate equity

Reducing the Cost of Risk

A captive insurance plan can reduce an organization's cost of risk over the long-run when compared to guaranteed-cost insurance because it involves retention; saves acquisition costs of obtaining insurance; reduces underwriting expenses; specializes claim adjusting functions; saves the cost of the commercial insurer's overhead and profit; and allows for investment income from premium, loss reserve, and collateral investment dollars. In addition, a group captive, if operated efficiently, can reduce a member organization's cost of risk by distributing the cost of administering the captive insurer among several members. Risk management professionals often consider reducing the cost of risk, and thereby preserving the resources of an organization, to be the most important advantage of a captive insurance plan.

Benefiting From Cash Flow

A captive insurer allows the insured(s) to benefit from the cash flow available on losses that are paid out over time because, under a funded plan, the captive earns investment income on premium funds that have not yet been paid out for claims. This includes investment income on loss reserves and unearned premiums. The insured benefits because it is part of the same economic family as the captive insurer.

However, the investment income earned by the captive is likely to be less than the insured's cost of capital. This constitutes an opportunity cost for the insured organization because it would realize a net savings if it could invest some or all of the cash tied up in the captive in its main business. The insured organization can retain some of the cash it would otherwise pay in premiums to the captive insurer by using a paid loss retrospective rating plan when paying premiums to its captive insurer. Also, some jurisdictions allow a captive insurer to lend funds back to its parent (the insured). This arrangement also overcomes the opportunity cost problem.

Obtaining Insurance Not Otherwise Available

Another advantage of a captive insurance plan is that its parent organization can obtain insurance coverage that is not available from commercial insurers. Such coverage includes liability insurance for environmental, products, and professional loss exposures. To obtain these kinds of coverage, the parent pays a premium to its captive, which then issues an appropriate insurance policy.

One could argue that using a single-parent captive to insure hard-to-place coverages does not constitute insurance because the parent owns the captive and, therefore, retains the premium and losses arising from its own loss exposures. However, in such cases, the captive may be able to negotiate a favorable reinsurance arrangement, which, in effect, transfers the parent's loss exposures just as a traditional insurance arrangement would.

Having Direct Access to Reinsurers

A captive insurer provides the insured organization direct access to the international market of reinsurers, which can be more flexible than insurers in terms of underwriting and rating. A captive insurer that uses reinsurance can capture any ceding commission on the reinsurance that would otherwise be paid to a commercial insurer. In addition, by removing the primary commercial insurer, the insured organization saves substantial markup costs. However, this advantage of gaining direct access to reinsurers is not as significant as it once was, because risk management professionals can often now deal directly with reinsurers, even in the absence of a captive insurance arrangement.

Negotiating With Insurers

The existence of a captive insurer can improve an insured's negotiating power with commercial insurers. Assume, for example, that an airline forms a single-parent captive insurer to retain a quota share percentage of its aircraft hull insurance. If premiums increase in the aircraft hull insurance market, the airline might increase the share it places in its captive. However, the fact that the airline has this option might increase its bargaining power with its commercial insurers, who might lower the airline's premium so as not to lose business to the captive.

Centralizing Loss Retention

Another advantage of a captive insurance plan is that the insured organization can use it to centralize retained losses that are spread throughout its subsidiaries. Centralization can result in savings to the insured organization because of the lower long-term cost of retention.

For example, if the management of a large multinational corporation wants to retain a significantly higher level of loss than each of its subsidiaries, it could use a single-parent captive to pool its losses on a worldwide basis and retain more losses than each of its subsidiaries, which purchase insurance from the captive. Exhibit 8-6 illustrates the operation of this type of plan.

EXHIBIT 8-6

Retaining Worldwide Risk of Loss in a Captive

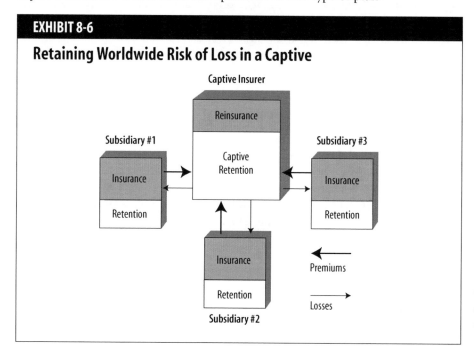

Subsidiaries #1, #2, and #3 each pay premiums to the captive, which takes a higher per occurrence retention than any of the subsidiaries.

Obtaining Potential Cash Flow Advantages on Income Taxes

Generally, a parent company may only deduct from its taxes the associated losses and other expenses that are paid by its captive insurer. In some cases, however, a parent company can achieve an even greater tax advantage by deducting from its taxes the premiums that it pays to its captive insurer. The Internal Revenue Service's (IRS) determination of whether premiums paid to a captive insurer are tax-deductible is based primarily on the following two factors:[2]

1. **Risk shifting**, which is the transfer of risk of loss to an insurer
2. **Risk distribution**, which is the sharing of risk by an insurer among its insureds

Risk shifting
The transfer of risk of loss to an insurer.

Risk distribution
The sharing of risk by an insurer among its insureds.

Brother-sister relationship
The relationship that exists when subsidiaries are owned by the same parent company.

The 1989 landmark Tax Court case involving Humana Corporation and its subsidiaries affirmed that the insurance premiums a parent company pays to its captive insurer generally are not tax-deductible. Humana owned a captive insurer to which it and each of its subsidiaries paid premiums. The Tax Court denied a deduction of the premiums paid by Humana to its captive insurer because it was the parent of the captive. It did, however, allow a deduction for premiums paid to the captive by each of Humana's subsidiaries. This allowance was based on the Tax Court's conclusion that the relationship between Humana's subsidiaries was a **brother-sister relationship**, which is the relationship that exists when subsidiaries are owned by the same parent company. If a brother-sister relationship exists, the risk shifting and distribution of loss exposures to the captive insurer are sufficient to allow the subsidiaries to deduct the premiums they pay to the captive insurer.

Based on prior rulings, a captive may need to insure as many as twelve subsidiaries that share a brother-sister relationship in order for its parent to deduct its premiums, but only if those subsidiaries transfer a roughly equal amount of loss exposures. Specifically, no subsidiary should absorb less than 5 percent or more than 15 percent of the risk distribution (per Ruling 2002-90).

Third-party business
Business that is not directly related to the captive's parent(s) or its subsidiaries.

The brother-sister relationship is one of several exceptions to the general rule of the Humana Corporation case that the insurance premium paid by a parent organization to its captive is normally not tax-deductible. Another exception involves **third-party business**, which is business that is not directly related to the captive's parent(s) or its subsidiaries. Some early tax rulings determined that if a large percentage of the captive's premiums are derived from third-party business, then the captive is considered to be operating at an arm's-length from its parent. In such a case, the premiums paid by the parent to the captive are tax-deductible. However, these early rulings did not determine how much of a captive insurer's premiums must be from third-party businesses in order to render the captive insurer an arm's-length insurer. In 1991, in three separate cases involving AMERCO, Harper, and Sears, the Tax Court allowed a deduction for premiums paid by each of the parents to their captives. In each case, the captive wrote substantial third-party business, ranging from 99 percent of the premium in the Sears case (Allstate was the insurance subsidiary in question) to less than 30 percent in the Harper case. These cases helped solidify the argument that substantial third-party business should enable a company to take tax deductions for premiums paid to its captive.

In May 2005, the IRS issued Ruling 2005-40, in which it held that a captive insuring one policyholder cannot accomplish adequate risk distribution to allow the premiums paid to the captive to be tax-deductible. In the same ruling, the IRS also stated that if the captive were to insure two policyholders, one of which absorbed a proportionately high amount of risk (a 90/10 split, for example), the premiums paid to the captive would again not be tax-deductible. The ruling did not address situations in which the split was more balanced.

Determining the tax-deductibility of the premiums paid to a captive insurer is complex. Tax Court cases and IRS rulings will continue to be applied to specific situations that will further define the conditions under which premiums paid to a captive insurer are and are not tax-deductible.

Many captive insurers are domiciled in offshore jurisdictions that have little or no income tax, such as the Bahamas, Bermuda, or Cayman Islands. Establishing a captive insurer in such a location allows a parent located in a high-income-tax country to save taxes if it deducts the premiums it pays to its captive and generates profits from the captive that are, in turn, subject to little or no income tax. In recent years, however, many countries, including the U.S. and the United Kingdom, have closed this loophole by requiring the parent company to pay tax in its home country on some or all of the profit generated by its offshore captive, even if the profit has not been paid as a dividend to the parent.

Controlling Losses

Because a captive insurance plan involves retention, an insured organization that controls its losses is able to save payments for losses and loss expenses. For a premium arrangement with a captive on a guaranteed-cost basis, the savings are immediately captured within the captive. For a premium arrangement with a captive on a retrospectively rated basis, much of the savings accrues directly to the insured organization. In addition, captive insurers can offer specialized risk control services that are similar to other commercial insurers.

Obtaining Rate Equity

An organization may have sufficient historical data to accurately predict its future losses with reasonable confidence. If the predicted losses are substantially lower than the premium being charged by its commercial insurer (taking into account the acquisition costs, overhead, and profit of the insurer) the risk management professional often concludes that the insured organization's premium is a result of the poor loss histories of other organizations with which it is pooled. In addition, raising the amount of retention does not always result in substantial premium reduction. A captive insurer has the rating flexibility to charge premiums that may more accurately reflect the predicted losses of its parent(s) and affiliates.

Disadvantages of Using a Captive Insurance Plan

When compared with other risk financing plans, a captive insurance plan presents several disadvantages, including the following, to the organization using it:

- Capital requirements and start-up costs
- Sensitivity to losses
- Pressure from parent company management
- Payment of premium taxes and residual market loadings

Capital and Start-Up Costs

A captive insurance plan involves a commitment of capital and start-up costs not incurred with other risk financing plans. Start-up and annual operating costs for a captive can range from $35,000 to more than $150,000.[3] Capital must be committed for several years. This requirement can, however, be met by using a letter of credit, which, in a captive insurance market, is a financial instrument issued by a bank at the request of a captive insurer in which the bank agrees to honor a demand for payment made by a third-party, which can be the captive's reinsurer or insurance regulator. Some captive domiciles' insurance regulators will allow letters of credit to satisfy the entire capital requirement.

Sensitivity to Losses

Captive insurance plans involve retention of losses, a potential disadvantage of their use. If the losses retained are higher than forecasted and exceed allocated funds, the financial solvency of the captive could be threatened. Financial insolvency would then prevent the payment of the parent company's losses. This disadvantage is especially relevant when the parent uses a group captive plan. Any of the insured members of a group captive that experience a particularly poor year of losses with high enough coverage limits could financially cripple the captive, regardless of the excellent loss histories of the other members. This peril of participating in a group captive can, at least partially, be prevented by using a rent-a-captive or a protected cell company captive, which segregate the underwriting account of each member.

Pressure From Parent Company Management

Captive insurers exist for the benefit of the parent organization. Consequently, another of their disadvantages is that they must insure the risks required by their parents. However, the pressure from the parent organization's management to insure risks in an economically advantageous fashion must be moderated. As previously discussed, the IRS requires an arm's-length relationship between the parent and its captive for the premiums paid to the captive insurer to be tax-deductible. Further, the reinsurer of the captive will likely be sensitive to overt pressure from the parent's management that may cause the captive's underwriting standards to be too lenient, its premiums too low, its claim payments too generous, or the lack of cooperation from the parent too easily ignored. This disadvantage may be of greater concern with a single-parent captive than with a group or association captive.

Premium Taxes and Residual Market Loadings

Another disadvantage of a captive insurance plan is that the losses retained by a captive insurer are paid for by the parent company as a premium on which premium taxes and residual market loadings are levied. However, these costs may be avoided or reduced by using a large deductible plan.

If, after considering these advantages and disadvantages, the organization's management decides to use a captive insurance plan, it must next conduct a feasibility study. A feasibility study will reveal how the proposed plan is expected to operate.

OPERATION OF CAPTIVE INSURANCE PLANS

An organization considering a captive insurance plan must first determine whether forming or joining a captive insurer is feasible by conducting a feasibility study. Many of the considerations crucial to operating a captive are addressed by such a study. If an organization deems a captive insurance plan feasible, it must resolve any remaining considerations, such as whether to operate as a reinsurer or direct writing insurer, selecting coverages, setting premiums, determining domicile, dedicating management resources of the parent company, administering the plan, and whether to write third-party business.

Conducting a Feasibility Study

An effective feasibility study should focus on senior management's goals for the captive insurance plan. This allows the risk management professional to optimize the plan's design. As a prelude to conducting the study, the risk management professional should also obtain an understanding with all his colleagues in senior management that the decision to enter a captive insurance plan requires careful consideration. It involves a multiyear commitment of substantial administrative and capital resources that could otherwise be invested at potentially higher rates of return elsewhere. This sacrifice of a possible higher return is often referred to as the opportunity cost. This cost can be measured, at least with respect to the capital resources used, by the parent company's borrowing rate or rate of return on investment.

The feasibility study should contain an analysis of the parent company's current risk financing structure, which includes the type of insurance coverages used, the amounts of coverage purchased, retention levels, premiums paid, supporting collateral, and type of rating plans applied. The goal is to understand the costs and benefits of the current risk financing plan.

The study should then assess the exposure basis of the parent company, which includes sales, payroll, and property values, for example. This assessment ideally should include several previous years in order to credibly project trends. Further, the study should consider any management plans that would affect the organization's loss exposures, such as, for instance, plans to merge with or acquire another company.

The study must also assess accidental losses. The parent company's history of losses (both retained and transferred) from at least the previous five years should be assessed in terms of the parent company's ability to perform risk control and to forecast expected future losses. Entering into a captive insurance plan will not resolve a risk control problem that must be separately addressed. Forecasting future expected losses will help the risk management professional determine the recommended level of retention verses transfer per occurrence and in the aggregate when structuring the captive insurance plan's coverage.

Forecasting losses will support the critical loss ratio assumption the organization uses in its pro forma financial statements. These statements should be prepared by a certified public accountant and include the following items:

- An income statement and balance sheet
- At least five years of projected pro forma financial results
- An accounting of the effects of all types of taxation (or an explanation of why a certain tax does not apply)
- At least one scenario that portrays worse than expected financial results and that demonstrates management has considered the possibility of financial impairment
- A detailed explanation of each assumption, such as expected loss ratio, interest rates, and year-to-year growth rates
- A model showing the minimum number of participants, premiums, and capital

Operating as a Reinsurer

Most countries have regulations requiring insurers to be licensed. For example, U.S. states require an insurer to be licensed to provide insurance for workers' compensation and automobile liability loss exposures. Most captive insurers are not licensed to provide these types of insurance in the U.S. In order to save the time and expense of obtaining such licenses, captive insurers usually operate as reinsurers behind U.S.-licensed insurers, which act as fronting companies.

Fronting company
A licensed insurer that issues an insurance policy and reinsures the loss exposures back to a captive insurer owned by the insured organization.

A **fronting company** is a licensed insurer that issues an insurance policy and reinsures the loss exposures back to a captive insurer owned by the insured organization. By having its captive reinsure a fronting company, the insured can benefit from using a captive insurer and at the same time comply with regulations that require the insurer to be licensed. In addition, a captive insurer that reinsures a fronting company usually satisfies other parties, such as mortgagees, loss payees, and business partners, that require the insured organization to purchase insurance from an established insurer with an acceptable claim-paying-ability rating from one of the rating agencies, such as A.M. Best or Standard & Poor's.

Exhibit 8-7 shows the relationships among the various parties when a captive uses a fronting company. Premiums are paid by the captive's parent (and its affiliates) to the fronting company, which issues an insurance policy. The fronting company deducts its fees and expenses and passes on the balance of the premium and the risk of loss to the captive insurer, which acts as a reinsurer of the fronting company. (In some cases, the fronting company retains a small quota share percentage of the loss exposures.) The captive insurer, in turn, retrocedes some of its risk to one or more reinsurers.

EXHIBIT 8-7

Operating a Captive as a Reinsurer

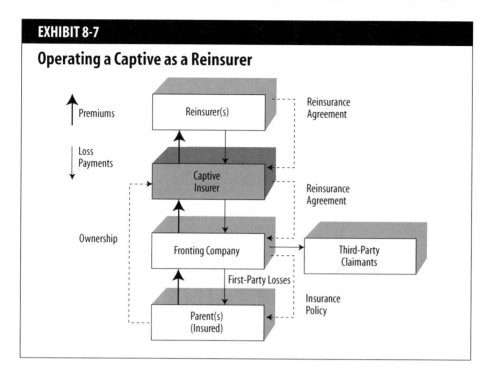

Because it issues an insurance policy, the fronting company is responsible for paying covered losses to the parent and third-party losses to other claimants. The fronting company is reimbursed for losses by the captive insurer. In effect, a licensed insurer (the fronting company) is guaranteeing the payment of losses covered by the captive insurer in order to satisfy jurisdictional regulations.

The relationship between the insured organization (the owner of the captive) and the fronting company is similar to the relationship between an insured and its insurer. The fronting company issues a policy to the insured, collects premium from the insured, and pays all losses, just as any other insurer would.

Yet a fronting company usually does not retain any underwriting risk (on a net basis) because it has a reinsurance agreement to transfer all premiums (less fees and expenses) and losses to the captive insurer. However, the fronting company does retain the credit risk that the captive may not have sufficient funds to reimburse it for payment of covered losses. To offset this credit risk, the fronting company usually requires a letter of credit or some other type of financial guarantee from the captive insurer.

A complication may arise if the fronting company decides to impose stricter collateral requirements that could make the captive's structure unfeasible. For example, the fronting company may require a separate letter of credit from every participant in a group captive, rather than a single letter for all the participants.

Another potential problem could arise if the fronting company charges an unreasonably high fee for its services or is unwilling to provide its services at any price. This can happen if the captive insurer is new to the industry and has no proven track record; the captive insurer is too small; the captive insures a line of business that has a history of problems; the type of captive is less desirable (some fronting companies may find a single-parent captive easier to underwrite than an association or group captive); or the number of commercial insurers in the fronting market has declined. Also, reinsurance may not be available at a level that sufficiently reduces the uncertainty of the captive insurer's retained losses.

The insured, through its ownership interest in the captive, is, in effect, retaining its own losses to the extent that they are retained by the captive. If the captive's premium (net of reinsurance premium) plus the investment income it earns on its cash flow exceeds its retained losses plus its expenses, the captive owner benefits because its ownership interest increases in value. The opposite applies if the captive's premium (net of reinsurance premium) plus investment income is less than retained losses plus captive expenses.

The fronting company often provides claim handling services for a fee, although sometimes the insured contracts with a third-party administrator to handle claims. The fronting company must pay expenses such as state premium taxes, license fees, service bureau charges, and residual market loadings, which it deducts from the premium before passing the balance to the captive.

As discussed, substantial expenses and other considerations, such as collateral requirements, are associated with obtaining a fronting company's services. These considerations have caused some organizations to limit their dependence on fronting companies. One alternative to using a fronting company is to operate as a direct writing captive insurer.

Operating as a Direct Writing Captive Insurer

Direct writing captive insurer
A captive that issues policies directly to its parent(s) and affiliates and does not use a fronting company.

For some types of insurance, a captive is able to operate as a **direct writing captive insurer**, which is a captive that issues policies directly to its parent(s) and affiliates and does not use a fronting company. For example, to provide many types of property, marine, and liability coverage in the U.S., an insurer does not need to be licensed. Therefore, a captive insurer can issue policies directly to its parent(s) and affiliates for these types of coverage. However, the captive insurer must comply with nonadmitted insurer regulations in each state and pay premium taxes. As another example, a captive insurer domiciled in Dublin, Ireland, does not need a license to sell insurance directly for its parent's (and affiliates') operations located throughout the European Union.

A major advantage of operating as a direct writing captive insurer is that a captive can save the fees charged by the fronting company, which range from 5 to 30 percent of premium.[4] This cost savings can make a direct writing captive insurance plan less expensive than commercial insurance and many other risk financing plans.

Selecting Coverages

Captive insurance plans are commonly used to cover losses that offer substantial cash flow, such as those covered by workers' compensation, general liability, and automobile liability policies. An advantage to covering these types of losses through a captive is that it can earn investment income on the substantial cash flow generated by the loss reserves. Captives are also used to cover property losses as well as losses that fall under specialized types of business, such as products and environmental liability.

Setting Premiums

The premium arrangement between the parent (and subsidiaries) and the captive insurer (with or without a fronting company) can be on a guaranteed-cost basis or a retrospectively rated basis. Under a guaranteed-cost arrangement, the insured organization pays a fixed premium rate, transferring the entire loss exposure to its captive. However, as mentioned, because the captive is part of the insured's economic family, any risk of loss retained by the captive is, in effect, retained by the insured. If the premium arrangement is on a retrospectively rated basis, the premium rate adjusts based on a portion of the insured's covered losses during the policy period. In this case, the insured and its captive share the loss exposure (again, with any residual loss retained by the captive, in effect, retained by the parent).

The retrospectively rated premium can be paid to the captive on a paid loss or an incurred loss basis. If the premium is on a paid loss basis, the cash flow benefit of the loss reserves for the insured's retained losses resides with the insured rather than with its captive insurer. The opposite is true if the premium is on an incurred loss basis.

A captive insurance plan is a funded plan if a guaranteed cost or an incurred loss retrospective rating plan is used to determine the premium paid by the insured. With these types of premium plans, funds are available within the captive to pay for losses as they become due. When a paid loss retrospective rating plan is used with a captive, the captive is unfunded for the portion of losses that the insured retains.

Using a Retrospective Rating Plan With a Captive Insurer

Assume that DKF Manufacturing (DKF) establishes a single-parent captive insurer and uses it to cover losses arising from its automobile liability and general liability loss exposures up to a limit of $1 million per occurrence/accident. To comply with regulatory requirements, DKF's captive insurer reinsures a fronting company, which issues the insurance policies to DKF.

Also assume that the insurance arrangement between DKF and the fronting company is an incurred loss retrospective rating plan with a loss limit of $100,000 per occurrence/accident. Therefore, DKF retains the first $100,000 of its own losses. DKF's captive reinsures the fronting company on the same retrospectively rated basis. Therefore, the deposit premium and retrospective adjustments are passed among DKF, the fronting company, and DKF's captive as follows:

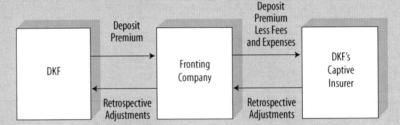

Assume that DKF's captive insurer purchases excess of loss reinsurance of $500,000 excess of $500,000 per occurrence/accident. (It does not purchase aggregate excess of loss reinsurance.) Therefore, the net loss exposure assumed by DKF's captive insurer is $400,000 per occurrence/accident excess of $100,000 per occurrence/accident, which is shown in the following diagram:

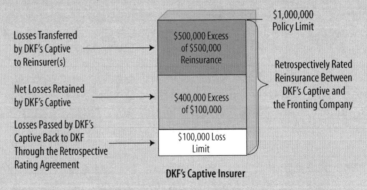

DKF's Captive Insurer

Because all retrospective rating agreements have a maximum premium, DKF's captive assumes the loss exposure that the losses subject to the loss limit of $100,000 will exceed the maximum premium under the retrospective rating plan between the fronting company and DKF.

To cover its reinsurance cost and its net retained loss exposure, DKF's captive builds an insurance charge (to account for the risk that the maximum premium might be exceeded) and an excess loss premium charge (to limit losses subject to retrospective rating to $100,000 per occurrence/accident) into the retrospective premium formula. In addition, DKF's captive includes its administrative costs and overhead in the basic premium, which is part of the retrospective premium formula.

Determining Domicile

Many jurisdictions encourage captive insurers to locate within their territories by offering favorable regulations and imposing little, or no, taxes. These jurisdictions see captive insurance as an industry that boosts their economies by providing employment and other income, such as annual registration fees.

The ten largest captive domiciles by number of captives (in descending order) are as follows:

1. Bermuda
2. Cayman Islands
3. Vermont
4. British Virgin Islands
5. Guernsey
6. Barbados
7. Luxembourg
8. Dublin
9. Turks & Caicos
10. Isle of Man

Bermuda has the largest number of captives by a considerable margin.

Although, theoretically, a captive insurer can be domiciled anywhere in the world, an organization usually chooses to place its captive insurer within a jurisdiction that is favorable for the formation and operation of captives. For example, some states require a single-parent captive to maintain a minimum capital and surplus of several million dollars, which is the same amount required of a commercial insurer. Tying up this much capital would make most single-parent captives uneconomical. By contrast, Vermont has a minimum capital and surplus requirement of $250,000 for a single-parent captive.

When evaluating a domicile for a captive insurer, the risk management professional should consider the following:

* Minimum premium requirements
* Minimum capitalization
* Solvency requirements
* Incorporation and registration expenses
* Local taxes
* Types of insurance that can be written
* General regulatory environment
* Investment restrictions
* Ease and reliability of communications and travel to and from the domicile

- Political stability
- Support infrastructure in terms of captive managers, claim administrators, bankers, accountants, lawyers, actuaries, and other services

Dedicating Management Resources of Parent Organizations

A captive insurer requires most, if not all, of the same management functions as any commercial insurer. For example, underwriting decisions must be made, policies must be issued, premiums must be billed and collected, and losses must be adjusted and paid. Other major functions include securing a fronting company, purchasing reinsurance, investing assets, and producing financial statements.

A single-parent captive, particularly one operating as a reinsurer, requires substantially less management than that needed for a group captive. A single-parent captive, by definition, is underwriting only its parent's (and subsidiaries') loss exposures, so it usually does not need to devote as many resources as a group captive would to underwriting and rating. For single-parent captives that operate as reinsurers, the fronting company performs many of the required functions, such as issuing policies, making filings, and adjusting claims.

Because of the limited amount of administration required, a single-parent captive usually finds it cost-efficient to hire a management company to oversee and coordinate tasks such as accounting, annual filings, purchase of reinsurance, and investment of assets. Dozens of companies, located in the widely used captive domiciles, specialize in managing captives. Many of these management companies are owned by a broker or an insurer, while others are independently owned.

Many group captives require the same amount of management as a large insurer requires, so a group captive can justify employing full-time staff. The volume of daily transactions can equal that of a large insurer. For example, some group captives insure (or reinsure) thousands of members, such as individual doctors or lawyers. A group captive must therefore frequently issue insurance policies and certificates and adjust and settle claims.

Administering the Plan

A single-parent captive plan can require more administration on the part of the insured (the parent) than do other risk financing plans that usually are applied to low- to medium-severity losses, such as retrospective rating or self-insurance plans. This is especially true in the formative stage, when the captive company must be incorporated and a domicile chosen. At this stage, relationships must be developed with captive managers, claim administrators, bankers, certified public accountants, lawyers, actuaries, regulators, and others. In addition, the parent must elect or appoint a board of directors and officers for the captive.

Requirements for Forming a Captive Insurer in Barbados[5]

Barbados is a domicile for many captive insurers. The following requirements illustrate Barbados' favorable regulatory and tax climate for establishing and operating a captive insurer:[6]

Requirement	Details
Minimum premium requirements	None.
Minimum capitalization requirements	$125,000 single-parent and group captives; letter of credit is permitted in place of cash.
Solvency requirements	Assets must exceed liabilities by $125,000 if prior year's premiums do not exceed $850,000. If premiums are between $850,000 and $5 million, assets must exceed liabilities by 20 percent of the premium and 10 percent for the portion of premium that exceeds $5 million.
Incorporation and registration expenses	$250 application fee; $390 incorporation fee; $2,500 initial license fee; $2,500 annual renewal fee.
Local taxes	None.
Types of insurance that can be written	All, subject to approval of superintendent of insurance.
General regulatory environment	Fairly lenient.
Investment restrictions	None.
Ease and reliability of communications and travel to and from the domicile	Good.
Political stability	Good.
Support infrastructure in terms of captive managers, claim administrators, bankers, accountants, lawyers, actuaries, and other services.	Good.

On an ongoing basis, the parent must oversee the management of its captive. Board meetings must be held annually, usually in the captive's domicile. The parent must oversee the adjustment of claims and make sure the fronting company (if used) is making the proper filings and passing on the premium to the captive promptly.

Group captives may or may not require substantial administration on the part of one of its members, depending on the degree of a member's involvement with the management of the group captive. In many cases, an individual member of a group captive has no more administration responsibilities than if it were purchasing insurance from a commercial insurer.

Insuring Third-Party Business

Many domiciles allow a captive insurer to insure third-party business. Often, a captive insures third-party business on a reinsurance basis because it is not licensed in the jurisdiction in which the third-party loss exposure is located.

Although third-party business potentially can generate profit for a captive, many captives have lost large sums of money insuring third-party business. This can occur when the captive insurer does not have a good understanding of the loss exposure involved.

Numerous organizations have found a benefit to insuring third-party business over which they have some control, such as warranties on the products they sell. In general, organizations understand this type of third-party business and, therefore, have a reasonable chance of making a profit by insuring it.

Understanding Financial Accounting Issues

As mentioned, because a single-parent captive insurer is a wholly owned subsidiary, its financial statements should be consolidated with those of its parent. Therefore, any profit or loss generated in the captive is reflected on the financial statements of its parent, similar to self-insurance.

Just as with any insurer, a captive insurer must recognize on its financial statements all losses as they are incurred. This includes an estimate for incurred but not reported (IBNR) losses if they can be determined with reasonable accuracy.

With a group captive, if risk shifting and distribution occur between the insured and the captive, the financial accounting treatment of the premiums is the same as with a guaranteed-cost insurance plan. The premiums are treated by the insured as an expense, and any dividends paid by the captive are treated as a return of premium to the insured.

SUMMARY

A captive insurer is a subsidiary that an organization forms to insure its own loss exposures. Organizations that are willing to retain a significant share of losses that offer substantial cash flow, such as those covered by workers' compensation, general liability, and automobile liability policies, often pursue a captive insurance plan to finance risk. These losses are usually retained by the captive insurer up to a certain point, beyond which they are transferred. This combination of retention and transfer classifies captive insurance plans as hybrid risk financing plans.

A variety of captive insurance plans exist, each of which is designed to address particular needs of its parent organization. A single-parent captive insurer is a subsidiary of only one parent company formed for the purpose of writing all or part of the insurance for its parent company. A group captive is a captive insurer owned by a group of companies, usually operating similar businesses, rather than a single parent. A risk retention group is a group captive that insures any type of liability coverage, except personal insurance, and employers' liability and workers' compensation. An agency captive is a type of group captive that is owned by insurance agents or brokers rather than by the organizations that are insured. A rent-a-captive is an arrangement in which an organization rents capital from a captive, to which it pays premium and receives reimbursement for its losses. A protected cell company is a group captive in which each participant pays premiums and receives reimbursement for its losses from, as well as credit for, underwriting profits and investment income, similar to a rent-a-captive.

The advantages of using a captive insurance plan include the following:

- Reducing the cost of risk
- Benefiting from cash flow
- Obtaining insurance not otherwise available
- Having direct access to reinsurers
- Negotiating with insurers
- Centralizing loss retention
- Obtaining potential cash flow advantages on income taxes
- Controlling losses
- Obtaining rate equity

The disadvantages of using a captive insurance plan include the following:

- Capital requirements and start-up costs
- Availability of fronting and reinsurance
- Sensitivity to losses
- Pressure from parent company management
- Payment of premium taxes and residual market loadings

If an organization's senior management weighs these advantages and disadvantages and decides to pursue a captive insurance plan, it must then conduct a feasibility study whose goal is to determine, based on management's goals, how to best operate the captive insurance plan. The captive insurance plan's operation includes deciding whether to design the captive to operate as a reinsurer through a fronting company, which is a licensed insurer that issues an insurance policy and reinsures the loss exposures back to a captive insurer owned by the insured organization. Depending on the loss exposures the captive insurance plan is designed to cover, management may instead choose to operate the captive insurer as a direct writing captive insurer, which is a captive that issues policies directly to its parent(s) and affiliates and does not use a fronting company.

Once this determination has been made, the organization selects the losses that the captive insurer will cover and sets the premiums accordingly. Additionally, the captive insurance company's domicile must be chosen. This decision often is based on a jurisdiction's financial and regulatory requirements for captives.

A captive insurer requires most, if not all, of the same management functions as any commercial insurer. Management must therefore dedicate resources accordingly to the plan's administration. Other considerations that affect the operation of captive insurance companies include the decision to insure third-party business and anticipating how a company's financial statements will be affected by the captive insurance company's accounting requirements.

Captive insurance plans provide organizations with flexibility that often rivals guaranteed cost insurance. Finite and integrated risk plans also present an organization with opportunities that may not exist with traditional insurance alone.

CHAPTER NOTES

1. International Risk Management Institute, *Risk Financing: A Guide to Insurance Cash Flow* (Dallas: International Risk Management Institute, Inc., 2000), 1st reprint, p. IV.K.5, March 1997.

2. For more information, including links to landmark court cases involving deductibility of premiums paid to captives, see www.assetprotectiontheory.com/captive_cases.htm.

3. Felix H. Kloman, "Captive Insurance Companies," in Harold D. Skipper, Jr., *International Risk and Insurance* (Burr Ridge, Ill.: Irwin/McGraw-Hill, 1998), p. 668.

4. Ibid., p. 681.

5. These are the requirements for an "exempt insurer," which is defined as a business (1) whose risks and premiums originate outside Barbados and (2) that is owned by persons resident outside the Caribbean Community.

6. International Risk Management Institute, *Risk Financing: A Guide to Insurance Cash Flow* (Dallas: International Risk Management Institute, Inc., 2000), p. B6, 2nd reprint, September 1998, and PricewaterhouseCoopers, "Barbados Insurance Companies" (PricewaterhouseCoopers, Inc., 2000), pp. 11–12.

Direct Your Learning

Finite and Integrated Risk Insurance Plans

After learning the content of this chapter and completing the corresponding course guide assignment, you should be able to:

■ Describe the characteristics of finite risk insurance plans.

■ Explain how finite risk insurance plans operate, including:

• Types of risks covered

• Experience fund terms and calculation guidelines

• Variations in the terms of plans

■ Describe the advantages and disadvantages of finite risk insurance plans.

■ Describe the financial accounting and tax implications of finite risk insurance plans.

■ Describe the characteristics of integrated risk insurance plans.

■ Explain how integrated risk insurance plans operate, including:

• Use of the plans

• Variations in the terms of plans

■ Describe the advantages and disadvantages of integrated risk insurance plans.

■ Describe the characteristics of insured organizations associated with successful finite and integrated risk insurance plans.

■ Define or describe each of the Key Words and Phrases for this chapter.

Develop Your Perspective

What are the main topics covered in the chapter?

Finite and integrated risk insurance plans are widely used by middle-market and large corporations that want to efficiently manage many of their traditional, nontraditional, and difficult-to-insure risks. This chapter describes how finite and integrated risk insurance plans are used, how they operate, and their advantages and disadvantages.

Review the characteristics of finite and integrated risk insurance plans.

- Which of the characteristics of these plans would benefit your organization?

- Who in your organization determines whether one of these risk financing plans would be appropriate?

Why is it important to learn about these topics?

Finite and integrated risk insurance plans offer several distinct advantages over traditional insurance products. The advantages include profit-sharing, investment income, higher limits, reduced cost of risk, and, for integrated risk insurance plans specifically, customization.

Examine the advantages and disadvantages of finite and integrated risk insurance plans.

- What advantages does a finite or integrated risk insurance plan have when compared with your organization's current risk financing plans?

- What disadvantages does a finite or integrated risk insurance plan have when compared with your organization's current risk financing plans?

How can you use what you will learn?

Analyze the effectiveness of the risk financing plans your organization currently uses.

- How well does the current strategy meet your organization's objectives?

- Which of your organization's risks may be covered more effectively by use of a finite or integrated risk insurance plan?

Chapter 9

Finite and Integrated Risk Insurance Plans

Finite and integrated risk insurance plans were once considered alternatives to traditional insurance during hard market conditions. They are now widely used by middle-market and large corporations that want to efficiently manage their traditional, nontraditional and difficult-to-insure risks.

For sophisticated, enterprise-focused risk management programs, a finite or integrated risk insurance plan can include financial or market risks, such as securities, interest rates, foreign exchange, and traded commodity price fluctuations. Both types of plans generally include multiyear terms and can be customized to meet an insured's individual risks. For example, an organization normally uses a finite and/or an integrated risk insurance plan for high-severity, high-volatility losses above a plan that involves retention, such as a self-insurance plan, a retrospective rating plan, or a captive insurance plan. However, under certain circumstances, an organization may use finite risk insurance to fund its working-level losses. Regardless of the plan's purpose, an insured must have a substantial annual cost of risk in order to justify the expenses involved with a finite and/or an integrated risk insurance plan.

CHARACTERISTICS OF FINITE RISK INSURANCE PLANS

A **finite risk insurance plan** is a risk financing plan that transfers a limited (finite) amount of risk to an insurer. A large percentage of the insured's premium in a finite risk insurance plan is used to fund the insured's own losses. The plans usually include a profit-sharing arrangement and are often characterized as hybrid plans because they combine the retention of self-insurance with the transfer of guaranteed-cost insurance.[1] Therefore, finite risk insurance plans are frequently referred to as "blended insurance" or "structured programs." If an insurer makes a profit under a finite risk insurance plan, it returns a portion of the premium to the insured organization, as specified by contract. This structure benefits an insured that is able to control its losses. Conversely, an insured that is not able to control its losses is protected because losses that exceed an aggregate retained amount are transferred to the insurer.

Finite risk insurance plan
A risk financing plan that transfers a limited (finite) amount of risk to an insurer.

Most finite risk insurance plans are somewhat similar in concept to a retrospective rating plan. However, a finite risk insurance plan usually covers an insured's high-volatility, high-severity losses over several years under a single contract, while a retrospective rating plan is usually applied to an insured's low- to medium-severity losses over a single year. Because events covered by finite plans tend to fluctuate over time, predicting finite plan results for a defined period can be challenging. Although no two finite risk insurance plans are exactly alike, most share the following characteristics:

- Coverage in the policy is often manuscript. In such a policy, the risk protection and policy language are negotiated between the insurer and the policyholder. Consequently, the policy is often tailored to meet the insured's individual needs. Coverage possibilities may be limited by lack of actuarial data necessary to underwrite the risk and by the insurer's appetite.

- Coverage is usually for multiple years, with terms of three to five years the most common. Contracts that specify terms in excess of ten years can be implemented for unique risks, including environmental risk and remediation coverages.[2]

- The limits of coverage apply on an aggregate basis. For example, a finite insurance policy might provide $150 million in limits over five years, with no more that $75 million in limits available in any single year or for any one occurrence.

- Coverage is normally noncancelable, except for breaches of contract.

- The premium is generally a substantial percentage of the policy limits. Premium percentages of finite risk insurance plans often exceed those of traditional insurance, because the charge is a function of the individual insured's frequency/severity risk profile. This high premium can result in an initial shock over the pricing of finite risk for insurance purchasers and their senior management who are not familiar with its purpose.

- The insurer shares profit, including investment income arising from positive cash flow.

- The insured is allowed to commute the plan within a specified time frame. A **commutation** is an agreement to extinguish all liabilities between the parties to an insurance or a reinsurance contract that usually involves a payment from the insurer to the insured (or from the reinsurer to the reinsured).

- Finite coverage may be accounted for as insurance under *FAS 113* (subsequently discussed). However, depending on the opinions of auditors and the amount of risk transfer, the structure may require other accounting and tax treatment.

- A finite risk insurance plan can be written as insurance or reinsurance. When written as reinsurance, a finite risk insurance plan can reinsure a captive insurer or a commercial insurer.

Commutation
An agreement to extinguish all liabilities between the parties to an insurance or a reinsurance contract that usually involves a payment from the insurer to the insured (or from the reinsurer to the reinsured).

OPERATION OF FINITE RISK INSURANCE PLANS

The operation of finite risk insurance plans can best be illustrated with an example. ABC Corporation is a publicly traded company whose primary business is the construction of single-family homes in the western United States. ABC's annual revenues are just under $300 million. The company sells approximately 1,000 homes per year whose average value is $275,000.

Insurance underwriters consider the home construction industry segment to be high risk from a liability standpoint as a result of the increasing number of construction defect lawsuits filed against homebuilders. This litigious trend has been most prominent in the western and southern U.S., where mold claims are now common. As their loss ratios have increased, a large number of insurers have decreased their capacity and increased the cost of coverage for homebuilders general liability policies.

ABC's high quality standards for home construction are reflected by its excellent twenty-year liability loss history. However, recent quotes it has received from insurers for general liability coverage have included relatively high premiums and low coverage limits, which are products of the industry's adverse experience, rather than of ABC's own loss history. ABC has substantial cash resources and is willing to retain a significant percentage of its homebuilders general liability risk. However, in the unlikely event that it suffers more than one significant loss over the next several years, its reported net income would drop significantly. This could cause the financial markets to bid down its share price.

ABC is undertaking a new corporate-wide risk management initiative to improve the rate of return on its deployed capital. Based on a comparison of the cost of traditional general liability insurance to the limits and terms of coverage provided, ABC decides to consider alternative risk financing plans. ABC asks its insurance broker to devise a structured insurance product that would enable it to spread the cost of any large losses over time. ABC's insurance broker suggests a finite risk insurance plan and obtains the quotation shown in Exhibit 9-1.

The quotation's higher limits are obtained, in part, because ABC is offering a multiple-year commitment while the insurer is assuming a limited (finite) amount of risk. A single large homebuilders liability loss or a series of moderately sized construction defect losses probably would not be fully paid for until many years after the occurrence. Therefore, the insurer has a period of several years over which to earn investment income on the net premium of $2.5 million, which is determined by deducting the insurer's fee of $500,000 from the deposit premium of $3 million. This fee is also referred to as the **margin**, which is an amount paid to the insurer under a finite risk insurance plan to compensate it for each type of risk it incurs and for its administrative expenses. The most that the insurer should ever have to pay over the five-year period is $5 million. The insurer's risk should be limited to $5 million minus the sum of the $2.5 million net premium and the earned investment income.

Margin

An amount paid to the insurer under a finite risk insurance plan to compensate it for each type of risk it incurs and for its administrative expenses.

EXHIBIT 9-1

ABC's Finite Risk Quotation

Coverage:	• General liability, including products-completed • Operations (construction defect) • Claims-made basis
Limits of liability:	$5 million per occurrence and aggregate for the coverage term
Attachment point (above a self-insured retention point)	$500,000 per occurrence
Deposit premium:	$3 million
Fee (paid to the insurer):	$500,000
Term:	Five years, noncancelable
Investment income credited:	Six-month Treasury bill (T-bill) rate
Commutation:	At the end of the five-year policy term and at each anniversary thereafter, ABC has the option to commute the agreement. Upon commutation, any funds returned to ABC (profit-sharing) are based on the following formula: $3 million deposit premium plus accrued investment income minus the $500,000 fee and the paid losses

Note that the plan shown in Exhibit 9-1 has many characteristics of a finite risk insurance plan. ABC pays a premium of $3 million at the beginning of the policy period to obtain a single aggregate limit of $5 million over the five years. By combining premiums and limits over five years, ABC can obtain a higher limit for its homebuilders general liability policy than it would be able to obtain with a single year's premium.

In exchange for assuming this limited amount of risk and to cover its expenses, the insurer receives the margin of $500,000 plus the opportunity to earn investment income that exceeds the rate of interest that it credits to the experience fund. The **experience fund** is a fund under a finite risk insurance plan that an insurer uses to share profit with the insured and whose amount is determined by adding the premium paid by the insured to the investment income earned and then subtracting the insurer's margin and paid losses. The investment income credited to the fund is earned at a negotiated rate, which, in ABC's case, is the rate for six-month Treasury bills (T-bills). The timing of the premium payment into the experience fund is frequently also negotiated. ABC's entire premium of $3 million is paid at the policy's inception, but the premium could have been negotiated to be paid over the policy's multiple-year term.

Experience fund

A fund under a finite risk insurance plan that an insurer uses to share profit with the insured and whose amount is determined by adding the premium paid by the insured to the investment income earned and then subtracting the insurer's margin and paid losses.

Upon commutation, any balance in the experience fund is returned to the insured. However, the insured would likely elect to commute the agreement only if the experience fund has a positive balance that is adequate to pay for the expected future losses that the insurer would no longer cover after the policy has been commuted.

The Experience Fund Concept and Mutual Insurance Companies

The experience fund concept is not unique to finite risk insurance plans. A common variation of an experience fund is applied within mutual insurance companies. The mutual insurer examines its losses on a portfolio basis and shares favorable loss results or profits with its members. Distributions are made fairly and equitably to members, frequently in the form of premium credits. A mutual insurer's application of the experience fund concept enables it to charge total premium at a level that ensures financial security, even in worst-case loss years, and develop and maintain loyalty from its membership base.

Exhibit 9-2 shows the relationship between retained losses (those paid out of the experience fund) and transferred losses under a finite risk insurance plan.

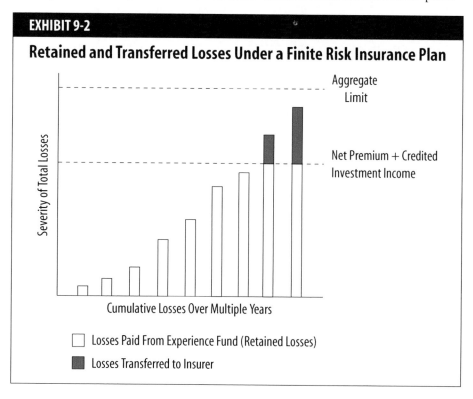

EXHIBIT 9-2

Retained and Transferred Losses Under a Finite Risk Insurance Plan

Because favorable financial accounting and income tax treatment add substantial value to a finite risk insurance plan, ABC hopes to be able to treat the deposit premium for the finite risk insurance plan in the same way it would treat the premium for a guaranteed-cost insurance plan. This treatment involves charging the $3 million deposit premium as an expense over the policy's five-year term for both financial accounting and tax purposes. This approach would provide ABC the benefit of a prorated tax deduction for paid premium over each of the five years and would also enable ABC to smooth the effect of a large loss on its financial statements over time with the creation of an off-balance-sheet fund[3] (the experience fund) that ABC could use to pay large general liability claims and settlements. However, as discussed subsequently, favorable financial and tax accounting treatments of a finite risk insurance plan are uncertain and depend largely on the design of a particular plan.

Types of Risk in Finite Risk Insurance Plans

Finite risk insurance plans, as well as most insurance transactions, involve varying degrees of three different types of risk:

1. Underwriting risk
2. Investment risk
3. Credit risk

Finite risk insurance can be better understood if it is analyzed in terms of these various types of risk.

Underwriting risk is the risk that an insurer's losses and expenses will be greater than the premiums and the investment income it expects to earn under the insurance contract.[4] For example, suppose an insurer receives $5 million in premiums for a finite risk insurance plan and expects to earn $3 million in investment income on the deposit premium. Therefore, the insurer expects to have $8 million available to cover losses and expenses during the coverage term. Also, suppose the limit of the finite risk insurance policy is $15 million, which is the maximum the insurer is required to pay. Based on these parameters, the insurer is assuming $7 million of underwriting risk under the finite policy.

Investment risk is the risk that an insurer's investment income will be lower than it expects and includes timing risk and interest rate risk. **Timing risk** is the risk, under an insurance contract, that the insured's losses will be paid faster or more slowly than expected. **Interest rate risk** is the risk that interest rates will be below the expected rate during the term of the insurance contract. Timing risk and interest rate risk together constitute investment risk. For example, an insurer's investment income will be lower than it expects if losses are paid sooner than expected and/or interest rates are lower than expected.

Credit risk is the risk that an insurer will not collect premiums owed by its insured. For example, under a paid loss retrospective rating plan, an insured pays premiums as the insurer pays losses. The insurer is responsible for paying all covered losses under the policy, even those losses not reimbursed by the insured. The insurer assumes a credit risk with this transaction because it may have to pay losses for which it is not reimbursed.[5] If an insurer has significant concerns about the creditworthiness of an insured, it may require full deposit

Underwriting risk
The risk that an insurer's losses and expenses will be greater than the premiums and the investment income it expects to earn under the insurance contract.

Investment risk
The risk that an insurer's investment income will be lower than it expects and includes timing risk and interest rate risk.

Timing risk
The risk, under an insurance contract, that the insured's losses will be paid faster or more slowly than expected.

Interest rate risk
The risk that interest rates will be below the expected rate during the term of the insurance contract.

Credit risk
The risk that an insurer will not collect premiums owed by its insured.

of premium prior to coverage inception, request some form of collateral, or decline to offer finite coverage.

A guaranteed-cost plan contains all three types of risk. When pricing a guaranteed-cost plan, an insurer calculates an expected amount of losses, expenses, and investment income. If actual losses and expenses on an individual policy are higher than expected, the insurer suffers an underwriting loss on the policy. Alternatively, if actual losses and expenses on the policy are lower than expected, the insurer realizes an underwriting gain. If actual investment income is lower than expected, the insurer suffers a loss due to investment risk. An insurer suffers a credit risk loss if the insured does not pay the premium.

When insurers underwrite on a guaranteed-cost basis, they usually issue a large number of policies, each covering similar loss exposures. Applying the law of large numbers on a portfolio basis, the insurer charges each insured a guaranteed-cost premium that reflects the expected, or average, annual amount of loss that will arise from each insured's exposures. If the insurer suffers an underwriting loss on one policy, it hopes to make it up with an underwriting gain on other policies. The insurer hopes to minimize its underwriting risk by spreading it out among the many policies it writes.

Finite risk insurance plans do not involve the same overall relationship between premiums and losses. Because each finite risk insurance plan tends to be unique, the insurer has to underwrite and manage each policy on an individual basis. Specifically, the insurer uses the premium and investment income from an individual finite risk policy largely to fund losses covered by that policy. The insurer charges a deposit premium that is a substantial percentage of the policy limits and sets aside a percentage of the deposit premium for the margin. The premium and limit are spread over several years, allowing for a large expected amount of investment income. Therefore, compared with a guaranteed-cost insurance policy, a finite risk policy involves a much higher degree of self-funding on the insured's part, and the insurer assumes a much lower degree of underwriting risk.

Exhibit 9-3 illustrates underwriting and investment risks for ABC's finite risk insurance plan. For ABC's finite risk plan, the net premium paid into the experience fund is $2.5 million. The most the insurer would ever have to pay in losses is $5 million. The term of the policy is five years (claims-made); however, any homebuilder liability claims will likely have a long settlement process. Therefore, losses covered by the finite risk plan are expected to be paid out over ten years. If the timing of loss payments and investment earnings is as expected, the cumulative investment income will equal $1 million over the ten-year period. Therefore, the net premium plus the investment income is expected to equal $3.5 million of total expected experience fund credits over the ten-year period. Under this scenario, the following would apply:

- The insurer is subject to a possible loss arising from underwriting risk, because the total losses could fall between $3.5 and $5 million.

- The insurer is subject to a possible loss arising from investment risk because the investment income may be lower than $1 million. (Note that, at lower loss levels, the insurer will probably not realize a loss arising from investment risk, because premiums plus investment income probably would be sufficient to fund losses.)

- The insurer has required that the premium be paid in one lump sum at the beginning of the policy period, rather than as annual payments throughout the policy period. This eliminates the possibility of loss associated with credit risk.

- To cover its administrative expenses, as well as to obtain compensation for taking the chance of a loss arising from underwriting, investment, and/or credit risk, the insurer receives a $500,000 premium (the margin) plus the chance to make an investment gain. The insurer makes an investment gain if it invests the funds at a rate that is higher than the six-month T-bill rate, which is the interest rate it credits to the experience fund.

EXHIBIT 9-3

Underwriting and Investment Risk Under ABC's Finite Risk Insurance Plan

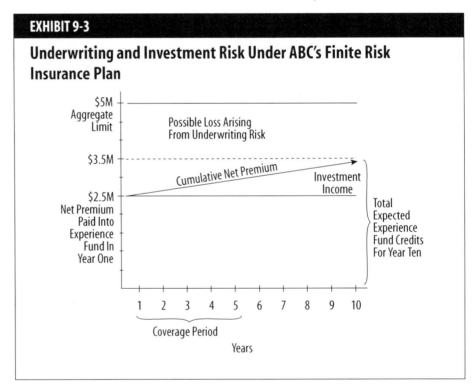

Experience Fund Terms and Calculation Guidelines

Because the majority of finite risk insurance policies are written to meet each insured's specific needs, terms for experience fund calculations can vary significantly. Some experience fund policy provisions are equation-based, while others are word-based, using timeline and settlement examples. The terms in the provisions tend to be very flexible and are negotiated in policy development.

This flexibility is partially because the experience fund calculation involves multiple components (for example, interest rates, margin, deposit premium, and losses) whose values change over time.

Before deciding to purchase a finite risk insurance plan, the insured organization must understand how the balance of the experience fund will respond under low, medium, and high levels of loss. Using scenario analysis, the insurer and insured can determine whether the fund will be sufficient to pay for losses at different levels and with different payment patterns. The insurer can use this information to measure its underwriting and investment risk. The insured also can use this information to determine the adequacy of coverage and the economic viability, or net cost, at various loss levels.

Use of Finite Risk Insurance Plans

Because the insurer assumes a carefully controlled, limited amount of risk, the underwriter of a finite risk insurance plan will usually agree to cover a broader range of exposures than it would cover under a traditional insurance plan. The coverage's breadth is governed by the availability of sufficient, unbiased risk information and underwriting data. In addition to covering commonly insured property and liability exposures, finite risk insurance plans can be used for many difficult-to-insure exposures, such as products recall, warranties, environmental liability (including cleanup), and illiquid commodity price fluctuations.

Finite risk insurance plans can be particularly beneficial for organizations involved in an acquisition or a merger. When the parties to an acquisition or a merger negotiate terms, they often must address an outstanding liability, such as a potential environmental cleanup exposure. A finite risk insurance plan that covers the potential environmental losses to fund an otherwise uninsurable exposure can help the parties complete their merger or acquisition agreement.

Regardless of the risks it covers, the value of a finite risk plan to an insured depends largely on the following factors:

- The cost effectiveness and availability of traditional insurance coverage
- Favorable financial accounting
- Beneficial income tax treatment
- Regulatory approval (if needed)
- Management's confidence that the program will provide a material benefit to the company's key stakeholders

Variations in the Terms of Finite Risk Plans

As stated previously in this chapter, finite structures are generally manuscript and tailored to each individual insured. ABC's policy's structure provides a finite insurance example that encompasses more common coverage features. Because the finite risk marketplace continues to evolve, it is difficult to present an exhaustive current account of all coverage options. However, the following section explores several less exotic variations of finite risk insurance coverage that have been consistently offered by insurers over the last decade.

Per Occurrence and/or Annual Aggregate Limits

In addition to an aggregate limit over the term of the agreement, a per occurrence limit can be placed on a finite risk insurance plan, reducing the insurer's risk. For example, ABC's finite risk insurance plan could have a per occurrence limit of $2.5 million as well as the aggregate limit of $5 million over five years. Therefore, if a single $5 million loss occurs, only $2.5 million of it would be covered under the plan.

In addition to a per occurrence limit and an aggregate limit over the term of the agreement, an aggregate limit can be placed over each year, further reducing the insurer's risk. For example, ABC's finite risk insurance plan could have an aggregate limit of $3 million per year as well as the per occurrence limit of $2.5 million and the aggregate limit of $5 million over five years. Therefore, if two $2.5 million losses occur in the first year, only $3 million would be covered under the plan.

For ease of reference, occurrence, annual aggregate, and policy term limits are frequently broken out and emphasized on a finite risk insurance policy's declarations page.

Limits on Annual Loss Payout

To lower the insurer's investment risk, a finite risk insurance plan can place limits on the annual payout of losses. For example, ABC's finite risk plan could impose a loss payout limit of $750,000 per year for the first five years so that during that period it is less likely that the insurer's cumulative loss payout will exceed the balance of the experience fund. Placing an annual limit on the loss payout guarantees that a minimum amount of investment income will be credited to the experience account. The annual limit on loss payout does not limit the amount of loss the insurer will pay over the term of the agreement; it just limits the amount the insurer will pay in any one year. Limits on annual loss payouts may create timing risk for the insured.

Contingent Sharing of Investment Income

A finite risk insurance plan can contain a provision to share investment income if the earned investment income exceeds the agreed-upon interest credit to the experience fund. For example, ABC's finite risk insurer could agree to credit the experience fund with one-half of the insurer's investment income to the extent that it exceeds the six-month T-bill rate.

Contingent sharing of investment income can be a key point of negotiation during the manuscripting of experience fund terms and calculations, particularly if a large interest rate spread is expected between T-bill rates and other securities in which the insurer intends to invest over the term. In addition, comprehensive investment income sharing can further align insurer and insured interests and enhance the finite risk transfer partnership.

Margin Based on a Sliding Scale

With ABC's finite risk plan, the insurer receives a fixed margin of 16.67 percent ($500,000 ÷ $3,000,000) of the deposit premium. Instead of being a fixed percentage, the margin could vary based on the loss ratio that falls under the plan, with the margin decreasing for favorable loss experience and increasing for unfavorable loss experience. This arrangement provides the insured with an additional incentive to control losses. The margin could be structured as follows:

Loss Ratio Percentage	Margin Amount	Margin Percentage
70–100	$750,000	25.00
30–69	$500,000	16.67
0–29	$250,000	8.33

Therefore, the margin falls to 8.33 percent if losses divided by the deposit premium are 29 percent or less and rises to 25 percent if losses divided by the deposit premium are 70 percent or more. Because the margin is subtracted in order to calculate the net premium, which is credited to the experience fund, decreasing the margin increases the amount available in the experience fund. Alternatively, increasing the margin decreases the amount available in the experience fund.

The application of this provision often depends on the frequency and severity profile of the risk being insured. If the finite coverage is for a single, high-severity risk whose probability increases with time, the desirability of this feature decreases for the insured, and it may also decrease for the insurer.

Additional Premium Requirement

A finite risk insurance plan might require that the insured pay an additional premium if total losses exceed a certain level. In such cases, the insured retains some of the risk that losses will exceed that level. This additional risk retention should be reflected through a lowering of the margin built into the plan.

The inclusion of an additional premium requirement can have substantial economic benefits for an insured. Due to the value of liquidity, many insureds prefer to maintain their cash as a current asset as long as possible instead of using it to meet premium payments. This is particularly true if the insured organization has significant business and growth opportunities that require near-term cash investment. In order to properly assess the risk and return trade-off of the additional premium provision, a potential insured can have the insurer price a finite risk insurance policy with standard terms and with an additional premium requirement. This requirement also stipulates that the deposit premium would be paid over the term of the agreement rather than at the policy's inception.

Prospective Versus Retroactive Plans

A **prospective plan** is a risk financing plan arranged to cover losses from events that have not yet occurred. A **retroactive plan** (sometimes called a retrospective plan) is a risk financing plan arranged to cover losses from events that have already occurred.

For example, a pharmaceutical company may be the subject of an uninsured multimillion-dollar lawsuit alleging that an injury was caused by one of its products. The pharmaceutical company does not know what the outcome of the suit will be and, therefore, is uncertain as to the magnitude, payout, and timing of the related loss. A finite risk insurance plan can be designed that covers this loss on a retroactive basis.

However, a retroactive plan may attract intense senior management and regulatory scrutiny regarding its qualification as insurance. For a retroactive plan to qualify as insurance, it must address an underlying uncertainty (such as the amount and timing of an adverse verdict in the pharmaceutical company's lawsuit), contain significant risk transfer, entail payment of risk premium, and be implemented for reasons beyond smoothing and earnings management. These characteristics are consistent with the features of traditional insurance contracts.

Loss Portfolio Transfers

A **loss portfolio transfer** is a type of retroactive plan that applies to an entire portfolio of losses. The losses usually have established reserves, but uncertainty exists as to the timing of the loss payments and the potential for further loss development. Loss portfolio transfers are frequently used as a risk transfer vehicle in the reinsurance sector and in self-insured organizations.

A loss portfolio transfer can be accomplished with a finite risk insurance agreement. For example, a captive insurer could transfer all of its outstanding workers' compensation losses from 2001, 2002, and 2003 with a finite risk insurance plan that provides an aggregate limit and returns funds to the captive if total losses are settled for amounts that are less than its outstanding reserves or if investment income is higher than expected.

An insured can usually negotiate a loss portfolio transfer for its working-level losses. These are losses characterized by low to medium severity and high frequency.

Prospective plan
A risk financing plan arranged to cover losses from events that have not yet occurred.

Retroactive plan
A risk financing plan arranged to cover losses from events that have already occurred.

Loss portfolio transfer
A type of retroactive plan that applies to an entire portfolio of losses.

ADVANTAGES AND DISADVANTAGES OF FINITE RISK INSURANCE PLANS

Finite risk insurance plans entail several advantages and disadvantages. The advantages include the following:

- Smooth out losses and premium costs over time
- Incorporate the features of retention and transfer
- Provide higher coverage limits
- Meet contractual and regulatory requirements
- Reduce the cost and time required for renewals
- Improve risk management budgeting
- Enhance market relationships

A finite risk insurance plan smooths out losses and premium costs over time. Given advantageous accounting treatment, a finite risk insurance plan can mitigate the effect of large losses on the insured's net income (profit) in its financial statements by treating the annual premium as an expense on its financial statements and on its income tax returns. Even with guaranteed-cost insurance, an insured that suffers a large loss in one year is likely to face an increase in premium the following year, which then lowers its net income. Finite risk insurance can help an organization avoid large swings in coverage costs because these policies fix costs over several years.

A finite risk insurance plan also incorporates the best features of retention and transfer. An insured that can control its losses under a finite risk insurance plan shares in the resulting profit, including investment income on the cash flow from the experience fund. The insured also is protected by a limited amount of risk transfer in the event that losses are much higher than expected.

Another advantage of a finite risk insurance plan is the higher coverage limits it offers. A finite risk plan often enables an insured to obtain higher limits than those provided by guaranteed-cost insurance plans. Underwriters are willing to provide these higher limits because a finite risk insurance plan combines premiums and limits over several years under a single plan.

In addition, a finite risk insurance plan can help the insured organization meet contractual and regulatory requirements by allowing it to certify to third parties that it has insurance coverage that might not otherwise be available. For example, many states require residential homebuilders to provide proof of general liability insurance. A hard market for homebuilders general liability coverage could make it cost-prohibitive to comply with this requirement. Therefore, homebuilders and insurers have developed and implemented finite risk insurance policies similar to the one used in the ABC Corporation example, whose higher limits allow for such coverage.

A further advantage of a finite risk plan is that it reduces the cost and time required for renewals. With traditional insurance plans, the insured, insurer, and broker spend a great deal of time each year renewing the insurance program. Underwriting information must be gathered and analyzed, and the premium must be negotiated. Although finite risk insurance plans involve these same tasks at renewal, renewal takes place only once every several years.

A finite risk plan also improves risk management budgeting by allowing the insured organization to better forecast insurance costs. The absence of annual renewals and the associated year-to-year fluctuations in premium creates greater certainty for the insured organization relative to a guaranteed-cost insurance plan's annual premium fluctuations.

A finite risk insurance plan enhances market relationships, another of the plan's advantages. Finite risk insurance plans require a close collaboration between the insured and the insurer during the underwriting, structuring, implementation, and settlement phases. This collaboration involves a substantial time commitment from both parties but ultimately enables the insurer to more comprehensively address the unique needs of the insured organization.

While there are substantial advantages associated with finite risk insurance plans, there are also tangible disadvantages to program implementation. Several of the disadvantages are as follows:

- Opportunity cost of capital
- Multiple-year aggregate limit
- Premium taxes
- Difficulty reentering the traditional marketplace
- Regulatory, auditor, and stakeholder scrutiny
- Potentially adverse accounting and tax treatment

An insured organization should carefully consider the disadvantages of the opportunity cost associated with having its capital tied up in an experience fund associated with a finite risk insurance plan. The cash balance in the experience fund usually is credited with a short-term investment rate based on the three- or six-month T-bill rate. The insured's cost of capital is almost certainly higher than the rate credited to the fund. This results in an opportunity cost to the insured because the insured could have otherwise used the funds as capital and earned a higher rate of return. Most finite risk insurance plans build up a large cash balance in the experience fund over time. A thorough assessment of the cost of capital spread can serve as a basis for negotiation prior to the binding of coverage.

Another disadvantage of a finite risk insurance plan is the multiple-year aggregate limit. If a full-limit loss occurs early in the term of a finite risk insurance plan, no further limits are available, even though the terms of the finite structure may require the insured to pay premiums for the remainder of the policy period. To combat this weakness, many finite policies now include an optional "limit buy-back" provision, often at a specified rate, if limits are exhausted in the first years of coverage. This provision reinstates the limit of coverage for subsequent losses.

Another disadvantage of a finite risk insurance plan is its related premium taxes, which can be a large expense. Depending on the structure of the finite risk insurance plan, state premium, surplus lines, or federal excise taxes may be due. For example, if a finite risk insurance plan is placed with an admitted insurer, then state premium taxes, which can be 2 to 3 percent of premium, are due. If a finite risk insurance plan is placed with a nonadmitted, offshore insurer, then a surplus lines or a self-procurement tax and a federal excise tax (for premiums paid to offshore insurers) may be due based on the premium amount.

A finite risk insurance plan may also present difficulties for an organization reentering the traditional marketplace. An insured organization may face additional time commitments associated with submissions and relationship development if it elects to reenter the insurance marketplace instead of renewing a finite risk insurance plan at expiration. Disparities between the finite risk insurance plan's coverage and cost and the coverage prices available in the traditional marketplace may also exist.

An additional disadvantage of a finite risk insurance plan is the regulatory, auditor, and stakeholder scrutiny its use may attract as a result of its financial accounting and tax implications. Both the insurer and insured may invest substantial time commitments and incur heavy costs to obtain approval and clarify treatment of a finite risk insurance plan from necessary regulators, auditors, members of senior management, and stakeholders.

Failure to obtain favorable accounting and tax treatment can constitute another disadvantage of a finite risk insurance plan. The loss of these advantages can adversely affect the insured and the insurer.

FINANCIAL ACCOUNTING AND TAX IMPLICATIONS OF FINITE RISK INSURANCE PLANS

A great deal of uncertainty exists regarding the financial accounting and income tax treatments of finite risk insurance plans. As mentioned, the value of a finite risk insurance plan to an insured organization depends largely on its ability to obtain favorable financial accounting and income tax treatments. However, the U.S. Financial Accounting Standards Board (FASB) has issued accounting standards and opinions that severely limit an insured's ability to treat the premiums under a finite risk insurance plan as it would treat premiums for traditional insurance.

An insured organization considers accounting and tax treatment for a finite risk insurance plan to be favorable if it is allowed to treat the premium as an expense on its financial statements and its income tax returns. Such treatment allows an organization to smooth out its reported expenses over time for its large losses and take a tax deduction on payments to fund those losses.

Because the premium for a finite risk insurance plan is used both to fund the insured's losses and to transfer a limited amount of risk, it is difficult to determine the appropriate accounting and tax treatments for the premium payments, regardless of whether the premium is paid in full at inception or in annual installments over the term. Many complex financial accounting and income tax issues affect treatment. Each finite risk insurance plan is different from others because it is customized for an insured's requirements. Therefore, the terms of each plan must be individually analyzed to determine whether it meets current accounting and tax guidelines.

Financial Accounting Issues

FASB statements and pronouncements have decreased opportunities to obtain favorable financial accounting treatment for a finite risk insurance plan. These statements and pronouncements include *Statement of Financial Accounting Standards No. 113 (FAS 113)*, *Emerging Issues Task Force (EITF) 93-6*, and *EITF 93-14*.

FAS 113: Accounting and Reporting for Reinsurance of Short-Duration and Long-Duration Contracts, applies specifically to reinsurance, including finite risk reinsurance. However, there is a widespread belief that auditors should apply its principles to finite risk insurance as well.

Treating Contracts as Reinsurance Under *FAS 113*

Two conditions must be met in order to account for a transaction as reinsurance under *FAS 113*:

1. The reinsurer assumes *significant* insurance risk under the reinsured portions of the underlying insurance contracts.

2. It is *reasonably possible* that the reinsurer may realize a significant loss from the transaction.[6]

To apply these two guidelines, the italicized words must be interpreted. "Insurance risk" is defined to include both timing risk and underwriting risk. "Reasonably possible" means that a chance exists that is more than remote. "Significant loss" is not defined in the statement. Therefore, the guidelines under *FAS 113* provide limited guidance as to whether a particular transaction can be accounted for as reinsurance.

If it is determined that a reinsurance transaction meets the standards specified by *FAS 113*, then the annual reinsurance premium is allowed as an expense on the insurer's financial statements each year.

If a reinsurance transaction does not meet *FAS 113*'s standards, then the insurer must account for the premium as a deposit to fund its losses; that is, the insurer cannot recognize the annual premium payments as an expense but instead must recognize its losses as an expense as they are incurred. As a result, the insurer's reported net income can vary significantly from year to year based on the timing and the size of actual incurred losses.

The provisions of *FAS 113* can be applied to finite risk insurance. *FAS 113* makes it clear that for a finite risk plan to be treated as insurance, it should transfer underwriting risk as well as timing risk. In addition, the plan should be designed so that it is "reasonably possible" that the insurer could realize a "significant loss" from the transaction. *FAS 113* provides no guidelines for defining a "reasonably possible significant loss." However, one method some insurance accounting professionals use to assess the applicability of *FAS 113*, known as the 10/10 Rule, states that there must be a 10 percent chance that the insurer could suffer a loss equal to 10 percent of its premium on the transaction on a present-value basis.

Some risk management professionals believe that the amount paid for the margin meets *FAS 113*'s standards because the margin functions like a guaranteed-cost insurance premium, which the insurer uses to fund the underwriting risk and timing risk on the transaction. Based on this reasoning, some risk management professionals assert it is reasonably possible for the insurer under a finite risk insurance plan to realize a significant loss on the margin. In this case, it is only the net premium for which uncertainty exists regarding financial accounting and tax treatments.

In 1993, FASB further clarified the financial accounting issues surrounding finite risk reinsurance by issuing *EITF 93-6*. (An *EITF*, an opinion issued by FASB's Emerging Issues Task Force, does not have the same authority as a Financial Accounting Standard.) Soon thereafter, the provisions of *EITF 93-6* were extended to insurance with the issuance of *EITF 93-14*.

EITF 93-6 (and **EITF 93-14** by extension) are two opinions issued by the Emerging Issues Task Force of the Financial Accounting Standards Board (FASB), which, taken together, require an insured under a finite risk insurance plan to recognize the retained portion of losses as they are incurred for financial accounting purposes. These two opinions suggest that an insurer and insured should make the following accruals at the end of each accounting period if treating a plan as insurance under *FAS 113*:

* The insured should accrue any experience-related obligations to pay cash or other consideration to the insurer as a liability in its financial statements.

* Conversely, the insurer should state the insured's experience-related obligations to pay cash or other consideration as an asset in the insurer's financial statements.

* The insured should state any experience-related right to payment from the insurer as an asset in its financial statements.

* Conversely, the insurer should state the insured's experience-related right to payment as a liability in the insurer's financial statement. Failing to do so would result in incorrectly stating a contingency reserve before the occurrence of the losses that are being transferred from the insured to the insurer.

EITF 93-6 and *EITF 93-14*
Two opinions issued by the Emerging Issues Task Force of the Financial Accounting Standards Board (FASB), which, taken together, require an insured under a finite risk insurance plan to recognize the retained portion of losses as they are incurred for financial accounting purposes.

Hence, if a finite risk insurance plan's structure meets *FAS 113*'s standards, then the plan can provide substantial loss-financing benefits to an organization.[7] Therefore, it is crucial that a finite risk insurance plan's design renders it "reasonably possible" for the insurer to realize a "significant loss" and does not create experience-related obligations for the insured to pay or receive cash

Tax Issues

In the U.S., the concepts that apply to financial accounting also apply to the tax treatment of finite risk insurance plans. Many tax accountants believe that *FAS 113*, while applying to financial accounting standards, is also a useful source of guidance for determining the tax deductibility of premiums.

Based on previous U.S. Tax Court cases and Revenue Rulings by the Internal Revenue Service (IRS), an insurance premium is tax-deductible if it entails both risk shifting and risk distribution. Therefore, the insurer must assume underwriting risk and use the profits it makes from some insureds to pay the losses it experiences with other insureds. A transaction that transfers only investment risk is not sufficient to enable an insured to take a tax deduction on the premiums.

CHARACTERISTICS OF INTEGRATED RISK INSURANCE PLANS

Integrated risk insurance plan
A risk financing plan that provides an insured with a single block of risk transfer capacity over several types of risk exposures and that is usually written for multiple years.

An **integrated risk insurance plan** is a risk financing plan that provides an insured with a single block of risk transfer capacity over several types of risk exposures and that is usually written for multiple years. Integrated risk insurance plans usually provide coverage for various types of significant hazard risk exposure. The most sophisticated plans may include coverage of financial/market risk exposures as well, such as movements in securities prices, commodity prices, interest rates, and foreign exchange rates. An integrated risk insurance plan is usually written on a guaranteed-cost basis; however, it may include features typically associated with finite risk insurance plans.

Many organizations manage their hazard, operational and financial risks in separate silos. Further, the manager of each department within an organization often is instructed to focus primarily on preventing or reducing the individual department's risk exposures. This narrow focus ignores the ripple effects of the diverse risks that cross departmental lines or that may have a cumulative effect on the entire organization's hazard, operational and financial risks.

Even inside the individual silos, a departmental manager's focus has become even narrower. They often analyze each individual risk exposure separately and decide on a combination of retention and transfer for each. To transfer hazard risk, most large organizations purchase separate annual insurance policies for property, general liability, products liability, automobile liability, marine liability, and directors and officers liability, as well as coverages for their other loss exposures. Organizations also routinely transfer their financial risk by hedging their securities price, credit, commodity price, interest rate, and foreign exchange rate risks with derivative contracts in the financial markets. An integrated risk plan can combine the transfer of both hazard and financial risks by providing a single block of risk-transfer capacity across these multiple types of hazard and financial risk exposures over multiple years (hence the word "integrated").

An organization can manage its risk effectively by retaining a portfolio of various types of risk exposures, allowing it to retain a large share of each of its risk exposures while reducing its overall retained risk level through diversification. The benefits of risk diversification also accrue to an insured that transfers risk in a large, single block across many of its risk exposures, rather than separately for each. This consolidated approach is more efficient than an exposure-by-exposure approach because the risk taker (the insurer) can diversify its risk across different types of risk exposures and across time (if the contract is for multiple years) and results in a lower premium.

An example helps illustrate the benefit of risk diversification and of considering risk on a portfolio basis. Assume that in Year 1, an organization suffers a $500,000 loss from its general liability exposure but that, in the same year, the organization realizes a $1 million gain from its foreign exchange (currency) exposure. In addition, assume that in Year 2, the organization has no general liability losses but realizes a $500,000 loss from its foreign exchange exposure. The organization's total net gain or loss over Year 1 and Year 2 for both exposures is $0. Therefore, its combined risk over two years is lower than its net gain or loss on any one risk exposure for any one year.

OPERATION OF INTEGRATED RISK INSURANCE PLANS

The following example illustrates the operation of an integrated risk insurance plan. Assume that an insured with two types of risk exposure purchases separate annual insurance policies for each. Each policy has a limit of $50 million per occurrence and a self-insured retention of $5 million per occurrence. Exhibit 9-4 illustrates the retention and limits for each policy. Note that the insured is willing to retain a large amount of total losses for a single year because it retains all loss occurrences up to $5 million under both Policy A and Policy B.

The loss exposures covered under Policy A and Policy B could be combined under an integrated risk insurance plan with a five-year period term, $10 million per occurrence self-insured retention, and $100 million per occurrence limit. Exhibit 9-5 illustrates how Policy A and Policy B can be combined.

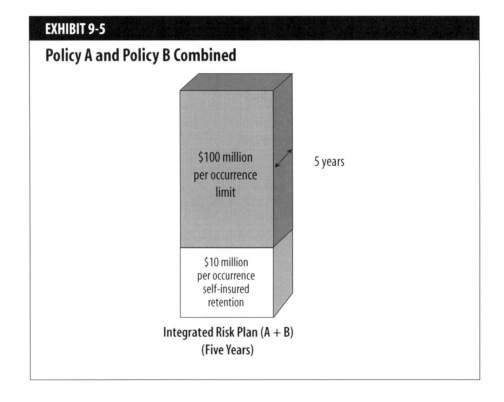

EXHIBIT 9-4

Efficiency of Transferring Risk on an Integrated Basis

$50 million per occurrence limit

$5 million per occurrence self-insured retention

Insurance Policy A (Single Year)

$50 million per occurrence limit

$5 million per occurrence self-insured retention

Insurance Policy B (Single Year)

EXHIBIT 9-5

Policy A and Policy B Combined

$100 million per occurrence limit

5 years

$10 million per occurrence self-insured retention

Integrated Risk Plan (A + B) (Five Years)

An insured that switches from a traditional insurance plan to an integrated risk plan engages in a tradeoff. The insured commits to a higher per occurrence retention: $10 million over a five-year period on a combined lines basis as opposed to $5 million for a single annual period for each separate line. In exchange, the insured receives a higher per occurrence limit of $100 million that applies to the combined exposures for the entire five-year period as opposed to $50 million for a single annual period for each separate line.

The five-year premium for the integrated risk plan is likely to be less than the sum of the annual premiums for Policy A and Policy B over the same five-year period. This is mainly because the insurer's risk attaches at a higher per occurrence attachment point ($10 million as opposed to $5 million).

As long as an integrated risk insurance plan provides an organization with a tolerable retention level, adequate limits, sufficient coverage language and policy terms, and appropriate servicing from the insurer, it can be an efficient way to transfer risk.

Use of Integrated Risk Insurance Plans

As mentioned, an integrated risk insurance plan can be used to cover various types of risk. To date, the vast majority of insureds have combined property and liability risks (hazard risks) in integrated risk insurance plans. These risks include property, business income, crime, ocean marine, general liability, automobile liability, crime/fidelity, and directors and officers liability, as well as many others.

In theory, almost any risk can be included in an integrated plan as long as the risks covered can be accurately modeled, exhibit low or no correlation, and have similar exposure sizes and loss probability profiles. Hence, some insureds are using the structure to manage enterprise-wide risks by combining financial or market risks with hazard risks in an integrated risk insurance plan.

Exhibit 9-6 shows one possible use of an integrated risk insurance plan for a large organization that takes a $25 million per occurrence retention for each type of risk. The integrated risk coverage applies to several hazard risks over a five-year period. There is a stop loss protection with a separate limit that applies above an annual aggregate retention for all the risks.[8] The integrated risk layer provides a limit of $50 million per occurrence that sits directly above the $25 million per occurrence retention for each type of risk. The integrated risk layer also has a $150 million aggregate limit that applies over the five-year coverage period. A monoline property coverage, purchased on an annual basis, sits above the integrated risk layer to ensure that an adequate limit is available to cover the property risk.

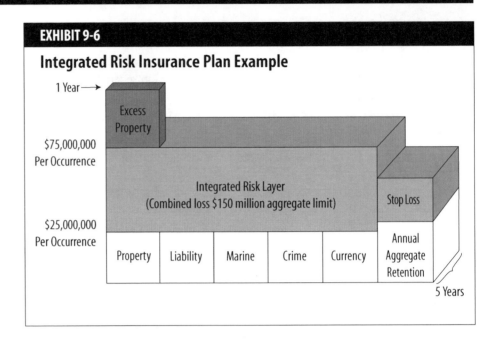

EXHIBIT 9-6

Integrated Risk Insurance Plan Example

Variations in the Terms of Integrated Risk Insurance Plans

Virtually unlimited variation of integrated risk insurance plans exists, though every integrated risk insurance plan is a single contract that covers more than one type of risk exposure. Two common term variations are basket aggregate retention and dual-trigger covers.

Basket Aggregate Retention

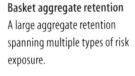

Basket aggregate retention
A large aggregate retention spanning multiple types of risk exposure.

A **basket aggregate retention** is a large aggregate retention spanning multiple types of risk exposure. Many integrated risk insurance plans are designed to provide coverage that sits above such a large aggregate retention.

The integrated risk insurance plan attaches at the point at which the basket aggregate retention is exhausted, and the basket aggregate retention itself usually sits above separate per occurrence retentions for each type of risk. The basket aggregate retention can apply separately to each annual period. This arrangement is illustrated in Exhibit 9-7. Note the basket aggregate retention is also above a nonhazard risk—specifically the financial risk of a fluctuating currency exchange rate.

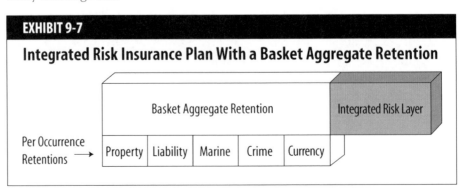

EXHIBIT 9-7

Integrated Risk Insurance Plan With a Basket Aggregate Retention

Dual-Trigger Covers

A **dual-trigger cover** is a type of integrated risk insurance plan in which the retention and limit are tied to two different types of risk and that requires the insured to incur a loss above a certain threshold under each of the two types of risk during the same time period in order to trigger coverage under the policy. Dual-trigger covers are sometimes referred to as multi-trigger covers. The distinguishing characteristic of a dual-trigger cover is that a loss above a certain retention threshold must occur under each of the two types of risk during the same period in order to trigger, or activate, coverage under the policy.

A dual-trigger cover provides a means for an organization to tie its retention and policy limit under its hazard risks to its other types of risks, such as its financial or market risks. It is best suited for an organization that is willing to take a high retention on each type of risk but that wants to transfer loss in the unlikely event that two large losses arising from different sources of risk occur during the same time period.

Consider the case of a large merchant electricity generator. The firm faces property and liability risks (hazard risks) from owning and operating power generation facilities, and it stands to lose a great deal of profit if the wholesale price of electricity suddenly increases (a financial/market risk). A dual-trigger cover could protect the electricity producer if it suffers generator downtime due to a property loss (the first trigger) and, during the same period, if it incurs a significant extra expense costs associated with an increase in the price of the replacement, purchased electricity used to supply its customer base (the second trigger). The insurer would reimburse the electricity generator for the combined loss to the extent that it exceeds a specified retention level.

Dual-trigger cover
A type of integrated risk insurance plan in which the retention and limit are tied to two different types of risk and that requires the insured to incur a loss above a certain threshold under each of the two types of risk during the same time period in order to trigger coverage under the policy.

ADVANTAGES AND DISADVANTAGES OF INTEGRATED RISK INSURANCE PLANS

The advantages of integrated risk insurance plans include the following:

- Flexibility of coverage
- Cost savings
- Stability
- Greater transparency

The first and perhaps the greatest advantage of integrated risk insurance plans is the flexibility of their coverage. An integrated risk insurance plan can be customized to fit an organization's risk appetite and its risk-bearing capacity. Traditional insurance plans, by contrast, are relatively inflexible. Integrated risk insurance plans, like finite risk insurance plans, can be crafted to address specific needs, improving the efficiency of risk transfer. Depending on the design of the plan, some esoteric and hard-to-insure risks may be included, allowing an insured to manage many of its enterprise-wide risks under one contract.

Another advantage of integrated risk insurance plans is the cost savings they offer. An integrated risk insurance plan provides cost savings that stem from the insured's bulk purchasing power and the absence of annual renewal negotiations. Also, an integrated risk insurance plan allows an organization to efficiently manage its retentions and limits by spreading them across different types of risk and multiple years. Therefore, the insured can reduce its aggregate retained risk through diversification and receive appropriate premium credits.

Integrated risk insurance plans also provide stability by enabling the insured to avoid the volatility of pricing, limits, and terms associated with insurance market cycles. An insured can achieve significant savings if a multiyear deal (usually three years) is locked in at the beginning of a hard market. A multiyear deal also guarantees long-term capacity. Risk management professionals can lock in large coverage limits for multiple years on risk exposures that may be difficult to insure, particularly in hard market conditions.

A further advantage of integrated risk insurance plans is the greater transparency they provide relative to other plans. A publicly held organization that implements an integrated risk insurance plan can demonstrate to shareholders and regulators that it takes a comprehensive approach to risk, allowing it to better withstand shareholder scrutiny.

The disadvantages of integrated risk financing plans include the following:

- Exhaustion of limits with a large loss
- Difficulties in premium allocation
- Complexity of pricing
- Delay in development of specialty policy language
- Reduction of additional services

One disadvantage of integrated risk insurance plans is that a large loss can potentially exhaust the policy's limits. A single multiyear aggregate limit may not be sufficient for an insured that experiences extremely high losses. A large loss in the first year of the plan could exhaust the aggregate limit, leaving no limit available for the remaining years of the contract. In order to offset this disadvantage, some integrated risk insurance carriers offer limit buy-back provisions.

Another disadvantage of integrated risk insurance plans is the difficulty posed by premium allocation. Allocating an integrated risk insurance premium among the divisions of a large organization may be difficult, because each division has its own unique risk exposures, making it difficult to allocate a composite premium that transfers risk for several lines together over multiple years under a single contract.

A further disadvantage of integrated risk insurance plans is the complexity of pricing, because they can include both financial/market and hazard risks spanning several years. Accurate pricing depends on an underwriter's ability to predict both the financial market and losses from hazard risks. This is difficult to do even for a one-year policy. It becomes increasingly complex the further into the future the underwriter tries to extend the prediction.

Integrated risk insurance plans also do not incorporate newly developed policy language as quickly as other plans. In specialized areas, such as products liability, aviation, or directors and officers coverage, stand-alone policies are highly tailored, with exceptions, exclusions, and settlement language written to provide optimal protection. Integrated risk plans do not always reflect specialty policy language needs and tend to incorporate changes in policy language more slowly than monoline markets.

Another disadvantage of integrated risk plans is that they do not provide additional risk-specific loss control, claim, and administrative services that are offered by insurers who provide primary-layer insurance for individual specialty lines. For example, insureds with high-value and high-risk property exposures frequently benefit from the industry-specific loss control expertise of specialty insurers.

CHARACTERISTICS OF INSUREDS ASSOCIATED WITH SUCCESSFUL FINITE AND INTEGRATED RISK INSURANCE PLANS

Integrated and finite risk insurance plans are not suitable for every insured. These plans require a minimum exposure size, time commitment, significant capital, and possible regulatory approval. Therefore, despite their customization and flexibility, these plans are more appropriate for insureds that have the following characteristics:

- It is exposed to difficult- or expensive-to-insure risks that are considered unattractive to the traditional insurance markets.
- It has a significant exposure whose associated loss could undermine business stability or have a material impact on net income or other key metrics.
- It is willing to assume substantial risk retention, such as through a high deductible or captive utilization.
- It desires an innovative, structured solution within the context of an insurance contract.
- Its senior corporate officials, including key members of treasury, finance, legal, and general management, perceive risk transfer to be a priority and are involved in initial phases of solution structuring and market meetings, including clearly defining the solution's motivation and objective.
- It has significant cash on hand (either idle or ineffectively invested in short-term, low-yield instruments) and will likely owe taxes.

SUMMARY

A finite risk insurance plan transfers a limited (finite) amount of risk from an insured to an insurer because a large component of the insured's premium is used to fund its own losses. An integrated risk insurance plan provides an insured with a single block of risk-transfer capacity over several types of risk exposures, which can include financial/market risk as well as hazard risk. Many structured insurance programs incorporate features traditionally associated with both finite and integrated risk insurance plans.

A finite risk insurance plan, which is categorized as a hybrid plan, can be thought of as a blend of self-insurance and guaranteed-cost insurance. Finite risk insurance plans share the following characteristics:

- The limits of coverage apply on an aggregate basis.
- The term of coverage is usually for multiple years (three to five years being most common) and is generally noncancelable.
- The premium is a substantial percentage of the policy limits.
- The insurer shares profit with the insured, including investment income arising from the cash flow.
- The insured is allowed to commute the plan within a specified time frame. Commutation extinguishes all liabilities between the parties and is the means by which the insurer shares profit on the transaction with the insured.

From an insurer's point of view, all insurance transactions involve varying degrees of three different types of risk: (1) underwriting risk, (2) investment risk, and (3) credit risk. Underwriting risk, for the purpose of analyzing a finite risk insurance plan, can be defined as the risk that an insurer's losses and expenses will be greater or less than its premiums plus the investment income it expects to earn, therefore exposing its capital to loss or gain. Investment risk is the risk that an insurer's investment income will be higher or lower than it expects. Investment risk can be broken down into timing risk, which is the risk that the insured's losses will be paid faster or more slowly than expected, and interest rate risk, which is the risk that interest rates will be above or below expected interest rates over the term of the contract. Credit risk is the risk that an insured will default on its premium payment to an insurer. Compared with a guaranteed cost insurance policy, a finite risk policy involves a much higher degree of self-funding on the insured's part, and the insurer assumes a much lower degree of underwriting risk.

A cumulative experience fund balance for a finite risk plan is calculated by adding each period's net premium and investment income and subtracting loss payments.

Some common variations of a finite risk insurance plan entail the addition of per occurrence and/or annual aggregate limits to the multi-year aggregate limit. Limits on the amount paid by the insurer for each year can be added.

The insurer can agree to share with the insured a percentage of any investment income that is higher than that credited to the experience fund under the plan. Also, the margin can be based on a sliding scale and, therefore, vary with the total losses that fall under the plan. Finally, a finite risk insurance plan may require the insured to pay an additional premium if total losses exceed a certain level.

A prospective finite risk insurance plan is arranged to cover losses from events that have not yet occurred. A retroactive finite risk insurance plan is arranged to cover losses from events that have already occurred. A loss portfolio transfer is a type of retroactive plan that applies to a defined portfolio of losses.

Because a carefully controlled, limited amount of risk is involved, an underwriter of a finite risk insurance plan may agree to cover a broader range of exposures than it would cover under a traditional insurance plan. Finite risk insurance plans can be used for many difficult-to-insure exposures, such as products recall, warranties, environmental liability (including cleanup), and illiquid commodity price fluctuations.

Assuming it receives favorable financial accounting treatment, one advantage of a finite risk insurance plan is that it smooths over time the effect of large losses on the insured's net income (profit) in its financial statements. As a hybrid plan, finite risk insurance also combines many of the advantages of both retention and transfer. An insured that can control its losses shares the insurer's profits, including investment income on the cash flow of the experience fund. In addition, the insured is protected by a limited amount of risk transfer in the event that losses are much higher than expected. A finite risk insurance plan often enables an insured to obtain higher limits than it could obtain under a traditional insurance plan. A finite risk insurance plan can also result in cost reductions as a result of the less frequent (non-annual) renewals it requires.

A disadvantage of finite risk insurance plans is that the insured's capital is tied up in the experience fund (an opportunity cost). A finite risk insurance plan has an aggregate limit that applies over multiple years. Therefore, if a full-limit loss occurs early in the term, no further limits are available, even though the insured may be obligated to pay premiums for the remainder of the term. Additionally, premium taxes on a finite risk plan can be a large expense.

A great deal of uncertainty exists regarding the financial accounting and income tax treatments of finite risk plans. In the U.S., accounting standards and opinions have been issued that severely limit an insured's ability to treat the premiums under a finite risk insurance plan as it would treat premiums for a guaranteed-cost insurance plan.

An integrated risk insurance plan is a single contract that covers more than one type of risk exposure, usually over multiple years. In general, integrated risk insurance plans combine various types of hazard risk. The most sophisticated plans may include various types of financial/market risk as well.

With an integrated risk insurance plan, an insured combines retentions and limits over multiple years. Such arrangements are likely to result in premium savings. As long as an integrated risk insurance plan provides an organization with a tolerable retention level, adequate limit, favorable policy language, and sufficient risk management services, it can efficiently transfer risk.

Integrated risk plans usually cover a layer of losses that sits above various per occurrence retentions. The limit usually applies on a per occurrence basis, and there is often an aggregate limit.

An integrated risk plan can be written above a basket aggregate retention, which is a retention that spans multiple types of risk exposure. An integrated risk plan also can be written as a dual-trigger cover, meaning that the retention and limit are tied to two different types of risk. The distinguishing characteristic of a dual-trigger cover is that a loss above a certain retention threshold must occur under each of the two types of risk during the same period in order to "trigger" coverage under the policy.

The most important advantage of an integrated risk insurance plan is that it can be customized to fit individual organizations' risk appetite and risk-bearing capacities. Another advantage is that an integrated risk insurance plan provides cost savings because of the insured's use of bulk purchasing power and avoidance of annual renewal negotiations. Also, an integrated risk plan can be an efficient way for an organization to manage its retentions and limits by spreading them over several types of risk and several years. It allows an insured to manage many of its enterprise-wide risks under a single contract. Depending on the design of the plan, the insurer might agree to cover some risks that are normally hard to insure.

However, the multi-year aggregate limit may not be sufficient for an insured that experiences high-severity losses, a potential disadvantage of such plans. A large loss in the first year of the plan could exhaust the aggregate limit, leaving no limit available for the remaining years of the contract. Another disadvantage of an integrated risk insurance plan is that allocating the premium among the divisions of a large organization might be difficult. Finally, the pricing of an integrated risk plan can be complex.

A number of insured characteristics are associated with the successful development, placement, and implementation of a finite or integrated risk insurance plan. These factors include: difficult- or expensive-to-insure risks, material risk exposure, appetite for substantial risk retention, desire for an innovative insurance solution, senior management commitment, and a cash-rich position.

Finite and integrated risk insurance plans provide organizations with alternative ways to obtain coverage for traditional, nontraditional and difficult-to-insure risks. Another approach to risk financing that extends beyond the traditional insurance marketplace is to deploy capital market risk financing plans.

CHAPTER NOTES

1. Although the application and treatment of finite risk plans has been a subject of debate in recent years, the basic definition of finite risk plans is consistent across the industry. For insurance structures, Warren Buffett defined it simply: "Finite insurance is insurance that carries limited amount of risk for the company that writes the policy." Buffett provided this and other insights regarding finite insurance during a Web-posted interview by Christopher Oster on April 29, 2005. This interview, "4 Tough Questions for Warren Buffett," can be found at moneycentral.msn.com (accessed January 28, 2006).

2. An outline of several specific finite risk applications for environmental and remediation issues was outlined in the testimony of Kenneth Cornell, Executive Vice President of AIG Environmental, before the Subcommittee on Superfund, Waste Control, and Risk Assessment of the U.S. Senate Environment and Public Works Committee on April 10, 2002. Cornell's testimony can be accessed at epw.senate.gov/ (accessed January 28, 2006).

3. Given favorable tax and accounting treatments, an off-balance sheet fund would exist because it is possible that a positive balance in the experience fund may not appear as an asset on the insured's balance sheet. However, a positive balance in the experience fund would be available to pay the insured's future losses.

4. An underwriting gain or loss is usually measured by comparing losses and premiums only. For the purpose of analyzing a finite risk plan, this definition of underwriting risk includes expected investment income as well.

5. To offset the credit risk under a paid loss retrospective rating plan, insurers usually require financial security such as a letter of credit.

6. Financial Accounting Standards Board, Statement of Financial Accounting Standards No. 113, "Accounting and Reporting for Reinsurance of Short-Duration and Long-Duration Contracts" (Norwalk, Conn.: FASB, December 1992), p. 7. Italics added. Available online at www.fasb.org/pdf/fas113.pdf, p. 6 (accessed January 27, 2006).

7. Deposit accounting outlines accounting for treatment of insurance and reinsurance contracts that do not transfer insurance risk. The American Institute of CPAs has produced Statement of Position (SOP) 98-7 to clarify application of FASB's position on deposit accounting. Copies of the Position paper are available for order on the Web at www.aicpa.org (accessed May 4, 2006).

8. A maintenance deductible, which applies to each loss, usually comes into play before the stop loss coverage pays for losses.

Chapter | 10

Direct Your Learning

After learning the content of this chapter and completing the corresponding course guide assignment, you should be able to:

- Describe the types of capital market products.

- Explain how securitization operates.

- Explain how insurance securitization operates, including:
  - The use of catastrophe bonds
  - The benefits to investors
  - The advantages and disadvantages of insurance securitization

- Explain how insurance derivatives operate, including:
  - The use of forwards and futures contracts
  - The use of swaps
  - The use of insurance options
  - The advantages and disadvantages of insurance derivatives

- Explain how contingent capital arrangements operate, including:
  - The use of a standby credit facility
  - The use of a contingent surplus note arrangement
  - The use of a catastrophe equity put arrangement
  - The advantages and disadvantages of contingent capital arrangements

- Analyze the concerns of organizations transferring risk and investors supplying capital.

- Explain the regulatory and accounting issues involved with insurance-linked securities and insurance derivatives.

- Define or describe each of the Key Words and Phrases for this chapter.

Develop Your Perspective

What are the main topics covered in the chapter?

This chapter examines the product innovations that enable organizations to access the capital markets to finance risks that are traditionally covered by insurance (or reinsurance). These capital market products include insurance-linked securities, insurance derivatives, and contingent capital arrangements.

Review each of the capital market products.

- Has your organization used one of these products?
- Who determines whether your organization will use one or more of these products?

Why is it important to learn about these topics?

Capital market products provide access to investors who are willing to accept risk. By knowing what capital market products are available, their use, and the advantages and disadvantages of each, the risk management professional can provide an organization with a competitive advantage over its rivals.

Examine the use of each capital market product.

- Identify a capital market product that your organization could use to transfer risk.
- What advantages and disadvantages would your organization incur by using that product?

How can you use what you will learn?

Consider your organization's use of traditional insurance.

- How well does the use of traditional insurance meet the objectives of your organization relative to capital market products?
- What changes might you suggest to improve the effectiveness of the use of your organization's assets to protect it from risk?

Chapter 10
Capital Market Risk Financing Plans

Some types of risk, particularly catastrophe risk (the risk of a large accumulation of losses stemming from a single event such as an earthquake or tornado), cannot always be suitably addressed through traditional risk financing methods. Capital market products, which are traded financial instruments (such as stocks and bonds) that mature in more than one year, have emerged as tools that organizations can use to finance risk as an alternative to insurance. These instruments were once used only to provide capital to insurers (or reinsurers), who then used the capital to underwrite their customers' risk as an alternative to insurance. The convergence of insurance with other financial services, however, has expanded the capital markets' role in risk financing to include insurance-linked securities, insurance derivatives, and contingent capital arrangements.

Some of these capital market products are rooted in the concepts of securitization and special purpose vehicles (SPV), which allow organizations to exchange assets for cash. Others are based on derivatives, which are financial contracts that derive their value from other assets. Each of the products involves advantages and disadvantages, many of which relate to risk transfer and retention. In addition to these considerations, risk financing professionals also must assess the accounting and regulatory ramifications associated with capital market products in order to determine whether they are appropriate for their organization.

TYPES OF CAPITAL MARKET PRODUCTS

Capital market products for risk financing fall into the following categories:

- Insurance securitizations
- Insurance derivatives
- Contingent capital arrangements

Capital market products have evolved from the convergence of insurance with other financial services. Noninsurance financial institutions, particularly investment banks, can expand their traditional business by offering the capital markets' capacity to organizations as an alternative to using insurance to finance losses, thereby allowing these institutions to enter the domain of insurers (and reinsurers) and insurance brokers. Likewise, insurers (and reinsurers) and insurance brokers can expand their traditional business by using insurance policies and/or capital market products to cover not only losses from traditionally insurable risks, but also losses from other types of risk, such as commodity price risk and interest rate risk.

Theoretically, capital market products can be used to finance any type of insurable risk. However, insufficient underwriting data for some categories of risk and regulatory and accounting uncertainty associated with the use of capital market products have limited their market and capacity growth. Each type of capital market product involves a great deal of time and expense to implement. Therefore, relatively few large organizations, mainly insurers and reinsurers, have used them to finance risk. Most successfully implemented capital market products finance catastrophe risk.

SECURITIZATION

Securitization
The process of creating a marketable investment security based on the expected cash flows from a financial transaction.

The concept of **securitization**, which is the process of creating a marketable investment security based on a financial transaction's expected cash flows, is central to the mechanics of insurance securitizations. An organization can use securitization to exchange income-producing assets for cash provided by the purchaser of the security, assuming that a market exists for the asset. This exchange allows the organization to transfer the asset from its balance sheet.

For example, a bank can securitize its mortgage loans. Most of the individuals who have received mortgage loans will pay them back. Therefore, the loans are recognized as an asset and referred to as mortgage receivables on the bank's balance sheet. Cash, however, is often a more desirable asset because of its versatility. For example, the bank could use cash to make more mortgage loans to individuals. Also, unlike mortgage receivables, cash does not carry credit risk, which is the possibility that the mortgage loan will not be repaid. If the bank wishes to convert the mortgage receivables asset to cash, it could sell it to an intermediary.

Special purpose vehicle (SPV)
A facility established for the purpose of purchasing income-producing assets from an organization, holding title to them and then using those assets to collateralize securities that will be sold to investors.

The intermediary that enables the bank to convert its mortgage receivables asset into a cash asset is referred to as a **special purpose vehicle (SPV)**, which is a facility established for the purpose of purchasing income-producing assets from an organization, holding title to them and then using those assets to collateralize securities that will be sold to investors. The SPV securitizes the mortgage receivables by using them as collateral for securities it sells to investors. The SPV then uses the interest and principal repayments on the mortgage receivables to fund the interest and principal repayments to the security investors. The securities carry the risks of the mortgage receivables held by the SPV. These risks include the possibility of default by the mortgagors (the borrowers) and the risk that the mortgagors might cancel their mortgages in order to refinance them at lower interest rates elsewhere. In essence, securitization transfers the risk inherent in the mortgage receivables from the bank to the security investors.

A major benefit of involving an SPV in a securitization transaction is that investors can decide whether to invest in the securities based solely on the risk presented by the income-producing assets held as collateral by the SPV. If an organization directly securitized its income-producing assets without using an SPV as an intermediary, investors would need to consider not only the risks presented by the income-producing assets but also the overall credit risk of the organization. Analyzing overall credit risk is complex because an organization holds many different types of assets and incurs many different types of liabilities. Even expert investors frequently have difficulty accurately analyzing the credit risk of an organization. An SPV reduces this associated credit risk.

Exhibit 10-1 depicts a generic securitization model. The organization sells income-producing assets to an SPV in exchange for cash. The income-producing assets are no longer owned by the organization but instead are owned by the SPV to sell to investors. The investors purchase the securities for cash and receive a return on their investment commensurate with the risk inherent in the income-producing assets that back the securities, not in the organization's credit risk.

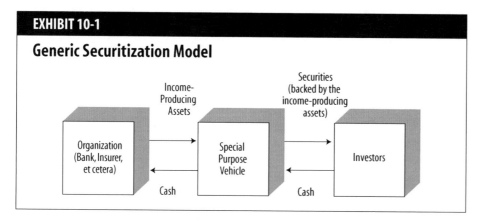

EXHIBIT 10-1

Generic Securitization Model

However, regulators, auditors, and potential investors closely scrutinize the use of SPVs, because they have been used to manipulate organizations' income statements and balance sheets. Therefore, a firm that uses an SPV for securitization must take the utmost care to meet all regulatory requirements and maintain a high level of disclosure regarding the SPV's assets, finances, purpose, and management.

Insurers can participate in a securitization transaction in a number of ways. For example, an insurer can securitize its premium receivables by transferring them to an SPV in exchange for cash. The SPV could then use those premium receivables to collateralize securities it sells to investors.

INSURANCE SECURITIZATIONS

An **insurance securitization** is a form of securitization that creates a marketable insurance-linked security based on the cash flows that arise from insuring loss exposures. These cash flows are similar to premium and loss payments under an insurance policy.

Insurance securitization
A form of securitization that creates a marketable insurance-linked security based on the cash flows that arise from insuring loss exposures.

In Exhibit 10-2, the SPV acts as an insurer (or a reinsurer). Cash is paid by an organization to the SPV in exchange for the promise to pay any losses that occur. The payments are similar to the premium and loss payments under an insurance policy.

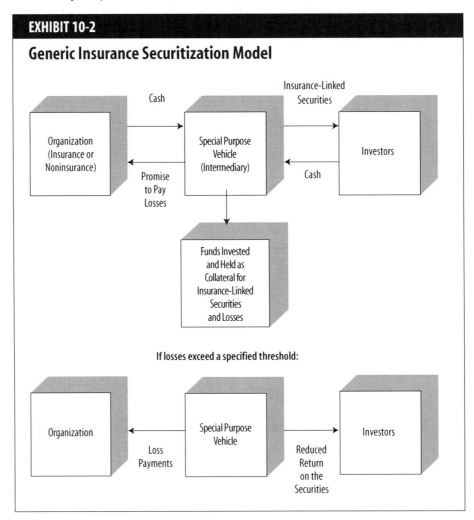

EXHIBIT 10-2

Generic Insurance Securitization Model

Insurance securitization differs from most other types of securitization. Instead of selling income-producing assets to an SPV and receiving cash, the organization engaging in an insurance securitization pays cash to the SPV and receives reimbursement for losses that occur. The reimbursement for losses can be determined by the organization's actual losses or an index of insured losses incurred by a group of insurers. When the reimbursement is based on the organization's actual losses, the insurance securitization transaction mimics a traditional insurance risk transfer.

An insurance securitization can be designed to cover an organization's losses either on a per occurrence or an aggregate basis. The definition of covered loss is specified in the contract between the investors and the SPV and in the contract between the SPV and the organization transferring its risk.

The Unique Role of an SPV in an Insurance Securitization

An SPV plays a different role in an insurance securitization transaction than it does in other types of securitization transactions.

- The SPV transforms insurable risk into investment risk.

- The SPV receives cash from both the investors and the organization that transfers the insurable risk. It holds the cash as collateral for its obligation to repay interest and principal on the insurance-linked securities and its obligation to pay any insured losses that occur.

- Depending on the domicile involved, the SPV may qualify as an authorized insurer (or reinsurer), which enables the organization transferring its risk of loss to treat the transaction as insurance (or reinsurance) for tax and accounting purposes. The advantages of treating the transaction as insurance (or reinsurance) are discussed subsequently.

Catastrophe Bonds

Even though insurance securitizations, which are also commonly referred to as insurance-linked securities, could, in theory, be applied to any insurable risk, the vast majority of insurance-linked securities issued to date are in the form of **catastrophe bonds**, which are a type of insurance-linked security that is specifically designed to transfer insurable catastrophe risk to investors. Catastrophe bonds were developed, in part, in response to the limited availability and affordability of catastrophe reinsurance.

These bonds are issued by the SPVs of large reinsurers, insurers, or large corporations and mimic traditional excess (catastrophe) insurance (and reinsurance). As such, they can be issued for any type of catastrophic insurable risk, including hurricanes, earthquakes, and other adverse weather and environmental risks.

The catastrophe losses that trigger payment under a catastrophe bond can be based on aggregate catastrophe losses over a defined period of time or the occurrence of a single catastrophic event. Losses triggered on an aggregate basis can be measured using an insurance industry loss index for catastrophes or the actual catastrophe losses of an organization, whether it is an insurance or a noninsurance organization. Losses can also be measured against a specific standard (such as a Category Four or greater hurricane). Computer models are used to measure the frequency and severity probabilities that determine the standards used to measure the catastrophic risk that is embedded in these kinds of bonds. Catastrophe bonds are typically structured to provide protection against infrequently occurring (1-in-100-year to 1-in-250-year) events. These frequencies appeal to both the organizations issuing the bonds and investors buying the bonds, because the issuers of the bonds want them to be triggered (and, consequently, priced) at a level that reflects a highly infrequent event. The investors who buy the bonds also want them to respond to highly infrequent events, which lowers the risk that they will lose money on the investment.

Catastrophe bond
A type of insurance-linked security that is specifically designed to transfer insurable catastrophe risk to investors.

Example of an Insurance-Linked Security

A property insurer has hurricane concentration risk in the southeastern and Gulf Coast regions of the United States. The property insurer is financially strong. A Category Three or higher hurricane that affects a densely populated area in the insurer's coverage region (Dade County, for example) could result in over $1.5 billion in paid insured losses for the firm. The insurer, therefore, wants to use a risk transfer mechanism that will reduce the variability of its financial results from one year to the next due to catastrophic events. It determines that traditional catastrophic reinsurance is not the most economically viable option for doing so, because previous hurricane events reduced reinsurer capacity and increased the year-to-year volatility of the cost of reinsurance.

The property insurer uses an SPV to issue $500 million in three-year catastrophe bonds to, in effect, reinsure its Gulf Coast and southeastern hurricane risks. The bond investors lose interest or interest and principal, depending on the bond series, if a Category Three, Four, or Five hurricane causes insured losses to the property insurer in excess of $1 billion during a twelve-month claims period. The property insurer, in turn, receives reimbursement for any catastrophe losses from the SPV. The bond offering is fully subscribed by investors.

The investors purchase the bonds from the SPV because they provide a premium rate of interest (that is, it is higher than that provided by a United States Treasury bond of comparable maturity) based on the expected frequency and severity of the embedded hurricane risk. In exchange for receiving a premium interest rate, the investors' return on the bond is linked to the risk of a Category Three or higher hurricane striking during the term of the bond. The bond investors underwrite the hurricane risk, which is an insurable risk because it could also have been underwritten with a traditional reinsurance policy. Therefore, the bond is an insurance-linked security. It is marketable because a secondary financial market exists, which is a market in which a bond can be sold to a subsequent investor during the bond's term. Therefore, through the process of insurance securitization, the property insurer's risk of a sizable loss due to a major hurricane has been "securitized" by linking it with the returns provided to investors in a marketable security. The securitization solution enables the property insurer to more effectively deploy its capital resources.

The prevalence of catastrophe bonds is attributable to issuing institutions and underlying catastrophe risks sharing several characteristics of successful insurance securitizations, including the following:

- A potentially large exposure is needed to make a securitization economically viable due to the significant time commitment and transaction costs it requires. Catastrophe bonds frequently have values in excess of $50 million.

- SPVs with high credit ratings or substantial assets that issue securities receive better pricing and subscription at issuance.

- Loss exposures with independent, accurate loss history data available for analyzing the frequency and severity may be underwritten and priced by investors. For many natural catastrophes, such as hurricanes, over 100 years of historical data is readily available.

Benefits to Investors

Insurance-linked securities differ from most other types of investments because the investor accepts only a specifically defined insurable risk and not the overall risks of an organization, as with investments in traditional stocks and bonds. Because insurable risk has a low level of correlation with the risks of traditional investment vehicles, such as the risk of interest rate or stock market movements, investors achieve the benefit of diversification and additional risk-return options.

Insurance-linked securities have gained acceptance by investors, and a small secondary market has developed for them. Rating agencies, such as Standard & Poor's and Moody's, report on the creditworthiness of many insurance-linked securities. The information contained in these reports is essential for selling these securities to investors, which include pension funds, mutual funds, banks, hedge funds, property-casualty insurers, and life insurers.

Advantages and Disadvantages of Insurance Securitizations

Insurance securitizations have a number of advantages and disadvantages. Their advantages include the following:

- They create additional risk transfer capacity.
- They lower credit risk.

One advantage of insurance securitizations is that they create additional risk transfer capacity. Insurance securitization supplements existing risk-transfer capacity and provides organizations with an alternative to traditional insurance and reinsurance. For example, an estimated 90 percent of the investment capital from catastrophe bond issuances is new to the property-casualty insurance industry.[1] However, the value of new capacity depends on the cost and supply of traditional insurance (and reinsurance), which vary over time.

Another advantage of insurance securitizations is that they lower credit risk. The obligation to pay losses to an organization and to pay interest and principal to investors is fully collateralized with investments held by the SPV, which can be readily converted into cash. This feature provides an organization with secure resources equal to the loss limits provided by its contract with the SPV. Some risk management professionals believe that the financial security provided by a typical insurance securitization is higher than that provided by a traditional insurance (or reinsurance) transaction because, in general, insurers (and reinsurers) maintain capital that is only a fraction of the total policy limits they sell.

The disadvantages of insurance securitizations include the following:

- They expose an organization to the volatility of the market's demand.
- They entail opportunity cost of collateralized assets.
- They involve substantial transaction costs.
- They subject organizations to basis risk.

An insurance securitization exposes an organization to the volatility of the market's demand, a potential disadvantage. Insurance securitizations have alleviated reinsurance capacity restrictions in the past; however, there is no guarantee that they will always be an economically effective risk transfer instrument. The relationship between the return demanded by securitization investors and premiums for insurance (and reinsurance) varies depending on two factors: the attractiveness of insurance-linked securities to investors when compared with their other investment opportunities and the state of the insurance underwriting cycle—that is, whether it is hard or soft—with its associated fluctuations in insurance (and reinsurance) pricing and market demand.

Another disadvantage of insurance securitization is that organizations that use an insurance securitization incur an opportunity cost for the assets that are used for collateral, because the funds held by the SPV are tied up in liquid assets and, therefore, earn a relatively low rate of return. If held in riskier investments, these funds, on average, would return a higher rate of return, potentially lowering the amount that the organization transferring its risk of loss would pay. Therefore, with an insurance securitization transaction, as with insurance and reinsurance, the insured faces a tradeoff between cost and financial security.

Insurance securitizations also involve substantial transaction costs. The security issuer and its business partners commit time and incur the significant financial costs associated with risk analysis and modeling, structuring, legal expenses, marketing, and subscribing to the insurance securitization. Analyzing and modeling risk involves gathering large amounts of data and using complex computer simulation programs that project the probability of various loss scenarios. Investors use this information to help them decide whether the expected return from an insurance-linked security is commensurate with its risk. Additionally, insurance securitization requires compliance with investment and insurance regulations.

Basis risk
The risk that the amount the organization receives to offset its losses may be greater than or less than its actual losses.

In addition to these disadvantages, an insurance securitization also can subject organizations transferring risk to **basis risk**, which is the risk that the amount the organization receives to offset its losses may be greater than or less than its actual losses. For example, an organization is subject to basis risk if it negotiates an insurance securitization transaction to cover its losses from hurricanes, but its contract with the SPV specifies that it will get paid based on the level of an insurance industry index of insured losses from hurricanes. In virtually all cases, the organization's actual losses suffered as a result of a hurricane will differ from the amount indicated by the insurance industry index. Although most organizations view basis risk in an insurance securitization to be a disadvantage, basis risk also offers the possibility that the amount an organization receives will exceed its actual losses.

> **Example of Convergence of Insurance and Banking Services**
>
> In 1999, Tokyo Disneyland arranged the transfer of its catastrophe earthquake risk through Goldman Sachs, an investment bank. Goldman Sachs accomplished this transaction with an insurance-linked security, in which it arranged for $200 million worth of "earthquake-linked" bonds to be sold to investors.[2] The sale was successful because Goldman Sachs was able to access a global financial market.

INSURANCE DERIVATIVES

A derivative, in general, is a financial contract that derives its value from the value of another asset, such as a commodity, or one that can derive its value from the yields on another asset or the level of an index, such as the Standard & Poor's 500 stock index.

An **insurance derivative** is a financial contract whose value is based on the level of insurable losses that occur during a specific time period. An insurance derivative increases in value as specified insurable losses increase and, therefore, the purchaser of the derivative can use this gain to offset its insurable losses. The buyer of an insurance derivative accepts insurable risk and receives a commensurate return for doing so.

Insurance derivative
Financial contract whose value is based on the level of insurable losses that occur during a specific time period.

The value of an insurance derivative can be based on the level of insurable losses experienced by a single organization or on the level of an insurance industry index of insured losses. An example of the latter is a financial instrument whose value is determined by all insured hurricane losses that occur in the southeastern U.S. during the third quarter of a particular year. Financial contracts based on the insurance derivative concept include the following:

- Forward contracts
- Swaps
- Insurance options

Forward Contracts

A **forward contract** is a contract that obligates one party to buy and another party to sell a specific financial instrument or physical commodity at a specified future date and price. A forward contract is the simplest and most commonly used form of derivative for financial risk management. A futures contract (discussed previously) is a forward contract that is exchange-traded and therefore standardized, openly available, and transferable. Because a forward contract enables a buyer and seller of a commodity to know its price

Forward contract
A contract that obligates one party to buy and another party to sell a specific financial instrument or physical commodity at a specified future date and price.

prior to delivery, it can serve to reduce the risk of price fluctuations of the commodity subject to the futures contract. Consequently, futures contracts enable organizations to plan and budget activities with less concern regarding price changes.

For example, in June, a small crude oil producer might enter into a forward contract with a refinery to sell 1,000 barrels of production for delivery in November at a price of $55 per barrel. In entering into the forward contract, the crude oil producer forgoes additional revenue if the November open market price of crude oil exceeds $55 per barrel, but is protected against decreased revenue if the November open market price is below $55 per barrel. Regardless of the variations in the price of crude oil in the actual market between June and November, the sales price for the producer's crude for 1,000 barrels will be $55 per barrel. The forward contract enables the crude oil producer to effectively manage its financial risk by eliminating the uncertainty of sales price at delivery.

Swaps

Swap
An agreement between two organizations to exchange payments based on changes in the value of an asset, yield, or index over a specific period.

A **swap** is an agreement between two organizations to exchange payments based on changes in the value of an asset, yield, or index over a specific period. A swap is a derivative because its value is determined by the value of an underlying asset, yield, or index. Swaps are frequently structured so that no money is paid up front between counterparties for the contract. Instead, cash flows are exchanged back and forth between the organizations throughout the term of the swap. Swaps are commonly used to manage interest rate and currency rate of exchange risk.

Insurers can spread their risks through swap arrangements. In such cases, the swap becomes an insurance derivative; the underlying asset is a portfolio of a specific class of insured risks for an individual insurer. For example, one insurer could exchange a portion of the cash flows (premium and losses) arising from its hurricane exposure in a particular geographic area with a portion of the cash flows arising from another insurer's tornado exposure in another geographic area. A swap arrangement between two insurers produces results similar to a reinsurance arrangement. The majority of swaps have been arranged to mimic reinsurance transactions.

Example of a Swap—Swiss Re and Mitsui Sumitomo Swap Transaction

In August 2003, Swiss Re and Mitsui Sumitomo Insurance Company entered into a swap agreement. The swap had a total value of $100 million. Two catastrophe risk exchanges took place, each with a value of $50 million. North Atlantic hurricane risk was swapped for Japanese typhoon risk and European windstorm risk was exchanged for Japanese typhoon risk. Via the swap, both insurers were able to limit exposure to specific geographic catastrophes and enhance the diversification of their portfolios.[3]

Insurance Options

An **option** is an agreement that gives its holder the right, but not the obligation, to buy or sell an asset at a specific price over a period of time. The **strike price** is the specific price at which the holder of an option can buy or sell the asset associated with the option. Options are available for stocks, commodities, foreign exchange rates, and other traded securities. A **call option** is an option that gives the holder the right to buy an asset. A **put option** is an option that gives the holder the right to sell an asset.

When the value of an option's underlying asset exceeds the strike price, the buyer can exercise (sell) the option and realize a gain. If the value of the underlying asset is less than the strike price, the buyer cannot realize a gain by exercising the option.

The seller is the party that issues the option and receives an up-front payment from the buyer. The payment compensates the seller for accepting the risk that it will have to pay cash to the buyer if the value of the underlying asset exceeds the strike price on an exercised option. As an example, assume ABC Corporation has an option to purchase 100 shares of stock at a strike price of $70 per share over the next year, and the current market price is $60 per share. If, during the year, the market price of the stock rises to $80 per share, ABC will likely exercise the option. By exercising the option, ABC can purchase 100 shares at $70 each for $7,000 and immediately sell those shares for $8,000 ($80 × 100). ABC would realize a $1,000 profit on the transaction.

An **insurance option** is a specialized type of option that derives its value from insurable losses—either an organization's actual insurable losses or an insurance industry index of losses. The value of an insurance option increases as the underlying insurable losses increase beyond the value of the strike price. Therefore, an organization can use a gain on an insurance option to offset its losses from insurable risk.

Many similarities exist between insurance policies and option contracts. The key features of the two risk transfer mechanisms are outlined in Exhibit 10-3.

Advantages and Disadvantages of Insurance Derivatives

With the development of the insurance derivatives market, a number of advantages and disadvantages have emerged. The advantages of insurance derivatives include the following:

- Additional risk capacity
- Lower in cost than insurance-linked securities
- Transparent pricing
- Opportunities for investors to exit during its term
- Standardized contracts
- Efficient claims and contract settlement

Option
An agreement that gives its holder the right, but not the obligation, to buy or sell an asset at a specific price over a period of time.

Strike price
The specific price at which the holder of an option can buy or sell the asset associated with the option.

Call option
An option that gives the holder the right to buy an asset.

Put option
An option that gives the holder the right to sell an asset.

Insurance option
A specialized type of option that derives its value from insurable losses—either an organization's actual insurable losses or an insurance industry index of losses.

EXHIBIT 10-3

Insurance Policies Compared With Option Contracts

Insurance Policy	Option Contracts—General and Insurance
Premium is paid by the purchaser prior to policy inception.	Premium is paid by the purchaser at the beginning of the contract term.
Deductible of self-insured retention can apply to a single occurrence or to aggregate losses for the policy period.	Strike price can apply to a single event, at regular time periods, or to the average or total experience over the entire contract period.
Purchaser is indemnified by the insurer if the level of insured losses exceeds the deductible or self-insured retention.	An option has value only if the underlying asset or index exceeds the strike price. Only then will the purchaser exercise the option for financial gain.
Has a policy limit.	Theoretically, has no limit of payout.

Example of an Insurance Option

Weather options derive their value from a measurement of weather conditions, such as average temperature or cumulative precipitation over a finite period. An organization can purchase these options to transfer weather-related risk.

For example, a midwestern U.S. basement repair contractor is most profitable during unusually wet summers—when cracks in basements are most likely to leak. Therefore, the worst-case weather situation for the basement contractor is a prolonged summer drought. The contractor determines that for every inch of precipitation shortfall below average for the months of August and September, the firm loses $10,000 in net income.

The basement repair contractor purchases a weather put option based on the measurement of rainfall during this period at the nearest weather station. The average precipitation for August through September is seven inches. The insurance option's put strike price is set at five inches. The put option is designed so that for every inch of precipitation below strike value (five inches), the option increases in value by $10,000. The precipitation cover is written as an insurance policy and has a limit of $40,000. If the cumulative precipitation between August and September is only three and one-half inches, the contractor will receive a payout of $15,000 [(5-3.5) × 10,000] from the weather insurer to help offset any lost profit from a reduction in the demand for basement repairs.

One advantage of insurance derivatives is that they create additional risk capacity. Insurance derivative markets supplement existing risk transfer capacity and provide an alternative to traditional insurance (and reinsurance). The degree of the advantage is dependent on the cost and supply of insurance (and reinsurance). During hard market periods, derivative markets enable companies to purchase protection for risks when no demand exists for structured insurance markets.

Insurance derivatives are also lower in cost than insurance-linked securities, another of their advantages. This is partially attributable to lower transaction costs, because they do not require the establishment of a SPV for claims settlement, management of cash flows, or collateral maintenance.

Another advantage of insurance derivatives is that they are transparent in pricing. A derivative is transparent in pricing if it has an open, high-volume market. Transparency is advantageous because it attracts more potential investors and assures them of liquidity.

An additional advantage of insurance derivatives is that they provide investors opportunities to exit a derivative during its term. This is an advantage because there may be opportunities to sell the contract in the secondary market during the derivative's term if the protection it provides its owner is no longer needed.

Insurance derivatives can be standardized contracts, a potential advantage over other risk financing techniques. Insurance derivatives that are traded on organized exchanges have standard contract terms and conditions, which assist buyers and sellers dealing in multiple contracts to implement and settle them consistently. Even structured derivative transactions retain a significant percentage of these standard terms and conditions.

Insurance derivatives also provide efficient claim and contract settlement. The final values of many insurance derivatives are readily determined with an independent, publicly available index or an agreed-upon value. Therefore, associated claim administration and end-of-term settlement processes are simpler and more expedient than with insurance.

There are also a number of disadvantages associated with insurance derivatives. These include the following:

- Underdeveloped markets
- Basis risk
- Credit risk
- Uncertain regulatory and accounting treatment

Insurance derivatives are sold in markets that are still underdeveloped. This may prevent an organization from purchasing the amount or type of coverage it desires. It also results in a small secondary market, which makes it difficult for an investor to exit an option contract during its term.

Insurance derivatives also subject the organization that is transferring risk to basis risk, a further disadvantage of their use. As with insurance securitization transactions, a derivative's structure may result in substantial basis risk for the purchaser. This could result in the payout from the derivative being much lower or higher than an organization's actual losses.

Another disadvantage of insurance derivatives is that they can expose an organization to credit risk. Some insurance derivative transactions are not collateralized, so the degree of credit risk depends on the financial security of the other party to the transaction (the counterparty). However, many swap and option contracts incorporate standardized terms and provide guidelines for recovery in case of default. Therefore, a large portion of the credit risk can be mitigated with standardized contracts, dealings with creditworthy counterparties, counterparty credit monitoring, exchange transactions, or use of an intermediary.

A final disadvantage of insurance derivatives is that they are subject to uncertain regulatory and accounting treatment. These issues are discussed subsequently.

CONTINGENT CAPITAL ARRANGEMENTS

Contingent capital arrangements
An agreement, entered into before losses occur, that enables an organization to raise cash by selling stock or issuing debt at prearranged terms after a loss occurs that exceeds a certain threshold.

A **contingent capital arrangement**, is an agreement, entered into before losses occur, that enables an organization to raise cash by selling stock or issuing debt at prearranged terms after a loss occurs that exceeds a certain threshold. The loss can arise from insurable risk, such as property damage resulting from an earthquake.

The organization agreeing to provide the contingent capital receives a commitment fee in exchange for its promise to reimburse the organization for its loss costs. The amount of the capital commitment fee is influenced by several factors, including likelihood of loss event, interest rates of alternative investments, and credit risk of the organization trying to arrange for the contingent capital.

Under a contingent capital arrangement, the organization does not transfer its risk of loss to investors. Instead, after a loss occurs, it receives a capital injection in the form of debt or equity to help it pay for the loss. Because the terms of the capital injection are agreed to in advance, the organization generally receives more favorable terms than it would receive if it were forced to raise capital after a large loss, when the organization is likely to be in a weakened financial condition and to pose a higher credit risk to potential lenders or investors.

The rate of the guaranteed capital infusion is normally discounted from current market pre-loss values. Investment banks and reinsurers assess the effect a catastrophic event will have on an organization and include in the interest rate on bonds or the agreed-upon stock purchase price the risk that the organization may be financially damaged beyond the contingent capital's ability to assist. Therefore, the organization still is charged an anticipated spread in credit risk, which is the higher interest rate or premium rate the organization has to pay the lender or investor in exchange for their promise to pay the contingent capital when it is needed.

Investors in a contingent capital arrangement become creditors of, or equity investors in, the organization following a loss. A contingent capital arrangement is usually set up as an option. Therefore, the organization that purchases a contingent capital arrangement is not obligated to exercise the option, even if its losses exceed the threshold specified in the agreement. However, the threshold usually is high enough to force the organization to use the agreement to supplement its own resources following the triggering event.

A contingent capital agreement generally falls into one of the following categories:

- Standby credit facility
- Contingent surplus note
- Catastrophe equity put option

Standby Credit Facility

A **standby credit facility** is an arrangement in which a bank or another financial institution agrees to provide a loan to an organization in the event the organization suffers a loss. The credit is prearranged so that the terms, such as the interest rate and principal repayment schedule, are known in advance of a loss. In exchange for this credit commitment, the organization taking out the line of credit pays a commitment fee.

Standby credit facility
An arrangement in which a bank or another financial institution agrees to provide a loan to an organization in the event the organization suffers a loss.

Many similarities exist between a standby credit facility and an insurance policy. In fact, these two risk financing techniques are often used together. For example, the owner of a group of fast food franchises may want to self-insure the first $10 million per year of its commercial general liability exposures using a standby credit facility and cover the next layer of $10 million in losses with an excess insurance policy. Alternatively, an organization may want to review the initial costs of making $10 million in funds available for losses with a standby credit facility as compared to insurance. Exhibit 10-4 shows this comparison.

At year-end, annual losses determine which of these combinations would have been the most effective. Despite the cash flow advantage of a standby credit facility, the risk management professional should consider the crucial difference between the two risk financing techniques. A standby credit facility obligates the organization to pay back, with interest, a loan it uses to cover losses. Losses paid by insurance, however, do not have to be repaid. Therefore, a standby credit facility entails loss retention, while insurance entails loss transfer.

Not accounting for the claim settlement, risk management, and other services an insurer provides, if an organization's resulting annual losses exceed the insurance premium, insurance is its best option. This underscores the importance of accurate loss forecasts.

EXHIBIT 10-4

Standby Credit Facility Compared With Excess Insurance

	Standby Credit Facility	Excess Insurance
Amount of funds available for losses	$10 million	$10 million
Initial cost of making funds available per year—prior to loss payments	$5,000 commitment fee	$200,000 premium
Interest rate on loan—if needed	5%	N/A
Length of loan—if needed	15 years	N/A
Largest possible cost in first year	$700,000 (Repay the loan = $10 million divided by 15 plus 5 percent interest)	$200,000 (premium payment)

Contingent Surplus Notes

Surplus notes
Notes sold to investors that are counted as policyholders' surplus rather than as a liability on an insurer's statutory balance sheet.

U.S. statutory accounting rules allow insurers to issue **surplus notes**, which are notes sold to investors that are counted as policyholders' surplus rather than as a liability on an insurer's statutory balance sheet. A benefit of surplus notes is that they increase an insurer's assets without increasing its liabilities. (Regular debt increases both assets and liabilities.) Although surplus notes have many of the characteristics of debt, their treatment as equity (policyholders' surplus) on an insurer's statutory balance sheet allows an insurer to increase its capacity to sell business. **Contingent surplus notes** are surplus notes that have been designed so that an insurer, at its option, can immediately obtain funds by issuing notes at a pre-agreed rate of interest.

Contingent surplus notes
Surplus notes that have been designed so that an insurer, at its option, can immediately obtain funds by issuing the notes at a pre-agreed rate of interest.

Catastrophe Equity Put Options

Catastrophe equity put option
A right to sell equity (stock) at a predetermined price in the event of a catastrophic loss.

Catastrophe equity put options are another way for an insurer or a noninsurance organization to raise funds in the event of a catastrophic loss. Whereas a put option is a right to sell an asset at a predetermined price, a **catastrophe equity put option** is a right to sell equity (stock) at a predetermined price in the event of a catastrophic loss. The buyer of a catastrophe equity put option pays a commitment fee to the seller, who agrees to purchase the equity at a pre-arranged price in the event of a catastrophic loss, as defined in the put agreement.

Risk Management in Practice—Horace Mann Committed Capital Agreement[4]

In 2002, Horace Mann Educators Corporation entered into a contingent capital arrangement with Swiss Re. The arrangement had a three-year contract period and an aggregate limit of $75 million. If Horace Mann experienced catastrophe property and casualty losses in the U.S. that exceeded a given threshold, then the firm would have the right to issue up to $75 million in convertible preferred securities to Swiss Re.

Exhibit 10-5 shows the relationship between an insurance or a noninsurance organization (the buyer) and an investor (the seller) in a catastrophe equity put.

EXHIBIT 10-5

Catastrophe Equity Put Arrangement

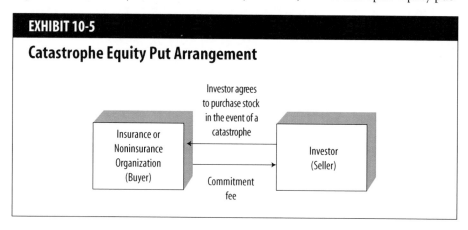

Advantages and Disadvantages of Contingent Capital Arrangements

As the market for contingent capital arrangements has developed, their advantages and disadvantages have become apparent. Advantages commonly associated with contingent capital arrangements include the following:

- Lower initial cost of making funds available to an organization per year

- Capital infusion at a predetermined price

One advantage of contingent capital arrangements is that the funds it makes available to an organization cost less than funds made available by insurance. The capital commitment fee required by the lender or equity investor is typically much lower than the premium charged for insurance. Although the commitment fee allows the organization to receive a loan on favorable terms, it still must repay the loan because it has retained the risk. With insurance, however, the organization does not pay back the losses paid because it has transferred the risk. The benefit of the risk retention element of a contingent capital arrangement is a lower initial cost, which lowers the organization's opportunity cost because, instead of using the funds to maintain a reserve fund for losses that may or may not occur, it can use them in production or in another investment opportunity that can earn a higher rate of return. In the event losses exceed an agreed-upon threshold, they will not have to be paid out of the organization's cash flow.

Another advantage of contingent capital arrangements is that they allow an organization to obtain capital infusion at a predetermined price. Contingent capital arrangements enable an organization to obtain funds (either through debt or equity) at a previously set price when it most needs it: immediately following a catastrophe. If an organization suffers a loss of capital due to a catastrophe, its increased credit risk would likely cause lenders to demand a higher interest rate on a loan. A catastrophe would also likely depress the organization's stock price, lowering the amount it would receive for newly issued stock. Contingent capital arrangements provide instant funds at a predetermined price to help an organization regain its capital following a catastrophe.

There are also disadvantages associated with contingent capital arrangements. These include the following:

- Loss sensitivity
- Ownership dilution

Funds received from a standby credit facility or contingent surplus note for losses are paid in the form of loans, not equity, and must be paid back to the lender with interest. In contrast, an organization that buys guaranteed-cost insurance pays a set premium that remains constant regardless of losses.

Another disadvantage of a contingent capital arrangement is ownership dilution. The amount of an organization's equity increases when a catastrophe equity put option is exercised, thereby reducing the existing shareholders' percentage of ownership. This dilution may also come at a crucial time in the management of the organization (that is, after a catastrophe). The additional owners introduced by a contingent capital arrangement, who may be unfamiliar with the issues and causes of the triggering event, may adversely affect the ability of the organization to recover, despite the injection of additional capital.

CONCERNS OF ORGANIZATIONS TRANSFERRING RISK AND INVESTORS SUPPLYING CAPITAL

Capital market products for risk financing can be analyzed in terms of various characteristics that determine their attractiveness to the organizations that use them to transfer risk and the investors that supply the risk capital.

Organizations Transferring Risk

The organizations that use insurance-linked securities and insurance derivatives to transfer risk are concerned with cost, the financial security (credit risk) of the parties supplying the risk capital, and the risk that the amount received may not match the amount of their loss (basis risk). Exhibit 10-6 compares insurance (and reinsurance), insurance-linked securities, and various types of insurance derivatives in terms of financial security and basis risk.

EXHIBIT 10-6

Insurance (Reinsurance), Insurance-Linked Securities, and Insurance Derivatives:[5] Financial Security and Basis Risk

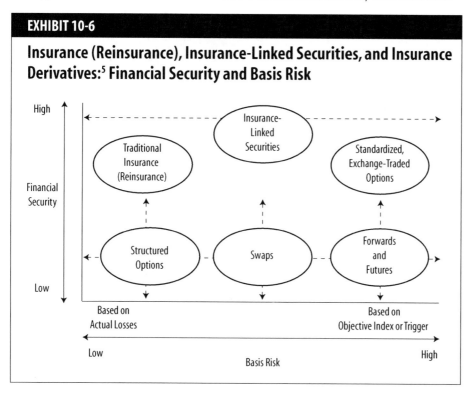

Insurance-linked securities, insurance (and reinsurance), and exchange-traded options provide a high level of financial security. Insurance-linked securities fall into this category because they are usually fully collateralized. The financial security of traditional and nontraditional insurance, including finite and integrated structures, varies depending on the strength of the balance sheet of the insurer (or reinsurer). The value of standardized, exchange-traded options is guaranteed by the exchange on which they are traded. The financial security of structured options and swaps varies depending on the financial strength of the other party (the counterparty) to the transaction. Therefore, these financial instruments provide a lower level of financial security.

Structured options and traditional insurance (and reinsurance) have a low level of basis risk. Structured options, like traditional insurance and reinsurance, are usually tailored to the organization. However, structured options have slightly higher basis risk than traditional insurance, as options normally settle to an index or are based on an agreed value, rather than providing indemnification for its actual losses.

Standardized, exchange-traded options tend to have higher basis risk because their value is based on a general industry or commodity index. Standardized options also have more rigid intervals of settlement; basis risk exists because the timing of settlement may not match the timing of the organization's actual loss and capital needs. Insurance-linked securities and swaps can be designed to have high or low basis risk, depending on whether their value is based on an index, an organization's expected losses, or actual losses.

When using insurance securitizations and insurance derivatives (swaps and options) to offset its losses, an organization must decide on the relative importance it places on financial security and basis risk. Products that provide high financial security tend to cost more than those that provide low financial security. Products that provide a perfect hedge (no basis risk) against an organization's losses tend to cost more than those that do not.

The purchasers of contingent capital arrangements have concerns that include cost, creditworthiness of the party supplying the risk capital, and adequacy and timing of the prearranged capital injection following a loss.

Investors Supplying Capital

The investors that supply risk capital for these capital market products are concerned with moral hazard, which is the degree to which an organization can influence the level of its insurable losses. For example, an organization could decide that, because it has transferred or otherwise financed its risk, it will not diligently prevent or settle its losses.

Objective trigger
A measurement that determines the value of an insurance-related capital market product based on a parameter that is not within the control of the organization transferring the risk.

Some capital market products are based on an **objective trigger**, which is a measurement that determines the value of an insurance-related capital market product based on a parameter that is not within the control of the organization transferring the risk. Objective triggers such as loss indices or earthquake severity parameters eliminate moral hazard. However, they also introduce basis risk. By contrast, when a transaction is based on an organization's own losses (that is, little or no basis risk exists), a degree of moral hazard could be involved. Therefore, a tradeoff exists between basis risk and moral hazard. In general, the lower the degree of basis risk, the higher the degree of moral hazard. This relationship helps explain why capital market products that have little or no basis risk tend to cost more than those that have basis risk.

REGULATORY AND ACCOUNTING ISSUES

A major issue associated with insurance-linked securities and insurance derivatives is whether they can be considered insurance and regulated as such. Insurance may be considered a contract that indemnifies an organization for its actual losses, and an insured organization must have an insurable interest that is the subject of an insurance contract. Based on these requirements, insurance securitizations and insurance derivatives (swaps and options) whose value is based on an organization's actual losses may be considered insurance and should be regulated as insurance. However, insurance securitizations and insurance derivatives whose values are based on an objective trigger, such as an index of insurance industry losses, may not be considered insurance and, therefore, should not be regulated as insurance.

If insurance-linked securities and insurance derivatives are determined to be insurance, then the organizations that use them to transfer risk, as well as the investors that supply risk capital, must comply with insurance regulations. State premium taxes would need to be paid. The amount paid (premiums) to transfer risk would probably be tax-deductible to the insured organization. In addition, it would not be required to record outstanding losses that are covered by the insurance on the liability section of its balance sheet.

If insurance-linked securities and insurance derivatives are determined not to be insurance, then their investors must comply with the requirements of the various regulators of securities and derivatives, such as the Securities and Exchange Commission (SEC) and the Commodities Futures Trading Commission (CFTC) in the U.S. An organization would probably not be able to deduct for tax purposes the amount it pays to transfer risk because that amount would be considered an investment in an asset rather than an insurance premium expense. In addition, the organization must record on its balance sheet outstanding losses that are meant to be covered by the proceeds from the insurance-linked security or insurance derivative. However, the organization can show a corresponding asset on its balance sheet for the fair value of the insurance-linked security or insurance derivative.

Insurance securitization transactions usually use a SPV. For a transaction involving a U.S. organization, the SPV usually qualifies as an insurer or a reinsurer under U.S. state insurance regulations. In this case, the organization transferring its risk of loss benefits from having the transaction treated as insurance (or reinsurance) because it overcomes the previously mentioned tax and accounting disadvantages. Although most SPVs to date have been formed in jurisdictions with limited regulation, such as Bermuda, U.S. insurance regulators are encouraging the formation of SPVs in various states.

In recent years, the determination of a capital market product's status as insurance has been central to several corporate finance and accounting scandals, contributed to the passage of the Sarbanes-Oxley Act, and been the subject of a higher level of scrutiny by various regulatory bodies. This issue is still evolving and will continue to test and refine the current definitions of insurance.

FAS 133 in the U.S.

In 1998, the Financial Accounting Standards Board (FASB) of the U.S. issued *FAS 133*, titled *Accounting for Derivative Instruments and Hedging Activities*. *FAS 133*, as amended by *FAS 137*, *138*, and *149*, requires that derivative instruments, except those that qualify for hedge accounting, be valued on an organization's balance sheet at fair value. Therefore, changes in the value of investments in speculative derivatives will show up immediately in the company's net worth.[6]

SUMMARY

Capital market risk financing plans allow organizations to access the capital markets to offset the risks that insurance (or reinsurance) policies have traditionally covered. These products include insurance securitizations, insurance derivatives, and contingent capital arrangements. The convergence of insurance with other financial services has spurred the development of these capital market products, and their future growth depends on their ability to deploy capital efficiently.

Securitization is a means to create a marketable security based on the expected cash flows from a financial transaction. Insurance securitization is a unique form of securitization because it involves creating a marketable insurance-linked security based on the cash flows that arise from the transfer of insurable risks. The insurance-linked securities issued to date are mainly in the form of catastrophe bonds, which can be designed to mimic an excess insurance (or reinsurance) layer. Investors are attracted to the portfolio diversification aspect of insurance-linked securities, as they constitute a distinct asset class with risk that normally has a low correlation with that of other asset classes, such as traditional stocks and bonds.

Insurance-linked securities created through insurance securitization supplement existing risk-transfer capacity and provide an alternative to traditional insurance and reinsurance. Another of their advantages is that the organization's obligation to pay losses is usually fully collateralized. A disadvantage is that capital used to fund insurance securitizations could earn a higher return, on average, if invested elsewhere in riskier securities. Other disadvantages include the volatility of market demand for securitizations, high transaction costs, and the possibility of basis risk.

A derivative is a contract that derives its value from another asset. An insurable derivative derives its value from the level of insurable losses that occur during a specific time period. Futures and forward contracts are the most common financial contracts used in risk management. The other two major categories of derivatives are swaps and options.

A forward contract obligates one party to buy and another party to sell a financial instrument or physical commodity at a specified future date and price. A futures contract is an exchanged-traded forward contract that is therefore standardized and transferable.

A swap is an agreement between two organizations to exchange their cash flows based on movements in the value of another asset, yield or index. Common examples are interest rate and foreign exchange rate swaps. An organization can use a swap that mimics an insurance policy to transfer its insurable risk. Insurance swaps are most frequently used by insurers to diversify catastrophe risk concentrations; these arrangements mimic reinsurance contracts.

An option is an agreement that gives the holder the right, but not the obligation, to buy or sell an asset at a specific price, called the strike price, during a period of time. A call option gives the holder the right to buy. A put option gives the holder the right to sell. Options can be structured between counterparties to minimize basis risk.

Users of derivatives face advantages and disadvantages. Advantages include additional risk capacity, lower cost than insurance-linked securities, transparency, ability to exit positions midterm, standardized contracts, and efficient claim and contract settlement. Disadvantages include underdeveloped markets, credit risk, basis risk, and regulatory and accounting issues. The applicability of various advantages and disadvantages varies significantly with each derivative's structure.

A contingent capital arrangement is an agreement that is entered into before losses occur that enables an organization to raise cash by selling stock or issuing debt at prearranged terms following a loss that exceeds a certain threshold. The major types of contingent capital arrangements are standby credit facilities, contingent surplus notes, and catastrophe equity put options. A standby credit facility is an arrangement in which a bank or another financial institution agrees to provide a loan to an organization in the event of a loss. The credit is prearranged so that the terms are known in advance of a loss. Contingent surplus notes are prearranged so that an insurer, at its option, can immediately obtain funds by issuing surplus notes that carry a predetermined rate of interest. A catastrophe equity put gives an organization the right to immediately sell equity (stock) at a predetermined price in the event of a catastrophic loss. The purchaser of a contingent capital arrangement pays a capital commitment fee.

Capital market products for risk financing can be analyzed in terms of various characteristics that determine their attractiveness to the organizations that purchase them and the investors that supply the risk capital.

Purchasers are concerned with cost, the creditworthiness (financial security) of the parties supplying the risk capital, and basis risk or, in the case of contingent capital arrangements, the adequacy and timing of the capital infusion following a loss. Traditional insurance and capital market instruments can be compared along two dimensions: financial security and basis risk. There is a tradeoff between cost and financial security and cost and basis risk. The purchaser of insurance (or reinsurance) or a capital market product must determine the relative importance it places in cost, financial security, and basis risk.

From the investor's (the capital provider's) perspective, a tradeoff exists between moral hazard and basis risk. In general, the lower the basis risk, the higher the moral hazard. However, the lower the basis risk, the higher the return received by the investor. The investor must decide whether it is willing to accept moral hazard in exchange for a higher return.

A major issue associated with insurance securitizations and insurance derivatives is whether they are considered insurance and should be regulated as such. If they are determined to be insurance, then the organizations that use them to transfer risk as well as the investors that supply risk capital must comply with insurance regulations. State premium taxes must be paid. Also, the cash paid (premium) to transfer risk is tax-deductible. If insurance-linked securities and insurance derivatives are not determined to be insurance, then the investors must comply with the requirements of the various regulators of securities and derivatives. Also, the cash paid to transfer risk is not tax-deductible when it is paid.

CHAPTER NOTES

1. The example case study and "new capital" estimation is drawn from Rhonda K. Aikens' of the United Services Automobile Association (USAA) presentation, "Securitization of Catastrophe Risk: A USAA Example" from The CAS Seminar on Financial Management on April 12, 1999. At the time of the presentation, Rhonda K. Aikens was an executive director, financial actuary at USAA.

2. Dan Lonkevich, "Tokyo Disney Securitizes $200M Cat Risk," *National Underwriter*, May 24, 1999, p. 3.

3. "Swiss Re and Mitsui Sumitomo Arrange USD 100 Million Catastrophe Risk Swap," August 4, 2003. www.swissre.com (accessed April 7, 2006).

4. "Swiss Re and Horace Mann Enter into USD 75 Million Committed Capital Facility." September 4, 2002. www.swissre.com (accessed April 7, 2006).

5. This exhibit is based on an exhibit presented during a lecture on April 28, 1999, given by Neil A. Doherty, PhD, professor of insurance and risk management, The Wharton School of the University of Pennsylvania.

6. The Financial Accounting and Standards Board (FASB) continually revises and updates guidance on the standards for accounting and reporting to reflect new market instruments and changing industry dynamics. Current information about FASB standards and Emerging Issues Task Force (EITF) statements is available at www.fasb.org.

Chapter | 11

Direct Your Learning

Noninsurance Contractual Transfer of Risk

After learning the content of this chapter and completing the corresponding course guide assignment, you should be able to:

- Describe the types of noninsurance risk transfers and several examples of each type.

- Describe noninsurance risk control and risk financing transfers categorized by type of transaction.

- Describe noninsurance risk financing transfers categorized by how they alter common-law liabilities.

- Describe the legal principles underlying noninsurance risk control and risk financing transfers.

- Explain how to manage noninsurance risk control and risk financing transfers.

- Define or describe each of the Key Words and Phrases for this chapter.

Develop Your Perspective

What are the main topics covered in the chapter?

This chapter examines noninsurance contractual transfers of risk. These transfers can be used independently or to supplement the protection provided by insurance. This chapter introduces several examples of both risk control transfers and risk financing transfers.

Review the examples of transferring risk.

- Which of the risk transfer techniques shown in the examples are used in your organization?

- Who in your organization oversees the use of each of these techniques?

Why is it important to learn about these topics?

Noninsurance risk control and risk financing transfers are often less expensive, more readily available, and have fewer exclusions than commercial insurance. Use of noninsurance contractual transfers can significantly affect an organization's financial health.

Describe the types of contractual transactions used by your organization.

- What risk control transfers could be implemented in these transactions?

- What risk financing transfers could be implemented in these transactions?

How can you use what you will learn?

Evaluate the effectiveness of the noninsurance contractual risk transfers used by your organization.

- How well do the strategies chosen support your organization's objectives?

- What changes would you make to the strategies?

Chapter 11
Noninsurance Contractual Transfer of Risk

Contract law allows contracting parties to transfer risks in several different ways besides through insurance. Two parties may agree, for example, that one party will reimburse the other for its loss. Alternatively, they may agree that one party will undertake an activity (and with it, absorb the accompanying risks) that the other party normally would perform. Another possible contractual arrangement entails one party waiving its rights to sue the other party for a tort related to the activity the contract covers. A tort is a wrongful act or omission, other than a crime or a breach of contract, for which the remedy is usually monetary damages.

This chapter discusses such agreements—contractual transfers of loss exposures (risk) or their financial consequences in which none of the parties operates as an insurer. Because many risk management professionals use the term "risk" in place of "loss exposure," the two terms are used interchangeably throughout this chapter.

A transferee in a noninsurance contractual risk transfer does not operate as an insurer. Consequently, it does not pool the risks of more than one transferor. A distinguishing characteristic of a noninsurance contractual risk transfer is that it is normally incidental to another larger transaction. The transferor can transfer either the loss exposure (or risk) itself or the cost of recovering from a loss.

From a transferor's perspective, transferring the risk itself is a risk control technique because it rids the transferor of some or all of the loss exposure. Transferring the cost of recovering from a loss is a risk financing technique (similar to traditional insurance) because it provides the transferor with a source of funds to finance recovery from an actual loss, but does not transfer the actual loss exposure.

When the transfer changes neither the frequency nor the severity of potential losses, but only who pays for losses when they occur, then the transfer involves only risk financing, not risk control. Although this is a text on risk financing, this chapter discusses noninsurance contractual transfer for both risk control and risk financing so that the more commonly used noninsurance risk transfers can be introduced and reviewed together.

TYPES OF NONINSURANCE RISK TRANSFERS

Insurance contracts allow an organization to transfer many of the financial consequences of accidental losses to an insurance company, which pools the risks of many insureds. The insured has the contractual right to receive (or to have provided on its behalf) indemnity or other benefits from the insurer under the same circumstances that the insurer has the duty to provide them. The typical insurance policy, therefore, creates certain conditional duties for one contracting party and correlative conditional rights for the other.

The common-law right to enter contracts allows organizations to transfer rights and duties associated with risk control and risk financing to parties other than insurers. When an organization (the transferor) contractually transfers risk control responsibilities to a party that is not an insurer (the transferee), it is essentially shifting the loss exposures associated with that risk to the transferee. This relieves the organization of most or all of the possibility of suffering a loss from the transferred risk. By contrast, when a transferor uses a contract as a risk financing technique, the underlying loss exposures are not transferred between the parties. Instead, the transferee is obligated to pay money to (or on behalf of) the transferor after the transferee or some third party has suffered a loss.

These kinds of agreements are known generally as noninsurance risk transfers. A noninsurance risk transfer is an agreement in which one party (the transferee), not acting as an insurer, accepts another party's (the transferor) exposure to loss or the financial consequences of the transferor's loss exposures as an incidental aspect of another business transaction.

Noninsurance risk transfers fall into the following two categories:

Noninsurance risk control transfer
A noninsurance transfer in which the transferor transfers a loss exposure to the transferee, thereby eliminating the possibility that the transferor will suffer a loss from the transferred exposure.

1. A **noninsurance risk control transfer** is a noninsurance risk transfer in which the transferor transfers a loss exposure to the transferee, thereby eliminating the possibility that the transferor will suffer a loss from the transferred exposure. Exhibit 11-1 depicts the relationships between parties in a noninsurance risk control transfer.

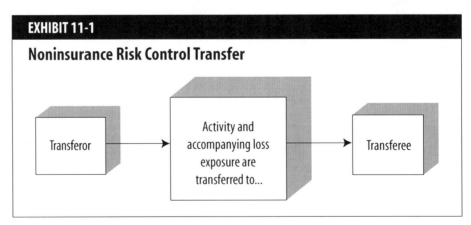

EXHIBIT 11-1

Noninsurance Risk Control Transfer

Transferor → Activity and accompanying loss exposure are transferred to... → Transferee

2. A **noninsurance risk financing transfer** is a noninsurance risk transfer in which the transferor transfers to the transferee the financial burden of losses by obligating the transferee to pay money to (or on behalf of) the transferor after the transferor or some third party suffers a loss. Exhibit 11-2 depicts the relationship between parties in a noninsurance risk financing transfer.

Noninsurance risk financing transfer
A noninsurance transfer in which the transferor transfers to the transferee the financial burden of losses by obligating the transferee to pay money to (or on behalf of) the transferor after the transferor or some third party suffers a loss.

EXHIBIT 11-2

Noninsurance Risk Financing Transfer

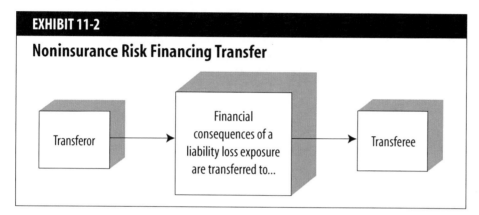

In both noninsurance risk control and noninsurance risk financing transfers, a contract is usually formed before any loss occurs. However, because noninsurance risk control transfers risk rather than the financial burdens of an actual loss, such a transfer becomes effective only when the transferee actually performs the action that rids the transferor of risk.

Noninsurance risk financing transfers provide the transferor with protection only after the funds to restore a loss are paid. Until a loss occurs, the transferor cannot be certain that the transferee will pay. If the transferee fails to provide the expected funds, the transferor receives no protection and has never truly transferred the risk's financial burden.

Another critical difference between a noninsurance risk control and a noninsurance risk financing transfer surfaces when a transferee becomes bankrupt or otherwise unable to fulfill the contractual transfer terms. In a noninsurance risk financing transfer, a bankrupt transferee provides no protection to the transferor, who must therefore pay for its own accidental loss. In a noninsurance risk control transfer, however, a bankrupt or uncooperative transferee may remain responsible for losses it caused, preserving the transferor's protection.

Both kinds of noninsurance risk transfers assume a variety of forms, each designed to meet the specific needs of the parties involved. The next section examines popular forms of noninsurance risk control transfers.

Noninsurance Risk Control Transfers

Many risk management professionals are experienced in insurance or financial matters and are therefore accustomed to dealing with contracts that indemnify losses. Noninsurance risk control transfer contracts, however, have frequently not been handled by risk management departments. For example, some risk management professionals do not manage leases or other similar written contracts. In such contracts, parties transfer risk of possible loss as an incidental part of the overall transaction. Examples of noninsurance risk control transfers include the following:

- Incorporation
- Leasing
- Contracting for services
- Suretyship and guaranty agreements
- Waivers
- Limitations of liability
- Disclaimer of warranties

Incorporation

Incorporation statutes in the United States, as well as in most western countries, stipulate that, in the absence of fraud, other intentional wrongs, or statutory violation by its founding stockholders, the most a corporation can lose because of a business venture, an accident, or a lawsuit is the value of its assets. These statutes also specify that any one stockholder's financial loss cannot exceed the value of his or her own shares, thereby insulating stockholders' personal assets. Therefore, a corporation is a legal entity distinct from its shareholders. In absence of fraud or overriding concerns for justice, a corporation is solely responsible for its own wrongs (including the wrongs of its agents).

A businessowner can use incorporation to insulate his or her organization from potential losses by designating a separate corporation to conduct each of his or her organization's major activities. For example, one corporation may manufacture and sell an organization's products, while another installs and services them. This practice is known as segregation. **Segregation** is a risk control technique that separates or duplicates an organization's activities or property so that no single cause of loss can simultaneously affect all the organization's activities or property. That is, the "divisions" between an organization's exposure units constitute the legal boundaries of separate corporations, thereby limiting loss potentials that arise from business risks, property losses, liability losses, and net income losses.

Segregation
A risk control technique that separates or duplicates an organization's activities or property so that no single cause of loss can simultaneously affect all the organization's activities or property.

Limiting potential liability losses is an important reason that, for instance, an owner of several taxicabs or trucks might form separate corporations according to vehicle activities. In such an instance, the individual entrepreneur transfers to the corporation risks that would otherwise threaten his or her personal finances, while the corporation itself is exposed to loss no greater than its assets. Similarly, stockholders can control the total value of the corporation's assets by contributing or withdrawing capital to or from the enterprise. The corporation is legally separate from any of its stockholders and serves as a transferee for risk that individual stockholders might otherwise face. As a transferee, and in exchange for stockholder capital, the corporation agrees to fulfill the business activities for which it was organized.

However, in some instances, courts might "pierce the corporate veil" by pursuing a major managing stockholder's personal assets in cases involving liability claims against corporations in the following situations:

- The corporate assets appear to have been manipulated to frustrate creditors of a corporation that seeks bankruptcy protection.

- The corporate form hides personal wrongdoings of a predominant stockholder or major executive.

In such cases, the courts often place greater importance on compensating individuals harmed by the corporation than on maintaining the usual separation between corporate liability and stockholders' personal assets.

Those who conduct business with small corporations (and regularly become their creditors) are aware of the limited personal liability of a corporation's owners. Therefore, to preserve their access to the stockholders' personal assets, creditors frequently require that the corporate owners personally cosign with the corporation all contracts, notes, and other credit obligations. This, in effect, "desegregates" corporate and personal finances.

Leasing

Property ownership legally entails several rights and duties. A leasehold is an example of one of these rights. A **leasehold** is the right to occupy or use real or personal property for a period of time. A leasehold right is asserted by a lessee, which is a person or organization that has the right to occupy or use the real or personal property for the period specified in the leasehold contract, commonly called a lease. Before and after a leasehold is placed in effect, the right to occupy or use the property remains with its owner.

Leasehold
The right to occupy or use real or personal property for a period of time.

Certain loss exposures accompany property ownership but do not accompany its use or occupancy. These loss exposures include loss from property destruction and liability to third parties for dangerous property conditions. A tenant (or lessee) does not normally have these exposures when leasing the property unless (1) the lease obligates the lessee to return the property to the lessor in the same condition in which it was received or (2) the lessee alone has caused a dangerous condition that has harmed others. Without specific language in the lease stating otherwise, if the leased property is damaged or destroyed during a lease's term, the lessee loses the ability to use the property for the remainder of the lease. The lessee often recovers this loss by leasing another property. The lessor, however, loses the property's value and rental income.

Real property owners may be liable for harm done to others because of the unsafe general condition of their property. A lessee, however, usually cannot be held liable to those harmed unless the harm arises from a condition the lessee has introduced to the leased property or unless the lessee has assumed liability under an agreement that excuses the lessor from liability.

Sale-and-lease-back arrangement
A transfer through which an organization that owns property transfers its risk by selling the property while retaining the right to occupy or use it under a lease with the new owner.

By leasing property rather than owning it, an organization practices risk control by allowing the property owner to retain the related loss exposures. A **sale-and-lease-back arrangement** is a transfer through which an organization that owns property transfers its risk by selling the property while retaining the right to occupy or use it under a lease with the new owner. Such an arrangement also allows the former property owner to convert its equity into cash. The new owner is often a corporation or other organization created or selected by the former property owner primarily for risk-transferring and financing purposes. The new owner may also be a real estate management firm, more able than the former owner to control or finance losses related to property ownership. If no fraud is involved, courts usually uphold such a transfer (except in cases in which dangerous property conditions were apparent before the property was sold and leased back).

Contracting for Services

An individual or organization that performs a particular activity is generally held primarily responsible for any losses caused by that activity. An organization that does not want to assume the risk of an activity can contract with another organization to perform the activity. This noninsurance risk control transfer method is called contracting for services or simply subcontracting. However, the party that transfers the risk need not be an independent contractor, and the party that accepts the risk need not be a subcontractor. Any contract requiring another party to perform a service and, implicitly, to assume the risk associated with that service, involves the act of subcontracting.

Generally, any property, net income, or personnel loss exposure associated with an activity can be transferred through subcontracting. However, the transfer agreement must meet the legal requirements for a fairly bargained transfer of both the loss exposures and the actual losses associated with the activity. In this case, both the loss exposure and the burden of financing recovery rest with the subcontractor.

Liability loss exposures associated with an activity, however, are not transferred easily, especially regarding harm to third parties. For example, if negligence by the subcontractor's employees creates a hazard (perhaps a large, unguarded hole) that causes injury to a pedestrian, the employees and the subcontractor would be primarily liable. However, the injured pedestrian would probably sue the landowner as the party responsible for the land's general condition.

Because the courts favor law that provides compensation to those who are injured, they also favor restricting the general rule that someone who hires an independent contractor is not liable for that contractor's torts. Several exceptions to this rule include the following:

- If the party that hired the contractor is negligent in selecting the contractor, giving directions, or failing to stop any unnecessary dangerous practices that come to the contractor's attention, the party is directly liable for such negligence.

- The responsibility that certain duties be performed safely cannot be delegated to another party. These duties may be created by statute, contract, or common law. The types of duties that are not delegable are not precisely defined but include the duty, for example, of common carriers to carry passengers safely and the duty of landowners to maintain lateral support for adjacent property.

- If the subcontracted work is inherently dangerous to others, the party who hired the contractor will retain liability for an injury to a third party caused by the contractor's negligence. This type of work includes such acts as blasting and excavating near a public highway as well as other acts that involve unusual risk of harm to others.

Despite the difficulties associated with using subcontracting to transfer liability loss exposures, organizations frequently use it to transfer loss exposures to organizations that are better able to control losses generated by a particular activity. Many organizations contract with specialty firms not only for building construction projects, but also for maintenance activities and transportation of raw materials and finished products. Organizations that contract temporary employees from agencies are relieved from the loss exposures associated with personnel, such as resignation and retirement. The contracting organization thus receives most of the benefits of temporary labor without assuming the associated employee benefits exposures.

Contracted activity usually requires resources unrelated to an organization's primary activities. Resources for such activities may be available less expensively and reliably through an outside source. Also, because contracted activities are the contractor's primary business, a competent contractor should be able to arrange more reliable and less expensive risk financing for the transferred losses than would the contracting organizations.

Suretyship and Guaranty Agreements

Surety agreements involve three parties. The first such party is the **surety**, who is a person or an organization that contractually guarantees to a party that another party will perform as promised. The second such party is the **obligee**, who is a person or an organization to whom a promised performance is owed from another party. The third such party is the **principal**, or **obligor**, who is a person or organization that has promised to perform an obligation to another party. Exhibit 11-3 depicts the relationship between these parties.

The surety's contractual guarantee is to perform or to hire someone to perform in the principal's place when the principal's failure or inability to perform becomes clear and the obligee demands performance from the surety. A surety agreement protects the obligee by providing a second source of performance.

Surety
A person or organization that contractually guarantees to a party that another party will perform as promised.

Obligee
A person or organization to whom a promised performance is owed from another party.

Principal, or **obligor**
A person or organization that has promised to perform an obligation to another party.

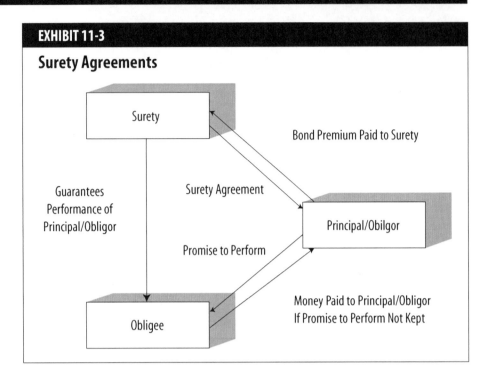

EXHIBIT 11-3

Surety Agreements

Surety

Guarantees Performance of Principal/Obligor

Surety Agreement

Bond Premium Paid to Surety

Principal/Obilgor

Promise to Perform

Obligee

Money Paid to Principal/Obligor If Promise to Perform Not Kept

A surety agreement permits the obligee to demand the surety's performance as soon as the principal's substantial failure to perform first becomes apparent. A guaranty agreement is similar to a surety agreement in that an obligee to whom a promise has been made relies on another party for performance. Such a party is called a **guarantor**, a person or organization that has promised to perform a duty in the event the party whose duty it was initially (the principal) fails to perform it. However, unlike a surety, a guarantor is obligated to perform only after the obligee has made every reasonable and legal effort to compel the principal's performance.

Guarantor

A person or organization that has promised to perform a duty in the event the party whose duty it was initially (the principal) fails to perform it.

Both suretyship and guaranty agreements allow the obligee to segregate loss exposures. Such an arrangement is analogous to having standby replacement machinery. If the principal does not perform, the obligee can rely on the surety or guarantor for performance.

Suretyship law, however, releases the surety from performance if the principal rightly refuses to perform. This might occur if the underlying promise had been secured through fraud or if the basic contract between the principal and obligee were otherwise defective. Whether a guarantor is released under similar circumstances depends on the guaranty agreement's wording.

Like other examples of noninsurance risk transfers, a surety agreement differs from most insurance contracts in two ways:

1. The surety's primary obligation is to perform as promised for the obligee, not to pay money to compensate the obligee for the principal's breach of contract.

2. A surety agreement is a three-party contract; virtually all insurance policies are two-party contracts.

Fidelity Bond

Insurers that issue performance bonds promising performance of an obligation are acting as sureties, not as insurers. However, insurance written for employee dishonesty is often called a fidelity bond. A fidelity bond is a two-party contract between an employer and an insurer that pays the employer for loss due to theft by an employee. This arrangement is not a true bond because an insured's employees are not direct parties to the insurance contract.

A surety has several rights that protect it against loss from the principal's misconduct or from collusion between the principal and the obligee. These rights include the following:

- Exoneration
- Subrogation
- Indemnity

Exoneration, the removal of a duty, applies if the obligee does not protect its rights against the principal but passively relies on the surety. For example, assume that a principal falls behind its project schedule, and the obligee fails to preserve its rights against the principal. In such a case, the surety is released from its liability to the extent that the surety can show that the obligee's inaction increased the surety's loss or otherwise harmed the surety.

Exoneration
The removal of a duty.

Subrogation (in a surety agreement) is the substitution of one party for another whose performance the substituting party satisfies and that entitles the substituting party to the rights that belonged to the defaulting party. Using subrogation in a surety agreement entitles the surety to the same payment the principal would have received. For example, if a principal defaults on a building's construction and a surety completes the construction, the building owner (obligee) must pay the surety for the portion of the work completed on the same basis on which it would have paid the contractor that defaulted.

Subrogation (in a surety agreement)
The substitution of one party for another whose debt or performance the substituting party satisfies and that entitles the substituting party to the rights that belonged to the defaulting party.

Indemnity (in a surety agreement) is the right of a surety to seek reimbursement from the principal for the resources the surety expended when it performed the principal's duty. The surety can proceed directly against the principal to recover the fair value of its effort or any funds it paid to the obligee as compensation for the principal's inaction. The principal must indemnify the surety for the costs of fulfilling the promise.

Indemnity (in a surety agreement)
The right of a surety to seek reimbursement from the principal for the resources the surety expended when it performed the principal's duty.

As mentioned, because a surety's contractual commitment is the same as the principal's, any justification (or legal defense) for nonperformance that releases the principal from the underlying contract also releases the surety. The surety can also be legally released if the original contract is modified without the surety's consent. Because the surety's promise is the same as the principal's, any attempt by the obligee and principal to alter the principal's commitments releases the surety from its original commitment.

Waivers

Waiver
The voluntary relinquishment of a known right.

Exculpatory clause
Contractual provision that relieves one party from liability resulting from a negligent or wrongful act.

An individual or organization that has the power to sue in contract or in tort can waive that right using a **waiver**, which is the voluntary relinquishment of a known right. An organization or individual who could be subject to a lawsuit no longer faces a liability exposure from those who have waived the right to sue. An **exculpatory clause**, a contractual provision that relieves one party from liability resulting from a negligent or wrongful act, is similar to a waiver. Both waivers and exculpatory clauses are intended to eliminate one party's liability loss exposure from another party. Many states use the terms "waive" and "exculpate" interchangeably. These types of clauses often are present in real property leases. For example, common law allows a real property lessee (tenant) to sue a lessor (landlord) for failing to maintain habitable premises. If, however, a lessee waives the right to sue, the lessor no longer faces the liability loss exposure from the lessee. Consider, for example, a lease provision that reads as follows:

> Lessee, as a material part of the consideration to be rendered to the Lessor hereby waives all claims against Lessor for damages to the goods, wares and merchandise in, upon or about said premises and for injuries to Lessee, his agents or invitees in or about said premises....

Unless improperly obtained or nullified by applicable state or local law, this lease provision lessens the concerns of the landlord that the tenant will sue for damages to any "goods, wares, and merchandise" or for injuries to the tenant or others who are on the premises at the tenant's request. As worded, the provision is broad, apparently excusing the lessor from liability even for intentional harm to the lessee.

By allowing an organization to rid itself of the applicable liability loss exposures, waivers can function as effective risk control mechanisms. For example, the previously discussed lease provision limits the landlord's loss exposures to lawsuits from the lessee. It does not, however, prevent others, such as the lessee's employees, guests, or other invitees, from suing the landlord. Nor does it obligate the lessee to hold the lessor harmless from lawsuits, that is, to provide the lessor with a legal defense and to pay any verdicts or judgments levied against the lessor.

To be effective, a waiver should comply with the following criteria:

• The waiving party must not have been forced to sign it by uneven bargaining power.

• It must be obtained honestly, not by deceit or concealment.

• It must state the specific right that is being waived in a clear and unambiguous manner.

• It must be supported by legal consideration paid to the party waiving the right.

Although the previous example was drawn from a lease, other kinds of contracts also can contain waivers. Some contracts contain a single provision granting mutual waivers, in which both parties agree to voluntarily relinquish their rights to sue each other. However, the courts do not generally require such reciprocity as long as some evidence of fair bargaining and reasonable disclosure is associated with the waiver.

Waivers are generally embodied in original contracts and are signed before the parties begin their contractual dealings or have suffered harm. However, an organization or individual may waive its rights to sue after it has suffered some harm for which it may have sued.

A **waiver of subrogation** is a special type of waiver that is a pre-loss voluntary relinquishment by an insurer of its right to seek reimbursement of its payment for damages that were caused by a party other than the insured. For example, a landlord's insurer frequently waives its right of subrogation against a tenant who may negligently cause a fire that damages the landlord's insured property. Note that the landlord cannot waive this right for the insurer. Only the insurer can do so.

Waiver of subrogation
A special type of waiver that is a pre-loss voluntary relinquishment by an insurer of its right to seek reimbursement of its payment for damages that were caused by a party other than the insured.

Limitations of Liability

In a situation in which transferor and transferee have equal bargaining power, the transferor may agree through contract negotiation to cap or limit the amount or type of its liability instead of insisting on a waiver of its liability entirely. The following is an example of a contractual clause that would accomplish this:

> In no event will (transferor) be liable to (transferee) or any third party for any incidental or consequential damages arising out of use or of inability to use (transferor's product which is being sold to transferee), or for any claim by any other party, even if (transferor) has been advised of the possibility of such damages. (Transferor's) total liability with respect to (transferor's product) shall not exceed the purchase price paid by the (transferee). (Transferee) acknowledges that these limitations permit (transferor) to provide this product at a lower cost than it otherwise could, and such limitations on liability are reasonable.

Disclaimer of Warranties

A disclaimer of warranties is often asserted by sellers of property. A disclaimer in a sales contract may serve several purposes. First, it may deny any express warranties made in conjunction with the property's sale. Second, it may deny several warranties that by default are often implied, including the following:

- The implied warranty for a particular purpose, which suggests that the seller is aware of the particular purpose for which the buyer will use the property and that the property is suitable for that purpose.
- The implied warranty of merchantability, which implies that the property is suitable for the purpose for which most buyers use it.

The following is an example of disclaimer language used in a software sales contract:

> (Seller's property) is provided "as is." To the maximum extent permitted by law, (seller) disclaims all warranties of any kind, either express or implied, including without limitation, implied warranties of fitness for a particular purpose and merchantability.

Without such a disclaimer, the seller may unknowingly provide an implied warranty that would expose it to contractual liability that it could have otherwise avoided.

Noninsurance Risk Financing Transfers

In all forms of noninsurance risk financing transfers, the transferor's protection is only as reliable as the transferee's ability and willingness to pay money when needed to restore the loss. Despite this potential drawback, such transfers can be highly effective and provide dependable protection for a transferor under the following conditions:

- Some loss characteristic renders the transferor beyond the scope of typical insurance contracts. For example, the cause of loss might not be covered in the only available or affordable insurance policy.
- The transferee's degree of commitment to fulfilling the general business contract with the transferor motivates the transferee to provide more complete indemnity because an insurer might question the indemnitee's right to payment.
- The transferee often has more direct and comprehensive knowledge of the risk it is accepting than an insurer's underwriter, as is the case for maintenance agreements and guarantees for services.

Noninsurance risk financing contracts transfer the financial burden of losses. If the transferee fails to provide the compensation the contract requires, the financial burden of the loss remains with the transferor. Two prevalent noninsurance risk financing transfers are the following:

- Hold-harmless agreements
- Risk transfer to the transferee's insurer

Hold-harmless Agreements

As discussed, a hold-harmless agreement is a contract under which one party (the indemnitor) agrees to assume the liability of a second party (the indemnitee). The liability assumed by the indemnitor is for the legal claims that may be brought against the indemnitee because of the activities the contract covers. The indemnitor often is referred to as the transferee and the indemnitee often is referred to as the transferor. Generally, any contractual party has the common-law right to agree to pay or indemnify the other party for any losses it suffers in fulfilling the contract's terms. The range of noninsurance transfers is extremely broad. However, the common law of contracts and the statutes of some jurisdictions limit a party's right to make another party pay for a loss. Under the indemnity clause of a hold-harmless agreement, one contractual party, the **indemnitor**, is the party that assumes an obligation by promising to indemnify another party. The other party is referred to as the **indemnitee**, who is the party whose liability the indemnitor assumes.

The indemnity clause of a hold-harmless agreement can provide a transferor with funds for restoring accidental losses to property, net income, liability claims, or the loss of the services of the transferor's key personnel. A broad array of indemnity clauses is found in hold-harmless agreements that cover the transferor's liability losses from contractual activities.

The following is an example of a hold-harmless agreement. Note that it includes both the terms "hold-harmless" and "indemnity:"

> The (transferee) shall hold harmless and indemnify (the transferor) for any losses, claims, damages, awards, penalties, or injuries incurred by any third party, including reasonable attorney's fees, which arise from any alleged breach of such indemnifying party's representations and warranties made under this agreement, provided that the indemnifying party is promptly notified of any such claims. The indemnifying party shall have the sole right to defend such claims at its own expense. The other party shall provide, at the indemnifying party's expense, such assistance in investigating and defending such claims as the indemnifying party may request. This indemnity shall survive the termination of this agreement.

A hold-harmless agreement can be difficult to understand. Those familiar with insurance often use the framework for interpreting an insurance policy to analyze hold-harmless agreements. In addition, most hold-harmless agreements do not indicate whether the transferee/indemnitor is obligated to pay punitive damages for which the transferor/indemnitee becomes liable or whether bankruptcy of the transferee/indemnitor relieves the transferee/indemnitor of any further liability. The effect of punitive damages and bankruptcy on both hold-harmless and other indemnity agreements varies greatly among jurisdictions. In some jurisdictions, the transferee's payment of punitive damages is included automatically within a hold-harmless agreement. In others, punitive damages are included only if specified. In still others, contractual transfer of the obligation to pay punitive damages is illegal. Bankruptcy excuses a transferee/indemnitor in some jurisdictions, often depending on the nature of the harm the claimant suffered.

Noninsurance risk financing transfers are largely unregulated. Therefore, the provisions and practices of hold-harmless agreements are not standardized. Generally, one party transfers the financial burden of losses in one or more of the following situations:

- One party has the bargaining power to require the other party to be its transferee.
- Such a transfer is standard practice for the particular transaction or industry.

Indemnitor
The party that assumes an obligation by promising to indemnify another party.

Indemnitee
The party whose liability the indemnitor assumes.

- The transaction requires that a risk financing transfer meet several criteria: legal enforceability of the transfer agreement, the relative ability of the contracting parties to manage risk, and the legal considerations paid for the transfer.

For many years, courts categorized indemnity agreements separately from hold-harmless agreements. Several courts viewed hold-harmless agreements as a special type of indemnity agreement that dealt only with specified activities. However, partly because the contractual clause typically includes both the terms "harmless" and "indemnity", many courts now view these as such similar agreements that they often refer to them simply as hold-harmless agreements.

Transfer of Risk to the Transferee's Insurer

Insurance agreements can be modified to allow the transferee's insurer to treat a specified third party as an insured. This can be accomplished through two kinds of endorsements—additional insured and named insured. Both of these endorsements obligate the transferee's insurer to pay (or pay on behalf of) the third party after it has suffered a loss.

Additional insured endorsement
An endorsement that adds coverage for one or more persons or organizations to the named insured's policy.

An **additional insured endorsement** is an endorsement that adds coverage for one or more persons or organizations to the named insured's policy. The endorsement offers a transferor several advantages. By being added to the transferee's insurance policy, the transferor acquires the following:

- Rights under the policy independent of the enforceability of the general business contract between the transferor and the transferee
- Benefit of the transferee's insurer waiving its right to subrogate against the transferor
- Additional source of funds to pay for the transferor's losses
- Right to demand that the transferee's insurer pay for the cost to defend the transferor for a covered liability loss
- Free coverage because the transferor often does not contribute funds toward payment of the transferee's insurance premium

Despite these clear advantages to the transferor, the transferee has a disadvantage. A request to an insurer to add a transferor as an additional insured to a policy can change the transferee's acceptability to its insurer's underwriter. Other than knowledge of the relationship between the insured transferee and the additional insured transferor, the underwriter usually has little information about the liability loss exposure that the additional insured presents. Although able to identify correctable problems that present a liability loss exposure, the underwriter often can do little to make the additional insured take corrective action. The underwriter may be forced to cancel or nonrenew the transferee's policy. Another disadvantage is that every policy has exclusions, and the transferor must still control or finance some loss exposures through another mechanism.

Named insured endorsement
An endorsement that, similar to an additional insured endorsement, adds coverage for one or more persons or organizations to the named insured's policy and elevates the new insured to the status of a named insured, giving it special rights and obligations.

A **named insured endorsement** is an endorsement that, similar to an additional insured endorsement, adds coverage for one or more persons or organizations to the named insured's policy and elevates the new insured to the status of a named insured, giving it special rights and obligations. This elevated status has several advantages, including the following:

- A transferor's agents, employees, officers, and directors are considered insureds and therefore are included in the transferee's coverage.
- The transferor, as the named insured, is likely entitled to receive notice if the transferee's policy is canceled or endorsed.

Several disadvantages also apply when a transferor is considered a named insured, including the following:

- The transferee's insurer may have a right to inspect the transferor's business and financial records.
- The transferor may unknowingly be agreeing to provide periodic reports to the insurer.
- The transferor may become involved in litigation unrelated to relevant insurance coverages.

Risk management professionals must weigh these advantages and disadvantages when considering these kinds of endorsements. Many risk management professionals have concluded that being added as an additional insured to the transferee's policy is preferable.

In practice, noninsurance risk transfers are often categorized in terms of the transaction they facilitate. The next section discusses both risk control and risk financing transfers in a variety of transactions.

NONINSURANCE RISK CONTROL AND RISK FINANCING TRANSFERS—TYPE OF TRANSACTION

Any written contract can contain a noninsurance transfer of risk control or risk financing. For example, the ticket a garage owner normally gives to those who park their cars in the garage contains a broad waiver of the car owner's common-law right to bring claims against the garage owner for vehicle and content damage. Automobile rental agreements require lessees to purchase insurance or otherwise bear the financial consequences of vehicle damage. Otherwise, the rental company, as the vehicle owner, would assume liability under common law in virtually all circumstances. Finally, two organizations agreeing to the sale, rental, or maintenance of a product can each include a provision in their agreements that makes the other party an indemnitor.

These contractual transfers for risk control or risk financing can be so enmeshed in the agreements exchanged that neither party may be aware of the mutual promise to indemnify the other. This situation creates contract interpretation conflicts that can render both the transfers and each party's attempt to collect indemnity from the other virtually meaningless. To avoid such problems, each organization's risk management professional, legal counsel, and key managers must recognize where to look for the more common forms of noninsurance risk transfers. Such agreements are typically included in the following contracts, each of which focuses on a different type of transaction:

1. Construction contracts
2. Service and maintenance contracts
3. Purchase order contracts
4. Lease of premises contracts
5. Equipment lease contracts
6. Bailment contracts
7. Sale and supply contracts

Construction Contracts

A building contractor's work creates many loss exposures, principally liability exposures, for the landowner and the building under construction. For example, a contractor's activities can harm its own, and a subcontractor's, employees, pedestrians, owners of adjoining properties, or even the entire community. As a landowner, the individual or organization for which the building is constructed is ultimately liable for all such harm. The owner is also liable for any breaches of building permit provisions or building codes that result from the contractor's or architect's decisions.

For protection against liability losses, landowners normally require that the building contractors or architects hold them harmless from certain construction-related claims. Contractors and architects usually cannot bargain to remove hold-harmless provisions from contracts because landowners can often find other contractors or architects who will agree to the hold-harmless provisions.

The exact extent of the claims against which the contractor or architect agrees to hold the landowner harmless can be determined only by carefully reading the hold-harmless agreement. However, the agreement may still leave some questions unanswered about the scope of losses the contractor agrees to assume.

Service and Maintenance Contracts

Constructing a building is a highly specialized type of service that results in a tangible product that, when finished, ends the contractor's services. Other services, however, frequently including maintenance, and transportation, are purchased on a continuing basis. The providers of such services often agree to a generic type of hold-harmless agreement. A contractor's obligation under such an agreement can be broad because (1) the contractor agrees to hold the owner harmless from virtually all property, liability, and other losses (except, most likely, revenue losses) the owner may suffer because of the contractor's errors and (2) the contractor agrees to be responsible even for those claims brought against the owner because of the owner's sole negligence.

Purchase Order Contracts

The raw materials, components, and supplies that manufacturers, wholesalers, or retailers purchase for use in their products can create products liability claims against purchasers. For example, the items purchased from a vendor may be defective, or they may be the wrong type or grade for the product. Common law gives the ultimate buyer or other product user the right to sue everyone involved in the product's production or sale, ranging from the raw material supplier to the retailer. Any organization in the distribution chain also has the right to ask any other party in the chain to provide it with protection against product liability claims. Traditionally, each purchasing organization may require its immediate supplier or vendor to hold it harmless through a contractual provision.

Like an insurance contract, many hold-harmless agreements also have "exclusions" and "conditions." For example, the provision in a purchase order agreement may exempt the indemnifying vendor from responding to claims brought against the purchaser based entirely on the purchaser's "sole negligence" without any fault of the vendor. The agreement also makes the vendor's promise conditional on the purchaser's immediately notifying the vendor of any claim. The vendor has authority to manage claims, while the purchaser is barred from making any separate settlement with a claimant. However, unlike an insurance contract, this agreement does not obligate the purchaser/indemnitee to cooperate with the vendor/indemnitor in the vendor's management of any claim.

Many hold-harmless agreements also protect the purchaser. The purchaser has enough bargaining power to obtain the vendor's promise of indemnity, and the vendor's eagerness to contract with the purchaser makes the agreement at least tolerable to the vendor. Those relationships can be reversed. A vendor who is the exclusive national manufacturer of a popular product may be able to require each wholesale or retail purchaser to agree to hold the manufacturer harmless from products liability or other claims, or even from other losses. Marketers throughout the distribution chain may have no choice but to provide the manufacturer with this promise of protection if they want to sell the product.

When several parties in the production-marketing chain enter into a series of hold-harmless agreements, considerable confusion can result. If all agreements transfer the financial consequence of losses one "link" back along the chain, then the original manufacturer (or even raw material supplier) could become obligated to finance the losses of all claims against other parties. In the opposite case, when the financial consequence is transferred forward, then the retailer could become burdened with the losses of all the parties in the distribution chain. If the agreement provides for indemnity from purchasers and from vendors, then the aggregate liability of all the producers and marketers could accumulate at various points along the chain. Even greater confusion can exist in construction situations, if a contractor and subcontractors sign agreements holding each other as well as the project owner harmless.

To guard against confusion and to ensure that financial responsibility is equitably and efficiently distributed, the agreements should be planned so that loss exposures are assumed by those most qualified to control them or so that losses that do occur are assumed by those qualified to finance their recovery.

Lease of Premises Contracts

Even if a lease of real or personal property contains no explicit risk transfer provisions, as discussed previously, it can be used for noninsurance risk control transfer. A lease by nature allows a lessee to enjoy the property's use for a specified period without having to be subjected to the many of the loss exposures inherent in property ownership. Although such exposures remain with the lessor, a lessor can attempt to use the lease to transfer to the lessee the financial burden of some losses, resulting in a noninsurance risk financing transfer. In effect, the lessee can use the lease for risk control transfer and the lessor can use the same lease for risk financing transfer.

A lessee frequently accepts the entire lease agreement as prepared by the lessor. Consequently, many lease agreements are written to substantially favor the lessor. Furthermore, unlike insurance contracts, which courts often interpret in an insured's favor, courts usually interpret leases assuming that the parties had equal bargaining power, especially if the lessee is an organization renting business space rather than an individual or a family renting personal space. Finally, a lessee that wants to do business in a particular location often has a limited choice regarding the number of available properties.

The lease obligates the lessee to respond to liability claims that may be brought against the lessor. The hold-harmless agreement is broad because the lessee's financial responsibility extends not only to the lessor's common-law liabilities but also to its statutory liabilities, including workers' compensation claims. In numerous states, an attempt to transfer risk to the lessee's workers' compensation insurance company or other statutory liability to the lessee's general liability insurer would be highly vulnerable to a court challenge by an injured employee of the lessor or by some third party injured on the lessor's premises. Both could claim that the financial security of their statutory protection had been jeopardized significantly by an attempted contractual transfer from the lessor to the presumably less financially able lessee.

Equipment Lease Contracts

An individual or organization that leases equipment usually promises to return the equipment in its original condition, often subject to certain exceptions. That promise protects the lessor against loss to equipment, which is often out of the lessor's direct control or supervision for substantial periods. The promise is not burdensome for the lessee because (1) the lessee does not assume any financial responsibility for liability claims against the lessor that may arise from the lessee's possession or use of the equipment and (2) the lessee is responsible only for the property value of the leased equipment and not for the revenue the lessor could have earned on the equipment had it remained undamaged and available for another rental.

Other equipment leases, however, obligate the lessee to hold the lessor harmless from liability claims related to the equipment while it is in the lessee's possession. The lessee might even be required to maintain insurance that provides the lessor with liability (and often other) protection.

Bailment Contracts

Many business transactions involve placing personal property in the custody of some other party, for example for repair, transportation, or safekeeping. **Bailment** is the temporary transfer of a property's custody. A **bailee** is a party having possession of another's personal property and a duty either to return it to the owner or to deliver or dispose of it as agreed. The **bailor** is the owner to whom property, in the temporary custody of another, is to be returned.

A **mutual benefit bailment** is an arrangement in which the bailor pays the bailee for work or service related to the bailed property and from which both the bailee and the bailor expect to benefit. A **gratuitous bailment** is an arrangement in which the bailee receives no compensation and owes a lower degree of care. Under common law, the bailee must exercise ordinary care for the safety of the bailor's property. In most cases, common law requires that a mutual benefit bailee return the property to the bailor in its original condition, excusing the bailee only for damage caused by acts of God and normal wear and tear.

A special class of mutual benefit bailment consists of common carrier transporters of others' goods, that is, carriers who transport anyone's cargo in accordance with an established schedule and set fees. A common carrier situation is a mutual benefit bailment. However, because of the public's interest in safe, efficient, and effective transport of goods, the degree of care required of common carriers exceeds that of an ordinary mutual benefit bailee. Any loss that results from an accident, or even from a third party's act, results in the carrier's liability. A common carrier is responsible for any damage to a bailor shipper's cargo except that caused by the following:

- Acts of God
- Warlike activities (usually described as involving acts of a public enemy, but not including rioting or terrorism)
- Exercise of public authority (as when police block the access to a particular neighborhood, thus depriving a business of its usual profits)
- Fault or neglect by the shipper (such as poor packaging or labeling)
- Any inherent vice of the cargo (any potential for the shipper's goods to destroy themselves, as when ice melts or explosives detonate because of improper packaging or labeling)

A bailor and bailee can contractually alter the common-law apportionment of their respective liability. For example, in many business situations, bailees

Bailment
The temporary transfer of a property's custody.

Bailee
A party having possession of another's personal property and a duty either to return it to the owner or to deliver or dispose of it as agreed.

Bailor
The owner to whom property, in the temporary custody of another, is to be returned.

Mutual benefit bailment
An arrangement in which the bailor pays the bailee for work or service related to the bailed property and from which both the bailee and the bailor expect to benefit.

Gratuitous bailment
An arrangement in which the bailee receives no compensation and owes a lower degree of care.

seek to limit their liability through posted notices or contract provisions stating that they are not responsible for damage to bailors' goods. Bailees can also attempt to limit their liability to a specified amount per item or only to the property's value (excluding any profits or loss of use the bailor would have earned from the property). In contrast, a bailor can seek to increase a bailee's liability by, for example, holding the bailee responsible for specified acts of God (such as windstorm).

Either party to a bailment contract can have business reasons for assuming liability that the common law usually places on the other party. Courts respect each party's freedom of contract to bargain fair apportionments of liability. However, they have been reluctant to enforce liability-transferring bailment contract provisions that are contrary to practice within the particular industry, not equitably negotiated, or less than adequately disclosed.

For example, the previously discussed statement on the back of tickets given to customers of a public parking garage is ignored by most courts as an inadequately disclosed and unbargained attempt to transfer the garagekeeper's liability, contrary to the bailor's reasonable expectation.

Sale and Supply Contracts

Contracts pertaining to the sale and supply of goods and services offer innumerable opportunities for transferring risk between buyers and sellers. The transfer usually favors the party with the greater bargaining power. For example, to maintain firm control of their products as they move through marketing channels, some manufacturers and processors sell their goods on consignment. Consignment places title to the property with the manufacturer or processor until the distributor sells the goods to the retailer or ultimate consumer. Also, the distributor, having never taken title to the goods, is never exposed to loss from their damage or destruction. Ownership, and the loss exposure, moves directly from the manufacturer or processor to the retailer or consumer, allowing the distributor to earn revenue only from its distribution.

Organizations also use sale and supply contracts to protect the buyer or other owner of substantial personal property against specified types of losses to or arising from that property. If the organization promises to provide services only but does not also agree to indemnify the property owner for losses, the agreement is one of risk control, not risk financing. If, in contrast, the organization agrees to hold the owner harmless from liability claims against the owner, then the agreement becomes a risk financing transfer.

Organizations become risk transferees under the following types of contracts:

- Contracts that provide a customer with a constant fuel supply, which obligate the fuel dealer to pay for any frozen pipes and certain other losses if the customer is ever without fuel
- Contracts to purchase data processing equipment, air conditioners, vehicles, or similar items with guarantees of maintenance and replacement as necessary

- Contracts of service under which real estate agents maintain specified equipment, such as heating systems, in homes they sell

Such contracts are similar to insurance if they go beyond guaranteeing the quality of the goods or the reliability of the supplier's performance and extend to other causes of loss. For example, courts have found organizations to be engaged in the business of insurance, making them subject to the provisions of the applicable state insurance code, in the following situations:

- A tire dealer agrees to give an allowance for unused mileage if a tire that it sold is damaged by road hazards.

- A glazier promises to replace plate glass windows broken by any cause.

Inadvertently becoming subject to an insurance code can be restrictive and costly for organizations. In effect, the organization can be forced to withdraw from the ambitious service or maintenance agreements through which it sought to attract customers by becoming the transferee of loss exposures that customers usually bear.

Sale and supply contracts can substantially modify the common law that distributes loss exposures between property buyers and sellers. The common law indicates that risk of loss, both to the property and from the property's loss of use, moves with the property's title. The owner always bears the exposures. Therefore, special risk transfer provisions aside, the time when ownership changes is important in identifying and managing an organization's loss exposures. For example, when Company S sells a product to Company B in another city, specifying when Company B acquires ownership is essential.

Company S may indicate in its standard sales contract that each sale is "F.O.B. Detroit," where Company S is located. **Free on Board (F.O.B.)** is a provision that absolves a seller of responsibility for goods sold once they have reached the designated location. Regardless of whether Company S delivers its products in its own vehicles or by common or contract carrier, the provision means that Company B acquires the goods (and the related loss exposures) as soon as the goods are aboard a carrier in Detroit. If, however, the specification is "F.O.B. Des Moines," which may be the location of Company B's warehouse or some central distribution point, then Company B owns and is responsible for the loss of the goods when they reach Des Moines and are ready to be unloaded.

Free on Board (F.O.B.)
A provision that absolves a seller of responsibility for sold goods once they have reached the designated location.

An alternative sales contract, particularly for a contract of sale for permanently installed equipment, may indicate that Company B does not become the owner until the property has been unloaded and installed and has passed a series of operational tests in the buyer's facility. Such an arrangement allows the seller to maintain control of the property and to ensure that it has been appropriately placed in service. If, in contrast, Company S wants Company B to be responsible for damage to the property throughout its transport, Company S may require that Company B take title to the property at Company S's shipping dock. The buyer's and seller's bargaining power, as well as industry custom, influences when loss exposures are transferred.

Cost-insurance Freight (C.I.F.)
A provision that includes in a good's price the cost of goods, insurance, and the freight charges to the destination.

Installment or **conditional sales contract**
A sales contract in which the seller commonly reserves ownership rights until the buyer meets all the contractual conditions, most notably the buyer's final installment payment.

Fungible goods
Commodities or bulk goods, all parts of which are presumed to be uniform.

Responsibilities for ownership loss exposures can be divided, with different responsibilities being transferred at different times. **Cost-insurance Freight (C.I.F.)** is a provision that includes in a good's price the cost of goods, insurance, and the freight charges to the destination. If the shipment between Company S and Company B is under C.I.F. terms, Company B acquires ownership as soon as the goods are on board a carrier. Company S, however, must purchase sufficient insurance and pay for the freight. If the insurance is less than the amount established by the custom of the trade or the sales contract specifications, Company S, because it has failed to fulfill the C.I.F. conditions, must compensate the buyer, Company B, for its loss. This arrangement illustrates how it is often possible to combine risk control transfers with risk financing transfers, in this case obligating the seller to provide insurance for, or to indemnify, the buyer directly.

Another frequent division of loss exposures in sales of property occurs in an **installment** or **conditional sales contract**, which is a sales contract in which the seller commonly reserves ownership rights until the buyer meets all the contractual conditions, most notably the buyer's final installment payment. Although the seller usually retains title, exposure to loss because of property damage can be transferred immediately to the buyer by the sales contract. The transfer can be achieved by a contract provision obligating the buyer to complete the contract by continuing installment payments even though the property might be lost or damaged before the buyer makes the final payment. Such an arrangement preserves the seller's right under an installment contract either to receive the full purchase price or, if the buyer defaults, to repossess the property. The buyer can also obtain insurance or other risk financing to protect its interests and obligations. During the time between the first and last installment payments, therefore, both the buyer and the seller are exposed to loss from damage and have an insurable interest in the property.

A common arrangement is for the seller to retain possession of property that has been sold for later delivery to the buyer. Valuable items of personal property, as well as substantial quantities of **fungible goods**, which are commodities or bulk goods, all parts of which are presumed to be uniform, are often sold in this way. The contract of sale becomes effective as soon as the buyer and seller agree on the particular items or quantity to be sold, the price, and the delivery date. The sales contract commonly specifies that property ownership transfers to the buyer at the time the agreement is reached. Although the ownership-related loss exposure to damage thus passes to the buyer, the seller having custody of the property still has a bailee's responsibility for the property's safety. In such cases, both the bailor's ownership interest and the bailee's liability for damage can expose each to loss and support each party's purchase of appropriate insurance or other risk financing arrangements. Exposures might be altered by specific agreement.

NONINSURANCE RISK FINANCING TRANSFERS— HOW THEY ALTER COMMON-LAW LIABILITIES

Noninsurance risk transfer agreements may define obligations of the transferor and transferee in a way that alters each party's common-law liabilities. Categorized by how they alter common law, such agreements can be grouped according to whether they achieve one of the following:

1. Transferring responsibility for joint fault (limited form)
2. Transferring all responsibility, except for transferor's fault (intermediate form)
3. Transferring all responsibility (broad form)

Although these types of agreements can be applied to any property, net income, liability, or personnel loss exposures, most pertain to a transferor's potential or actual liability loss exposures.

Transferring Responsibility for Joint Fault (Limited Form)

Two or more individuals or organizations working together to fulfill their contract may jointly harm a third party. Or, they may be joined as defendants in a civil suit charging them both with fault for a breach of contract or a tort. The facts of the situation may not reveal which party is at fault or the extent to which the parties share fault. Determining who is responsible and to what extent can be a difficult, time-consuming, and contentious process.

However, this process can be eliminated if one contracting party transfers its common-law responsibility for joint civil wrongs to the other contracting party. The one to which joint responsibility is transferred (the transferee) must agree to hold the other party (the transferor) harmless from claims arising from their joint fault. Such a transfer is embodied in the italicized portion of the following hold-harmless clause:

> Lessee shall be liable for, and shall hold the Lessor harmless with respect to, all claims relating to damage or injury to the property or persons of others alleged to have occurred on or have been caused by the condition of the leased premises, if such injury or damage is alleged to have been caused by an act or neglect of the Lessee (including anyone in the Lessee's control or employ) *or the joint act or neglect of the Lessee and Lessor*.

This agreement is noteworthy because the italicized words pertaining to joint responsibility are surrounded by many other provisions describing the lessee's responsibility not only for liability claims but also for damage to the premises. The italicized words are designed to transfer the otherwise joint responsibilities for harm to others, making what was once joint the transferee's sole responsibility. This responsibility could be overlooked easily by the lessee, especially if this part of the agreement is typed or otherwise prepared individually for each agreement and not made a part of the preprinted form. Both the transferor and the transferee must be sure that the agreement expresses their shared intent.

Transferring All Responsibility Except Transferor's Fault (Intermediate Form)

Most of the agreements discussed previously would not apply if the contracting parties and a third party all were named defendants in a civil suit. The agreement does not mention the third party's fault. Nor does it refer to claims arising from more complex chains of causation, like lawsuits for bodily injury or property damage involving the transferor's fault, coupled with the plaintiff's fault or the wrongful acts of a civil authority. In these more complex cases a transferee (such as the previously discussed lessee) could maintain, with some reasonable chance of success, that it was not obligated to hold the transferor harmless from the claims of others.

A hold-harmless agreement that protects the transferor in such cases would be phrased to apply to all claims except those arising from the transferor's sole fault. The following is an example of such a provision in a building construction contract:

> The contractor shall indemnify and hold harmless the owner from and against all claims attributable to bodily injury unless caused entirely by the owner's act or omission.

Under the agreement, the contractor is not obligated to respond to a lawsuit against the owner if the contractor could show that, regardless of any allegations, the owner solely caused the plaintiff's bodily injury. If the concluding words of this provision had read "…alleged to have been caused entirely by…," then the wording of the plaintiff's complaint, rather than the case's actual facts, could determine whether the contractor had been obliged to hold the owner harmless.

Transferring All Responsibility (Broad Form)

Beginning with a relatively simple restatement of common law, the two preceding hold-harmless agreements have sought to progressively improve the transferor's position, transferring ever greater financial consequences to the transferee.

The broad form of the hold-harmless agreement attempts to place all financial consequences of potential losses on the transferee. Many state courts have held that it is inappropriate to include indemnification for the acts the transferor is solely liable for and therefore have not enforced such agreements. To illustrate a broad form of a hold-harmless agreement, assume that the provision used in the previous section was amended to read as follows:

> The contractor shall indemnify and hold harmless the owner from and against all claims…attributable to bodily injury or property damage… whether or not caused in part by the owner.

The words following "whether" do not limit the contractor's duty to respond. In fact, the provision seeks to make the contractor financially responsible for all bodily injury and property damage claims against the owner.

LEGAL PRINCIPLES UNDERLYING NONINSURANCE RISK TRANSFERS

The legal principles underlying noninsurance risk transfers allow certain freedoms and impose certain limitations. Contracting parties have the freedom of contract. This freedom is important because it promotes commerce and facilitates business transactions. Contracting parties are also limited by common law and statutes. The limitations are important because they protect the public by preventing contracting parties from engaging in unacceptable behavior.

Freedom of Contract

Legally competent parties are free to bargain, that is, they have freedom of contract, as long as the contract does not unreasonably interfere with the rights of others. Contracting parties can mutually bind one another to the contract, and courts can enforce a contract against a contracting party who decides not to abide by its terms. A contractual provision can assign responsibility for risk control or risk financing to various parties. Courts enforce contract terms by requiring parties to comply with the contract's risk-transferring provisions.

Despite the latitude historically enjoyed by contracting parties through freedom of contract, courts increasingly refuse to enforce noninsurance transfers that meet the following criteria:

- Have been unfairly imposed
- Unreasonably interfere with the rights of others who are not parties to the contract, making the transfer against public policy or contrary to public interest

Many state statutes attempt to preserve fairness and to foster economically appropriate allocations of loss exposures and of actual losses by doing the following:

- Prohibiting certain types of transfers in some contracts (particularly hold-harmless agreements)
- Prohibiting certain wording in some forms of contractual transfers
- Prescribing the wording of transfer provisions

Common-Law Limitations

A fundamental goal of common law is to balance the competing interests of individuals and society, whose actions, if based on self-interest, can create conflict and infringe on others' rights. For contractual transfers of risk or for the cost of losses, that goal requires balancing the potentially competing interests of contracting parties and the collective rights of contracting parties against those of society and the economy. Unconscionability is a key concept when balancing competing interests between contracting parties. Public policy is key when balancing the competing interests of contracting parties and society.

Unconscionability

When courts enforce contracts, they generally assume that to fulfill the contracting parties' original intentions, each party can be held to its original, freely made promise as indicated in the contract. Consequently, consent of the parties is an essential prerequisite of any valid contract. Without it, the courts have little basis for requiring a party to perform a contract.

Unconscionable provision
A contract provision that is so intolerably offensive to the court's sense of basic justice that the court cannot, in good conscience, enforce it.

Some contract provisions contain terms that are so unfavorable to one party that their presence implies that the party could not have willfully consented to their inclusion. Such a provision is known as an **unconscionable provision**, a contract provision that is so intolerably offensive to the court's sense of basic justice that it cannot, in good conscience, enforce it. For a contract to be deemed unconscionable, one party must have been physically, psychologically, or economically coerced into signing it. Holding that party to such a bargain would be unconscionable, even though the contract appears to be valid. For example, an employee waives all rights to workers' compensation benefits shortly after suffering a seriously disabling injury but has not reclaimed the common-law right to sue the employer. This is an example of a noninsurance risk control transfer. A court would probably refuse to enforce the waiver and would allow the employee to pursue statutory workers' compensation benefits. A court can reason that the employee would have agreed to such a waiver only by being misled or coerced and that the waiver agreement was not the result of a genuine accord between the employer and the employee. This lack of mutual consent indicated by the inequity of the waiver would render the waiver unenforcable.

Public Policy

In determining whether a contract or provision is unconscionable, a court examines the bargaining relationships between parties. A court must also consider the economic and social consequences that would result if entire groups of people or organizations were to enter into contracts with similar provisions. The **public policy** of a given country, state, or other jurisdiction is the set of assumptions and principles (often unstated) on which the laws and court decisions of that jurisdiction are based.

Public policy
In a given country, state, or other jurisdiction is the set of assumptions and principles (often unstated) on which the laws and court decisions of that jurisdiction are based.

Many contracts courts consider to be unconscionable are also contrary to public policy. For example, the previously discussed injured employee's waiver of workers' compensation benefits, described as unconscionable, is contrary to the public policy goal of workers' compensation statutes. One goal of those statutes and one public policy mandate is to relieve the government, and ultimately the taxpayers, of the responsibility of financing losses an employee incurs when injured on the job. Given that goal, any agreement between an employer and an employee that waives the employee's statutory right to workers' compensation benefits without providing alternative compensation to the employee in return would probably not be honored by the courts. Such a waiver puts the responsibility of the loss on society rather than on the employer. Therefore, the contract is also contrary to public policy.

Another example of how a risk control transfer can be limited by unconscionability or for public policy considerations is an agreement between a common carrier and a cargo shipper that excuses the carrier from liability for cargo damage caused by the carrier's negligence. The Federal Interstate Commerce Act makes a common carrier liable for all damage to goods except for that due to specified causes. Therefore, any dilution of liability by a noninsurance risk control transfer agreement is contrary to the act's goal of protecting the public by encouraging common carriers to safely transport goods. Moreover, because common law traditionally requires that a common carrier exercise a high standard of care, a court would likely infer that a shipper would excuse a carrier from negligence only if the shipper were coerced into doing so. The coercion would make the contract unconscionable, thus negating the shipper's waiver.

Statutory Limitations

Many states have statutes dealing with hold-harmless agreements. Various states prohibit the agreements, forbid the use of certain wording in certain agreements, or specify precise wording of the agreements. The statutes reflect legislative questioning of one contracting party's attempt to limit its liability for negligence or other wrongdoing by compelling another party to waive its right to sue or to pay the transferor's losses. The statutes reflect public concern for preserving incentives for organizations to act carefully to prevent harm to others. Some statutes also provide a source of adequate compensation for those harmed, especially compensation from financially strong organizations, which likely have the bargaining power to enforce an unconscionable hold-harmless agreement.

Statutory limitations on hold-harmless agreements are noteworthy for their diversity, especially regarding the following variables:

- The types of noninsurance transfers to which the statutes apply (generally for risk financing, not risk control)
- The parties the statutes regulate regarding who can be a transferor or a transferee
- The scope of the loss exposures (particularly liability loss exposures) whose transfer the statutes seek to regulate

Each statute must therefore be carefully read to determine how it treats those variables. For example, a Georgia statute states the following:

> A covenant, promise, agreement, or understanding in, or in connection with, or collateral to, a contract or agreement relative to the construction, alteration, repair, or maintenance of a building structure, appurtenances, and appliances including moving, demolition, and excavating connected therewith, purporting to indemnify or hold harmless the promisee against liability for damage arising out of bodily injury to persons or damage to property caused by or resulting from the sole negligence of the promisee, his agents or employees, or the indemnitee, is against public policy and is void and unenforceable provided that this section shall not affect the validity of any insurance contract, Workers Compensation agreement, or other agreement issued by an admitted insurer.[1]

That statute applies only to hold-harmless agreements that do the following:

- Relate to building construction/demolition
- Seek to transfer the promisee's/indemnitee's sole negligence
- Apply only if the transferee/indemnitor is not an insurance company admitted in Georgia

Executives and their legal counsel or risk management professionals draft creative hold-harmless agreements for a broad range of circumstances. Drafting a statute that applied equitably and unambiguously to all contracts would be a legislative challenge. For example, unlike the previously discussed Georgia statute, other state statutes specifically state they apply not only to the building structure, appurtenances, and appliances but also to roads, highways, and bridges. Therefore, whether the statute in the preceding provision applies to contracts involving roads, highways, and bridges is not clear.

Despite these obstacles to determining applicability, the statutes that apply to hold-harmless agreements can be classified into those that prohibit transfer (all-inclusive statutes), those that prohibit particular wording, and those that prescribe the precise wording in provisions the contracting parties include in their agreement.

All-Inclusive Statutes

Some statutes prohibit virtually all hold-harmless agreements in order to protect certain classes of people. One example of such a statute reads as follows:

> Indemnification Agreements Prohibited. Any agreement or provision whereby an architect, engineer, surveyor or his agents or employees is sought to be held harmless or indemnified for damages and claims arising out of circumstances giving rise to legal liability therefore on the part of any said persons shall be against public policy, void and wholly unenforceable.

This New Hampshire statute is very broad. It bars hold-harmless agreements (including indemnification) that might apply to "circumstances giving rise to legal liability," regardless of the type of wrongdoing or the extent of fault of involved parties. Perhaps significantly, the statute is also narrow in denying protection only to architects, engineers, surveyors, and their associates. Any hold-harmless agreement involving, for example, a building owner, contractor, or subcontractor is presumably valid in this jurisdiction.

Statutes Prohibiting Particular Wording

Some statutes prohibit a narrowly defined class of hold-harmless agreements, such as those that refer to the transferor's "sole negligence." Parties responsible for composing hold-harmless agreements under such a statute must use alternate phrasing, such as referring to the transferee/indemnitor's "joint fault," or "shared legal responsibility."

Other statutes more directly address the wording of risk control and risk financing transfers. For example, one statute used by several states indicates the following:

> No agency of this state nor any political subdivision, municipal corporation or district, nor any public officer or person charged with the letting of contracts for the construction, alteration or repair of public works shall draft or cause to be drafted specifications for bids, in connection with the construction, alteration or repair of public works:
>
> (a) In such a manner as to limit the bidding, directly or indirectly, to any one specific concern or…
>
> (b) In such a manner as to hold the bidder to whom such contract is awarded responsible for extra costs incurred as a result of errors or omissions by the public agency in the contract documents.

The statute is subject to two crucial limitations:

- It applies only to public entities and their officials and agents who draft bids for contracts that hold the bidder "responsible for extra costs incurred as a result of errors or omissions by the public agency in the contract documents," not for other errors or omissions.
- It applies only to building/demolition contracts for public works.

The statute does not apply to private organizations or individuals, public contracts unrelated to public works, or errors and omissions of the public agency that are not reflected in the contract documents.

Statutes prohibiting particular wording in risk transfer agreements are generally very narrow. Compliance with these statutes primarily involves avoiding the prohibited words and other related phrases. Precise contract wording can usually achieve the contracting parties' intentions almost as fully as if this kind of prohibitory statute did not exist.

Statutes Prescribing Certain Wording

To prevent a transferee/indemnitor from undertaking burdensome commitments in a hold-harmless agreement, some states specify that if a particular type of contract does contain any such provision, the provision's wording must incorporate certain phrases. The following statute used by many states illustrates this limitation:

> Any portion of any agreement or contract for, or in connection with, any construction, alteration, repair, or demolition of a building, structure, appurtenance, or appliance, including moving and excavating connected with it, or any guarantee of, or in connection with, any of them, between an owner of real property and an architect, engineer, general contractor, subcontractor, or between any combination thereof, wherein any party referred to herein obtains indemnification from liability for damages to persons or property caused in whole or in part by any act, omission, or default of that party arising from the contract or its performance shall be void and unenforceable unless:
>
> (a) The contract contains a monetary limitation on the extent of the indemnification and shall be a part of the project specifications or bid documents, if any.
>
> (b) The person indemnified by the contract gives a specific consideration to the indemnitor for the indemnification that shall be provided for in his contract and section of the project specifications or bid documents if any.

Legislatures that have passed this or similarly worded statutes may have reasoned that a hold-harmless agreement for building construction/demolition is fairly bargained if the indemnitor's obligation has some monetary limit and the transferor gives specific legal consideration to the transferee for the promise of protection. This entire provision applies only to construction/ demolition projects, not to any bailment, equipment lease, sales or service contract, or any other contractual transfers for risk financing or risk control. Nor does the statute require that every construction contract contain this provision. The statute demands only that, if a hold-harmless agreement is included, then it must contain the specified wording.

Understanding the legal principles underlying transfer of risk is part of the overall task of managing both risk control and risk financing transfers. Several of the more critical factors to consider in the management of such transfers are discussed in the next section.

MANAGEMENT OF NONINSURANCE RISK CONTROL AND RISK FINANCING TRANSFERS

An organization's risk management professional has many uses for noninsurance transfers for risk control and risk financing and should be aware of the legal restrictions that govern their use. He or she should develop a consistent, feasible program to manage such contractual transfers. The risk management professional also should be aware that transferring or assuming risk is not always an organization's best alternative. The organization may instead allow common or statutory law to apportion the loss exposures and financial consequences of specified types of losses. In general, consistent and effective control of noninsurance transfers requires the following:

- An analysis of factors affecting appropriate use of risk transfers
- A clearly written and widely disseminated organizational policy with general administrative controls and specific control measures for managing noninsurance transfers

Factors Affecting Appropriate Use of Noninsurance Risk Transfers

Some risk management professionals use the negotiation of noninsurance transfers, especially those for risk financing, as a way to reduce the organization's liability loss exposures and loss costs. Such an approach is possible because contract provisions, especially liability-related hold-harmless agreements not connected with construction contracts, are largely unregulated.

However, the goal of sound risk management is to use noninsurance transfers in ways that efficiently apportion loss exposures and the loss cost for the transferor, the transferee, and the economy as a whole. Here, efficiency refers to both organizational and economy-wide cost of risk. Therefore, the most efficient transfer lowers the cost of risk for each contracting organization.

Because the parties drafting and using noninsurance transfers can benefit from the transfer's negotiation by obtaining more favorable terms than the other involved parties, a risk management professional should participate not as a competitor but as a referee, seeking fairness and mutual benefit for all participants. As such, the risk management professional should consider the following three factors.

1. The legal enforceability of contract provisions
2. The relative abilities of the parties to manage risk (that is, to keep losses from occurring and to pay for those that do)
3. The price or other legal consideration the transferor explicitly or implicitly pays or gives to the transferee

Enforceability

Legal enforceability is one factor that determines a contract's appropriate use and whether the contract can be used at all. First, a contract is not enforceable if it is unconscionable or in violation of public policy or statutes. Second, attempts by the contracting parties to rid themselves of the same or related loss exposures or financial consequences could make it difficult to enforce the contract. For example, contracts in which risks have been transferred and retransferred can make it almost impossible for a court to tell who has agreed to accept what risk and may be unenforceable as a result.

Ability to Manage Risk

Another factor to consider in risk transfer is the transferee's ability to pay major losses when they occur, specifically, whether the transferee has accepted in this and other contracts more responsibility than it can handle. Construction companies, in particular, are a common target for hold-harmless agreements. As a group, they are also subject to sudden and severe financial strains in the ordinary conduct of their business.

Generally, transferees must receive enough benefits from their contracts to cover the obligations assumed under them. However, a benefit that is fair for the transferee may not always be reasonable for the transferor to offer. In such a case, noninsurance transfer may not be the most efficient method for handling a given loss exposure. Moreover, transfers could make it impractical to handle a loss exposure in a more efficient way or could even preclude such a possibility. For example, the transferee may be unable not only to pay for large losses but also to effectively reduce losses.

Limitations on the efficacy of transfer apply particularly when the negligence loss exposure is transferred and can violate the fundamental general management principle of assigning authority and its related responsibility to the same party. When liability for the negligence of one's own employees is transferred, the responsibility (and therefore the incentive) to control negligence is disconnected from the authority to do so. The transferor retains the authority to control employee negligence, whereas the transferee acquires the responsibility and the incentive to do so.

Consideration Paid

The third factor related to contract fairness is the price or other consideration the transferor gives to the transferee. Regarding cost, the greatest efficiency is commonly achieved when the responsibility for risk financing and the authority for risk control rest with the same party. This result requires arrangements such as having manufacturers rather than distributors assume the full financial responsibility for losses arising from faulty products and for defective materials used in the manufacturing process. It also requires manufacturers to assume full responsibility for claims arising from their advertising statements. However, distributors should have full financial responsibility for claims arising from their own statements in selling and advertising and for their own acts of assembling, disassembling, mixing, storing, and packing products. Similarly, contractors should have full financial responsibility for their employees; for their agents' activities; and for the condition of their premises, equipment, and materials. On the other hand, the building owner should have full responsibility for losses arising from items such as specifications and from any use the owner makes of the premises on which the contractor is working. Because dividing lines between responsibilities are not always clear, the underlying contract, in the interests of economy and ease of enforcement, should be specifically and carefully worded.

In determining who can best manage loss exposures and pay for losses, the contractual transfer should not be considered by itself. How one transfer relates to another should be considered. This sometimes leads to exceptions to the general rule of merging responsibility and authority. Consider the responsibility of a single tenant in a large office building for damage to the entire building. The general rule would require the tenant to assume liability for all damage arising from the small portion of the premises the tenant actively controls. But that rule would make it necessary for the tenant to buy insurance against its possible liability for severe fire damage to the building, duplicating the owner's insurance covering the same property.

Once a risk management professional considers the factors in determining contract fairness, risk management efforts should concentrate on establishing an effective program for controlling noninsurance transfers.

Elements of a Noninsurance Risk Transfer Program

The first and most important element of a sound noninsurance risk transfer control program is a consistent transfer strategy. Such a strategy ensures that the organization does the following:

1. Becomes a transferor when this role serves both the organization and the general economy
2. Becomes a transferee when this role is similarly appropriate
3. Avoids assuming both roles simultaneously when appropriate

A defensive approach to noninsurance risk transfer requires an organization to avoid inadvertently becoming a transferee. Such a defensive strategy should reflect an understanding of the conditions under which it is unwise for an organization, and thus economically inefficient for society, to become a transferee.

The opposite position, the offensive approach, entails taking advantage of other organizations by using economic power to impose transfers. This frequently is an inappropriate strategy for an organization and for society. Unwavering pursuit of an offensive strategy is regarded by many risk management professionals as unethical. An unduly aggressive strategy could prompt others to consistently follow a defensive strategy and could prompt legislatures and the courts to look suspiciously on transfers that are handled under such circumstances.

A more balanced and productive strategy is neither consistently defensive nor consistently offensive. Instead, it examines the implications of alternative noninsurance transfer arrangements for the contracting organizations and the economy. Consequently, transfers are used only when they benefit all contracting parties without, at the very least, harming the economy. Therefore, a sound policy rests both on a good general administrative program and on specific controls to secure appropriate transfers while avoiding inappropriate ones.

General Administrative Controls

Regardless of the organization's size, an organized administrative program must control noninsurance transfers. The risk management professional must cultivate an understanding with everyone who is involved with contracts, including those who design them and those who accept them. These individuals should also be encouraged to stay in close touch with the risk management department and to inform it of the status of all contracts.

The initial goal of controls should be to help all contract-related personnel clearly understand the loss exposure that could be hidden in the most simple contracts and the need to have such documents reviewed by experienced personnel. In practically every organization, most contracts are, for the most part, routine. Wording should be standardized. To illustrate, some weeks or months of careful scrutiny will probably indicate that purchase orders, service contracts, and other routine contracts contain only a standard hold-harmless agreement. Once the responsible executives determine this, appropriate decisions can be made about dealing with the liability involved. Contracts can then be left to periodic auditing.

Contracts that cannot be classified as routine can be troublesome. With these contracts, effective education and training for all responsible personnel are of major importance. Noninsurance risk transfer agreements are not easy to spot, are not easy to evaluate, and can be hazardous to the organization. The risk management professional or other official with responsibility for controlling such transfers must be given an adequate opportunity to read and interpret each contract. Unlike routine contracts, these types of contracts require more attention than periodic auditing.

Even the most imaginative and thorough administrative program for controlling noninsurance transfers should be reviewed periodically. Procedures that are customary can become unnecessarily cumbersome or imprecise. Similarly, the cost of administering the program must be known and monitored. Control, which depends on accurately assessing the current situation, is the goal.

Records of Contractual Transfers

Detailed, current records of all the written contracts into which an organization has entered are crucial for properly managing noninsurance transfers. These records should include the contracts themselves, the identities of the parties to whom the organization is bound by these contracts or from whom the organization is entitled to protection, and the legal bases (statutes or court cases) for the enforceability of these noninsurance transfers.

These records are likely to be voluminous and to change constantly. The great variety and number of contracts into which an organization enters and the diversity of state and federal laws on the content and interpretation of noninsurance transfers mean that a risk management professional needs a great deal of information to determine the meaning of these transfers. Furthermore, legal counsel for the organization or for others with whom the organization deals often drafts new transfers in response to recent court rulings for legislative mandates dealing with these transfers.

These records and related information should be included within an organization's computerized risk management information system (RMIS). RMIS can be helpful in several ways. It can help to maintain current records of these transfers to track recent court decisions and statutes germane to the transfers, and to generate revised wording for the noninsurance transfers in an organization's own contracts in ways that best fulfill the organization's offensive or defensive strategy for managing these transfers.

Specific Control Measures

Having identified and evaluated the loss exposure in the noninsurance transfers, the risk management professional must decide how to treat loss exposures or must present recommendations to management. A risk management professional should review all contracts before they are finally executed and reject inappropriate ones. When reviewing a contract, the risk management professional should ask the following questions:

- To what extent can the assumption of loss exposure be reduced?
- What loss exposures can the organization safely assume?
- To what extent should contractually assumed loss exposures be transferred by insurance?
- Can specific contract provisions be deleted, particularly those involving loss exposures that can be neither safely retained nor transferred?
- Can clearer contract language be negotiated, especially to clarify points that seem likely to be disputed?

Some agreements may present loss exposures the organization is willing to assume without insurance. Such loss exposures usually involve only minor and remote hazards, free of any element of catastrophe. However, if the risk management professional determines that loss exposures introduced by the contract are dangerously severe, retention might be unwise.

For loss exposures to be covered by insurance, the risk management professional must be as certain as possible of the available coverage. The risk management professional must also examine the other contracting party's insurance protection, if any. Needed coverage must be obtained as well as a clear explanation of coverage and the insurer's legal defense obligations.

Even the best use of risk control and risk financing can fail to control contractual transfers. Rather than avoid such contracts, management can remove some of their provisions. Examples include eliminating transfers of liability related to acts of God (a contingency for which no insurance can be obtained) and claims caused entirely by the transferor's alleged fault without wrongdoing by any other party (transferor's sole negligence). The ability to make such changes depends on the bargaining strengths of the parties and the importance of their contractual relationship.

Wherever possible, contract language should be clarified. Although often omitted from contracts, definitions are also very important.

Fundamental Guidelines

The following fundamental guidelines for managing noninsurance transfers for risk control or risk financing apply the principles presented throughout this chapter:

- Ensure that the indemnitor can fulfill its commitment financially. Legal precedent mandates that the commitment be backed by insurance of at least $1 million per occurrence.

- Require a certificate of insurance for contractual liability coverage before contract operations begin. The certificate should clearly state that the insurer must provide at least thirty days' notice of cancellation or material change in coverage.

- Be named as an additional insured on the transferee's policy. Although being added as an additional insured can pose problems, such as an increased possibility of having the policy canceled or nonrenewed, its advantages far outweigh the disadvantages.

- Avoid being too severe. If a contractual transfer is too extreme, the courts may construe it as invalid because it is unconscionable or contrary to public policy. The further apart the two parties are in their bargaining power and knowledge of contract terms, the greater the probability that the contract will be unenforceable.

- Avoid ambiguity. The courts do not favor contracts that indemnify individuals or organizations against the consequences of their own negligence or intentional wrongdoing. If contract language is ambiguous, courts generally construe a hold-harmless agreement to make it consistent with common law and public policy. Generally, this means that a person or an organization is indemnified for liability, especially if the person or organization was only passively negligent in causing property damage or bodily injury.

- Become more actively involved in legislation. Many of the present statutes limiting noninsurance indemnification are the products of lobbying efforts. Risk management professionals have an obligation to their organizations and to the public to present compelling reasons for laws that can benefit an organization, the economy, and society.

SUMMARY

The two types of noninsurance risk transfer are risk control and risk financing. Risk control transfers a loss exposure from transferors to transferees and rid transferors of most or all of the possibility of suffering a loss from the transferred exposure. Risk financing transfers the financial burden of losses and creates the transferee's duty to pay money to (or on behalf of) transferors after the transferor has suffered a loss.

Risk control transfers include the following: incorporation, leasing, contracting for services, suretyship and guaranty agreements, waivers, limitation of liability, and disclaimer of warranties. Risk financing transfers include hold-harmless agreements.

In noninsurance risk financing transfers, generally one party transfers the financial consequence of losses when any one of the following occurs: one party has the bargaining power to require the other party to be its transferee; such a transfer is standard practice for the particular transaction or industry; the transaction requires a risk financing transfer to meet several criteria, including legal enforceability of the transfer agreement, the relative ability of the contracting parties to manage risk, and the legal consideration paid for the transfer.

Noninsurance risk transfers are classified in two ways. One classification is by type of transaction. Examples include transactions involving construction contracts, service and maintenance contracts, purchase order contracts, lease of premises contracts, equipment lease contracts, bailment contracts, and sale and supply contracts.

Agreements can also be classified by responsibility transferred. Responsibility can be transferred by transferring responsibility for joint fault; by transferring all responsibility, except for transferor's fault; and by transferring all responsibility.

Common and statutory law impose some restrictions on noninsurance transfers. Those restrictions protect the public by preventing unconscionable behavior by contracting parties. Legally competent parties are free to bargain as long as the bargaining does not unreasonably interfere with the rights of others. Common-law limitations include unconscionability and violation of public policy.

An organization's risk management professional should develop a consistent, feasible program to manage noninsurance transfers of risk control and risk financing. A consistent and effective program analyzes factors affecting appropriate use of risk transfers and uses a clearly written and widely disseminated organizational policy.

When negotiating noninsurance transfers, a risk management professional should consider the following factors, which are relevant to contract fairness and the mutual benefit of the contracting parties: enforceability, ability to manage risk, and consideration paid.

The first and most important element of a sound noninsurance risk transfer control program is to develop a consistent transfer strategy. Developing a strategy ensures that the organization becomes a transferor when that role is appropriate, becomes a transferee when appropriate, and avoids assuming both roles simultaneously when appropriate.

The following basic guidelines for using noninsurance transfers in risk control and risk financing apply the principles that were presented throughout the chapter:

- Ensure that the indemnitor can fulfill its commitment financially
- Require a certificate of insurance for contractual liability coverage before contract operations begin
- Be named as an additional insured on the transferee's policy
- Avoid being too severe
- Avoid ambiguity
- Become more actively involved in legislation

CHAPTER NOTES

1.   Ga. Code Ann. § 20-504.

Chapter | 12

Direct Your Learning

Purchasing Insurance and Other Risk Financing Services

After learning the content of this chapter and completing the corresponding course guide assignment, you should be able to:

- Describe the six steps in purchasing insurance and other risk financing services.

- Explain the marketing considerations for risk financing plans.

- Describe the types, roles, required characteristics, and compensation of risk financing plan intermediaries.

- Describe the opportunities for unbundling the services that are part of an insurance package.

- Explain how to evaluate proposal responses, including:

  - Services offered

  - Financial stability of insurers

  - Costs

- Describe the legal principles of insurance contracts.

- Define or describe each of the Key Words and Phrases for this chapter.

Develop Your Perspective

What are the main topics covered in the chapter?

This chapter examines the processes involved in purchasing insurance and other risk financing services. The six steps involved in purchasing insurance allow the risk management professional to manage the placement of new and renewal insurance coverages systematically.

Review the six steps in purchasing insurance.

- Is the entire process practiced at your organization? If not, what steps are used?

- Who oversees this process at your organization?

Why is it important to learn about these topics?

Insurance is one of the most prevalent methods organizations used to transfer risk. Frequently, more than one insurer is willing to accept the transfer of an organization's risk. A risk management professional must be able to select the right insurer, use the right insurance marketing intermediary, and purchase only the services needed among all the proposals solicited and received.

Examine the processes used by your organization when purchasing insurance.

- What characteristics does your organization require from its insurance marketing intermediaries and how are those intermediaries compensated?

- How does your organization determine which insurer services to accept, reject, or obtain from another vendor?

How can you use what you will learn?

Evaluate the effectiveness of the processes used by your organization when purchasing insurance.

- How well do the strategies chosen support your organization's objectives?

- What changes would you make to the process your organization uses to purchase insurance?

Chapter 12
Purchasing Insurance and Other Risk Financing Services

Many risk financing transactions require risk management professionals to interact with one or more insurers or with other providers of risk financing services. This chapter is most useful to those risk management professionals who have assessed their organization's loss exposures, evaluated the risk financing alternatives for dealing with potential losses from each significant exposure, and determined that purchasing insurance is the most appropriate risk financing plan for the organization to pursue.

After reaching this conclusion, the risk management professional must then select or renew an existing insurance policy that is most compatible with the organization's needs. The wide variety of insurers and policy types available can make this determination difficult. The risk management professional may also investigate opportunities to reduce insurance costs by pursuing alternatives to the incidental services an insurer generally charges for in the policy's premium. A systematic approach to insurance selection often yields the best result. The six-step process for purchasing risk financing services involves an organization determining its insurance needs and then communicating them to insurers and relevant third parties. To ensure that this process produces the best results for the organization, a risk management professional should be familiar with the marketing, legal, and economic considerations that affect each of its steps.

STEPS IN PURCHASING INSURANCE AND OTHER RISK FINANCING SERVICES

Organizations commonly purchase risk financing services by entering into a new insurance contract or renewing an existing one. The ideal insurance contract satisfies both the insured's (or the applicant's) need for protection and the insurer's need for premium income. Arriving at such a contract requires the cooperation of the organization seeking coverage, the prospective insurers, and insurance intermediaries. An **intermediary** is an insurance agent, broker, or other marketing channel for an organization seeking to sell its loss exposures to insurers. Each of these parties plays a role in the following six-step sequence, which is depicted in Exhibit 12-1:

1. The organization determines its insurance needs and develops specifications for coverage.

Intermediary
An insurance agent, broker or other marketing channel for an organization seeking to sell its loss exposures to insurers.

2. The organization presents its proposal to insurers through intermediaries.
3. Insurers and their intermediaries develop and present coverage proposals to the organization.
4. The organization evaluates the coverage proposals.
5. The organization enters into a contract with the insurer.
6. The organization implements steps related to the new coverage.

EXHIBIT 12-1

General Chronology of an Insurance Placement or Renewal

Step	Months Before Placement/Renewal
1. The organization determines its insurance needs and develops specifications for coverage.	6
2. The organization presents its proposal to insurers through intermediaries.	5
3. Insurers and their intermediaries develop and present coverage proposals to the organization.	4 (If initial placement) 3 (If policy renewal)
4. The organization evaluates the coverage proposals.	2
5. The organization enters into a contract with the insurer.	1
6. The organization implements steps related to the new coverage.	0

Determination of Insurance Needs and Development of Specifications for Coverage

In the first step in the risk financing purchase process, an organization determines its insurance needs and develops specifications for coverage. This step should begin with the first two steps in the risk management process: identifying and analyzing the organization's loss exposures. The organization's risk management professional must assess the organization's loss exposures and evaluate the risk financing alternatives for dealing with potential losses from each. The risk management professional can then specify the types and potential amounts of the possible accidental losses facing the organization that will not be retained or transferred to a noninsurance transferee. The risk management professional must then develop insurance specifications for those exposures.

Deciding whether to formulate general or detailed coverage specifications can pose a dilemma for an organization's risk management professional. General specifications give the insurance intermediaries or the insurers considerable opportunities to creatively meet the organization's needs. However, the resulting variations among insurers' proposals can make it difficult for the risk management professional to compare and choose among proposals. Alternatively, requiring insurers and their intermediaries to comply with detailed specifications can stifle their innovation and prevent the risk management professional from learning about new insurance-based risk financing alternatives not originally considered in developing the specifications.

One way to resolve this dilemma is to require all insurers and their intermediaries to submit proposals that meet exact specifications and also to encourage insurers and intermediaries to propose innovations that could be incorporated into subsequent specifications. However, that approach can extend the time needed to secure coverage.

If the organization suddenly faces a new potentially major loss exposure that its risk management professional has not had time to assess, the risk management professional should obtain some standard form of generally applicable property-casualty coverage for a brief period. With coverage in place, the risk management professional has time to analyze the general coverage and eliminate any coverage that proves unnecessary and/or to add necessary coverage. The risk management professional also may conclude that the organization's existing policies provide similar coverage for the new loss exposure.

Presentation to Insurers Through Intermediaries

In the second step of the risk financing service purchase process, the organization presents its needs to insurers through intermediaries. How best to make contact with those intermediaries depends on the insurer's marketing channels. Sometimes an organization's risk management professional contacts a broker, an independent agent, or an exclusive agent who acts as an insurer's marketing intermediary. At other times, the risk management professional may not use a marketing intermediary at all, but instead deal directly with the insurer. (This is subsequently discussed.)

The risk management professional may spend several days or weeks presenting the organization's insurance specifications to one or more intermediaries. Ideally, presentations should occur at least five months before existing coverage is scheduled to end. Presentations should be uniform, clear, and complete so that potential insurers can develop proposals that respond to the same coverage needs based on the same information. The risk management professional may schedule a series of meetings with individual intermediaries of particular insurers or a single meeting with several insurers' intermediaries.

When several intermediaries are responding to the presentations by developing coverage proposals (discussed subsequently), some potential difficulties must be addressed in advance of the presentations. For example, if two intermediaries represent the same insurers, the risk management professional should reach agreements with those intermediaries about which insurers each will approach for a coverage proposal. Such an agreement can eliminate confusion on the part of the insurer. The risk management professional should also ensure that the proposal addresses any changing needs during this period, which, as indicated, can span several months. Changing needs can otherwise render the coverage proposal obsolete and result in unnecessary or inappropriate coverage. For example, as events occur within the organization that would affect an underwriter's decision to cover the exposure, such as the acquisition of a new subsidiary, the risk management professional should update the proposal to reflect the changing conditions accordingly.

Development and Presentation of Coverage Proposals by Insurers and Intermediaries

In the third step in purchasing risk financing services, insurers and intermediaries develop and present coverage proposals to the organization. Depending on the urgency and complexity of the organization's coverage needs, the insurers and the intermediaries may need one or two months to develop coverage proposals. Typically, proposals are presented three or four months before expiration of the organization's existing coverage. During that interval, some insurers may withdraw from consideration, particularly if they cannot be competitive.

Alternatively, some insurers or intermediaries may raise questions or make suggestions about the effectiveness of the original coverage specifications. In such cases, the risk management professional may ask an insurer or intermediary (1) to develop a proposal based on the original specifications, so that the proposal can be compared with those developed by other insurers and (2) show how its recommendations alter the original proposal. This information allows the risk management professional to make valid proposal comparisons and assess the merits of the alterations to the original proposal.

Evaluation of Coverage Proposals by the Organization

In the fourth step in purchasing risk financing services, the organization evaluates the coverage proposals. The risk management professional should receive proposals about two months before the organization wants its coverage to take effect. After receiving each insurer's offer and confirming that each offer is complete and conforms adequately to the specifications, the risk management professional may either personally decide which proposal(s) to accept or confer with senior management before deciding. Final decisions should be based on the goals of the organization's risk management program and should be consistent with its other financial and operating goals. Also, an organization's operating and senior management should understand and support the insurance-buying decision as fully as they support other resource-allocation decisions.

Entrance Into an Insurance Contract Between the Organization and the Insurer

In the fifth step of the risk financing service purchase process, the organization enters into a contract with the insurer. Once the organization's risk management professional or senior management has decided which coverages to purchase, the risk management professional must notify all the insurers or intermediaries who were involved. Usually, the risk management professional first contacts the insurers or intermediaries who have been chosen in order to confirm that their proposals (offers) remain open and to communicate acceptance of the proposals. The proposal's wording, the insured organization's operating procedures, and customary business practices between an insurer and its insured determine who has authority to accept each insurer's proposal and the written or oral process for communicating that acceptance.

After mutual assent creates a binding insurance contract, the organization's risk management professional should then contact the insurers or intermediaries whose proposals were not accepted as a matter of professional courtesy and to provide them with feedback.

Implementation of the New Insurance Coverage

After the proposal responses have been evaluated, the risk management professional has made a recommendation that is accepted by top management, and the insurance contract is finalized, an orderly transition must be made to the new insurer before the expiration of the current coverage. For example, new certificates of insurance must be given to vendors and lenders, identification cards for any insured vehicles have to be prepared, and a new accident investigation kit has to be provided for any insured vehicle. Managers and supervisors of each business unit must be given the name of the new insurer and policy numbers so that appropriate first reports of accidents and of claims can be made promptly to the insurer's nearest claim representative. Orientation meetings should be arranged with the new insurer's regional claim manager and with the adjusters assigned to the insured's account.

RISK FINANCING PLAN MARKETING CONSIDERATIONS

A risk management professional should evaluate the following marketing considerations when placing or renewing insurance as part of a risk financing plan:

- Nature of insurance marketing
- Market timing considerations
- Insurance specifications
- Competitive bidding

Nature of Insurance Marketing

Marketing is generally a seller-initiated activity. Sellers initiate the marketing of goods and services that buyers accept. However, in insurance, the party who initiates the marketing activity is not always the same. The typical commodity in the insurance market is the loss exposure that organizations attempt to "sell" to underwriters. The basic risk management goal is to convince underwriters to "buy" or accept those loss exposures in exchange for the lowest "placement fee" (insurance premium).

Frequently, organizations seeking protection initiate commercial insurance transactions, not the insurers that are competing to provide it. Insurance agents, brokers, and other marketing channels typically act as intermediaries for organizations seeking to sell their loss exposures to insurers.

Sometimes, especially when cash flow underwriting prevails in certain phases of the underwriting cycle, the incentive for insurance marketing is reversed, and insurers initiate policy sales to gain more investable funds. In those circumstances, a risk management professional's efforts to make an account attractive to underwriters are focused on the goal of qualifying for lower premium rates or broader coverage, not on simply obtaining basic coverage from the insurer.

Regardless, most of a risk management professional's activities in marketing an organization's insurance account (the group of insurance policies protecting the organization at any one time) focus on making the organization's insurance needs attractive to underwriters. In doing so, the risk management professional combines efforts with agents, brokers, or other insurance marketing intermediaries, who should all direct their marketing work toward communicating the nature of the organization's exposures in the most favorable yet accurate light. In this marketing effort, a risk management professional should perform the following activities:

- Play an active role in seeking needed coverage. In most cases, the risk management professional is the primary "salesperson" for the account and is ideally situated to initiate the marketing process.

- Establish criteria for selecting insurers, insurance marketing intermediaries, intermediaries' account executives, and providers of other risk management services.

- Assess the organization's loss exposures and identify which insurance contracts can best cover those exposures if insurance is desired—or assist insurance marketing intermediaries and others in doing so.

- Assist with making oral or written presentations to selected underwriters about the organization's loss exposures and insurance requirements, when requested.

- Negotiate the final terms and the premium rates of each insurance contract the organization purchases.

During hard markets, an organization and its risk management professional might feel fortunate to have obtained any adequate insurance at an affordable premium. Yet, even in such insurer-dominated markets, the marketing of an organization's insurance account is critical. When underwriters believe they can provide only limited coverage, they are most likely to first insure accounts that promise the greatest underwriting profit (or the least underwriting loss).

Market Timing Considerations

Unless substantial changes have occurred from one policy period to the next (such as in an organization's loss exposures or in insurers' products or premium rates), a risk management professional does not normally market an organization's account at every renewal of an annual policy. When active marketing is planned, it should be scheduled far in advance of the expiration of the existing insurance. The following section discusses marketing frequency and scheduling considerations.

Frequency

Marketing an organization's insurance account can cost tens or hundreds of thousands of dollars. The largest costs are salary expenses for the risk management professional and support personnel, as well as fees paid to outside consultants. Because of these costs, marketing efforts should be performed only when a benefit greater than the costs can be expected. Moreover, continuous marketing of an insurance account can give an organization a reputation as a "shopper," which can be a disadvantage in a hard market and inhibit future marketing efforts.

Even when not actively marketing an insurance contact, a risk management professional should maintain contact with insurance marketing representatives. Given no specific reason to change insurers, most risk management professionals choose to market their accounts no more than every three to six years. They can, however, conduct brief monthly or quarterly marketing reviews without preparing full-scale specifications or contacting numerous insurance marketing representatives. Through such reviews, a risk management professional can learn about significant changes in the following:

- Available coverages
- Pricing of those coverages
- Characteristics of available risk-financing alternatives

Scheduling

Although small accounts can be marketed in one month, the routine marketing of a large account (or an account of a small organization that faces risk financing challenges) normally requires six months, roughly scheduled as follows:

- Six weeks to prepare insurance specifications
- Six to twelve weeks to negotiate with intermediaries and underwriters
- Two to four weeks to complete any transition to new insurers

Account Sizes

Because the size of an account is an indication of how soon a risk management professional should start marketing an organization's account, the risk management professional should know what constitutes a small, medium, and large account. Small accounts typically have premiums of up to $50,000; medium accounts typically have premiums of between $51,000 and $100,000; and large accounts typically have premiums of more than $100,000. Of course, these are not rigid premium ranges because different organizations define small, medium, and large accounts differently. Also, the amount of time required to renew an account depends on the types of coverages that need to be renewed. For example, in some cases, renewing workers' compensation coverage requires relatively less work and, therefore, less time than other commercial coverages, such as commercial general liability coverage and commercial property coverage. Additionally, some intermediaries may classify account sizes by a combination of commission and fee income as opposed to premiums.

This schedule can sometimes be shortened. However, insurance intermediaries typically function more effectively and maintain a more favorable impression of an organization when allowed four to six months for marketing. Additional time should be allowed for renewals occurring near the end of a calendar year (or other fiscal year) because of the high volume of renewals at those times. Still more time should be allowed when markets are hard and insurance is particularly scarce or costly.

When an organization wants quotations from more than one insurance marketing intermediary, the risk management professional should begin informal discussions several months before the earliest insurance policy expiration date. Dealing with several potential intermediaries is time consuming. The intermediaries must be familiar with the organization's insurance needs and be given guidance about which insurers they may approach without unduly interfering with the other intermediaries' efforts. Giving such guidance is often called "assigning markets." Also, the organization seeking insurance needs time to evaluate all of the proposals.

Insurance Specifications

Preparing written insurance specifications is the joint effort of an organization's risk management professional and its insurance marketing intermediary, usually with the risk management professional taking the lead. Although that work is costly and time consuming, it generates specifications that can be updated, corrected, and used for future renewals. The specifications include the underwriting information needed to comprehensively evaluate the risks the organization wishes to insure. To develop sound, enduring specifications, the professionals preparing them should carefully consider their format and content.

Format

Properly prepared specifications allow an underwriter to read as little or as much about a potential account as necessary. Essential underwriting information should be presented succinctly in an introductory overview, often called an executive summary. Detailed information should be presented throughout the specifications in exhibits or in appendices. As a whole, the specifications should be brief but complete.

It is usually preferable to arrange the specifications so that supporting information moves from the general to the specific. For example, the specifications could begin with aggregate losses incurred by line of insurance, followed by tabulations of individual losses, more detailed analyses of particularly large losses, and risk control measures to prevent their recurrence. An efficient format is often enhanced by developing separate sections describing the organization's structure, operation, and risk financing philosophy. Financial statements should also be included as a separate section. Those sections should be written without reference to specific lines of insurance, so they can be used in different combinations as parts of specifications for various lines of insurance. Consequently, only relevant information is included in the specifications for each particular line of insurance. Also, the likelihood of inconsistencies in the background information accompanying each set of specifications is reduced.

To prevent errors in specifications and thus to minimize coverage gaps, overlaps, or other mistakes, specifications should be edited by persons who are competent in risk management and who did not participate in the original drafting. If an oral presentation accompanies the written specifications, rehearsing at least the outline of the oral presentation with the editors' specifications is recommended to ensure that the ideas and facts presented aloud are consistent with the written specifications.

Proper packaging is also important. For example, an attractive presentation of the insurance account can often be made in a binder marked with the organization's name and corporate logo. The name and logo should appear not only on the cover but also on the spine, so that an underwriter can find the binder in a pile of other submissions. Also, all pages should be numbered for easy reference and updating. The following items should precede the table of contents:

- A short note about the contents
- The name of the organization that developed the presentation and the name of the insurer that is receiving it
- The name, mailing address, e-mail address, and telephone numbers of the risk management professional (or other representatives) marketing the account

Each set of specifications should also be accompanied by a cover letter that does the following:

- Identifies a desired schedule for receiving proposals for, negotiating the terms of, and implementing any new insurance program

- Specifies any unusual circumstances underlying requests for high limits of coverage and for reinsurance

- Describes the existing insurance program and specifies the present premium if (1) the underwriter or the insurance marketing intermediary requested this information and (2) the risk management professional is comfortable with providing current premium information to all underwriters from whom quotations are sought

- Lists additional sources of technical information for the underwriter, such as quality control manuals, product warranties and users' manuals, manufacturers' procedural manuals for the materials or equipment used by the insured organization, and in-house safety records

- Offers the underwriter an opportunity to visit the organization's facilities and talk with its risk management professional and other appropriate personnel

Content

Exhibit 12-2 depicts the order in which insurance specifications should be presented in the proposal. Although fairly standard, this order can be modified to address organizational or insurer preference.

The Insuring Forms Desired section is structured by type of exposure. Clearly stating the organization's contract expectations helps to prevent misunderstandings and minimizes the need for further negotiations after an apparent agreement has been reached. The risk management professional should provide as much detail as possible in this section, specifying policy form numbers (if readily available) or attaching samples of policies (especially manuscript policies).

Competitive Bidding

Many organizations obtain their insurance through competitive bidding. Some organizations, such as public entities, are required by statute or by business contracts to purchase insurance through competitive bidding. Others are required to follow a specific bidding process to obtain insurance. Bids can be sought either to select a new insurance marketing intermediary or to control the cost and quality of insurance.

EXHIBIT 12-2

Outline for Underwriting Specifications

Description of Operations

- Overview of operations by subsidiaries, divisions, and branches
- Financial statements
- SEC Form 10K and most recent Form 10Q
- Annual report

Description of Risk Management Department

- Organization and structure
- Functions provided—cost allocation, claim handling, and risk control
- Services contracted with external vendors

Property Loss Exposure Analysis

- Basis of values: replacement, market, or actual cash value, plus date of valuation
- Total values by location and by type of coverage
- Source of valuations—who made them and when
- Maximum probable loss and the amount subject (maximum possible loss) by location
- Individual fire protection reports, pictures, and diagrams for large locations
- Values for property in transit and unscheduled locations
- Business interruption worksheets
- Other time element value estimates

Liability Loss Exposure Assessment

- Quantified underwriting data: revenues, payrolls, advertising expenditures, and so on
- Products that develop loss exposures

Loss Analysis

- Description of claim handling: insurer, contract adjuster, or in-house
- Total incurred losses by type of coverage
- Description and analysis of all large (for example, more than $10,000) losses, even if not yet paid
- Loss stratification by type of coverage and in total. Exhibit should show losses at varying levels depending on size of risk; for example, losses from $0 to $10,000; $10,001 to $50,000; $50,001 to $100,000; and more than $100,000.
- Loss forecasting and retention analysis. Trend future losses or use regression analysis to project probable future loss levels.

Insuring Forms Desired—and Completion of Corresponding ACORD (or Similar) Application

- Property loss exposures
- Net income loss exposures
- Liability loss exposures

Incidental or Umbrella Loss Exposures

- Care, custody, and control loss exposures
- Professional liability loss exposures
- Potential liability loss exposures under specified federal statutes
- Watercraft and aircraft loss exposures
- Other perceived loss exposures

Open bidding
A process in which advertisements are placed in insurance-related media or publications requesting bids from all intermediaries who meet certain qualifications.

Closed or **selective bidding**
A process in which only specific intermediaries who meet certain qualifications are invited to submit bids.

The two broad categories of bidding are open and closed. **Open bidding** is a process in which advertisements are placed in insurance-related media or publications requesting bids from all intermediaries who meet certain qualifications. These qualifications often specify that the intermediary have a particular experience level, a certain staff size, minimum premium volume requirements, and service facilities in appropriate cities. Open bidding can become unwieldy unless the eligibility qualifications are rigorous. Although open bidding is not the norm among profit-seeking organizations, public organizations whose insurance placement procedures and costs are subject to public scrutiny use it frequently in order to maintain transparent processes. Exhibit 12-3 illustrates an open bidding request for insurance proposals. In contrast, **closed**, or **selective bidding** is a process in which only specific intermediaries who meet certain qualifications are invited to submit bids.

EXHIBIT 12-3

Typical Open Bidding Notice

ABC Corporation
Request for Proposal
Insurance Agent/Broker/Consultants
for
Property-Casualty Insurance
Proposals Due: October 1, 20XX
5:00 P.M.
150 Main Street
Anytown, NY 10000
(555) 555-5555

Notice is hereby given that ABC Corporation is accepting proposals for an insurance agent, broker, or consultant who will provide risk management and insurance brokerage services for ABC Corporation.

Interested parties should complete the attached Request for Proposal and return it to ABC Corporation at the above captioned address. Sealed proposals must be received by October 1, 20XX.

During the evaluation process, ABC Corporation reserves the right to request additional information from bidders who submit proposals, including oral presentations, or to allow corrections of errors or omissions.

Insurance contracts may be awarded to more than one bidder. Accepted proposals will be announced no later than October 21, 20XX.

Contact: Lena T. Ruiz
Comptroller
(555) 555-555
lruiz@abccorp.zzz

An organization seeking to buy commercial insurance typically approaches the insurance market through various intermediaries who may be associated with a large international organization, a smaller regional firm, or an independent local agency or brokerage having offices in only one city (typically agents or brokers).

Some commercial insurers market coverage through several types of intermediaries; some use only one or a few. Therefore, the choice of an insurer and an intermediary are often closely linked. An organization that wants to deal with a particular insurer often has a limited choice of intermediaries. Moreover, regardless of the intermediary chosen, the qualifications and character of the intermediary are of paramount importance. Therefore, a risk management professional must understand the different types of intermediaries and determine if the intermediary has the required characteristics.

RISK FINANCING PLAN INTERMEDIARIES

Different types of intermediaries differ by who they represent, their size, and in the services they provide. A risk management professional should understand each of these types. However, there are certain characteristics a risk management professional should be certain exist in every intermediary selected, regardless of type, as a prerequisite to the intermediary's hiring and as a condition of continued association. The intermediary's compensation must also be determined.

Types of Intermediaries

The four primary types of intermediaries are as follows:

1. Broker
2. Independent agent
3. Direct writing insurer
4. Risk management consultant

Broker

A **broker** is a marketing intermediary who is an authorized representative of the *insured*. When risk management professionals consider buying insurance, many approach large brokerage firms that have offices worldwide. However, brokerage size alone does not guarantee that an intermediary can satisfy all of an organization's coverage needs, render exemplary service, and select insurers offering competitive premiums. Also, different offices of the same firm can vary significantly in their capabilities.

Broker
A marketing intermediary who is an authorized representative of the *insured*.

Brokerage firms often have specialized departments, such as marine, aviation, or energy-related operations, as well as safety, actuarial, and general risk management services. The influence that international brokerages have in the insurance marketplace is important. Because of the premium volume these brokers can direct to various insurers, they can often negotiate highly favorable coverage terms, conditions, and premiums for their clients.

Regional brokerage firms are smaller and less expansive than international brokerages. They differ in the number of offices they maintain to serve clients. As the term "regional" implies, such firms concentrate their operations in a particular area, such as within a state or several contiguous states.

Agent

An **agent** is a marketing intermediary who is an authorized representative of the *insurer*. A few states, including Pennsylvania, have modernized the licensing of insurance agents and brokers by creating one insurance producer license that covers both functions.[1] Therefore, the distinction between these two intermediaries is becoming blurred. Agents generally concentrate their activities in a particular city and stress their ability to provide personalized service. Because of long-standing, face-to-face relationships with their clients and knowledge of their operations, agents remain a major marketing channel. An agent can often provide a level of service for clients that is difficult for larger competitors to match.

Direct Writing Insurer

A **direct writing insurer** is an insurer that markets its coverages directly through its own employees rather than through intermediaries. Direct writing insurers account for a sizable percentage of property and liability insurance written for business organizations. The coverage available through direct writing representatives depends primarily on the insurer's specialized technical capabilities or the underwriting capacity for each line of insurance. Sometimes, direct writing insurers can pass some operating expense savings on to insureds through lower premiums.

Risk Management Consultant

Many organizations rely on risk management consultants to help with insurers' representatives or other risk financing and risk control concerns.

A **risk management consultant** is an individual who does not sell insurance directly but who provides advice for a fee about a variety of risk management matters. These matters can include drafting insurance specifications, evaluating insurance proposals, and reviewing insurance coverages relative to what is available in the insurance marketplace. The benefits of a risk management consultant's service are the consultant's expertise and objectivity.

Some consultants specialize in performing certain activities, such as loss exposure analysis or claim administration, while others specialize in particular industries, such as building construction or hospitals. Risk management consultants frequently are hired to perform the following activities:

- Study an organization's loss exposures and recommend an appropriate risk management program
- Draft specifications for bidding an insurance program and analyze proposals
- Review the insurance coverages included in the organization's risk management program and compare them to those generally available in the current insurance market
- Audit an organization's risk management activities (similar to an accountant's audit of financial records)
- Conduct a feasibility study of proposals for establishing a captive insurance affiliate or a pool

- Draft a risk management procedures manual
- Design or conduct employee safety training programs
- Confirm the recommendations of an organization's own risk management professional

If one or more of these risk management activities is deemed better performed by a consultant due to the additional expertise or objectivity the consultant can apply to the activity, then the purpose and the scope of the consultation must be determined. A request for proposal (RFP) for consulting services is often drafted. The RFP should, of course, describe the purpose and scope of the activities and provide enough information about the organization to enable a consultant to determine whether it wants the organization as a client. That information should include the following:

- The organization's annual report or another description of its activities
- A 10K financial disclosure form or comparable document filed with federal and state securities regulators
- A listing of the organization's loss exposures, actual losses, and insurance policies and premiums
- A brief summary of the organization's past risk management activities

The final step is to interview and hire the best available consultant.

A consultant is not compensated in the same manner as brokers, agents, or direct writing insurers. A consultant often charges an hourly or a daily fee, a monthly or an annual retainer, or a per-assignment fee. Regardless of the compensation system, both the client and the consultant must believe that the consultant's service is worth the fee. Judging a risk management consultant's competency is often more difficult and subjective than evaluating the qualifications of a broker, of an agent or of direct writing insurers. Some states require the licensing of risk management consultants, while other states require only that a risk management consultant register with the state insurance department. A few states do not regulate risk management consulting. Education and experience indicate ability, as do references from agents, brokers, insurers, and the consultant's previous clients.

Required Characteristics of Intermediaries

The following are required characteristics of the broker, agent, direct writing insurer, or risk management consultant from whom an insurance product or service is purchased:

- Technical expertise
- Financial resources
- Creativity
- Agreement on claim settlement approach
- Integrity

Technical Expertise

It is reasonable to ask prospective brokers, agents, or other intermediaries to provide biographical sketches of the key personnel who will be involved with an account. Key personnel should hold professional insurance designations such as the Chartered Property Casualty Underwriter (CPCU), Chartered Life Underwriter (CLU), Associate in Risk Management (ARM), Accredited Adviser in Insurance (AAI), Certified Safety Professional (CSP), Certified Employee Benefits Specialist (CEBS), Professional Engineer (PE), Certified Industrial Hygienist (CIH), or other relevant designations. Individuals also should have practical experience that applies to the organization's needs and should be able to handle the loss exposures that are characteristic of the client's industry. Their expertise should be readily available. The existence of a peer review system or an account feedback process and the intermediary's relationship with its errors and omissions insurer are additional signs of the intermediary's quality.

An account representative should be able to design an affordable risk management program and to assist the organization in claim management and risk control activities. That individual must also stay abreast of market availability, especially when considering specialized coverages. Someone in the intermediary's organization should also be well versed in all coverages the client organization requires.

Financial Resources

Apart from the financial strength of the particular insurers it represents, an intermediary's own financial strength is also a required characteristic. The intermediary should have the financial strength to continue to function effectively and be able to expand the scope of its business to meet evolving client needs, if necessary.

Creativity

Intermediaries must also be creative. Purchasing guaranteed-cost insurance (traditionally coupled with a full range of insurer-provided services) is no longer routine. Risk management professionals recognize that they will eventually pay for their own losses through insurance or retention. Therefore, they seek creativity from intermediaries in designing loss-sensitive plans or using other cash flow techniques that minimize the outflow of corporate funds.

Agreement on Claim Settlement Approach

Those involved in the insurance transaction should agree on how insured claims should be handled. The risk management professional should review past data concerning the organization's loss frequency and severity with each prospective intermediary. The intermediary should then ask the claim department and the insurers' attorneys how they would deal with such claims.

Any organization, whether self-insured or insured through traditional insurance, can adopt several different approaches to third-party claims (when someone seeks payment for damages suffered). Third-party claims that can be settled for less than the cost to defend them can simply be settled, regardless of fault. The major disadvantage of this approach is that the public and the plaintiff's counsel may then exploit the organization, based on the perception that the organization will settle claims in lieu of contesting them. Consequently, the organization may pay significant claims for which it is not legally liable, which raises the cost of retained losses or the organization's liability premiums.

An organization may adopt the opposite approach and decide to pay only claims for which it was clearly at fault and aggressively defend the rest. Typically, the organization's insurer does not pay until the organization's liability is clearly established. This approach can generate numerous lawsuits, many of which third parties may be unwilling to pursue because of the expense and time required to obtain a verdict.

The risk management professional must also recognize that an occasional adverse verdict can become more expensive than paying every claim. Most organizations combine the two approaches and accept the challenge of finding a balance between selecting which claims to defend (to discourage unfounded claims) and which to settle (to avoid severely adverse court verdicts). If the insured organization is liable to the plaintiff, every attempt should be made to settle the claim outside the court system. An insurer or insured should agree on the approach the insurer will take in adjusting the insured's third-party claims so that the expenses incurred in settling a loss or paying a court judgment are more likely to appear reasonable to both the organization's management and the insurer.

Integrity

Complete confidence in the integrity of all parties is essential to any financial transaction. Insurance transactions are executed in utmost good faith. Integrity in this context means that the parties should be confident that all relevant compensation information, such as contingent commissions and all other forms of remuneration, are transparent to the client and that confidential information is appropriately safeguarded. Any doubts about an intermediary's willingness to place the best interests of the client above its own should weigh heavily in the selection process.

Compensation of Intermediaries

Intermediaries, whether they are agencies or brokerages, typically receive commissions from the insurers with whom they place coverage. The commissions are calculated as a percentage of the premiums collected by the insurers. Commission percentages often vary by insurer and by line of insurance. The percentage commission system has long been considered as an equitable means of accomplishing the following:

- Adequately compensating intermediaries for their services
- Motivating intermediaries to place greater marketing emphasis on the accounts and lines of insurance that insurers want to underwrite (and for which they are willing to pay higher commission rates)
- Permitting intermediaries to share in the insurers' growth, which is reflected in higher premium writings and greater commission income for the intermediaries

However, increasing emphasis on offering a total range of risk management services, only one of which is placing insurance, has broadened many insurance intermediaries' activities to include designing risk retention programs, providing safety and actuarial services, and administering claims. Such activities are valuable to the intermediaries' business clients but are not directly related to the volume of premiums generated. Therefore, an increasing number of intermediaries and many risk management professionals consider flat fees a more appropriate compensation method than commissions. Such fees are paid directly by clients, reflect the value of the intermediaries' services, and are negotiated by the client and the intermediary.

Moreover, eliminating intermediaries' commissions from premiums paid by insureds and compensating intermediaries with more clearly identifiable fees allow many organizations to account more accurately for the true cost of insurance. Such a system fairly and clearly compensates intermediaries for the time spent and expenses incurred on behalf of the insured. Because their compensation is not a function of a premium, intermediaries can be more objective in recommending noninsurance risk management techniques to best serve the client.

Some intermediaries receive compensation through a combination of commissions and fees. Commissions paid in combination with fees are usually earned at a lower percentage than if the intermediary's total compensation were paid through commissions. Fees can be charged on an hourly or a monthly basis. Additionally, annual retainers or specific fees for particular activities can be charged. Such an activity might be assessing the client's loss exposures or establishing a captive insurance subsidiary. To negotiate the appropriate type of compensation for intermediaries in different situations, a risk management professional should understand the reasoning supporting both the insurer's paying commissions and the insured's paying fees.

The following arguments are among those that support commissions:

- Intermediaries perform many services that are not directly related to any one insured's account. Therefore, no particular insured should be charged for those services. An intermediary can provide those services because the commission system distributes the cost of services among the intermediary's clients. Without commissions, intermediaries could not afford to perform those services.

- An intermediary's effort in securing and servicing a large account is greater than for a small account, especially because of the added risk assessment, rating, and claim administration activities required for a large account. Percentage commissions tend to provide an intermediary with compensation commensurate with its efforts and the value of the services it provides, both to insurers and to insureds.

The following reasons are among those that support negotiated fees:

- The fee-for-service system minimizes the conflicts of interest that insurance marketing intermediaries might experience when a sound risk management recommendation reduces their commission income. For example, recommending that a client adopt higher deductibles or risk control measures, which both lower the client's cost of risk and make the client's account more attractive to underwriters, reduces the intermediary's commission income by either lowering premium rates or decreasing the amount of coverage the client purchases. However, if a fee were provided, the intermediary would not have to sacrifice income for the client's welfare.

- Intermediaries' traditional percentage commission from an account is not proportional to their efforts on that account. Particularly for property insurance, the extent of an intermediary's insurance placement activities is not related to the amount of insurance written on an account. With liability insurance, however, the potential for more frequent and extremely large losses often requires more intensive marketing of large policies than of small ones. Placing and servicing a $5 million premium property insurance policy does not normally require five times the effort needed for placing and servicing a $1 million premium policy on the same type of exposure. However, the traditional percentage compensation system pays the intermediary five times more for the former account than for the latter. A fee for such activities compensates the intermediary more equitably.

Because of potential deficiencies in both systems of compensation, some insurers and their intermediaries have explored alternatives that combine elements of both systems. For example, numerous insurers use a **sliding scale commission**, which is a compensation system in which commission rates decrease for policies with large premiums, thus generating lower total compensation for such policies than are generated by fixed-rate commission schedules. Such rates are used most often with workers' compensation insurance. In this line of insurance, an intermediary's work is not entirely proportional to the amount of premium generated.

Another option intermediaries have introduced is the **management fee**, which is a compensation system in which the intermediary waives the normal percentage commission and negotiates a minimum annual fee with each client. The client and the intermediary agree that the annual fee represents the total annual revenue that the intermediary needs to service the account properly and to generate a reasonable profit. This system resulted from intermediaries' awareness of clients' concerns that commissions generate

Sliding scale commission
A compensation system in which commission rates decrease for policies with large premiums, thus generating lower total commissions for such policies than are generated by fixed-rate commission schedules.

Management fee
A compensation system in which the intermediary waives the normal percentage commission and negotiates a minimum annual fee with each client.

conflicts of interest and foster mediocrity. Those concerns arose because an agency or a brokerage can raise its income merely by selling clients excessive amounts or unnecessary insurance without fully considering the clients' risk management needs.

The commissions the intermediary receives from insurers are credited against (deducted from) the negotiated fee, and the client is responsible for paying only the fee remaining at the year's end. If the year-end total commissions exceed the negotiated fee, the client owes no further fee for that year. If commissions fall short of the fee, no refund is owed to the client because the intermediary was entitled to at least that fee. Because of "anti-rebating" statutes in most jurisdictions, the client cannot also receive a refund for any deposits or installments on the negotiated payment made to the intermediary.

Commissions and management fees can often be averaged over a period of several years to account for annual variations in premium payment schedules, changes in commission and premium rates, and the insured's loss experience under loss-sensitive premium rating plans. In some of the states that do not permit an insurance agent or broker to receive both commission and fee income, fee-for-service work can be channeled through a subsidiary corporation.

OPPORTUNITIES FOR UNBUNDLING SERVICES

Traditionally, property-casualty insurers have included in their coverage additional incidental services that are related to the protection a policy provides, such as expert claim administration and risk control services. The cost of these services is included in the insurer's premium. An organization that removes such services (and their related costs) from its insurance coverage can conserve capital by eliminating its need for the services, providing its own services internally, or purchasing them from third parties.

Unbundling
The removal of an insurer's incidental services from insurance coverage.

Unbundling is the removal of an insurer's incidental services from insurance coverage. Unbundled insurance polices have allowed third-party providers of claim, risk control, and other insurance-related services to compete for business that was once the exclusive domain of insurers, though, in some cases, insurers provide the best and most economical services related to their insurance policies. This competition has reduced the cost of incidental insurance-related services and has, in turn, made unbundled insurance policies economically attractive to many insured organizations.

Provided an unbundled policy does not render an insured an unacceptable underwriting risk because of the reduced revenue it provides for the insurer, a policy's services can be unbundled whenever the insured deems it cost effective to do so. When considering unbundling a policy, an organization should evaluate the available alternatives to the following unbundled services:

- Claim administration services
- Risk control services
- Risk management information services

- Financial management services
- Multiple intermediary marketing services
- Actuarial services

Claim Administration Services

Claim administration services are well-suited to unbundling because many organizations' operations generate claims that require special skills to control, evaluate, and settle. A commercial insurer serving many insureds may not have enough claim representatives (adjusters) to meet each insured's needs. Therefore, the organization itself or a firm specializing in contract claim administration might better handle claims.

A third-party (contract) claim administrator must be acceptable to the organization's insurer. Settling claims properly, promptly, and cost effectively requires cooperation among the insurer, the insured, the agent/broker or other insurance marketing intermediary, and any outside contract claim administrator.

The cost of a contract claim administrator's services can be negotiated. Some administrators prefer their compensation to be a percentage of the settlement value of the claims they handle. However, many risk management professionals question this approach because it appears to encourage paying claims that might not be in the insured's best interest and paying them at a higher amount. However, alternative compensation methods are available.

First, based on an insured organization's loss experience, a contract claim administrator may charge an annual retainer that reflects the expected volume of work regardless of the value of the claims handled during the contract period. Several large international claim management firms use annual retainers for organizations with domestic and international claim activity. Such firms also use annual retainers to handle distant claim activity for an organization whose activity is typically local. The annual retainer is subject to annual change (or change from one contract period to the next), based on the volume of work, the types of claims, and the number and types of claims likely to be litigated.

Second, a contract claim administrator may also charge for services on a per claim basis. This method is used when the client organization generates claims related to local business activities, perhaps with an occasional more-distant claim. Like an annual retainer, charges on a per claim basis vary by type of claim and by the number and types of claims likely to be litigated. Because of the difficulty in anticipating the outcome of complex liability claims, however, claim administrators are reluctant to provide pricing for the life of the claim.

Risk Control Services

Although many property-casualty insurers provide risk control services to a variety of insureds, the growth of technical knowledge about and specialties within this area has allowed many organizations to establish themselves as risk control specialists. In addition, many large industrial organizations have developed an in-house staff to provide specially-tailored risk control services. Therefore, risk control has become a cost-effective noninsurance alternative and provides an excellent opportunity to unbundle the insurance package.

Independent risk control specialists can assist with property protection. For example, they can design automatic sprinklers for fire protection, identify and train in-house fire-fighting personnel, coordinate safety training programs, and prepare safety manuals. Comparable expertise is available in other areas of property protection, such as vehicle and cargo safety, crime prevention, and crisis management planning.

Risk control specialists can also help a risk management professional obtain management support. For example, an external safety specialist can assist with training supervisors and managers in risk control. Because an on-staff safety specialist's resources are limited, all managers and supervisors must also be committed to safety and be familiar with practical risk control procedures. An external safety specialist can often convey and help implement these procedures more quickly than can an on-staff person alone, regardless of the staff person's competence.

Risk Management Information Services (RMIS)

Although many insurers make computerized claim reports available to their large insureds, those reports are often not tailored to an organization's risk management needs and slow to arrive, lessening their usefulness. Independent information systems can be tailored to the needs of most organizations' risk management professionals. Many large organizations have developed comprehensive, state-of-the-art systems through which risk financing and risk control data can be tied directly into the data repository of an independent risk management information service. These data can be processed promptly to generate useful decision-making information.

Some insurers and independent risk management information service firms have formed joint ventures to enable insurers to extend their service repertoire and, therefore, to increase their ability to attract and retain insureds. For instance, an insurer can have the option of either (1) providing a particular service (here, RMIS applications) for a fee to insureds who want that service or (2) providing that service at no extra charge (with the cost of the service built into the insurer's premium rate structure). Undertaking broad joint ventures with well-established and widely recognized independent service firms might also enable some insurers to recapture revenues they lost by unbundling traditional insurance packages.

Financial Management Services

Managing a risk financing program requires answering several questions, including the following:

- How many and which loss exposures should be retained?

- What are the appropriate policy limits and deductibles for primary and excess insurance?
- In what financial instruments can any funded loss reserves be invested?
- How can an organization's captive insurance subsidiary be managed?

Answering these questions requires insight and skills not always found within an organization. (In fact, the management of some organizations might not recognize that these questions must be answered.) Furthermore, some organizations are reluctant to rely solely on their insurers or on the insurers' intermediaries to keep them abreast of the latest developments in risk financing alternatives to insurance. Several types of independent firms can assist in answering these questions.

Numerous agencies and brokerage firms offer risk financing management services separately from their insurance marketing activities. They might charge an hourly fee, an annual retainer, or a negotiated fee for each service. Risk management consulting firms also offer a broad spectrum of such services. They assert that their complete independence from the insurance product heightens their objectivity. Several service firms, including most large brokerages, also specialize in helping organizations establish and operate their own captives or insurance pools. In short, an organization that wants a sophisticated risk financing program does not have to develop it in-house or through its insurer. Rather, the organization can contract for risk financing on particular services or for a complete menu of risk financing services.

A risk management professional should work with the organization's senior management to determine when and from whom to obtain risk financing services. Any external source used for these services should do the following:

- Thoroughly understand the organization's operations and goals
- Share the organization's risk financing philosophy
- Demonstrate an established record of reliability and fiduciary responsibility
- Maintain excellent communication with the key risk management professional and other executives of the organization

Multiple Intermediary Marketing Services

Different intermediaries have significantly different levels of expertise and access to insurers. Therefore, in unbundling an organization's insurance package, the risk management professional may decide to place different coverages through different agents or brokers. Often, large organizations have one agent or broker to handle property coverages, another for liability coverages, a third for workers' compensation coverage, and a fourth for the employee benefits program. While agents or brokers may be able to place all coverages, the risk management professional purchases highly specialized insurance placement services from different intermediaries by dividing the organization's insurance program among them.

This method of unbundling is not without its difficulties, particularly in coordinating coverages (minimizing gaps and overlaps), minimizing disputes about which insurer covers which loss, and planning how the insurers will work together. Recognizing and resolving these difficulties require that the risk management professional take a leadership role in dealing with intermediaries and insurers. Also, those insurers' representatives must communicate and cooperate with the risk management professional and with one another.

Actuarial Services

Organizations that have substantial retention programs need access to expertise similar to the access their insurers would need if the loss exposures were commercially insured. Retained and insured losses must be "adjusted" through appropriate claim administration activities. Thus, both retained and insured loss exposures require that loss costs be estimates of the present costs of future losses. Those loss costs may be the basis for insurance premiums or for internal budgetary charges for the organization's own risk management cost-allocation system. Determining those estimates requires persons with considerable actuarial skills. Therefore, several independent service organizations provide data-gathering, analytical, and decision-support services to the risk management departments of many organizations, including large agencies and brokerages, actuarial consulting firms, and the mathematics or business departments of universities.

Unbundling the actuarial element from the insurance package is much like separating the aforementioned financial management services needed for risk financing. Thus, any actuarial firm or individual expert should have qualities comparable to those sought from a financial management service. Moreover, an organization should discuss with each candidate the feasibility of doing actuarial work and whether the candidate can find sufficient data from the organizations' records or elsewhere from which to draw useful conclusions about loss experience.

In summary, unbundling the insurance package presents an organization with cost and service benefits. However, unbundling services must not cause the organization's risk management program to become fragmented and thus jeopardize the profitability, if not the survival, of both the client organization and the firms that have committed their resources to serving the client.

EVALUATION OF COVERAGE PROPOSALS

After the selected intermediaries have presented their coverage proposals and services have been unbundled as appropriate, the risk management professional must next evaluate the coverage proposals. Evaluation is often performed using the following three criteria:

1. Services offered
2. Financial stability
3. Costs

Services Offered

The risk management professional should ensure that each proposal received includes the same requested incidental services. However, just because the same services are included in each of the proposals does not mean those services will be of equal quality. For example, certain insurers are particularly adept at delivering claim administration and risk control services. Other insurers may have developed a particularly advanced interface with the insured's RMIS that allows the risk management professional to more quickly identify loss trends that could become problematic if not addressed in a timely manner. Insureds that purchase bailee's coverage to protect their customer's property while it is in their care typically depend on their insurer's fast and fair claim service to retain the goodwill of their customers.

When coverage is being renewed, the insured is likely already familiar with the insurer's level and quality of service. However, if the proposal is from an insurer with which the risk management professional is unfamiliar, then additional investigation is warranted. Despite the possible conflict of interest, the intermediary who is suggesting the organization use an unfamiliar insurer should be asked for contact information for the insurer's other insureds that are local to the area, that are in the same or closely-related industry, and that have similar coverages and services as listed in the proposal response being evaluated. Contacting the insurer's previous and current insureds is often an effective way to accurately assess the insurer's quality of service. The quality and effectiveness of incidental services are among the important criteria to consider when evaluating an insurer's response to the coverage proposal.

Financial Stability

Proposals should also be evaluated by reviewing the five most recent annual ratings of each prospective insurer as reported by the rating services of A.M. Best Company; Standard & Poor's Corporation; Demotech; Weiss Ratings; Moody's Investors Services; or other widely respected, reliable sources of insurer financial data. It is particularly important to look carefully at the financial ratings when a single insurer provides a large percentage of the insured's total coverages or if the insurer provides nonstandard policies, which are not guaranteed by the state's guarantee fund if the insurer were to become insolvent. The rating services each provide similar financial ratios to measure the financial condition of an insurer based on profitability, liquidity (the ability to convert assets to cash at or near market price in order to pay losses in a timely manner) and leverage (the amount of and type of debt owed on its assets). Additional qualitative factors may also be considered, which include the insurers' insurance product and geographic diversification, competitive position in the insurance market, exposure to volatile lines of insurance, identity of any parent insurance company, adequacy of reserves, and stability of financial performance.

Costs

In addition to services offered and insurer financial stability, costs should also be evaluated. The risk management professional can use a spreadsheet to compare the costs of the proposal responses that have met the services offered criterion. Exhibit 12-4 illustrates the evaluation of seven different proposal responses on retrospective rating insurance plan coverage. The characteristics of retrospective rating plan insurance generate several objective factors, as indicated in Exhibit 12-4, including the following:

- *Basic premium.* The cost for the "pure insurance" portion of the coverage (the minimum retrospective premium) would be the fixed cost for each proposal response, as shown in Column 2, assuming that the insured had no insured losses.

- *Loss conversion factor (LCF).* The loss conversion factor (LCF) is shown for each proposal response in Column 3. Notice that six of the seven presentations quoted claim administration costs on a percentage basis. Proposal C, which has the lowest maximum total cost, quoted claim administration costs as a fixed dollar amount per claim. Pricing claim administration services as a percentage of claims paid can raise questions about the incentive an insurer's claim department has to settle claims for the lowest reasonable amounts.

- *Maximum chargeable losses.* This amount, in Column 4, represents the maximum aggregate amount of insured losses for which the insured would have to pay a retrospective premium. If losses exceeded that maximum in a given coverage period, the insurer would continue to provide indemnity (up to the maximum aggregate amount), but the insured would not have to pay any additional premium for that coverage period. Instead, the retrospective rating formula would raise future premiums to cover past losses.

- *Maximum possible total cost.* This amount, shown in Column 5, represents the maximum the insured would have to pay for insurance in a given coverage period. This amount is calculated as the fixed cost plus the product of the maximum chargeable losses multiplied by the sum of one plus the loss conversion factor.

After carefully reviewing all the proposals in light of the services offered, financial stability, costs, and other decision-making criteria, the risk management professional may conclude that no proposal is clearly superior to all of the others. When the risk management professional discusses these matters with the organization's senior management, the consensus may be to accept Proposal G because all criteria except costs were essentially equal. Although Proposal G is only the second lowest bid in terms of fixed initial cost, it has one of the lower maximum possible total costs and lower claim administration costs (LCF).

EXHIBIT 12-4

Factors of Retrospective Rating Insurance Plan Proposals

Column 1	Column 2	Column 3	Column 4	Column 5
Proposal Response	Basic Premium	Loss Conversion Factor (LCF)	Maximum Chargeable Losses	Maximum Possible Total Cost Col. 2 + [Col. 4 × (1 + Col. 3)]
A	$424,322	16.00%	$1,780,715	$2,489,951
B	325,000	13.50%	1,021,500	1,484,403
C	313,416	$85,000*	1,000,000	1,398,416**
D	414,661	14.28%	2,126,270	2,844,562
E	356,159	11.40%	1,541,872	2,073,804
F	538,619	11.40%	2,230,000	3,022,839
G	318,600	9.00%	1,100,000	1,517,600

*   Fixed dollar amount, not a percentage of losses
** Sum of Columns 2, 3, and 4

LEGAL PRINCIPLES OF INSURANCE CONTRACTS

Once a coverage proposal response has been selected, an insurance contract effects the coverage. A risk management professional should be aware that to be legally binding, insurance contracts are subject to the same laws that govern all contracts, such as requiring a legal purpose, an offer and acceptance, an exchange of valuable consideration, and legally competent parties. However, because insurance contracts include many unique characteristics, an additional body of law governs issues exclusive to insurance. Most insurance policies are subject to the following three legal principles:

1. Disclosure
2. Equity
3. Indemnity

This section describes these three principles as they apply to insurance contracts.

Disclosure

Every insurance contract is a contract of **utmost good faith**, which is an obligation to act in complete honesty and to disclose all relevant facts. The contracting parties are entitled to rely on, possibly to their detriment, the truth of all statements they make to each other in negotiating and establishing an insurance contract. Utmost good faith is fundamental to the **principle of disclosure**, a principle of law indicating that every insurance

Utmost good faith
An obligation to act in complete honesty and to disclose all relevant facts.

Principle of disclosure
A principle of law indicating that every insurance applicant has a duty to disclose to the insurer and its legal agents all material information, which is information that could reasonably affect the insurer's underwriting decisions about whether and on what terms to insure the applicant.

applicant has a duty to disclose to the insurer and its legal agents all material information, which is information that could reasonably affect the insurer's underwriting decisions about whether and on what terms to insure the applicant. Courts of law support this principle in insurance contracts. Therefore, the insurer has a right to expect full disclosure from each applicant.

Misrepresentation

Representation
A statement of fact or opinion made by the insured when applying for insurance, usually in response to a question from the insurer.

A **representation** is a statement of fact or opinion made by the insured when applying for insurance, usually in response to a question from the insurer. The truthfulness of an insured's representations is critical. An insurer may deny coverage for an insurance claim at the time of a loss if it can demonstrate to a court that the insured made a **misrepresentation**, which is a statement of fact that is incorrect and material.

Misrepresentation
A statement of fact that is incorrect and material.

For example, a hardware store's insurance application asks whether the insured has ever had its insurance canceled. The question generally requires a statement of fact. The insured in fact has had its previous insurer cancel its coverage because of a poor loss history; however, a risk manager for the hardware store answers "no" to the question. The untrue statement of fact would probably give the insurer a valid basis for denying a claim because the statement of fact is incorrect and is material to the insurer's underwriting decision.

Concealment

Concealment
The insured's intentional failure to reveal certain facts to the insurer.

Concealment is the insured's intentional failure to reveal certain facts to the insurer. The legal doctrine of concealment applies to virtually all types of insurance. The concealed fact need not have contributed to the loss that the insurer refuses to pay. For example, that an insured concealed the fact that a particular cargo was radioactive would give the insurer grounds for denying coverage of unrelated water damage to the cargo. The insurer could claim that had it known the information the insured concealed, it would have changed its underwriting of the policy, even though the loss was unrelated to the concealed fact.

However, insurers, for all but ocean marine policies, must prove that the applicant intentionally concealed facts that were known to be material and that would not be apparent by inspecting the loss exposure. This additional requirement substantially reduces the insurer's reliance on the doctrine of concealment because the intent to fraudulently deceive an insurer is often difficult to prove.

Breach of Warranty

Warranty
A policy condition that must be satisfied for coverage to apply.

In an insurance context, a **warranty** is a policy condition that must be satisfied for coverage to apply. A representation becomes a warranty if it is a condition of the insurer's promise of coverage. Courts are not likely to interpret a representation as a warranty unless the contract clearly indicates that the representation is a policy condition. Warranties can be either affirmative or promissory. An **affirmative warranty** is a policy condition that is supposed to exist on the date that the warranty is made. A **promissory warranty** is a policy condition that should exist throughout the policy period. For example, an automobile insurance policy contains an affirmative warranty stating that no insurer has canceled an automobile insurance policy covering the insured during the past three years. A burglary policy contains a promissory warranty stating that during the policy period, the burglar alarm system described in the policy will be maintained properly.

To void a contract for breach of warranty, an insurer must prove that the condition has not been met. Unlike with the doctrine of misrepresentation, the insurer need not prove materiality of the condition. Furthermore, courts are more likely to require compliance with a warranty than with a representation.

Affirmative warranty
A policy condition that is supposed to exist on the date that the warranty is made.

Promissory warranty
A policy condition that should exist throughout the policy period.

Statutory Modifications

The previously discussed legal doctrines were historically used by insurers to wrongfully deny claims based on immaterial breaches of contract. Consequently, many state legislatures enacted statutes modifying these doctrines in order to more effectively protect insureds. The statutes fall into the following four classifications:

1. Statutes declaring that all statements the insured makes, in the absence of fraud, are considered representations and not warranties.

2. Statutes permitting the insured to recover unless the breach of warranty or the fact misrepresented either substantially increased the risk or materially affected the hazard.

3. Statutes permitting the insured to recover unless the breach of warranty or the fact misrepresented contributed to the loss.

4. Statutes permitting reduction in the amount paid for an insured loss if the insured makes a nonfraudulent misrepresentation that does not contribute to the loss. The reduction depends on the premium paid relative to the premium that would have been paid had the fact not been misrepresented.

The scope of these four types of statutes can also differ depending on how the individual statute is worded. For example, several state statutes refer only to insurance against designated causes of loss rather than all causes of loss. A statute may distinguish between affirmative and promissory warranties. Therefore, each statute must be studied before being applied to a particular case.

Equity

The **principle of equity** is a legal principle that requires the parties to an insurance contract to deal fairly with one another. It is a broad principle with many applications. For example, in contesting the insurer's right to void a contract because the insured violated a policy condition or concealed information, the insured can cite the equity-related doctrines of waiver and estoppel.

Principle of equity
A legal principle that requires the parties to an insurance contract to deal fairly with one another.

Waiver and Estoppel

Estoppel
A legal principle that prohibits a party from asserting a claim or right that is inconsistent with that party's past statement or conduct on which another party has detrimentally relied.

Waiver and estoppel were once two distinctly different legal doctrines. A waiver (discussed previously) is a legal doctrine that allows the voluntary relinquishment of a known right. An **estoppel** is a legal principle that prohibits a party from asserting a claim or right that is inconsistent with that party's past statement or conduct on which another party has detrimentally relied. A waiver often occurs when an insurer's representative tells an insured that complying with a policy condition or disclosing certain information is unnecessary.

Most courts no longer distinguish between waiver and estoppel. Courts instead use the two doctrines in conjunction with one other. For example, if an insurer waives an insurance policy right, the insurer is estopped from later asserting that right. Used in this text, waiver refers to both doctrines. Whether a waiver exists depends partly on when the waiver allegedly occurred. Generally, courts are more likely to find a waiver of a breached condition (that is, to rule that the insurance remained in force despite the breach) when any of the following occurs:

- The policy language expressing the condition was highly ambiguous.
- The insurer's representative, who allegedly waived the condition, had actual or apparent authority to do so.
- The actions of the insurer's representative were clearly intended to be a waiver or could reasonably have been interpreted to be a waiver.
- The additional hazard created by the breach was slight.

If any of these conditions does not occur, then many courts would find that a waiver does not exist, that the policy condition has been breached, and that no coverage applies.

Contract of Adhesion

Contract of adhesion
A contract to which one party must adhere as written by the other party.

Another aspect of equity is that an insurance contract is a contract of adhesion. A **contract of adhesion** is a contract to which one party must adhere as written by the other party. The insured seldom participates in drafting the insurance contract. (An exception to this involves risk management professionals of large firms, who occasionally do so.) Typically, the insurer offers the insured a contract on a take-it-or-leave-it basis. Courts frequently refer to this characteristic of insurance contracts when they interpret ambiguous provisions (that is, a term or a phrase in a contract that can be reasonably interpreted to have more than one meaning) in the insured's favor.

The courts reason that the party that is in the best position to avoid an ambiguity is the party that drafts the contract. Because the insurer, not the insured, typically drafts an insurance contract, the insurer is in the best position to avoid ambiguity. Therefore, in fairness and equity, if the court finds an ambiguity, it will apply the meaning that is most favorable to the insured.

Unconscionable Advantage and Reasonable Expectations

Two additional doctrines explain many court decisions. Under the previously discussed doctrine of unconscionable advantage, an insurer is not allowed to take undue advantage of an insured's lack of information or vulnerable bargaining position. The doctrine of **reasonable expectations** is a legal doctrine that states that the insurance applicant's reasonable expectations about benefiting from the insurance should be honored even if those expectations would not have been fulfilled if the applicant had fully understood the policy. The reasonable expectations doctrine also applies to decisions in which the insurer delivers a policy that significantly deviates from the coverage for which the insured applied or the insurer reduces coverage in a renewal policy without informing the insured.

A frequently applied corollary to the doctrine of reasonable expectations is that the policy language will be interpreted from the layperson's, not the underwriter's, point of view. This approach places increased importance on the policy's definitions section. If a key term is not defined within the policy, the insurer can anticipate that the court will refer to layperson's dictionaries or other references readily available to the layperson when interpreting the term, regardless of how the term is commonly used in the insurance industry.

Reasonable expectations
A legal doctrine that states that the insurance applicant's reasonable expectations about benefiting from the insurance should be honored even if those expectations would not have been fulfilled if the applicant had fully understood the policy.

Correction of Mistakes

Insurance and some other contracts are subject to specific legal rules for correcting mistakes. An insurance policy may not express the actual agreement between the insured and the insurer. For example, if an oral contract is made with the intent to follow it with a written contract, and a mistake is made in the written contract, then an aggrieved party can ask the court to reform the contract to represent the true agreement. However, under any other circumstances, oral evidence before or at the time of the written agreement cannot alter the agreement as written. Once the agreement is reduced to writing, no oral evidence can contradict its terms. Enforcing the contract as written is consistent with the **parol evidence rule**, which is a rule of evidence that limits the terms of a contract to those expressed in writing. This legal rule of contract interpretation applies if the written contract is complete on its face and contains no obvious errors or omissions and the court finds no strong, independent evidence of fraud or duress committed by the party who seeks to interpret the written provisions for its benefit.

Parol evidence rule
A rule of evidence that limits the terms of a contract to those expressed in writing.

Conditional Contracts

Although equity can force the insurer to perform only after the contract is effective, the insurer can refuse to perform if the insured does not satisfy certain contractual conditions. For example, the insurer need not pay a claim if the insured increases the chance of loss in some manner prohibited under the contract or fails to submit a proof of loss within a specified time period.

Conditional contract
A contract under which performance is only required under certain conditions.

Consequently, an insurance contract is often called a **conditional contract**, a contract under which performance is only required under certain conditions. The courts, in equity, allow the insurer to refuse to perform unless the contractual conditions are met. For example, the insurer may have charged a lower premium, assuming that the insured would meet certain conditions or may have issued the policy based on the insurer's reliance on the enforceability of the conditions.

Indemnity

Principle of indemnity
A legal principle that holds that an insured's proceeds should not exceed its financial losses from an insured event.

Most property and liability insurance contracts are governed by the **principle of indemnity**, which is a legal principle that holds that an insured's proceeds should not exceed its financial losses from an insured event. Provisions designed to enforce this principle help reduce the economic incentives the insured may have to cause a loss. The following sections examine how this principle functions in an insurance context.

Insurance contracts are contracts of indemnity because they perform the following functions:

1. Pay for actual loss
2. Require an insurable interest
3. Prevent duplicate coverage
4. Allow subrogation

Pay for Actual Loss

Insurance contracts uphold the principle of indemnity because they pay for actual loss. Property insurance contracts, which insure against direct loss of property, have traditionally promised to pay the insured no more than the actual loss—that is, the actual cash value of the loss. The actual cash value of a loss is the cost of repair or replacement minus an allowance for physical depreciation and economic obsolescence. Therefore, if properly enforced, property insurance contracts do not over-indemnify the insured. Replacement cost insurance, however, does not reduce the payment to the insured by the amount of the insured item's physical depreciation or economic obsolescence. To reduce the likelihood that insureds will benefit from a loss with this type of protection, insurers usually require actual replacement of the property and the insurance coverage limit to be close to the replacement cost of the property.

Most states have statutes requiring that insurance covering most types of real property against most causes of loss be written through "valued policies." Under such policies, the insurer must pay the contract's face value for a total loss, even if the face amount exceeds the actual loss. Some state statutes apply payment proportionally to partial losses so that, for example, if an insured building is one-third damaged, the insurer must pay one-third of the face amount of the valued policy. Without the valued policy requirement, the insurer would have to pay only the amount of the loss. The insurer would keep the premium for the over-insurance but would pay no extra loss payments. Valued policy legislation encourages insurers to reduce the likelihood of over-insurance by inspecting property before they insure it.

Valued policies are common for rare articles because they are valued more easily and accurately before a loss than after one. Valued policies are also common in marine insurance. However, values in marine insurance policies are often based on invoice cost or another objective measure, rather than replacement cost, and seldom violate the principle of indemnity.

Property insurance contracts covering net income losses resulting from damage to property usually limit recovery to the actual loss sustained. Some valued policies also exist, but the values in those policies are usually fixed at reasonable levels. Liability insurance contracts provide the insured with defense services and a promise to pay whatever the court or statutes award the claimant up to the policy limits or, more commonly, the negotiated settlement. Although the insurer could pay a claimant more than the insured would have been able to pay, the insured does not benefit from the insurer's payment.

Require an Insurable Interest

Insurance contracts also uphold the principle of indemnity by requiring an insurable interest. Property insurance contracts promise to pay the insured no more than its insurable interest at the time of the loss. An **insurable interest** is an interest in the subject of an insurance policy that is not unduly remote and that would cause the interested party to suffer financial loss if an insurance event occurred. The extent of the possible financial loss indicates the degree of insurable interest. A sole owner's insurable interest is the total possible loss to the insured property, whereas a part owner's insurable interest is a share of the total loss. A secured creditor, such as a mortgagee, has an insurable interest equal to the debt plus the cost to the creditor, if any, of the insurance protection. Other examples of insurable interests are the liability interest of a bailee in the property that is in the bailee's care, custody, or control, and the interest of persons holding judgments against the owner. Although the interest of a general creditor is too distant to justify an insurable interest, a creditor acquires an insurable interest in a debtor's property if a court judgment against the debtor is obtained.

> **Insurable interest**
> An interest in the subject of an insurance policy that is not unduly remote and that would cause the interested party to suffer financial loss if an insurance event occurred.

Unlike life insurance, an insurable interest in property need not exist when insurance is purchased because, for example, the buyer of certain real property may not have title yet but will soon based on the terms of a sales contract. The buyer, understandably, wants to be sure the coverage is in effect the moment he or she has ownership and, consequently, an insurable interest in the property. The insurable interest is also lost when the same property is sold by the insured to another party. Therefore, for the insurable interest requirement to be met, it must exist at the time of the loss to preserve the principle of indemnity.

Prevent Duplicate Coverage

To uphold the principle of indemnity, insurance contracts also need ways to prevent duplicate coverage. Limiting an insured's recovery under any one insurance contract to the actual loss might be insufficient to ensure indemnity. The insured can still purchase several insurance policies and collect under each unless provisions prevent this duplicate recovery. Such provisions are also needed to clarify each insurer's obligations regarding an insured loss to which several policies might apply. Property-casualty insurance contracts contain at least one of the following three types of provisions, collectively called "other insurance" clauses, which handle the duplicate coverage in the following ways:

1. Prorating coverage among insurers
2. Establishing primary/excess arrangements among coverages
3. Prohibiting other insurance

The most common type of provision dealing with duplicate insurance prorates liability for a loss among all the insurance policies that would provide coverage if no other insurance applied. Liability is frequently prorated among insurers by dividing the loss equally among all policies, by the face amount of the policies, or by the limit of liability for a particular loss. In no case, however, does an insurer pay more than the policy's face amount.

The second type of provision dealing with duplicate insurance stipulates that the coverage in one policy is excess (or sometimes primary) regarding the other insurance covering the same loss. For example, most automobile insurance contracts state that an insured is protected while operating someone else's automobile, but this insured must first exhaust any of the vehicle owner's insurance before the insured's coverage for nonowned automobiles applies. This provision makes an operator's coverage for nonowned automobiles excess over the automobile owner's coverage. When each of two or more policies stipulates that coverage is excess (or primary) relative to all other coverage, those policies typically prorate coverage, most frequently in proportion to their respective limits of liability for the particular loss.

A third type of provision dealing with duplicate coverage prohibits other insurance, which makes purchasing other insurance a breach of a warranty and excuses the insurer whose policy prohibits such coverage from any liability. An insurer can achieve the same result by excluding from its policy any loss to which other insurance applies. If all applicable policies contain such provisions, then those policies typically prorate liability in proportion to their respective limits of liability for the particular loss.

Allow Subrogation

The final way that insurance contracts uphold the principle of indemnity is to allow subrogation (discussed previously in the context of a surety agreement). The principle of indemnity could be violated if the insured collects from its own insurer and then a second time from the third party who is responsible for the loss. However, **subrogation** is the process by which an insurer recovers payment from a liable third party who has caused a property or liability loss that the insurer has paid to, or on behalf of, an insured. The insurer's right is limited to the extent of its payment, and most courts have held that the insurer can recover only after the insured has been fully indemnified.

Subrogation
The process by which an insurer recovers payment from a liable third party who has caused a property or liability loss that the insurer has paid to, or on behalf of, an insured.

Although the insurer's right is based on statutory and/or common law, property-casualty insurance contracts also contain subrogation clauses that indicate that interference with this right could result in the insurer's denying liability. The insurer sometimes waives this right. For example, in a policy protecting a landlord, the insurer might agree to waive subrogation rights against a tenant.

In addition to preventing the insured from collecting twice and violating the principle of indemnity, subrogation increases the probability that responsible parties will be held accountable and lowers the losses ultimately paid by the insurer.

SUMMARY

The six steps in purchasing risk financing services are as follows:

1. The organization determines its insurance needs and develops specifications for coverage.
2. The organization presents its proposal to insurers through intermediaries.
3. Insurers and their intermediaries develop and present coverage proposals to the organization.
4. The organization evaluates the coverage proposals.
5. The organization enters into a contract with the insurer.
6. The organization implements steps related to the new coverage.

The first step of this process, in which the organization determines its insurance needs and develops specifications, can be complex and time-consuming. Whether obtaining new coverage or renewing existing coverage, the organization's risk management professional must assess the organization's loss exposures and evaluate the risk financing alternatives for dealing with potential losses from each significant exposure.

Once the organization has determined its needs, it must then present its proposal to insurers and marketing intermediaries, the second step in the process. Ideally, these presentations should occur at least five months before existing coverage is scheduled to end and should be uniform, clear, and complete. Most of a risk management professional's activities in marketing an organization's insurance account focus on making the organization's insurance needs attractive to underwriters. This is accomplished by combining efforts with insurance marketing intermediaries.

The four primary types of intermediaries are brokers, independent agents, direct writing insurers, and risk management consultants. A broker is a marketing intermediary who is an authorized representative of an insured. An agent is a marketing intermediary who is an authorized representative of the insurer. A direct writing insurer is an insurer that markets its coverages directly through its own employees rather than through intermediaries. A risk management consultant is an individual who does not sell insurance directly, but who often provides advice for a fee about a variety of risk management matters.

Each of these types of intermediaries should possess technical expertise, adequate financial resources, creativity, agreement on claim handling, and integrity. Intermediaries may be compensated in a variety of ways, including through fees, commissions, or a combination of the two.

During the risk financing service purchase process, the risk management professional also may seek to reduce the organization's insurance costs by eliminating the charges for incidental services that insurers embed in a policy's premium. Unbundling is the removal of an insurer's incidental services from insurance coverage. If an organization unbundles a particular service from its coverage, it can purchase a comparable service from other sources, use its own personnel to provide the services, or eliminate its need for the service.

After the selected intermediaries have presented coverage proposals and services have been unbundled where appropriate, the risk management professional must next evaluate the coverage proposals. This evaluation should focus on the services offered, the financial stability of the insurer, and the associated costs.

Once a proposal has been selected, the organization enters into an insurance contract with the insurer in order to effect coverage. Most insurance policies are subject to the legal principles of disclosure, equity, and indemnity. Disclosure imposes on every insurance applicant a duty to disclose to the insurer and its legal agents all material information. Material information is information that could reasonably affect the insurer's underwriting decisions about whether and on what terms to insure the applicant. Equity requires the parties to an insurance contract to deal fairly with one another. Indemnity holds that an insured's proceeds should not exceed the insured's financial losses from an insured event.

CHAPTER NOTE

1. Act 147 of 2002, Producer Modernization Act, modeled in part after the NAIC's Producer Licensing Model Act.

Direct Your Learning

Allocating Risk Management Costs

After learning the content of this chapter and completing the corresponding course guide assignment, you should be able to:

- Describe the purposes of allocating risk management costs.

- Describe the types of risk management costs an organization may want to allocate.

- Describe the prospective and retrospective approaches to allocating risk management costs.

- Describe the exposure bases and experience bases used to allocate risk management costs.

- Describe the practical considerations of selecting an allocation basis.

- Given a case, justify how risk management costs may be allocated among an organization's departments.

- Define or describe each of the Key Words and Phrases for this chapter.

Develop Your Perspective

What are the main topics covered in the chapter?

This chapter examines the process of allocating risk management costs, including the purpose of the process, which costs to allocate, and how the costs should be allocated.

Review the type of costs an organization should allocate.

- Is each type of cost allocated by your organization? If not, which costs are not allocated?

- Who oversees which costs are allocated in your organization?

Why is it important to learn about these topics?

A properly designed and implemented allocation of risk management costs among the departments of an organization can promote risk control, facilitate risk retention, prioritize risk management expenditures, reduce costs, distribute costs fairly, balance risk-bearing and risk-sharing, and provide managers with cost information.

Examine why your organization allocates risk management costs.

- Which objectives are most important to your organization?

- Which objectives are least important to your organization?

How can you use what you will learn?

Evaluate the effectiveness of the allocation of risk management costs for your organization.

- How well do the strategies chosen support your organization's corporate objectives?

- What changes might you make to the process your organization uses to allocate risk management costs?

Chapter 13
Allocating Risk Management Costs

An organization must budget and pay for the costs of its risk management function. How it assigns those costs to individual business units or departments within the organization can significantly affect each department's financial results. An ideal risk management cost allocation system is a balance between departmental risk bearing and risk sharing across all the organization's departments. In addition, a risk management cost allocation system should promote effective risk management by encouraging risk control and effective claim management. It simultaneously should allow for cost-based product and service pricing. This chapter explains the purposes of a risk management cost allocation system, the types of costs that must be allocated, the approaches to cost allocation, and the bases on which costs can be allocated.

PURPOSES OF A RISK MANAGEMENT COST ALLOCATION SYSTEM

A risk management cost allocation system should focus on the following risk management costs:

- Retained losses
- Insurance premiums
- Risk control costs
- Administrative expenses for the risk management function

These risk management costs should be clearly identified and properly attributed to the organization's departments, products, or activities. Effective risk management programs require that most costs be allocated to the departments that generate them.

An effective risk management cost allocation system should serve the following purposes:

- Promote risk control
- Facilitate risk retention
- Prioritize risk management expenditures

- Reduce costs
- Distribute costs fairly
- Balance risk-bearing and risk-sharing
- Provide managers with risk management cost information

Promote Risk Control

The primary purpose of a risk management cost allocation system is to promote risk control throughout an organization by allocating the costs of a loss or potential loss to the responsible department. Therefore, each department is either held accountable or rewarded for its risk control efforts. For example, a department that effectively controls its property losses will realize a reduction in its allocated property insurance premiums. If a department's risk control measure, such as an investment in risk control equipment, benefits the entire organization, then its cost is allocated across all of the organization's departments.

Facilitate Risk Retention

A risk management cost allocation system implemented by the organization throughout all departments allows the entire organization to benefit from an optimal risk retention level. As a result, individual departments are not unduly exposed to excessive fluctuations in their cost of risk, and, consequently, they are encouraged to increase their risk retention.

Prioritize Risk Management Expenditures

A risk management cost allocation system, because it assigns responsibility for risk management costs to individual departments, prioritizes risk management expenditures within departments. The method used to allocate risk management expenditures, particularly if the expenditures are allocated to a single department as opposed to all departments within an organization, has a direct bearing on how a department manager determines which risk control measures get funded. If a department must pay for a risk control measure by itself, it may more carefully scrutinize the measure's cost effectiveness. The department may also more carefully prioritize among the competing measures to fund those that provide the greatest return on investment.

Reduce Costs

A risk management cost allocation system effectively reduces an organization's costs. As risk control is promoted, losses are prevented or reduced. As risk retention is facilitated, the organization can more easily retain risk at an optimal level, which reduces its cost of risk. Finally, as risk management expenditures are prioritized in terms of cost effectiveness and return on investment, an organization's cost of risk is again lowered. This, in turn, allows the risk management professional to apply additional resources to other risk management goals or return funds to the organization's operational budget.

Distribute Costs Fairly

A risk management cost allocation system also should distribute costs fairly. Departmental managers may object if there is no direct correlation between departmental losses and the risk management costs allocated to their units. For example, a manager whose unit has considerably fewer departmental losses than another department may believe it unfair for his or her department to contribute toward high limits of coverage for the entire organization.

As another example, an organization's accounting department may be assigned just one company vehicle, which only the manager uses. The manager has a good claim history but still exposes the company to auto liability. By comparison, the distribution department of the same company uses several dozen long-haul trucks that incur many minor and several severe claims a year. The company purchases commercial auto liability coverage with high limits that insures all its vehicles. The accounting manager may believe the department should contribute little, if anything, toward the organization's commercial auto liability insurance premium. An effective cost allocation system would address the accounting manager's concerns by reducing the allocated amount charged to the accounting department on the basis of both the amount of the department's auto liability exposure and its claim experience.

Balance Risk-Bearing and Risk-Sharing

A **risk-bearing system** is a risk management cost allocation system that allocates losses to the individual department that generates them. Such a system creates a direct correlation between a department's loss exposures and the amount of risk it bears and is therefore responsive to a department's risk control efforts. However, it does not distinguish between risk that is directly attributable to a department's management and risk that is an unavoidable product of a department's function. Additionally, because a risk-bearing system assigns costs only to the responsible department, it can cause fluctuations in a department's financial results from one accounting period to the next, particularly when losses are catastrophic.

Risk-bearing system
A risk management cost allocation system that allocates losses to the individual department that generates them.

A **risk-sharing system**, which is a risk management cost allocation system that allocates losses among all of an organization's departments, can alleviate individual departments' burdens. Risk-sharing systems stabilize risk management costs across departments but are not as responsive to risk control efforts within individual departments.

Risk-sharing system
A risk management cost allocation system that allocates losses among all of an organization's departments.

Most risk management cost allocation systems are a combination of risk-bearing and risk-sharing systems. Such a balance distributes risk management costs across the organization while also allowing departments to benefit from their own loss experience and other changing conditions.

An effective risk management cost allocation system should balance the two types of plans in a manner that encourages risk control activities (accomplished through the risk-bearing element of a balanced plan) while minimizing departmental cost fluctuations (accomplished through the risk-sharing element of a balanced plan). Because risk control usually takes precedence over cost stabilization, most organizations use risk management cost allocation systems that consist primarily of risk-bearing.

Provide Managers With Risk Management Cost Information

Another purpose of a risk management cost allocation system is to provide managers with risk management cost information. Accurate allocation and reporting of cost of risk to the department responsible for the loss generation compels managers to focus on areas in which the cost of risk can be reduced. Consequently, the risk management cost allocation system may direct managers to address situations in which the cost of risk can be controlled more effectively.

Risk management cost allocation reporting systems that become too complex do not provide clear incentives for performance and cannot be administered easily. Claim runs (detailed listings of incidents causing particular types of losses, the dates and amounts of payments for each loss, and the development of reserves for each loss), exposure reports, and other documents providing data for allocating costs should follow a clear format. The system should also be explained in writing by the risk management professional and discussed in presentations to each department's management.

The information generated by a risk management cost allocation system can be useful to an organization only if it can be independently verified and has not been manipulated either within individual departments (internal manipulation) or by an organization's owners or senior management (external manipulation).

Two prevalent examples of internal manipulation are the suppression of claim reporting and the deliberately inaccurate presentation of loss-related facts. The first tactic is effective if the risk management cost allocation system is based on reported claims and does not correct claims based on subsequent reporting. The second tactic bases the risk management cost allocation system on loss reserves and does not correct for subsequent case valuations in allocating costs. The risk management cost allocation system can discourage or prevent internal manipulation by requiring losses to be reviewed or audited in order to confirm that they were reported in a timely fashion and that subsequent changes to reserve amounts are not attributable to facts that should have been revealed at the time of the loss.

External manipulation is performed by an organization's owners or senior management and generally occurs when a risk management cost allocation system does not meet the overall financial objectives of the organization's owners or senior management. For example, assume that an organization prices its products to reflect production costs, with the exception of one department that produces a loss leader for the rest of the organization. If risk management costs are allocated to that department, senior management might argue that such costs should be absorbed by the rest of the organization, because the department's product is designed and priced exclusively to generate revenue for other departments. Senior management may reason that because the department producing a loss leader is meant to operate at a loss for the benefit of the organization, it would be inappropriate for that department to be allocated part of the organization's risk management costs. To do so would force it to operate at an even greater loss. The best way to prevent external manipulation is to design the risk management cost allocation system to reflect the organization's overall objectives and to obtain prior approval of the system from senior management.

TYPES OF RISK MANAGEMENT COSTS TO BE ALLOCATED

A risk management cost allocation system can fully or partially allocate four types of risk management costs, which together constitute an organization's cost of risk, as follows:

1. Costs of accidental losses not reimbursed by insurance or other outside sources
2. Insurance premiums
3. Costs of risk control techniques
4. Costs of administering risk management activities

Any combination of the preceding costs, or portions of them, can be allocated to any department. Costs that are most beneficial to allocate to a particular department are those that are clearly incurred by and beneficial to a given department and that are wholly within that department's control. The organization must determine or estimate the value of each cost category for the period for which it is to be allocated and must also determine how to allocate the costs. Consistent costs, such as guaranteed-cost insurance premiums, are more easily allocated than complex costs, such as retained losses, which vary over time.

An organization can assign a different allocation method to each type of cost. For example, it can use distinct allocation systems for general liability, automobile liability, workers' compensation, and property losses. Some of these costs can be fully allocated to the department that generated the exposure or losses. Other costs can be partially allocated to the department that generated them and partially absorbed by the entire organization. Still other costs can simply be charged as general overhead.

Costs of Accidental Losses Not Reimbursed by Insurance or Other Outside Sources

Most accidental loss costs not reimbursed by insurance or other outside sources are apportioned to the responsible department by the risk management cost allocation system. Other losses, or portions of losses, are charged to the organization as a whole (losses not allocated are treated as overhead). Losses to be allocated to a department are measured by the dollars incurred as a result of the occurrence. Departments can fund such retained losses with an explicit retention program, alternative risk financing plans, retrospective rating insurance plans, a retrospective rating insurance pool, or any other loss-sensitive risk financing technique.

Some costs of accidental losses, such as loss adjustment expenses, can be attributed to a particular loss or claim. Others cannot. Allocated loss adjustment expenses (ALAE) can be specifically related to and/or identified with a particular loss or claim. Such expenses include investigation, negotiation, and legal costs, as well as salvage, debris removal, and similar costs associated with administering claims. If retained by the organization, the ALAE should be allocated either within the responsible department or to the organization as a whole.

Some retrospective rating insurance programs and pools do not handle ALAE through the general risk management allocation system but instead treat them as part of the program's or pool's overhead cost. Normally, to be included in an organization's risk management cost allocation system, a loss adjustment expense should be identified as being incurred to adjust a particular claim.

Unallocated loss adjustment expenses (ULAE) are not easily identified with a particular claim; however, they should be charged to a particular department. For example, an organization that retains its workers' compensation losses may pay a third-party administrator to handle claims. The administrator's fee may be charged to each department that generates claims handled by the administrator.

To determine how much of each retained loss to allocate, it is important to first select an appropriate basis for calculating the values and loss costs. Loss costs can be calculated by one of the following three bases:

1. **Incurred loss basis**—the calculation of loss costs by adding the amounts paid for losses to reserves for pending claims, to the additions to those reserves and to the estimated amount of incurred but not reported losses.

2. **Claims-made basis**—the calculation of loss costs by adding the actual payments to changes in reserves for claims made during the accounting period.

3. **Claims-paid basis**—the calculation of loss costs using the amount paid on losses during the accounting period, regardless of when the losses were incurred.

Incurred loss basis (for allocating costs)
The calculation of loss costs by adding the amounts paid for losses to reserves for pending claims, to the additions to those reserves and to the estimated amount of incurred but not reported losses.

Claims-made basis (for allocating costs)
The calculation of loss costs by adding the actual payments to changes in reserves for claims made during the accounting period.

Claims-paid basis (for allocating costs)
The calculation of loss costs using the amount paid on losses during the accounting period, regardless of when they were incurred.

Each basis for calculating losses can include a risk charge. A risk charge is an amount added to an organization's expected losses to cover potential adverse fluctuations in experience. If an organization's loss experience is worse than expected, the risk charge will help pay for those additional, unexpected losses. Some organizations accumulate a risk charge for the organization as a whole, and others establish annual department risk charges for each accounting period. During an accounting period, if a department does not have worse than expected losses and, consequently, does not require the risk charge, the risk charge amount is returned to the organization.

According to generally accepted accounting principles, an organization should indicate on its financial statements its **incurred but unpaid liabilities**, which are those liabilities that reflect both the reserve amount of reported losses and the incurred but not reported losses that the organization anticipates financing through retention. A risk charge, however, is not a liability and should not be shown as such on financial statements. The risk charge should be shown as a segregated part of the organization's equity.

Incurred but unpaid liabilities
Liabilities that reflect both the reserve amount of reported losses and the incurred but not reported losses that the organization anticipates financing through retention.

Insurance Premiums

Insurance premiums are payments made to an insurer to transfer risk. Premiums are generally fixed for a policy year and can usually be attributed directly to a department. For example, aircraft product liability premiums can be allocated directly to a department that manufactures aircraft or aircraft components. In contrast, certain coverages, such as directors and officers liability insurance, provide a more general benefit for the entire organization. Costs associated with such coverages do not have a specific source of exposure and therefore are usually allocated equally across the whole organization.

Costs of Risk Control Techniques

Costs of risk control techniques include either long-term capital investments (such as a fire detection and suppression system) or expenditures to purchase less expensive loss control measures (such as safety shoes or driver-training instruction). Capital investments create or add to depreciable assets; occasional expenditures are usually charged against the accounting period in which they produce services or other benefits for the organization. In either case, most loss control expenditures are clearly allocable to a particular department. When a risk control expenditure is not closely linked to a particular department, the cost is usually treated as part of administrative overhead for the risk management function.

Costs of Administering Risk Management Activities

Costs of administering risk management activities include the following:

- The operating budget of the risk management department
- Cost of executives' time from other departments
- Other resources from other departments devoted to risk management

Some organizations allocate all operating costs of some or all central departments, such as risk management, to other departments. Other organizations allocate to other departments only those costs associated with certain types of exposures clearly attributable to those departments. Costs can include the salary and benefits for people working in workers' compensation claim administration departments and the cost of their furniture, supplies, and other needs. Allocated costs can also include the portion of the risk management professional's salary and benefits that represents the time that person spends on the workers' compensation program for each department.

Other administrative expenses are not so easily attributable to a particular department or departments and therefore are often not charged as such. Examples include a consultant's audit of the entire risk management program, an actuarial evaluation of a risk retention proposal, and management services for the organization's captive insurer.

APPROACHES TO RISK MANAGEMENT COST ALLOCATION

After an organization determines which risk management costs to allocate and to whom they will be allocated, it must then decide the allocation method it will use. There are many approaches to risk management cost allocation. This section discusses two widely used, but mutually exclusive, approaches.

Prospective cost allocation
A cost allocation approach in which estimated costs are allocated at the beginning of the accounting period during which they are expected to be incurred.

The first approach, **prospective cost allocation**, is a cost allocation approach in which estimated costs are allocated at the beginning of the accounting period during which they are expected to be incurred. Once they are allocated, costs are not changed for that period, regardless of actual losses incurred.

Retrospective cost allocation
A cost allocation approach in which estimated costs are allocated at the beginning of the accounting period during which they are expected to be incurred but can then be reallocated one or more times during or after the close of the period, with payments or returns made retrospectively according to changes in loss experience.

The second approach, **retrospective cost allocation**, is a cost allocation approach in which estimated costs are allocated at the beginning of the accounting period during which they are expected to be incurred but can then be reallocated one or more times during or after the close of the period, with payments or returns made retrospectively according to changes in loss experience. Both systems seek a balance between loss experience and loss exposure. In a prospective system, costs are allocated primarily on the basis of potential exposures to loss and secondarily on the basis of recent actual loss experience. In a retrospective system, the opposite is true; actual loss experience is the primary basis for allocation, and potential loss exposures are the secondary basis.

Prospective Cost Allocation Approach

The primary advantage of prospective cost allocation is a stable budget in which costs are assumed to be known before the beginning of the accounting period and are not changed. The corresponding disadvantage is that actual costs can differ substantially from those allocated. Although the differences can be corrected in subsequent periods, the corrected costs are not associated with the output of the period to which they are charged. Another disadvantage of prospective allocation is that an increase (or a decrease) in risk control activity can be separated by several accounting periods from the corresponding reduction (or increase) in allocated costs, which can delay the positive influence a cost allocation system may have on a departmental manager's risk control efforts.

Retrospective Cost Allocation Approach

The primary advantage of retrospective cost allocation is that costs are more accurately attributed to the period and the department with which they are associated. Consequently, an increase (or a decrease) in risk control activity and a corresponding reduction (or increase) in loss costs are immediately recognized in terms of allocated costs, facilitating the evaluation of the risk control program's effectiveness. The corresponding disadvantage is that final allocated risk management costs are not determined until well after the end of the period during which the losses were incurred, which complicates risk management budgeting.

BASES FOR RISK MANAGEMENT COST ALLOCATION

After an organization determines the types and amounts of its costs of risk, which it may approach prospectively or retrospectively, it must determine the bases on which it will allocate the costs among its departments. Costs can be allocated based on loss exposure or loss experience. An **exposure-based system** is a system that allocates costs to departments on the basis of their exposures, regardless of loss experience. Under such a system, the proportionate costs charged to any department do not change as long as its exposures do not change. An **experience-based system** is a system that allocates costs to departments according to their pro rata portion of past losses. This system can subject small departments to significant fluctuations in costs from one accounting period to the next if their loss experience fluctuates significantly.

Rather than exclusively relying on one system or the other, many organizations use a combination of exposure and experience to allocate costs of risk throughout the organization's departments, a practice known as blending allocation. Generally, systems for allocating costs for exposures that generate frequent claims (such as workers' compensation) rely more on loss experience than on exposures. Furthermore, managers of larger, more financially capable departments generally want their costs to be allocated by experience rather than by exposures because loss experience can decrease their allocated costs to an amount less than what their department's size alone suggests.

Exposure-based system
A system that allocates costs to departments on the basis of their exposures, regardless of their loss experience.

Experience-based system
A system that allocates costs to departments according to their pro rata portion of past losses.

For example, consider an organization composed of two departments, one that generates $100 million in revenues and another that generates $50 million in revenues. Risk management costs associated with property can be allocated to both departments, based 90 percent on their exposure and 10 percent on their loss experience. In contrast, workers' compensation costs can be allocated 75 percent on experience (25 percent on exposure) for the larger-revenue department and 50 percent on experience (50 percent on exposure) for the smaller-revenue department. Percentages should reflect the relative degree of confidence placed in the organization's past experience as a predictor of its future experience. The greater the correlation between past losses and future losses, the more closely the loss experience approaches 100 percent credibility. In practice, credibility is often determined by judgment or by actuarial calculations.

The costs of loss-sensitive insurance (such as a retrospective rating plan) can be apportioned not in percentages, but in layers. For example, in a system that allocates the costs of insuring liability loss exposures, each department can be responsible for paying all relatively small losses within its individual deductible. Costs for losses above the deductible, but within the organization's overall retention, can be allocated to each department, based 50 percent on experience and 50 percent on exposure. The costs for liability insurance above the organization's retention can be allocated wholly on the basis of each department's exposure.

Exposure Bases

The bases for determining and allocating risk management costs differ by type of exposure. For example, different bases are used to allocate general liability costs than are used to allocate workers' compensation costs. Each basis selected should, to the extent practical, reflect the underlying exposures. For each risk management cost category mentioned earlier, exposure can generally be measured by size, nature of operations, and territory, which, in turn, can be measured by some easily verified gauge. Size, for example, can be measured by revenues, number of employees, or square footage. A department with twice the revenues of another with identical operations can be considered to have twice the exposure and, thus, twice the allocated costs.

The nature of a department's operations also determines the extent of the exposure. A department making pharmaceutical products has a greater products liability exposure than one that manufactures soap because of the greater risk of health complication for consumers from pharmaceutical products. Therefore, the products liability risk management charges per dollar of revenue that are allocated to the pharmaceutical department should be greater than the risk management charges for each dollar of revenue allocated to the soap-manufacturing department.

The geographic location of the exposure can also be used to estimate the cost of risk for the exposure because it can reflect the difference in benefit levels and expected legal costs to be incurred. For example, a person injured in the United States would probably receive greater compensation than a person similarly injured in Brazil. Consequently, general liability risk management charges for each dollar of an organization's output in the U.S. should exceed charges for revenues generated in other countries.

Another type of exposure basis is rate per unit of exposure. Insurance premiums for guaranteed-cost coverages for a particular department are usually calculated on a rate per unit of exposure. The rate for each department can differ substantially from the premium rate that an insurer charges the organization as a whole because each department's degree of hazard differs from the organization's composite rate.

The exposure bases used by the insurer are usually helpful in determining an appropriate exposure for the type of risk management cost being allocated. The following types of costs are common to many organizations and require a variety of exposure bases:

- General liability
- Automobile liability
- Workers' compensation
- Property
- Other exposures

General Liability

General liability loss exposures vary widely among different types of organizations. For some organizations, general liability exposure arises primarily from premises and operations. For others, it comes primarily from products or the activities of independent contractors. Commonly used bases for measuring an organization's dominant general liability exposure and for allocating general liability costs include square footage of floor space, annual budget, payroll, full-time-equivalent workers, and sales. If an insurer charges an extra premium for a special exposure, such as mobile communication systems, the premium is usually charged directly to the department responsible for it.

At times, an organization may have to modify an insurer's exposure basis to better reflect the degree of exposure associated with a particular department's activities. For example, department budgets can indicate the premises liability exposure for each department. However, if a department has extremely high research and development costs, and those costs generate no significant premises liability exposure, the department's budget (which is large) does not accurately reflect its exposure (which is small). For cost allocation purposes, the department's research and development costs may be excluded from its budget because they do not increase the department's premises liability exposure.

Automobile Liability

Automobile liability loss exposures differ by departments and by types of vehicles operated by those departments. Some departments use small trucks; some, large trucks; some, only passenger vehicles; and some, essentially no vehicles at all. The most commonly used exposure basis for allocating automobile liability costs is the number of vehicles used, with some adjustments for differences in types of vehicles. For example, a department operating both private passenger automobiles and delivery trucks might assign to private passenger automobiles an exposure basis, which is also referred to as a relativity in this circumstance, of 1.00, and to delivery trucks a relativity of 5.00 (if, hypothetically, it is assumed that the trucks typically generate five times the losses of an equal number of the private passenger automobiles). Therefore, the number of vehicles serving as the allocation basis for the department would be computed as the number of private passenger automobiles plus five times the number of trucks.

Workers' Compensation

Workers' compensation loss exposures differ by department and by job classifications within departments. A workers' compensation loss exposure can involve highly hazardous mining operations or much safer office operations, for example. The two most common exposure bases for allocating workers' compensation costs are payroll and full-time-equivalent number of employees. For both, rates are commonly adjusted for differences in exposure by job classification. For example, office workers might have a payroll relativity of 1.00, and firefighting personnel might have a relativity of 12.00. Therefore, a department that employs fifty office workers and two firefighters would be shown as having a total of seventy-four employees in the organization's workers' compensation cost allocation system. The National Council on Compensation Insurance provides exposure bases, called "rate relativities," which can be modified for particular departments.

Property

Property loss exposures vary by organization and by type of building and occupancy within an organization. For some organizations, manufacturing plants are the dominant property exposure; for others, office buildings. The two most common exposure bases for allocating risk management costs for property are square footage and property values (either replacement cost or actual cash value). When an insurer charges an extra premium for a particular loss exposure, such as a chemical mixing operation, the premium is often charged directly to the department responsible for it.

The exposure basis for property must often be modified to accurately reflect the associated exposure. For example, although property values are good general indicators of exposure, one department might operate in a building containing inflammable chemicals. The property values for that department, when used in the cost allocation system, should reflect the degree of hazard created by the presence of the chemicals. The effects of location, such as a building located in a hurricane zone, should also be considered. Again, the relativities used by property insurers are often germane but are usually modified for each organization.

Other Exposures

Activities within the risk management program related to other exposures, such as crime and fidelity, should have corresponding exposure bases for cost allocation, to the extent practical. For example, risk management department overhead can be allocated in different ways, including the following:

- In proportion to the total of other risk management department costs allocated for particular exposures
- As a fixed percentage of some other basis, such as sales
- As a combination of a flat fee per department (to cover fixed costs) and a percentage of some base, such as sales (to cover variable costs)

Using the most desirable exposure basis in all situations might not be possible because of one or more of the following problems:

- The data that form an exposure base, such as the number of full-time equivalent employees for allocating workers' compensation costs, are not available readily or at a reasonable price.
- Department managers disagree on how to calculate a particular exposure basis (for example, total operating expenditures excluding capital investments).
- Desired data, such as replacement cost property values, cannot be calculated each year in time to be used in a prospective cost allocation system.

However, in situations that effectively prohibit using the desired exposure base, finding an adequate, practical alternative is usually possible. For the three preceding problems, acceptable alternative exposure bases are payroll for workers' compensation, payroll for general liability, and replacement cost property values for the previous year. For building values, it may be necessary to adjust for more recent building acquisitions and disposals (again valued at the previous year's replacement cost).

Experience Basis

Loss experience is another basis that has been used effectively to allocate costs among departments within an organization. Loss experience is also often used as an indicator of the success of a risk management program and is measured by frequency or aggregate severity limited to some dollar amount. Frequency of losses indicates the quality of most loss control programs better than severity of losses because frequency is usually easier to control than severity.

Aggregate severity, which is the cumulative losses for a given period, is commonly used to indicate each department's claim experience. Each loss charged to a department is limited to a certain amount. The amount, for example $25,000 per occurrence, is often meant to be high enough to include the majority of a department's losses but low enough to prevent a rare large loss from detrimentally affecting a department's loss experience that otherwise was good. Each loss, up to the limit, is added to the department's loss experience. All claims reported for a given period are then accumulated to determine the department's experience.

Once a department's claim experience has been measured by severity, its future losses and related costs can be projected. The three primary criteria used for doing so are the following:

1.   Changes in claims paid
2.   Changes in payments plus loss reserves
3.   Changes in projected ultimate incurred losses

When cost of risk allocations are made according to changes in claims paid, the costs to a department tend to fluctuate by accounting period. Allocations based on changes in payments plus loss reserves typically fluctuate less (assuming the individual incurred losses are limited) than the most recent claim payments. However, loss reserves may be poorly estimated, which can artificially influence a department's allocated costs. (But if that artificial influence is uniform across departments, the cost distribution among departments will not be altered.) Also, using payments plus loss reserves avoids difficulties that can arise because of different reporting and payment patterns for claims that are characteristic of different departments. In such situations, estimated ultimate incurred losses, which are estimated total payments for open claims, could be a better choice. If presumably incurred but unreported losses are allocated to departments in proportion to reported claims (as measured by payments plus case reserves), allocations based on payments plus cash reserves and allocations based on projected ultimate losses will produce the same results.

Regardless of the experience criteria used, several considerations are useful in calculating the aggregate severity of a department's claims, including the following:

•   Per occurrence limit
•   Aggregate limit
•   Experience period

Per Occurrence Limit

Effective risk management programs work to reduce both the number of occurrences that result in claims and the amount of each claim that arises. As mentioned, claim frequency is usually easier to control than claim severity. Consequently, most risk management cost allocation systems are designed to be more sensitive to loss frequency than loss severity. By limiting losses to a specified amount per occurrence, the cost allocation system directs management's attention to where frequency of losses is a problem rather than to a department that has incurred a large loss that may never reoccur.

The amount of each loss and related ALAE in excess of the per occurrence limit can be allocated among all departments based on their exposures, rather than experience, to reflect the fortuitous nature of catastrophic events and losses. Alternatively, the excess amount of losses can be absorbed by the organization as a whole rather than by its departments.

Aggregate Limit

In addition to capping per occurrence limits, some risk management cost allocation systems further cap annual losses by using an annual aggregate limit. Aggregate limits should be set high enough so that a manager is directly penalized for poor aggregate loss experience. A high aggregate limit ensures that more costs can be allocated to each department.

Experience Period

Any experience-based cost allocation system distributes current claims and related ALAE among departments proportionally to each department's claims and related ALAE experience. An **experience period** is the length of time available to collect loss costs. For prospective plans, experience periods usually range from two to five previous years. For retrospective plans, the allocation is based on the losses for the current year.

Experience period
The length of time available to collect loss costs.

The shorter the experience period, the more responsive the cost allocation formula is to changes in recent past loss experience. Consequently, a short experience period more quickly reflects the results of recent changes in risk management activity. However, a short experience period also tends to subject individual departments to more widely fluctuating charges resulting from unusually good or bad claim experience. That fluctuation can be mitigated by placing maximums and minimums on the claim amounts that can be included in any one department's experience base. Furthermore, multi-year experience periods can be weighted to more heavily count recent experience. Therefore, experience accumulated over five years can be used to develop a weighted average in which each of the two most recent years is weighted by 30 percent, the third year 20 percent, and each of the two most distant years 10 percent.

Practical Considerations When Selecting an Allocation Basis

Many practical considerations affect selection of an allocation basis and the actual or perceived fairness of that allocation. One such consideration is that an organization's accounting system can influence allocation. Exposure bases often rely on exposure-based data, such as sales and payroll, which are maintained as part of the organization's overall accounting system. However, the desired data may not be readily available per department or activity. Also, the data may be available but unusable by the risk management professional to allocate costs because they were collected for purposes other than risk management cost allocation. For example, the organization's accounting system must follow certain statutory and regulatory guidelines when collecting and reporting the data.

Another practical consideration is that some of an organization's operations may be subject to more than one tax system, such as when an organization operates internationally or with foreign subsidiaries. Allocating costs among internationally operating departments and subsidiaries can have unfavorable tax consequences for the organization as a whole. Consequently, cost allocation systems must consider tax implications on an aggregate basis.

In some organizations, each department should be charged at least a minimum amount for risk management services regardless of its exposures or claim experience. Charging a minimum amount incorporates an exposure basis within the risk management cost allocation system. For example, when allocating costs associated with a workers' compensation retention program, each department may have the following as a minimum charge:

• Risk control costs
• Risk management department overhead
• Excess insurance premiums

These costs could be allocated by payroll and adjusted for differences in job classifications. The services and protection afforded by excess insurance benefit all departments regardless of experience. Similarly, it may be appropriate to establish a maximum that a department can be charged despite the worst possible experience. The usual purpose of establishing a maximum charge is to reduce the fluctuations in allocated costs from one accounting period to the next. Such a maximum is often expressed as a percentage of the prior year's allocated risk management costs.

An additional practical consideration is that if an organization is highly decentralized, department managers may be allowed to purchase their own insurance rather than participate in a centralized risk management cost allocation system. This is likely not to be as cost effective as buying insurance for the organization as a whole because it does not leverage the combined purchasing power of all the departments to negotiate lower expense factors and service fees from an insurer. Gaps in coverage or duplications of coverage also may result. Consistent application of umbrella or excess liability insurance policies also presents a challenge when departments are allowed to purchase their own coverage.

Also, for an organization with a small aggregate cost of risk relative to its total budget, the results of cost allocation can be insignificant. In this case, a risk management cost allocation system is probably not needed at all. For instance, a $10,000 or $25,000 charge for workers' compensation coverage will have little effect on a department with a $10 million budget.

Another practical consideration is that a risk management cost allocation system should penalize or reward each department manager according to that department's risk management costs. This can be accomplished if managers' bonuses reflect their allocated risk management costs as well as other operating results. Moreover, a department's total budget should not be adjusted to compensate for changes in risk management results; doing so tends to cushion or cancel the manager's penalty or reward. For example, if a department's workers' compensation cost allocation increases from $1 million to $5 million because of its deteriorating experience, increasing its total budget by $4 million does not penalize its manager appropriately and fails to motivate improvement of the department's workers' compensation results.

Department and senior managers should support the risk management cost allocation plan that is selected. Having the support of department and senior managers is necessary to collect the data for cost allocation and to foster cooperation. Cooperation can also be encouraged by including managers in the development of the risk management cost allocation plan.

An additional practical consideration is that the use of computerized risk management information systems (RMIS) has become standard in many industries, particularly in the application of experience-based risk management allocation systems. Many RMIS gather cost information and allocate costs among departments, products, or functions. Department and senior managers should agree in advance, if possible, on the allocation bases, formulas, and limits of the RMIS.

A final practical consideration when selecting an allocation basis is that cost allocation systems should remain as consistent as possible from year to year. Risk management cost allocation systems usually use past loss and claim data as a benchmark to evaluate current performance. Consequently, changes in the underlying data may make the current performance evaluation meaningless. Changes in risk management cost allocation systems can be necessary, however, because the organizations they monitor are dynamic. The ramifications of any changes should be considered and communicated to the affected managers. Situations that typically trigger system changes include the following:

- Material shifts in the organization's operations (for example, purchasing a large subsidiary, discontinuing operations, or deciding to make one product a loss leader)
- Change in expected losses due change in legal climate, inflation, or some other factor, which can create the need to change the per occurrence limit
- Restructuring of the organization's departments or lines of authority

CASE STUDY IN RISK MANAGEMENT COST ALLOCATION

Applying a risk management cost allocation system to a specific organization requires the risk management professional to perform the following six steps:

1. Review the attributes of an effective risk management cost allocation system and determine the organization's objectives for such a system.
2. Identify the costs that will be allocated by the risk management cost allocation system.

3. For each category of cost, determine whether a prospective or retrospective allocation would best show where risk management techniques should be used.

4. Determine the value and the way each cost will be allocated based on one or more of the following:

   • Exposure basis

   • Experience basis

   • Per occurrence limit

   • Aggregate limit

   • Experience period

5. Consider the opportunities and challenges of each of the following when implementing a risk management allocation system:

   • Accounting system

   • Organization's tax situation

   • Minimum and/or maximum limits on costs to be allocated for each accounting period

   • Decentralized departments

   • Significance of risk management costs to each department's budget

   • Ways in which cost allocations may penalize or reward a department manager according to that department's costs to influence motivation and performance

   • Level of support and cooperation from management

   • RMIS used

   • Consistency of allocation system

6. Perform trial calculations to determine whether the proposed system meets the organization's needs. If it does not, make adjustments and repeat this step as necessary.

The remainder of this section presents an example of how a hypothetical organization, Lorac Management Corporation (Lorac), may apply the preceding six steps when developing its risk management cost allocation system for its general liability risk financing program. The case illustrates the need for an organization-specific system and demonstrates that no right or wrong approach to risk management cost allocation exists, only one that makes sense for a given organization within the preceding guidelines.

Lorac is a privately held organization that owns and manages five commercial properties located in three U.S. cities, as shown in Exhibit 13-1. Each property is treated as a profit center, and each maintains separate accounting information in the form of profit and loss statements. Each property manager is on an incentive compensation system that reflects the profitability of each property and that takes into account all expenses, including risk management expenses.

Last year, Lorac purchased guaranteed-cost, occurrence-basis, primary general liability insurance for a premium of $300,000. The premium had been allocated as shown in Exhibit 13-2. Using square footage as an allocation basis limited fluctuations in allocated costs to the changes in annual premiums because the square footage at each property remained fairly constant.

After last year's allocations, some of Lorac's property managers complained about general liability insurance costs. The manager of the Houston hotel, which had a significantly lower occupancy rate than the other two hotels, believed that the Houston property was subsidizing the cost of risk for the hotels in Denver and Los Angeles. In contrast, the managers of the apartment and office buildings, which historically had fewer claims, believed that they were subsidizing the hotels.

EXHIBIT 13-1

Listing of Lorac Properties

Location	Occupancy
Los Angeles	Hotel
Los Angeles	Apartment building
Denver	Hotel
Denver	Office building
Houston	Hotel

EXHIBIT 13-2

Allocation of Costs Based on Square Footage

(1)	(2)	(3)	(4)	(5)
Location	Occupancy	Square Footage	Percentage of Total	Cost Allocation
Los Angeles	Hotel	200,000	20%	$ 60,000
Los Angeles	Apartment building	300,000	30	90,000
Denver	Hotel	200,000	20	60,000
Denver	Office building	100,000	10	30,000
Houston	Hotel	200,000	20	60,000
Total		1,000,000	100%	$300,000

For the forthcoming renewal, Lorac's risk management professional realizes that, because of market conditions and deteriorating claim experience, Lorac's guaranteed-cost general liability premium will probably increase from $300,000 to $500,000. The risk management professional also realizes that allocation according to square footage may not encourage risk control activities at the properties. In addition, the risk management professional worked with an outside consultant to develop a basic risk control program that addresses many of the causes of past accidents, which the risk management professional believes may reduce future losses. The risk management professional confirms that senior management would support a risk management cost allocation process that influenced property managers' bonuses so that each manager would have a personal incentive to reach the goals of the new risk control program.

The program recommended by the outside consultant includes a $10,000 per occurrence liability deductible for the general liability coverage. Lorac's acceptance of the deductible induced the underwriter to lower the guaranteed-cost premium for the coming year to $250,000. The risk management professional determines that annual losses within the $10,000 per occurrence deductible could be expected to aggregate to $150,000. She consequently estimates that the total primary general liability risk financing cost for the coming year would be $400,000, consisting of $250,000 in premiums and $150,000 in retained losses (including loss adjustment expenses for both insured and uninsured claims). The risk management professional also concludes that maintaining a prospective cost allocation system is important because property managers want risk management costs that can be determined in advance. As a result, changes in loss experience for each year will influence only cost allocations for the next year.

The risk management professional evaluates how costs would be allocated for the coming year and decides that the projected $150,000 in retained losses should be allocated by the last three years of losses, up to $10,000 per occurrence. In contrast, the guaranteed-cost insurance premium should be allocated principally on relative exposure, with some adjustment for large losses. She believes this blended approach should reflect her contention that the frequency of losses within the $10,000 deductible is controllable.

She next performs the cost allocation calculations. For the $150,000 projected annual losses within the $10,000 per occurrence deductible, she calculates by location the past three years of paid and reserved losses, which were increased to reflect inflation and were capped at $10,000 per occurrence. The calculations are shown in Columns 3, 4, and 5 of Exhibit 13-3. The sum of those three Columns appears in Column 6. The amounts in Column 6 have been used to calculate the percentages in Column 7. Each percentage in Column 7 has been computed by dividing the total loses at each location by the $400,000 of losses at all locations. The allocated costs in Column 8 apportion the $150,000 of projected retained claims by the percentages in Column 7.

EXHIBIT 13-3

Allocation of Retained Claims by Three Years' Cumulative Claim Experience Capped at $10,000 per Occurrence

(1)	(2)	(3) Least Recent Year 1	(4) Year 2	(5) Most Recent Year 3	(6) Total Claims (Col. 3 + Col. 4 + Col. 5)	(7) Percentage of Total	(8) Cost Allocation (Col. 7 × $150,000)
Location	Occupancy						
Los Angeles	Hotel	$ 75,000	$ 75,000	$40,000	$190,000	47.5%	$ 71,250
Los Angeles	Apartment building	30,000	25,000	15,000	70,000	17.5	26,250
Denver	Hotel	40,000	40,000	20,000	100,000	25.0	37,500
Denver	Office building	8,000	2,000	0	10,000	2.5	3,750
Houston	Hotel	2,000	10,000	18,000	30,000	7.5	11,250
Total		$155,000	$152,000	$93,000	$400,000	100.0%	$150,000

The risk management professional also notes that the Los Angeles hotel has generated a large portion of the claims that would have fallen within the $10,000 deductible. Although the hotel represents 20 percent of Lorac's total square footage, it sustained 47.5 percent of all inflation-adjusted claims capped at $10,000. The risk management professional believes that square footage does not sufficiently indicate exposure. Although square footage represents size relativities, it does not reflect differences in the operational exposures of hotel, apartment, and office occupancies. Furthermore, square footage does not account for territorial relativities—for example, the differences in the legal environments of Los Angeles, Denver, and Houston.

The risk management professional relies on insurance premium rates for different occupancies in the states in which Lorac's buildings are located to reflect the relativities shown in Column 4 of Exhibit 13-4. (Notice that those relativities are weighting factors that, unlike percentages, need not add up to 1.00.) Applying the relativities to the square footage in Column 3 of Exhibit 13-4 enables the risk management professional to adjust square footage so it more closely reflects exposure, as shown in Column 5. Column 6 shows the resulting changes in the percentage of the total premium allocated to each location. The actual cost based on those percentages is shown in Column 7. The calculations conclude the exposure-based allocation of retained losses.

To build an experience-based allocation of the guaranteed-cost insurance premium, the risk management professional decides to use large losses (that is, inflation-adjusted claims between $10,000 and $50,000) as the allocation basis and five years of experience because of the low frequency of large claims. The results are shown in Exhibit 13-5. Column 8 totals the relevant claims from Columns 3 through 7. Column 9 indicates the experience basis for each location as a percentage of their $400,000 total. The allocated insurance premium in Column 10 is based on those percentages.

The risk management professional considers the amount of loss experience that should be reflected in cost allocation figures to motivate division managers to improve loss control. A high percentage based on losses could lead to fluctuations in divisional costs that would not always reflect the long-term effects of loss control. The risk management professional thus decides to allocate 80 percent of the $250,000 premium by exposure and 20 percent by the claim experience from Exhibit 13-5. The results shown in Exhibit 13-6 were obtained by taking the exposure percentages from Column 6 of Exhibit 13-4 and multiplying them by 80 percent. The risk management professional then uses the experience percentages from Column 9 of Exhibit 13-5 and multiplies them by 20 percent. The sum of the two percentages, the overall allocation percentage, is shown for each property in Column 7 of Exhibit 13-6. Applying those percentages to the $250,000 premium generates the insurance costs allocated to each location, as shown in Column 8 of Exhibit 13-6.

The risk management professional decides to use the costs in Column 6 of Exhibit 13-7 as a first approximation of the final allocation for the coming year. She knows that a lively discussion will ensue concerning the significant shifts in cost, particularly toward the Los Angeles and Denver hotels. The risk management professional considers this the ideal means to draw senior and operating management attention to the costs of claims as well as to the new risk control measures to reduce those claims. Although the final cost allocations may not represent such a dramatic departure from the previous year, they should improve and justify Lorac's risk control efforts and overall risk management program.

EXHIBIT 13-4

Allocation of Insurance Premium Based on Adjusted Square Footage

(1) Location	(2) Occupancy	(3) Square Footage	(4) Rate	(5) Adjusted Square Footage (Col. 3 × Col. 4)	(6) Percentage of Total	(7) Allocation of Insurance Premium
Los Angeles	Hotel	200,000	0.225	45,000	30%	$ 75,000
Los Angeles	Apartment building	300,000	0.100	30,000	20	50,000
Denver	Hotel	200,000	0.200	40,000	27	67,500
Denver	Office building	100,000	0.050	5,000	3	7,500
Houston	Hotel	200,000	0.150	30,000	20	50,000
Total		1,000,000		150,000	100%	$250,000

EXHIBIT 13-5

Allocation of Insurance Premium Based on Five Years of Claim Experience Between $10,000 and $50,000 per Occurrence

(1) Location	(2) Occupancy	(3) Least Recent Year 1	(4) Year 2	(5) Year 3	(6) Year 4	(7) Most Recent Year 5	(8) Cumulative Total Claims	(9) Percentage of Total	(10) Allocation of Insurance Premium
Los Angeles	Hotel	$ 0	$60,000	$60,000	$30,000	$30,000	$180,000	45%	$112,500
Los Angeles	Apartment building	20,000	0	10,000	10,000	40,000	80,000	20	50,000
Denver	Hotel	40,000	10,000	20,000	40,000	10,000	120,000	30	75,000
Denver	Office building	0	0	0	0	0	0	0	0
Houston	Hotel	10,000	0	0	0	10,000	20,000	5	12,500
Total		$70,000	$70,000	$90,000	$80,000	$90,000	$400,000	100%	$250,000

EXHIBIT 13-6

Allocation of Insurance Premium Based on Experience and Exposure

(1) Location	(2) Occupancy	(3) Exposure Percentage	(4) Exposure Percentage (80% of Col. 3)	(5) Experience Percentage	(6) Experience Percentage (20% of Col. 5)	(7) Total Percentage Allocation (Col. 4 + Col. 6)	(8) Premium Allocation (Col. 7 × $250,000)
Los Angeles	Hotel	30%	24.0%	45%	9%	33.0%	$ 82,500
Los Angeles	Apartment building	20	16.0	20	4	20.0	50,000
Denver	Hotel	27	21.6	30	6	27.6	69,000
Denver	Office building	3	2.4	0	0	2.4	6,000
Houston	Hotel	20	16.0	5	1	17.0	42,500
Total		100%	80.0%	100%	20%	100.0%	$250,000

EXHIBIT 13-7

Comparison of Final to Initial Cost Allocation

(1)	(2)	(3)	(4)	(5)	(6)	(7)
		Final Premium Allocation	Final Retained Claim Allocation	Final Total Cost Allocation (Col. 3 + Col. 4)	Initial Cost Allocation (Ex. 13-2)	Percentage Change
Location	Occupancy					
Los Angeles	Hotel	$ 82,500	$ 71,250	$153,750	$ 60,000	156%
Los Angeles	Apartment building	50,000	26,250	76,250	90,000	(15)
Denver	Hotel	69,000	37,500	106,500	60,000	78
Denver	Office building	6,000	3,750	9,750	30,000	(67)
Houston	Hotel	42,500	11,250	53,750	60,000	(10)
Total		$250,000	$150,000	$400,000	$300,000	33%

SUMMARY

Effective risk management cost allocation systems require that most costs be allocated to the departments that generate them. A properly designed risk management cost allocation system does the following:

- Promotes risk control
- Facilitates risk retention
- Prioritizes risk management expenditures
- Reduces costs
- Distributes costs fairly
- Balances risk-bearing and risk-sharing
- Provides managers with cost information

The four types of costs that can be fully or partially allocated, which together constitute an organization's cost of risk, are as follows:

1. Costs of accidental losses not reimbursed by insurance or other outside sources
2. Insurance premiums
3. Costs of risk control techniques
4. Costs of administering risk management activities

Any combination of these costs, or portions of them, can be allocated to any department. Costs that are clearly incurred by and beneficial to a given department, or wholly within that department's control, are easily allocated to that department. Other costs, such as retained losses, valuation, and allocation, are more complex.

The two widely used approaches to risk management cost allocation are prospective and retrospective. The distinction refers to differences in determining both the initial allocation and the final payment of losses and other risk management costs. In a prospective cost allocation approach, costs are estimated and allocated at the beginning of the accounting period during which they are expected to be incurred. Once allocated, costs are not changed for that period. In a retrospective cost allocation approach, costs are also estimated and allocated at the beginning of the accounting period during which they are expected to be incurred. However, they can be reallocated one or more times during or after the close of the period.

The initial step in the risk management cost allocation process is to determine the types and amounts of an organization's risk management costs. The next step is to decide the basis on which they should be allocated to each department. Costs can be allocated by loss exposure or loss experience.

Each basis selected should reflect the underlying exposures. Exposure can generally be measured by size, nature of operations, and territory. Loss experience is often used as a direct measure of a risk management program's success. It is measured by frequency or aggregate severity limited to some dollar amount.

Several practical factors affect the design of a risk management cost allocation system. The risk management professional designing a risk management cost allocation system should consider that an organization's accounting system can affect the plan's design, because exposure bases often rely on exposure-based accounting data, such as sales and payroll. Also, some of an organization's operations may be subject to more than one tax system. Therefore, risk management cost allocation systems should consider tax implications on an aggregate basis. Likewise, the plan also should charge each department at least a minimum amount for risk management services, regardless of individual exposures, and reward departmental managers for risk control efforts by incorporating related bonuses in their compensation.

A risk management cost allocation system may not be necessary for an organization that has a small aggregate cost of risk relative to its total budget. If a risk management cost allocation system is necessary, departmental managers and an organization's senior management must support its implementation and also should agree on the extent to which risk management information systems (RMIS) should be used to determine bases, compute formulas, and allocate costs.

A risk management professional should perform the following six steps when developing a risk management cost allocation system:

1. Review the attributes of an effective risk management cost allocation system and determine the organization's objectives for such a system.
2. Identify the costs that will be allocated by the risk management cost allocation system.

3. For each category of cost, determine whether a prospective or retrospective allocation would best show where risk management techniques should be used.

4. Determine the value and the way each cost will be allocated based on one or more of the following:
   - Exposure basis
   - Experience basis
   - Per occurrence limit
   - Aggregate limit
   - Experience period

5. Consider the opportunities and challenges of each of the following when implementing a risk management allocation system:
   - Accounting system
   - Organization's tax situation
   - Minimum and/or maximum limits on costs to be allocated for each accounting period
   - Decentralized departments
   - Significance of risk management costs to each department's budget
   - Ways in which cost allocations might penalize or reward a department manager according to that department's costs to influence motivation and performance
   - Level of support and cooperation from management
   - RMIS used
   - Consistency of allocation system

6. Perform trial calculations to determine whether the proposed system meets the organization's needs. If it does not, make adjustments and repeat this step as necessary.

Index

Page numbers in boldface refer to definitions of Key Words and Phrases.